# Phantoms
of the Other

SUNY series in Contemporary Continental Philosophy

Dennis J. Schmidt, editor

# Phantoms
of the Other

Four Generations of Derrida's *Geschlecht*

DAVID FARRELL KRELL

The cover shows a detail of a photograph of three of the Trakl children taken *circa* 1897. Georg is at age 10, Gretl at age 5. The photograph is in the collection of the Forschungsinstitut Brenner-Archiv of the University of Innsbruck, which generously granted permission to reproduce it here. The concept for the cover design is by David Matthew Krell, of dmkdesign.

Published by State University of New York Press, Albany

© 2015 State University of New York

All rights reserved

Printed in the United States of America

No part of this book may be used or reproduced in any manner whatsoever without written permission. No part of this book may be stored in a retrieval system or transmitted in any form or by any means including electronic, electrostatic, magnetic tape, mechanical, photocopying, recording, or otherwise without the prior permission in writing of the publisher.

For information, contact State University of New York Press, Albany, NY
www.sunypress.edu

Production, Eileen Nizer
Marketing, Anne M. Valentine

**Library of Congress Cataloging-in-Publication Data**

Krell, David Farrell.
    Phantoms of the other : four generations of Derrida's *Geschlecht* / David Farrell Krell.
        pages cm. — (SUNY series in contemporary continental philosophy)
    Includes bibliographical references and index.
    ISBN 978-1-4384-5449-8 (hc : alk. paper)  978-1-4384-5450-4 (pb : alk. paper)
    ISBN 978-1-4384-5451-1 (ebook)
    1. Heidegger, Martin, 1889–1976.  2. National socialism and philosophy.
3. Poetry.  4. Derrida, Jacques.  I. Title.

B3279.H49K75 2014
193—dc23
                                                                          2014007245

10 9 8 7 6 5 4 3 2 1

*for*
*Elena Sophia and Elias Dylan*
*and their dream*

Does not the dream, all by itself, demonstrate that of which it is dreaming, which is there precisely to make us dream?
—Jacques Derrida

# Contents

Preface ix

Abbreviations of Works Cited xiii

Introduction 1

1. *Geschlecht I*: Sexual Difference, Ontological Difference 19

2. *Geschlecht II*: Heidegger's Singular Hand 47

3. Of Spirit 69

4. *Geschlecht IV*: Heidegger's Philopolemological Ear 107

5. *Geschlecht III*: A Truncated Typescript 131

6. *Geschlecht III*: The Phantom of the Other 171

7. The Magnetism of Georg and Gretl Trakl 223

Appendix A: Poems Discussed in the Present Volume 257

Appendix B: Poems Undiscussed 311

Index 349

# Preface

During the 1980s, Derrida wrote four major texts on the word and the things called, in German, *Geschlecht*—roughly, clan, tribe, race, generation, genus, lineage, coinage, sex, and a few things more—in relation to Heidegger's thought. Derrida published the first, second, and fourth of these long pieces, whereas the third was never completed and never published. This "missing" generation of *Geschlecht*, however, can be reconstructed on the basis of an incomplete typescript Derrida himself prepared in 1985, along with lecture notes from his 1984–85 seminar in Paris, "Philosophical Nationality and Nationalism: The Phantom of the Other." Each of these texts, the four generations of *Geschlecht*, both the published and the unpublished, focus on the years 1928 and 1953 in Heidegger's career of thought.

In 1928 Heidegger speculated on the relation of the neutral and neuter term *Dasein* or mortal existence to sexuality and sexual difference; in 1953 he reflected once again on the nature of sexual difference, this time in Georg Trakl's singular "poem." Even though the 1953 Heidegger text, "Language in the Poem: A Placement of Georg Trakl's Poem," served right from the start as the second magnetic pole of Derrida's entire *Geschlecht* project, Derrida himself never published his most detailed reflections on that text. Along with the published works *Of Spirit, Aporias,* and volume two of *The Beast and the Sovereign,* the *Geschlecht* series, in my view, represents Derrida's most penetrating reflections on Heidegger. The incompleteness of the series is a sign not of failure on Derrida's part but of a fundamental reserve, a reserve that has to do with the necessary reticence of all thinking, including the thinking of deconstruction, in the face of poetry. The present book is about Derrida's achievement—and that reserve. My letters to and from Derrida, and my conversations with him about the *Geschlecht* series throughout the 1980s and 1990s, may offer some otherwise inaccessible insights into the project as a whole.

Not many years ago, I published two brief accounts of Derrida's entire *Geschlecht* series, desiring to focus there on the third and missing generation of that series, that is, the *Geschlecht* that deals with Heidegger's reading of Georg Trakl.[1] The three published generations of Derrida's series, namely, the first, second, and fourth, were so rich that by the time I arrived at my proper subject in the first account I found that I had left myself too little room. The result was a mere four pages of commentary on *Geschlecht III*, which I then expanded in the second piece, albeit only slightly. I still regard the "missing" third *Geschlecht*—however remarkable the other three in the series may be—as the most thought-provoking of the *Geschlechter*. Why? Because, to repeat, that particular *Geschlecht* more than any of the others focuses on Heidegger and Trakl. More specifically, it takes up Heidegger's very long and very difficult 1953 essay, "Die Sprache im Gedicht: eine Erörterung von Georg Trakls Gedicht," the essay that, as Derrida himself often reiterates, incites and "magnetizes" the entire *Geschlecht* series. This third *Geschlecht*, which never truly came to term, and which Derrida himself never published, is the subject of the fifth and sixth chapters of the present book and in effect the entire book's raison d'être.—But allow me to backtrack a bit.

My first careful reading of Derrida's work began quite late, in June 1979. Until then I had been critical of the few avatars of "deconstruction" I had met and heard, those who spoke in Derrida's name but who perhaps were speaking too soon. In any case, at the time I was underwhelmed by "Derrida," especially when confrontations between "deconstruction" and Heidegger were being discussed. My friends at the Warwick Workshops organized by David Wood during the 1970s—David himself, John Llewelyn, and Robert Bernasconi—were not fooled by these avatars; they became serious students of Derrida's work long before I did. In June 1979, however, John Sallis pressed a copy of Derrida's *Éperons: les styles de Nietzsche* into my hot little hands. "I think you'd better read this," he said. After John continued on his travels, I took the book up into my hillside garden and in a single day, prodded by purple knightspur, I read the whole thing. I have not stopped reading Derrida since.

My first reading of Georg Trakl, thanks to Heidegger's two Trakl essays in *Underway to Language*, had occurred in the early 1970s. My first published article on Trakl and Heidegger, written in 1976–77, appeared in

---

1. See D. F. Krell, "One, Two, Four—Yet Where Is the Third? A Note on Derrida's *Geschlecht* Series," *Epoché* 10, no. 2 (Spring 2006): 341–57, esp. 351–54; and Krell, "Marginalia to *Geschlecht III*," *The New Centennial Review* 7, no. 2 (2007): 175–200.

1978.[2] I sent the piece to Derrida on January 4, 1983, after having read the first of his *Geschlecht* essays in typescript. Some weeks earlier, John Sallis had brought me a copy of the typescript, which Ruben Berezdivin was translating into English for the journal *Research in Phenomenology*, and I read it with great interest, not to say enthusiasm. At that time, as now, not many students of Heidegger were commenting on the Trakl essays, and I was struck by the fact that the themes and problems that Derrida had selected for discussion often dovetailed with my own. First among these was the theme of *Geschlecht* itself and the odd (not to say striking) way in which Heidegger uses the words *Schlag* and *schlagen* (the roots of *Geschlecht,* meaning "to strike a blow," "to beat," "to coin") in his second Trakl essay. It was not false modesty when I remarked to Derrida in the January 1983 letter that my own essay, "Schlag der Liebe, Schlag des Todes," was "undisciplined and not very critical." Along with an even earlier essay on the theme of "rhythm" in Heidegger's second Trakl essay, this essay was something of a first try.[3] I rescue one or two facets of it in the final chapter of the present book. In any case, the point I want to emphasize is that my contact with Derrida, and our eventual friendship, had Trakl—Heidegger's Trakl—at its very center. We talked about it endlessly. And it seems to me now, as I look back on Derrida's extraordinarily productive career, that his work on *Geschlecht* stands out as exceptional in an oeuvre that is altogether exceptional. It will take students of Heidegger decades to absorb that work, I suspect. And I feel certain that nothing will be more rewarding for them—if confrontation with enigmas and even phantoms can be rewarding.

In the present book, *Geschlecht III* will be considered anachronically, that is to say, only after the "completion" of the *Geschlecht* series—in *De l'esprit* and *Geschlecht IV*—has been interpreted. The book turns to *Geschlecht III* in chapters 5 and 6, even though the typescript and the seminar date from the years 1984–85, some four or five years earlier than the fourth and final *Geschlecht*. Chapter 7, the concluding chapter of the

---

2. "Schlag der Liebe, Schlag des Todes: On Heidegger and Trakl," in *Radical Phenomenology: Essays in Honor of Martin Heidegger,* ed. John Sallis (Atlantic Highlands, NJ: Humanities Press, 1978), 238–58. With some excisions, and a dedication to Derrida added, this piece became the final chapter of *Intimations of Mortality* (IM 163–76), published in 1986.

3. For the essay on rhythm, written also in the mid-1970s, see "The Wave's Source: Rhythms of Poetic Speech," in *Heidegger and Language,* ed. David Wood (Warwick, UK: Parousia Press, 1981), 25–50. The essay, revised and expanded, appeared many years later as the third chapter of my *Lunar Voices* (LV 55–82), published in 1995.

book, attempts to continue the meditation on Trakl, now engaging both Heidegger and Derrida in a *Zwiegespräch*, one in which Trakl remains the principal partner—hence, a *Drei-* or even *Viergespräch*, if I dare to include myself. I take it that such a conversation responds to Derrida's own wish and holds him to his own promise—death serving as no excuse—to return to the questions posed in the third generation of *Geschlecht*. The present book can be no more than an invitation to others, some of them surviving as phantoms, others still living, to join in the conversation.

Because I have written so often on the *Geschlecht* series in earlier years, I succumbed to the temptation, while preparing this book, of reading my own earlier work, especially the work on *Of Spirit* in chapter 8 of *Daimon Life* and on "the voice of the sister" in *Lunar Voices*. Some of what was written in those places appears here again, with my apologies, but I hope also with some refinements, some signs of having listened a bit more carefully during the intervening years.

In what order should these chapters be read? I am uncertain. For those who know little of and about Trakl's poetry, I suggest reading the Appendices first. Perhaps then a look at the final chapter, the seventh, which tries to say something about the lives of the poet and his gifted and beloved sister Gretl. At that point Heidegger's preoccupation with Trakl, and Derrida's with Heidegger's Trakl, may make more sense.

I owe many debts of gratitude. Had Ulrich Halfmann not spent all those hours on my translations of Trakl's poems in the Appendices, the result would have been catastrophic. In dozens upon dozens of cases, Halfmann brought the translations closer to the German, closer to Trakl. It was an education to work with him, and I am more than grateful for that education. My thanks to Walter Brogan and to the reviewers for SUNY Press for their reading and their suggestions, and to Andrew Kenyon, Eileen Nizer, and the entire staff at SUNY Press for help at every stage. And once again to my son David Matthew Krell for the design of the cover.

D. F. K.<br>
Strobelhütte, St. Ulrich

# Abbreviations of Works Cited

## Works by Derrida

A     *L'animal que donc je suis*. Paris: Galilée, 2006. Translated by David Wills as *The Animal That Therefore I Am*. New York: Fordham University Press, 2008.

AP     *Apories*. Paris: Galilée, 1996 [1992]. Translated by Thomas Dutoit as *Aporias*. Stanford: Stanford University Press, 1993.

B1     *Séminaire: La bête et le souverain, Volume I (2001–2002)*. Edited by Michel Lisse, Marie-Louise Mallet, and Genette Michaud. Paris: Galilée, 2008. Translated by Geoffrey Bennington as *The Beast and the Sovereign*, Volume I. Chicago: University of Chicago Press, 2009. Cited by volume and page of the French edition.

B2     *Séminaire: La bête et le souverain, Volume II (2002–2003)*. Edited by Michel Lisse, Marie-Louise Mallet, and Genette Michaud. Paris: Galilée, 2010. Translated by Geoffrey Bennington as *The Beast and the Sovereign*, Volume II. Chicago: University of Chicago Press, 2011. Cited by volume and page of the French edition.

C     *Circumfession*. In Geoffrey Bennington, *Jacques Derrida*. Paris: Seuil, 1991; English translation published by University of Chicago Press, 1993.

CP     *La Carte postale de Socrate à Freud et au-delà*. Paris: Aubier-Flammarion, 1980. Translated by Alan Bass as *The Post Card from Socrates to Freud and Beyond*. Chicago: University of Chicago Press, 1987.

DE   *De l'esprit: Heidegger et la question.* Paris: Galilée, 1987. Translated by Geoffrey Bennington and Rachel Bowlby as *Of Spirit: Heidegger and the Question.* Chicago: University of Chicago Press, 1989.

DG   *De la grammatologie.* Paris: Minuit, 1967. Translated by Gayatri Chakravorty Spivak as *Of Grammatology.* Baltimore: Johns Hopkins University Press, 1976.

ED   *Écriture et la différence.* Paris: Seuil, 1967. Translated by Alan Bass as *Writing and Difference.* Chicago: University of Chicago Press, 1978.

É    *Éperons: Les styles de Nietzsche.* Paris: Flammarion, 1978.

G 1–4 The four "Geschlecht" papers: (1) and (2) are published in *Psyché,* while (4) is in *Politiques de l'amitié,* with English translations as follows: (1) by Ruben Berezdivin in *Research in Phenomenology* XIII (1983): 65–83; by Ruben Berezdivin and Elizabeth Rottenberg in *Psyche 2: Inventions of the Other,* ed. Peggy Kamuf and Elizabeth Rottenberg. Stanford: Stanford University Press, 2008, 7–26; (2) translated by John P. Leavey Jr. in *Deconstruction and Philosophy: The Texts of Jacques Derrida.* Edited by John Sallis. Chicago: University of Chicago Press, 1987, 161–96; by John P. Leavey and Elizabeth Rottenberg in *Psyche 2,* cited above. The third "Geschlecht" is not yet published. The fourth, "L'oreille de Heidegger: Philopolémologie (*Geschlecht* IV)" appears in *Politiques de l'amitié.* An English translation by John P. Leavey Jr. appears in *Commemorations: Reading Heidegger.* Edited by John Sallis. Chicago: University of Chicago Press, 1993.

Gl   *Glas.* Paris: Galilée, 1974. Translated by John P. Leavey Jr. and Richard Rand. Lincoln: University of Nebraska Press, 1986.

M    *Marges de la philosophie.* Paris: Éditions de Minuit, 1972. Translated by Alan Bass. Chicago: University of Chicago Press, 1985.

MA   *Mal d'Archive: Une impression freudienne.* Paris: Galilée, 1995. Translated by Eric Prenowitz as *Archive Fever.* Chicago: University of Chicago Press, 1996.

O    *Otobiographies: L'enseignement de Nietzsche et la politique du nom propre.* Paris: Galilée, 1984. Translated (in part) as *The Ear of the Other: Otobiography, Transference, Translation,* by Peggy Kamuf,

|      | edited by Christie V. McDonald. New York: Schocken Books, 1985. |
|------|---|
| PA   | *Politiques de l'amitié.* Paris: Galilée, 1994. Translated as *Politics of Friendship* by George Collins. New York: Verso, 1997. |
| PM   | *Papier machine.* Paris: Galilée, 2001. |
| Po   | *Points de suspension . . . Entretiens.* Edited by Elisabeth Weber. Paris: Galilée, 1992. Translated by Peggy Kamuf as *Points: Interviews 1974–1994.* Stanford: Stanford University Press, 1995. |
| Ps   | *Psyché: Inventions de l'autre.* Paris: Galilée, 1987. English translation by Peggy Kamuf and Elizabeth Rottenberg. Stanford University Press, forthcoming. |
| S    | *Schibboleth: Pour Paul Celan.* Paris: Galilée, 1986. Translated by Joshua Wilner and Thomas Dutoit in *Sovereignties in Question: The Poetics of Paul Celan,* edited by Thomas Dutoit and Outi Pasanen. New York: Fordham University Press, 2005. |
| SM   | *Spectres de Marx.* Paris: Galilée, 1993. Translated by Peggy Kamuf as *Specters of Marx: The State of the Debt, the Work of Mourning, and the New International.* New York: Routledge, 1994. |
| V    | *Voyous.* Paris: Galilée, 2003. Translated by Pascale-Anne Brault and Michael Naas as *Rogues: Two Essays on Reason.* Stanford: Stanford University Press, 2005. |

## Works by Heidegger

| BW    | *Basic Writings.* 2nd ed. San Francisco: HarperCollins, 1993. |
|-------|---|
| EGT   | *Early Greek Thinking.* 2nd ed. San Francisco: HarperCollins, 1984. |
| EHD   | *Erläuterungen zu Hölderlins Dichtung.* 4th, expanded ed. Frankfurt am Main: V. Klostermann, 1971. |
| EM    | *Einführung in die Metaphysik.* Tübingen: M. Niemeyer, 1953. |
| G     | *Gelassenheit.* Pfullingen: G. Neske, 1959. |
| H     | *Holzwege.* Frankfurt am Main: V. Klostermann, 1950. |
| N I–II | *Nietzsche,* 2 vols. Pfullingen: G. Neske, 1961. |

Ni 1–4  *Nietzsche*, 4 vols. 2nd ed. San Francisco: HarperCollins, 1991.

SB  *Die Selbstbehauptung der deutschen Universität; Das Rektorat 1933/34: Tatsachen und Gedanken.* Edited by Hermann Heidegger. Frankfurt am Main: V. Klostermann, 1983.

SCH  *Schellings Abhandlung über das Wesen der menschlichen Freiheit* (1809). Edited by Hildegard Feick. Tübingen: M. Niemeyer, 1971.

SZ  *Sein und Zeit*, 12th ed. Tübingen: M. Niemeyer, 1972.

US  *Unterwegs zur Sprache*. Pfullingen: G. Neske, 1959.

VA  *Vorträge und Aufsätze*. Pfullingen: G. Neske, 1954.

W  *Wegmarken* (Frankfurt am Main: V. Klostermann, 1967.

WhD?  *Was heißt Denken?* Tübingen: M. Niemeyer, 1954.

20  *Prolegomena zur Geschichte des Zeitbegriffs*. Gesamtausgabe vol. 20. Marburg lecture course, Summer Semester 1925. Frankfurt am Main: V. Klostermann, 1979.

24  *Die Grundprobleme der Phänomenologie*. Gesamtausgabe vol. 24. Marburg lecture course, Summer Semester 1927. Frankfurt am Main: V. Klostermann, 1975.

26  *Metaphysische Anfangsgründe der Logik im Ausgang von Leibniz*, Gesamtausgabe vol. 26. Marburg lecture course, Summer Semester, 1928. Frankfurt am Main: V. Klostermann, 1978.

27  *Einleitung in die Philosophie,* Gesamtausgabe vol. 27. Freiburg lecture course, Winter Semester, 1928–29. Frankfurt am Main: V. Kostermann, 2001.

29/30  *Die Grundbegriffe der Metaphysik: Welt—Endlichkeit—Einsamkeit,* Gesamtausgabe vol. 29/30. Freiburg lecture course, Winter Semester, 1929–30. Frankfurt am Main: V. Klostermann, 1983.

39  *Hölderlins Hymnen "Germanien" und "Der Rhein."* Gesamtausgabe vol. 39. Freiburg lecture course, Winter Semester 1934–35. Frankfurt am Main: V. Klostermann, 1980.

52  *Hölderlins Hymne "Andenken."* Gesamtausgabe vol. 52. Freiburg lecture course, Winter Semester 1941–42. Frankfurt am Main: V. Klostermann, 1982.

53  *Hölderlins Hymne "Der Ister."* Gesamtausgabe vol. 53. Freiburg lecture course, Summer Semester 1942. Frankfurt am Main: V. Klostermann, 1984.

54  *Parmenides.* Gesamtausgabe vol. 54. Freiburg lecture course, Winter Semester, 1942–43. Frankfurt am Main: V. Klostermann, 1982.

55  *Heraklit: (1) Der Anfang des abendländischen Denkens; (2) Logik: Heraklits Lehre vom Logos.* Gesamtausgabe vol. 55. Freiburg lecture courses, Summer Semesters 1943 and 1944. Frankfurt am Main: V. Klostermann, 1979.

61  *Phänomenologische Interpretationen zu Aristoteles: Einführung in die phänomenologische Forschung.* Gesamtausgabe vol. 61. Early Freiburg lecture course, Winter Semester 1921–22. Frankfurt am Main: V. Klostermann, 1985.

63  *Ontologie (Hermeneutik der Faktizität).* Gesamtausgabe vol. 63. Early Freiburg lecture course, Summer Semester 1923. Frankfurt am Main: V. Klostermann, 1988.

65  *Beiträge zur Philosophie (Vom Ereignis).* Gesamtausgabe vol. 65. From the years 1936–38. Frankfurt am Main: V. Klostermann, 1989.

94  *Überlegungen II–VI (Schwarze Hefte 1931–38).* Gesamtausgabe vol. 94. Frankfurt am Main: V. Klostermann, 2014.

95  *Überlegungen VII–XI (Schwarze Hefte 1938–39).* Gesamtausgabe vol. 95. Frankfurt am Main: V. Klostermann, 2014.

96  *Überlegungen XII–XV (Schwarze Hefte 1939–1941).* Gesamtausgabe vol. 96. Frankfurt am Main: V. Klostermann, 2014.

## Works by the Author

AO  *Derrida and Our Animal Others: Derrida's Final Seminar, "The Beast and the Sovereign."* Bloomington and London: Indiana University Press, 2013.

AT  *Architecture: Ecstasies of Space, Time, and the Human Body.* Albany: State University of New York Press, 1997.

DL   *Daimon Life: Heidegger and Life-Philosophy*. Bloomington and London: Indiana University Press, 1992.

IM   *Intimations of Mortality: Time, Truth, and Finitude in Heidegger's Thinking of Being*. 2nd ed. University Park: Pennsylvania State University Press, 1991.

LV   *Lunar Voices: Of Tragedy, Poetry, Fiction, and Thought*. Chicago: University of Chicago Press, 1995.

PB   *The Purest of Bastards: Works of Mourning, Art, and Affirmation in the Thought of Jacques Derrida*. Pennsylvania State University Press, 2000.

TA   *The Tragic Absolute: German Idealism and the Languishing of God*. Bloomington and London: Indiana University Press, 2005.

## Works by Other Authors

7, 8   F. W. J. Schelling, *Abhandlung über das Wesen der menschlichen Freiheit und die damit zusammenhängenden Gegenstände*, in vol. 7 of *Sämtliche Werke*. Stuttgart et Augsburg: J. G. Cotta, 1860. The third (1815) version of *Die Weltalter (Die Vergangenheit)* is published in vol. 8 of the same edition. Cited by volume and page in the body of my text, e.g., 7:399, 8:260.

BP   Benoît Peeters, *Derrida*. Paris: Flammarion, 2010.

CHV 1–3   Works by Hölderlin are cited from Friedrich Hölderlin, *Sämtliche Werke und Briefe*. 3 vols. Edited by Michael Knaupp. Munich: Carl Hanser Verlag, 1992.

DK   Hermann Diels and Walther Kranz, *Die Fragmente der Vorsokratiker*, 3 vols. 6th ed. Zürich: Weidmann, 1951. Cited by fragment number.

És   Jacques Lacan, *Écrits*. Paris: Éditions du Seuil, 1966.

HP   Hermann Paul, *Deutsches Wörterbuch*. 6th ed. by Werner Betz. Tübingen: Max Niemeyer Verlag, 1966.

KSA   Works by Nietzsche are cited from Friedrich Nietzsche, *Kritische Studienausgabe*, 15 vols. Edited by Giorgio Colli and Mazzino

|   | Montinari. Berlin and Munich: Walter de Gruyter and Deutscher Taschenbuch Verlag, 1980. |
|---|---|
| OB | Otto Basil, *Trakl*. Reinbek bei Hamburg: Rowohlt, 1965. |
| PG | G. W. F. Hegel, *Phänomenologie des Geistes*, 6th ed. Edited by Johannes Hoffmeister. Hamburg: F. Meiner, 1952. |
| RC | Roberto Calasso, *Le nozze di Cadmo e Armonia*. Milan: Adelphi, 1988). Translated by Tim Parks as *The Marriage of Cadmus and Harmony*. New York: Alfred A. Knopf, Borzoi Books, 1993. |
| SA 1–10 | Works by Sigmund Freud are cited from the *Studienausgabe*, 10 vols., with an *Ergänzungsband*. Edited by Alexander Mitscherlich, Angela Richards, and James Strachey. Frankfurt am Main: Fischer, 1982. |
| T | I cite Trakl's poems from Georg Trakl, *Dichtungen und Briefe*, 3d ed., edited by Walther Killy and Hans Szklenar (Salzburg: Otto Müller Verlag, 1974), which is based on the first volume of the historical-critical edition by these same editors. |

# Introduction

Four generations of an unpronounceable German word? An unpronounceable German word that is irreducibly multiple in its meanings? This cannot be good.

I sympathize with the reader. Derrida too, himself the heart and soul of generosity, would have sympathized. Yet he devoted a decade of his life to the study of this word, or, as he preferred to say, of "the word and the things." He did not underestimate the difficulty of proceeding from the word *Geschlecht* to all the things it means. The word and the things appear at two moments in the life and work of Martin Heidegger, first in 1928, then in 1953. Only two moments, it seems. Yet in Derrida's view they are decisive moments. Decisive for what? First, for the fundamental ontology of Dasein, that is, for Heidegger's entire project of an existential analytic in the 1927 *Being and Time* and in the lecture courses immediately preceding and following it; second, for Heidegger's later effort to think in dialogue with poetry, especially the poetry of Georg Trakl.

Let us begin as we used to do back in elementary school each time we had to write an essay, namely, by dashing off to the dictionaries. *Geschlecht*: noun, neuter, deriving from the Old High German *gislahti*, from which the English words *slay* and *slaughter* are formed. (This, again, cannot be good.) The prefix *gi-*, today *Ge-*, refers to a collectivity, and means "all things involving or surrounding the root in question." The root of *Geschlecht*, that is, *slahti*, derives from early forms of the verb *schlagen*, "to beat," "strike," "smite," "stamp," "coin," but also to "play a stringed instrument," "strike up a tune," or, if the musician is a blackbird, "warble." The oldest sense of *Geschlecht*, according to Hermann Paul's *Deutsches Wörterbuch*, is equivalent to the Latin word *genus*, that is, a group of persons who share a common ancestry, especially if that group or family belongs to the Patrician class. *Schlagen* in this case means as much as "to cause to resemble," or "to imprint or coin," with particular reference to the passing on of family likenesses. Such a family might also expand to form a clan, tribe, or class. The Grimm Brothers emphasize that the blood relations and the clan ties of a *Geschlecht* found the state. *Geschlecht* and even *Schlag* might also indicate a *species* of animal, more properly designated by the German *Gattung*, or even a particular herd of animals, say, of magnificent horses. Furthermore, the community of persons may expand to include all of humanity, *das Menschengeschlecht*, "the human race." It later comes to mean the entire assemblage of human beings who are alive for an identical period or era, a "generation." At the same time, it refers to the *genus masculinum* and *genus femininum*, the two genders that, one might speculate, are somehow already implicated in all the other meanings. Thus the "sexual" sense of *Geschlecht* is as archaic as all the others, such that the word serves as the root for an entire series of words involving sexuality and reproduction: *Geschlechtsglied, -teil*, or *-organ*, the genitalia; *Geschlechtlichkeit*, the erotic and the sexual in general; *Geschlechtstrieb*, the sex drive; *Geschlechtsverkehr*, sexual congress or intercourse, and so on. Finally, the "natural" *Geschlechter*, male and female, masculine and feminine, come to be applied to matters grammatical, namely, the masculine, feminine, and neuter genders of nouns and pronouns. The neuter gender poses a special problem, to be sure, and it is referred to in various ways, early on as *das unbenahmte Geschlecht*, the "undeclared" or "unnamed" gender, or *das sächliche Geschlecht*, the gender having to do with "things" or "states of affairs," and later simply as *geschlechtslos*, "genderless." When, late in the history of this word, Heidegger notes that *das Dasein*, a neuter noun, is *geschlechtslos*, he may merely be following the guidelines of grammar. Or he may be thinking something else, something more archaic than grammar; it is difficult to say.

In the present book, more will have to be said of Derrida's *Geschlecht I* than of *Geschlechter II* and *IV*, but most will have to be said of his *Geschlecht III*. The very first generation of *Geschlecht*, not yet numbered by him, is the one that is most drawn to, or most "magnetized by," the themes of the never completed and never published *Geschlecht III*.

Derrida's *Geschlecht* series, along with the books *Of Spirit, Aporias*, and the second volume of *The Beast and the Sovereign*, constitute his most sustained close-readings of Heidegger. To repeat, three essays of the four-part *Geschlecht* series were published during Derrida's lifetime, namely, the first, second, and fourth; these, taken together, comprise some 130 book pages. The third *Geschlecht* exists *in nuce* as a thirty-three-page typescript prepared sometime before March 1985 and distributed to the speakers at a colloquium in Chicago organized by John Sallis. These thirty-three pages are among the 100 to 130 pages of typescript that Derrida by his own account devoted to Heidegger's 1953 essay on Georg Trakl's poetry ("Die Sprache im Gedicht"); however provisional and fragmentary it may be, the typescript tells us much about the themes that "magnetize" the entire *Geschlecht* series. Yet it now seems clear that the core of the missing *Geschlecht III* is the 1984–85 seminar held in Paris under the title, "Nationalité et nationalisme philosophiques: le fantôme de l'autre."

In terms of Derrida's published work, it is as though the third generation of *Geschlecht* had gone missing, or had been skipped over. Whether the editorial committee that is preparing the seminars for publication has plans to publish the 1984–85 seminar I do not know. That seminar is of considerable importance, however, because it indicates both the questions that "magnetized" Derrida from the start, that is, from the first generation onward, and the way in which his path toward the second magnetic pole split off in multiple directions—or, to keep the metaphor of *Geschlecht*, the way in which the third generation itself dispersed into multiple tribes, clans, coinages, stirpes, generations, lineages—and perhaps even sexes. The present Introduction offers a chronology of Derrida's *Geschlecht* publications and then recounts something of the "ancestry" of the *Geschlecht* project, taking a look at some—but only some—of Derrida's work on Heidegger during the 1960s and 1970s.

The first *Geschlecht*, subtitled "Sexual Difference, Ontological Difference," appeared under the title *Geschlecht*, without any numerical designation, in Michel Haar's collection of essays on Heidegger for the *Cahier de l'Herne* in 1983. Ruben Berezdivin translated the piece for John Sallis's journal, *Research in Phenomenology* 13 (1983): 65–83. Today the French text appears on pages 395–414 of *Psyché: Inventions de l'autre* (Paris: Galilée, 1987), edited and translated into English by Peggy Kamuf and Elizabeth Rottenberg. The second *Geschlecht* (the subtitle is "Geschlecht II," set in parentheses), entitled "The Hand of Heidegger," translated by John P. Leavey Jr., was delivered at a conference organized by John Sallis at Loyola University of Chicago in March 1985 and published by the University of Chicago Press in 1987 under the title *Deconstruction and Philosophy: The Texts of Jacques Derrida*, edited by John Sallis, on pages 161–96. The French text of this second *Geschlecht* too is published today in *Psyché*, immediately after the first, on pages 415–51. One notices immediately the difference in length: the second is almost double the length of the first. This tendency toward proliferation continues with the fourth generation of *Geschlecht*, "The Ear of Heidegger: Philopolemology (*Geschlecht IV*)," originally presented at a second conference at Loyola organized by John

Sallis in September 1989; this piece too was translated by John P. Leavey Jr., and was published in a volume edited by John Sallis entitled *Reading Heidegger: Commemorations,* released in 1993 by Indiana University Press. The French text is published today as the second part of *Politiques de l'amitié* (Paris: Galilée, 1994), pages 341–419; as though following the predictions of Malthus, it is more than double the length of the second *Geschlecht,* the second almost double the length of the first.

Perhaps it is fitting that the generations and tribes of *Geschlecht* should increase and multiply in this way. Yet this burgeoning of the project precludes anything like a thoroughgoing analysis in the present volume of the three generations that exist in published form. In this limited space it will be possible to present only very brief synopses of the available *Geschlechter,* offering a somewhat more detailed analysis of the first and most succinct of them. For in the very first *Geschlecht* Derrida gives us several indications concerning the missing third. Later, at the end of the thirty-three-page typescript, he notes that the typescript itself is a preliminary and provisional transcription of notes from a seminar held in Paris, and that for lack of time five sessions of that seminar have not been taken into account. He estimates that some one hundred pages of material remain to be transcribed. Apart from some important references to *Geschlecht III* that appear toward the end of *Geschlecht II,* this is all we know about the third, and missing, *Geschlecht.*

As for the larger picture of the chronology, let us say three things. First, if the series begins about the time Derrida has been focusing on the ear of the other, specifically, Nietzsche's delicate ears (of which Nietzsche was inordinately proud) and the questions of woman, sexual difference, and mourning or ob-sequence (*Éperons,* 1979; *L'oreille de l'autre,* 1982; *Otobiographies,* 1984), it moves toward Heidegger's ear—and his politics; second, the series begins in seminars on philosophical nationality and nationalism, the first of these in 1983–84 on "Nation, Nationality, Nationalism," and it culminates in the 1987 *Of Spirit: Heidegger and the Question,* a work that raised the remarkably low level of the contemporary discussion of Heidegger and politics to its highest and philosophically most demanding level; third, further points of culmination for the *Geschlecht* series are the seminar of 1988–89, "The Politics of Friendship," and those of 1989–1993, on "the secret" and "witness" (PA 11).

Perhaps this is the place for a brief review of Derrida's preoccupations with Heidegger prior to the *Geschlecht* series, a brief and highly selective review, since it would be fair to say that the books and essays by Derrida in which Heidegger is *not* mentioned are rare. Here it can only be a matter of sampling some of the early work. Fortunately, with the recent publication of Derrida's 1964–65 seminar on Heidegger and historicity, we catch a glimpse of Derrida's earliest concerns with Heidegger, concerns that led to Derrida's quite famous essays of the late 1960s.[1]

All we can say about Derrida's fascination with Heidegger prior to the decade of the 1960s is the following. Derrida apparently first learned of Heidegger from one of his philosophy instructors, Jan Czarnecki, during the year of his *hypokhâgne* in Algiers, 1948–49 (BP 47–48). The only volume of Heidegger in French translation at the time was a selection by Henry Corbin that included Heidegger's 1929 inaugural address, "What Is Metaphysics?" Heidegger's analysis there of "the nothing" as prior to and more powerful than any negative assertion, along with his dramatic depiction of anxiety as the key to an experience of "the nothing," impressed the young student who at the end of the 1940s, not yet twenty years old, found himself wavering between philosophy and literature as his life choices. Even if Husserl was to become the object of his first serious studies in philosophy, it was Heidegger who gripped him from the start. His philosophy instructors at the lycée Louis-le-Grand in Paris had no real interest in Heidegger, but on his own Derrida was able to read French translations of Heidegger's *Kant and the Problem of Metaphysics* and the first division of *Being and Time* (BP 72). At the Husserl Archive in Louvain in 1954, Derrida, by that time a student at the École Normale Supérieure, worked on Husserl's "Origin of Geometry." There he befriended Rudolf Boehm, a student of Gadamer's, who told him a great deal about Heidegger (BP 91).

Ten years later, in 1964–65, Derrida conducted a seminar titled "Heidegger: the Question of Being and History," the seminar mentioned a moment ago. The recently published transcription of Derrida's handwritten lecture notes is a volume of more than three hundred pages. Only the most cursory summary is possible here—and that is regrettable, inasmuch as the text is remarkable. Above all, it shows how much of Heidegger's work, from *Being and Time* to the books and essays of the 1950s, Derrida had absorbed, and how penetrating his reading of that work is. His focus in the seminar is a few sections of *Being and Time*, namely, sections 6 and 72–76, which are the sections in which Heidegger develops the themes of "the *Destruktion* of the history of ontology" and the "historicity" of a temporalizing Dasein. Yet Derrida treats both themes with a view to

---

1. Jacques Derrida, *Heidegger: la question de l'Être et l'Histoire (Cours de l'ENS-Ulm 1964–1965*, ed. Thomas Dutoit and Margueritte Derrida (Paris: Galilée, 2013). An English translation by Geoffrey Bennington is in preparation.

"Part Two" of *Being and Time,* that is, the part that was never written as such; he also refers in detail to many of the later texts that we associate with Heidegger's "turning," the so-called *Kehre,* from the question of being and time to that of time and being. To be more precise, Derrida shows no interest in the much-discussed *Kehre* as such. Rather, he argues that from the outset Heidegger's focus is the *Da* of *Da-Sein,* the temporality of *being,* and the *history* and *historicity* of Dasein and being.

While it is safe to say that no specific reference to *Geschlecht* appears in these pages—the 1928 course by Heidegger has not yet been published and Derrida does not seem to have read the 1953 Trakl essay as yet—this early seminar foreshadows many of Derrida's own later themes. Moreover, the seminar transcript shows us a Derrida who is not concerned to attain critical distance from Heidegger, nor even to "deconstruct" his texts. Here Derrida prefers the word *sollicitation,* a word that suggests both an invitation to read Heidegger with engagement and to dismantle or perhaps even "undercut" its theses in a thoughtful manner. One may say that Derrida's relation to Heidegger parallels Heidegger's relation to the tradition of metaphysics: to "solicit" it, in both senses of the French word, is to respect it even as one "undoes" it. One may perhaps isolate a dozen steps in Derrida's *sollicitation* of Heidegger's question of being and the themes of history and historicity.

1. Even if Heidegger is pursuing a "fundamental ontology" by means of "phenomenology" and "hermeneutics," he is already on the verge of discovering that ontology, onto-theology, phenomenology, and hermeneutics alike are saturated by the metaphysics of *presence,* that is, by a metaphysics that has run its course and is no longer sustainable.

2. Heidegger's debts to both Hegel and Husserl (the texts of both are examined in detail during the seminar) cannot obscure the fact that Heidegger's *Seinsfrage* and his budding sense of the *history* of being break decisively from the phenomenologies of both predecessors.

3. Heidegger's sensitivity with regard to the question of the grammar and syntax of the word *being* and to the metaphysical foundations of *metaphor* compels his radical overcoming of metaphysics; the "philosophical novel" that "recounts stories" about being (recall Plato's complaints in

*Sophist* and *Timaeus* concerning the philosophical giants of his own past) from antiquity through Hegel has come to an end.

4. The principal "story" for the history of philosophy has been the unwavering dominion of *presence* and *the present*, whether in Greek antiquity (οὐσία, πάρουσία) or in Cartesian-Hegelian modernity (the "I think," self-consciousness, subjectivity, etc.).

5. The "fact" that Dasein understands *Sein* in a vague and general manner, along with the temporal structure of the "always already" in its understanding of the "is," are the lynchpins of (a) the question of being and (b) the temporal horizon of historicity, including all its "epochs."

6. Heidegger's suggestion that an understanding of being (*das Gefragte*) can be "read off" of the being of the questioner (*das [or, better, der] Befragte*), along with his later celebration of language as "the house of being," indicate that Dasein itself is a text and that a *grammatology* and a new examination of *metaphoricity* will become crucial for the questions of being and history.

7. The text, tissue, or weave of language will disclose itself, not as a past that is a past-present or that can be presentified, but as *trace*—and as a trace whose *origin* has vanished.

8. The history of being and the historicity of a finite, temporalizing Dasein are imbricated indissolubly, although the *origin* of the imbrication itself remains an *enigma*.

9. The primacy of the future ecstasy in Heidegger's existential analytic is challenged by the emphasis (in chapter 5 of division two of *Being and Time*) on the finite temporality of historicity, or *Geschichtlichkeit*, which stresses the having-been of Dasein.

10. The enigma of Da-sein expresses itself in the primacy of the ecstasy of the *future* and the significance our of being-*toward*-death, and yet also in the apparent primacy of the *past* in one's birth and communal inheritance (*das*

*Erbe*); the only thing that remains clear is that the ecstasy of the *present,* which is born of both future and past, can no longer hold onto some enduring, standing, "eternal" or "infinite" presence.

11. If there is something aporetic and even "short of breath" about the final sections of *Being and Time,* that is because Heidegger is still crossing the threshold of the question of the (finite) historicity of (finite) being, confronting there an aporia that no form of *vorlaufende Entschlossenheit,* or "precursory resolve," can dissipate—inasmuch as the "origin" of historicity, to repeat, pertains to a past and a passivity that never were *present* and that never can be *presentified* phenomenologically.

12. The enigma of historicity and the history of being cannot be solved by reference to the oppositional structures of authenticity-inauthenticity or of "vulgar" as opposed to "primordial, originary" time. The occurrence of history and of destiny (*Geschehen, Geschichte, Geschick*) is scarcely explained by Heidegger's appeals to the retrieval of past possibilities (*Wiederholung*), precursory resolve (*vorlaufende Entschlossenheit*), thrownness (*Geworfenheit*), the passivity of Dasein as "moved" (*Bewegtheit*), or the metaphorical name bestowed on the ownmost possibility of a finite Da-Sein, to wit, "death."

There is, of course, much more to the 1964–65 seminar. Yet because the themes of *Geschlecht,* from sexual and ontological differences to a poetics of these differences, are not broached at this early date, we may proceed with our own brief history of Derrida's earlier involvements with Heidegger.

Yet let it be said once again: by the end of the 1960s, Derrida's mastery of the Heideggerian text and his critical appreciation of Heidegger's project as a whole are nothing short of astonishing. In the January 1968 lecture to the French Society of Philosophy, "La différance," it is the first letter of the alphabet, the pyramidal "A" of *différance,* that is Derrida's theme, along with the *trace* structure of writing. After working through a series of issues involving Hegel (the thinker of the pyramidal "A"), Koyré, and Saussure, in which the structure of the Latin *differe* as both differing and deferring is developed, Derrida turns to Nietzsche, Freud, and—last not least—Heidegger. Nietzsche's rejection of all the putatively self-identical concepts of metaphysics and morals is found everywhere in his work; perhaps less visible, at least until one studies Gilles Deleuze's *Nietzsche and Philosophy*, is the differential nature of *force* and *forces* in that work. Freud's emphasis on trace (*Spur*) and effraction (*Bahnung, frayage*) is briefly discussed in "La différance," but then quickly brought to the decisive question concerning the economic problem of the "detour" in the pleasure principle (the detour sign that is held in the hand of the reality principle) and the radical interruption of the pleasure principle by the death-and-destruction drives. After a brief reference to Levinas's challenge to ontological thinking, Derrida turns to Heidegger. Here the problem is whether *différance* can be said to refer to, or even be subsumed under, Heidegger's "ontological difference," the difference between being and beings, or between presencing and the things that come to presence. Derrida's first foray is perhaps the most decisive: *la différance n'est pas*, differance (with an *a*) *is not*. It cannot be capitalized, it governs no realm, and it cannot be reduced to an element in the story of the *epoch* of metaphysics. Epochality, discussed at length already in the 1964–65 seminar, will prove to be one of the four threads in that weft of issues, the *Geflecht*, which structures the 1978 *Of Spirit*. In the present essay, Derrida is tempted to think of the entire history of metaphysics, up to and including Heidegger, as that epoch in which the Heraclitean "one differentiating itself" is lost in the traces of what Heidegger calls "ontological difference." Yet, for Derrida, thinking the trace of differance does not participate in Heidegger's quest for the "truth of being": the trace does not present itself in the history of presencing. Always differing, the trace defers presence. "It effaces itself in presenting itself, becomes voiceless as it resonates, like the *a* that is written, inscribing its pyramid in differance" (M 24).

At this point Derrida introduces Heidegger's "Anaximander Fragment," examining there the appearances of the word *Spur*, "trace," in Heidegger's own text. For already in Heidegger's text the trace resists presence. Oblivion of being is the having-been-forgotten or the already-having-withdrawn of the difference between being and beings or between presencing and the beings that present themselves. Such oblivion, which according to Heidegger dominates metaphysics from beginning to end, leaves not a trace of itself. Yet a certain equivocation enters Heidegger's text precisely here: what disappears, he says, is "the early trace" of the difference, *die frühe Spur* that Heidegger nevertheless does find in the earliest fragments of Western thinking, above all in this oldest of fragments, "the saying of Anaximander." True, the trace of presencing, or the trace of the difference between presencing and beings, is not itself present—it never really took place. And yet, lost in invisibility, a streak of dawn's light is somehow retained, guarded, and regarded. "In a text," Derrida adds (M 26). The trace of the ontological difference is sealed, as though in a pyramid, and thus "remains preserved" (*so eine Spur geprägt hat . . . gewahrt bleibt*). This leads Derrida to a crucial question that the *Geschlecht* series will take up: the trace of the ontological difference appears to have vanished from "our language" (whether *notre langue* or *unserer Sprache*), and so seems to force us to go beyond the idioms of our own tongues to what Heidegger identifies simply as "language." Heidegger tries to rescue the vanished sense of τὸ χρεών, traced in Anaximander's thinking, by turning to an old German word, *der Brauch,* which is related to both need and usage, hence also to custom—a word that is related to the English word *to brook* and that is translated by the French as *le maintien*. In *Geschlecht III* the theme of the early trace—of the dawn, of morning—will return: there it will be the promise of an early experience of a sexual duality that is not yet struck by discord and dissension. The dawn "to come" is always for Heidegger our only hope in the night of our present, and yet that dawn is somehow "earlier" than our nocturnal present. Heidegger insists that these early traces "immediately disappear" and are lost forever in the history of being as metaphysics. Lost forever and yet *preserved* as being's note-to-self, as it were, a note in the margins of one or other ancient text, at least if "our language" may succeed in translating itself over to that early, obliterated text. Lost forever, however, it vanishes *as such*. The early trace, both obliterated and preserved, thus "threatens the authority of the *as such* in general" (M 27). This "as such," which in his final seminar Derrida discusses in terms of what Heidegger, following Aristotle, calls "apophantic discourse," will draw Derrida's attention from this point on up to the end of his life.

In 1972, Derrida adds a long note to his "Differance" on the problem of "the proper" and "property," this time not in Heidegger's fundamental ontology of Dasein but in his later thinking of *Ereignis*. Needless to say, the trace—as Derrida understands it—will not yield any sense of appropriation, property, and propriety, not even in the *Ereignis* that seems to be "beyond being." Neither "trace" nor "ontological difference" nor "being" nor "the event of appropriation and expropriation" will serve as a means of ownership or ownness: "There will not be a unique name, not even the word *being*. And one will have to think this word without *nostalgia*, which is to say, outside the myth of a purely maternal or purely paternal language, of the lost fatherland of thought" (M 29). Especially *Geschlecht*

II and III will focus on the matter of philosophical nationality and nationalism as ensconced in "our" language, especially if "our" language happens to be Heidegger's German. Heidegger remains caught up in the search for the perfect word, the word for *being*, even if the word becomes *Ereignis* or *Lichtung* or *das Gewähren* of time and being, the granting of clearing and presencing. In all these cases, Heidegger remains caught up preeminently in his own—the German—language. If, as Heidegger asserts at the end of his Anaximander essay, "being speaks always and everywhere throughout all language," Derrida will pose questions concerning such "speech," which turns out to be written, and such "language," which turns out to be more multifarious, differing, deferred, and disseminated than Heidegger ever allows in and for his "own" language.

By examining a long note near the end of *Being and Time* (SZ 432–33), a note that anticipates the "second half" of Heidegger's magnum opus, the half that is never written, Derrida's "Ousia and Grammè" is able to challenge Heidegger's account of the "vulgar" understanding of time and the very horizon of "original time" upon which that opus is projected. An entire series of words that one might translate as "presence" (οὐσία, παρουσία, *Anwesenheit, Gegenwart, [Ver]gegenwärtigung, Vorhandenheit*), introduced at the outset of *Being and Time*, is never fully clarified in the course of that long work. Furthermore, close readings of Aristotle's *Physics* IV, 10–14, and Hegel's *Encyclopedia* and the early "Jena Logic" (along with other works) do not sustain Heidegger's claim that in the long history of metaphysics, from Aristotle to Hegel and Bergson, the "vulgar" understanding of time is based on the notion of time as a line of "now-points." As in the lecture "Différance," Derrida here too suggests that the problem of "presence" devolves upon that of the trace, indeed, the "written trace" (M 37, 76–77). The *line* of time and of the written trace therefore becomes the focus of Derrida's study. That study concludes by challenging the notion of a "derivative," "vulgar" temporality, one that would somehow have fallen away from an "original" temporality, a distinction that seems to Derrida to arise from a classic metaphysical gesture.

The only thing that is missing from Derrida's analysis in "Ousia and Grammè," it seems to me, and it is something I discussed with him often, is a detailed analysis of what Heidegger calls the *ecstatic* interpretation of temporality. The ecstases of time, of "original," "authentic" time, themselves seem to derive from a reading of chapter 14 of Book IV of the *Physics*, where words for "suddenness" and "existence" at least *seem* to be the source of Heidegger's notion. It has always seemed to me that a close reading of sections 65–68 of *Being and Time* would be needed not only to make the argument of "Ousia and Grammē" telling but also to provide the context for Derrida's own notion of the *spacing* of the trace. In other words, even if Heidegger's metaphysical gesture of distinguishing an "appropriate" from an "inappropriate" temporality for Dasein inevitably falters, his analysis of the "raptures" of time, that is, of the ecstases and their *Entrückungen,* still seems to be the most creative and revolutionary analysis of *Being and Time*. It will not do to ignore ecstatic temporality. (Perhaps the most detailed reflection on ecstatic temporality that we have from Derrida appears in his early 1964–65 seminar, even if the relevant pages of *Being and Time* are not read there.) Rather than pursue what would no doubt be a long and complex reading, however, Derrida concludes his article by once again challenging "the enigmatic proximity" of Dasein to the question of being. He adds a note to his "Note":

> The originary, the authentic, is determined as the "proper" (*eigentlich*), that is to say, the *near* (proper, *proprius*), the present in the proximity of presence to self. One could show how this value of proximity and of presence to self intervenes at the beginning of *Being and Time* and elsewhere in the decision to pose the question of the meaning of being by taking as one's point of departure an existential analytic of *Dasein.* And one could show the momentum of metaphysics in such a decision and in the credit here accorded the value of presence to self. This question could propagate its movement to include all the concepts implying the value of the "proper" (*eigen, eigens, ereignen, Ereignis, eigentümlich, das Eignen,* etc.). (M 74 n. 26)

No doubt the *locus classicus* of the theme of proximity and propriety in Heidegger's thinking is Derrida's "The Ends of Man," written in May 1968 and delivered as an address to an "international colloquium" in New York City in October of that year. The "ends" in question extend from the Kantian distinction between means and ends in the treatment by man of man, via Sartre's phenomenological ontology and its discussion of "human reality," to Michel Foucault's prediction that *l'homme*, an "invention" of "recent date," is about to expire, and above all to Heidegger's fundamental ontology of Dasein. Derrida's initial reflection on the "international colloquium" evokes the notion of "philosophical nationalities," a notion that dominates his seminars during the 1980s and the second and third of his *Geschlechter*. The final fifteen pages of "The Ends" develop in great detail a certain "magnetism" in Heidegger's thinking of *Mensch* and "the truth of being." The word *l'aimantation,* "magnetism," is used twice there; it will be applied to the *Geschlecht* series itself, and from the outset. As Derrida's own series is "magnetized" by Heidegger's 1953 Trakl interpretation, "Die Sprache im Gedicht," so here Derrida is sensitive to the magnetic force of a certain nearness—namely, the proximity of Dasein to being, a proximity that would constitute the proper essence of Dasein. The propriety of proximity is nothing other than the closeness and even immediacy of Dasein to being as the *questioner* of being. Such immediacy, argues Derrida, in spite of Heidegger's protestations to the contrary, arises from the presence-to-self that defines humankind in and for philosophy at least since Descartes. Even if the question of being is ontologically remote from Dasein, swathed as it is in an everydayness that has endured throughout the epoch of metaphysics, the question is as close to Dasein as anything can get. "One thus sees that the *Dasein,* if it is *not* man, is nevertheless *not anything other than* man" (M 151). Even if Heidegger emphasizes *Ferne* (remoteness) every bit as much as *Nähe* (nearness), argues Derrida, what is proper to the essence of man is that he and she close the distance—either by interrogating themselves in order to solicit the meaning of being or, later, by standing in the truth of being. In spite of the metaphorics of *Unheimlichkeit* and the oblivion of being, man's "nearness to being" elaborates the metaphorics of "neighborhood, shelter, house, service, safeguarding, voice and hearing" (M 156). Even if Heidegger subjects the meaning of being as *presence* (*Gegenwart, Anwesenheit*) to a dismantling, the language of presence—especially the presence of the spoken word to thinking, which hears and understands what it says—comes to prevail in his own thought.

Yet Derrida notes something startling about the language of proximity and propriety, something that gets lost in a footnote of "The Ends of Man" (M 159 n. 19) and that even *Geschlecht III*, which is devoted to the question of what can be said best in a "foreign" language, fails to recall. Heidegger's German words, which otherwise guide his thinking without fail, increasingly so as the years go by—such that, apart from the Greek, no other language offers food for thought—here do not serve: in the words *Nähe,* "proximity," and *das Eigene,* the "proper," it is not easy to hear the relation that the Latin (*prope, proprius*) and even the French (*proche, propre*) make clear. It is as though Heidegger, when thinking his own most magnetic thought, the thought that the *nearness* to being of Dasein is all its *own,* would have to think in French. Whether early or late, and whether or not because of its encapsulation within "our" language, Heidegger's thinking overlooks the debt it owes to the metaphysics of presence. Derrida writes: "The proximate is the proper; the proper is what is closest (*prope, proprius*). Man is the proper of being, which, quite close, whispers in his ear; being is the proper of man; it is the truth that speaks to him; such is the proposition that grants the *there* of the truth of being and the truth of man" (M 160). It is the confidence in such proximity and propriety, confidence in the intimacy and ownership between being and man, that from both the inside and the outside is coming to an end.

I confess—if I may add a rejoinder—that Derrida's insistence on proximity and propriety in Heidegger, while convincing me most days of the week, on other days needs to be balanced by the realization that Heidegger early and late thinks *within* anxiety. That is to say, the proximity that is surely there in Heidegger's thought is tempered by notions of distancing, remoteness, uncanniness, abyss, and ecstasis. There was thus always a tension between Derrida and me, each of us emphasizing one side of the coin while knowing we both had to examine Heidegger whole coin. In my own earliest work, such as it is or was, I stressed what I called "thinking-within-anxiety" even in Heidegger's later work, that is, even in the apparently Olympian thinking of *Ereignis* and the destiny of being. Perhaps it was an amulet on my part, attempting to hold at bay the suspicions that Derrida was rightly raising. Yet when we recall section 40 of *Being and Time* and its analysis of the fundamental *Befindlichkeit* of anxiety, we remember that anything like a confidence-boosting "self-presence" is quite foreign to what Heidegger is describing: in anxiety, nothing at all threatens us, even as it—the nothing—grows near; no source of comfort or assuredness prevails in that nearness. *Das Nichts* encroaches precisely because it comes from nowhere and has nowhere else to go. The region of disclosedness that opens up in anxiety offers no solace: it is no spark of divine light, no cogito, and no transcendental unity of apperception. Rather, anxiety "is already 'there' ['*da*']—and yet nowhere; it is so close that it corners us and stops our breath—and yet it is nowhere" (SZ 186). To be sure, Derrida is aware of such hauntings throughout Heidegger's work; otherwise he would never have been interested in it. Yet his reading of proximity as self-presence underplays and even underestimates the haunting power of anxiety. Here more than ever the Derridian "double reading" is needed. If the *wovor der Angst* ("that in the face of which we are anxious") and the *worum der Angst* ("that for the sake of which we are anxious") coalesce, so that the disclosing and the disclosed are one and the same, revealing the tenuous and fragile possibility of our being in the world, this is no mere reflexivity of the modern metaphysical sort. "In anxiety, it is 'uncanny' for one," writes Heidegger (SZ 188). Every sort of familiarity and comfort zone the world has to offer comes crashing down, or quietly crumbles in *Unheimlichkeit*. Our being-in (the world) is a being *un-zuhause*. Self-presence? Heigh ho, nobody home. That does not sound like Descartes, or Kant, or even Hegel. Nietzsche, perhaps.

In the 1980 paper "Envoi," seldom discussed in the Heidegger literature, we have a truly remarkable piece of analysis of language and idiom. Originally an address to the Societies for Philosophy in the French Language, meeting that year in Strasbourg, it focuses on the meaning of *representation,* the word and the thing. A large part of the address is devoted to a reading of Heidegger's 1938 essay, "The Age When All the World Becomes an Image," *Die Zeit des Weltbildes.* Particularly important for the *Geschlecht* series is the fact that here Derrida insists on the significance of Heidegger's work for French philosophy—and the significance of Heidegger's essentially untranslatable *language*. Because the *Geschlecht* series, especially in its third generation, stresses the limitations of Heidegger's appeal to his "own" language, whereby Heidegger often misses the richness of the Romance languages for the very themes he is trying to develop, we might have assumed that Derrida is interested only in pointing out such limitations. In the 1980 address to the French philosophers the reverse is the case. Derrida chooses the title of his address carefully: *envoi* is an envoy, but also the message that the envoy is to report and represent. The envoy is "sent," and the Heideggerian *Geschick*, the destinal sending of being, is here on Derrida's mind. Yet Derrida spends even more time and devotes even greater pains to note the differences between the dubious French word *représentation* and the German *Vorstellung,* a word and concept that both Hegel and Heidegger view askance, since it designates a thinking that has not advanced to *genuine* thought. Perhaps all we must note here is the importance of the idiomatic nature of *stellen* and *vor-stellen*, as opposed to *re-praesentatio*, and the thought-provoking untranslatability or at least dissymmetry of the two. If in the *Geschlecht* series Derrida is concerned to show how philosophical nationality and nationalism can, in Heidegger's case, foreclose possibilities for Heidegger's "own" thought, here he is urging the French philosophers to cross the Rhine, and even to engage the language he here calls—oddly, and without commenting on it—*germain*. As though it were *germane* to French philosophy.

There is one further item in the address that has to concern us, one that has to do with a kind of *dissension* in the very notion of *Anwesenheit*. On the one hand, Heidegger calls for the overcoming or at least the letting-be of metaphysics, which has always identified being as "presence"; on the other hand, his own radically other thinking does nothing other than try to think the same thing, "presence." Because the missing *Geschlecht* has much to do with *dissension,* not as ontological difference but as sexual difference, we will have to keep Derrida's "Envoi" in mind throughout later chapters of the present book, especially chapters 5 and 6. Yet now we must turn from the singular "Envoi" of 1980 to the maddeningly multiple and wildly disseminating *Envois* of *The Post Card,* published that same year, 1980.

Many more essays, including "The Supplement of Copula" and "The Retreat of Metaphor," to mention only two, would doubtless need to be recalled here. Yet it is gradually becoming clear that the *Geschlecht* series also has at least two largely extra-Heideggerian sources (in addition to Derrida's Nietzsche books) that need to be mentioned, namely, the 1974 *Glas* and the 1980 *Post Card.* In each of these a concatenation of themes links us to *Geschlecht,* although here we will have to satisfied with a mere list: in *Glas,* the theme of the sister, whether her name be Christiane or Mary Magdalene, and whether she be Hegel's sister or the sister of Christ, and whether she be a wife or a professional virgin; and, along with the sister, the family and the holy family, which sometimes includes a mother who often, especially when it comes to the legacies of fathers and sons, is reduced to something like a room, a room that can be rented only once; and, along with the family, whether holy or profane, the fulfillment of the law in love, even if love is constantly bestrewn with the flowers of sexual and genital love; such flowers include "broom," which the French call *Genêt;* something like forbidden loves, then, loves that do not fulfill but violate the law, if incest prohibition and exogamous, monogamous heterosexuality are the law.[2]

One would have thought that Heidegger is even less likely to play a role in such a love story than Hegel. Heidegger would be the pious sacristan's son who pulls the rope of the death knell. Yet in *The Post Card from Socrates to Freud and Beyond* Heidegger plays a more grownup and more confusing role, at least in the *Envois* that open the text. There Heidegger is

---

2. Another place to look for anticipations of the *Geschlecht* series, especially the first of the essays, is Derrida's correspondence with Christie V. MacDonald during the autumn of 1981. There we see something of Derrida's hope for a sexuality that is not trapped in and by dualities and duels—later in the present book we will refer to that hope. Although the 1953 Trakl essay is not yet mentioned in the correspondence, Derrida has clearly already developed his response to Heidegger's 1928 Leibniz-logic course. See "Choreographies: An Interview with Jacques Derrida," ed. and trans. Christie V. MacDonald, *Diacritics* 12, no. 2 (Summer 1982): 66–76. See now *Points de suspension,* PS 95–115, especially 109–11.

proclaimed one of the two grandfathers of our time, one of the two *Pépés* or pleasure principles—or Primary Processes or Penmen/Postmen, Penny Posts, and so on (CP 91; 206). True, these two, Freud and Heidegger, never met, neither at Vienna nor, to be sure, in London; not even, one must say, at Zollikon. They never exchanged letters or postcards. Entire worlds separate them. And yet. Together they constitute in Derrida's view "the grand epoch," the epoch that sees metaphysics—commencing with a Plato who backs a writing Socrates—entering into its end. There is, as far as I recall, no explicit mention of *Geschlecht* in these love letters without destination, these postcards pleading for a rendezvous that never happens. There is a great deal of *Geschick*, that is, of skillful thought concerning a tragic destiny and an unreachable destination, but no *Geschlecht*. Perhaps the most striking clairvoyance in this regard, however, comes at the very end of the *Envois*, which as a whole serve as a modest 260-page preface to two essays and an interview on Freud. There, at the end (CP 271–72), Derrida recalls Hegel's correspondence with his sister Christiane, presented at length in *Glas*, along with Hegel's assertion in the *Phenomenology of Spirit* that in the eminently ethical brother-sister relationship the blood is never agitated. And, oddly, Derrida concurs. His own sister is the one person with whom he has never had "even the smallest beginnings of a quarrel." Years later, both publicly and privately, Derrida confirms this fact. "It's true, I swear it," he says, discounting as a mere aberration of childhood an early attempt to immolate her. If the *Envois* of *La Carte postale* are filled with dissension and discord, along with desperate love, it could be that Derrida is particularly susceptible to dreams of a love where no quarrel can ever arise. And such dreams of love would never leave "the sister" altogether out of account. So saying, we find ourselves upon the very verge of the four generations of *Geschlecht* and their multiple phantoms of the other.

Chapters 1 and 2 of the present book treat the first two of the *Geschlechter*. Chapter 3, which treats *Of Spirit: Heidegger and the Question*, only seems to interrupt the series; in reality this small monograph, one of Derrida's most remarkable achievements, is very much a part of the *Geschlecht* project. My own chapter 4 comments on the final, the fourth, *Geschlecht*, in which the themes of Derrida's seminar, "Philosophical Nationality and Nationalism," come to dominate. Only then, in chapters 5 and 6, does the missing *Geschlecht*, the third, the unpublished *Geschlecht*, make its appearance, first as a reading of the thirty-three-page Loyola typescript, then as an account of the 1984–85 seminar, "The Phantom of the Other." Finally, chapter 7 returns to the poetry of Georg Trakl—and to the lives of Georg and Gretl Trakl—both of which clearly "magnetize" the *Geschlecht* project as a whole. Because Trakl's poetry is not all that well known in the Anglophone world, the book ends with two appendices, the first presenting in German and English *en face* a number of the poems discussed by Heidegger and Derrida, the second a number of poems I wish they had discussed, poems that evoke figures of "the sister" and of "the lovers." In the end, as in the beginning, what magnetizes is the poetry.

1

# *Geschlecht I*

## Sexual Difference, Ontological Difference

Derrida confesses himself riveted by Heidegger's use of the word *Geschlecht*. Derrida's two principal sources in the initial *Geschlecht* article are, to repeat, Heidegger's 1928 logic lectures, especially the tenth and eleventh sections of the course, and the 1953 essay on Trakl, "Language in the Poem: A Placement of Georg Trakl's Poem." The more positive side of Derrida's reading claims that Heidegger is seeking something like a pre-dual sexuality, that is, an erotic power that is not married, as it were, to binary difference and male-female opposition. The less positive side of his reading wonders whether the "order of implications" that Heidegger tries to institute in fundamental ontology—for example, his desire to distinguish ontological semination or bestrewal (*die Streuung*) from ontic dispersion and dissemination (*die Zerstreuung*), and yet to prevent the "ontic" from becoming something merely negative and nugatory on account of that distinction—can be sustained. *Geschlecht I* therefore closes by confronting the method of "privative interpretation" in and for existential analysis and the vast problem of *just-plain-life,* that is, of life as *nur-noch-Leben,* interpreted *per impossibile* as Dasein minus care—*per impossible* since Dasein minus care equals zero. Yet a more detailed synopsis is called for.

Derrida begins his *Geschlecht* article by noting that it is easy to see and to say that Heidegger nowhere writes about sex and sexual difference. All too easy. Perhaps facile, therefore—whether in discussions among "Heideggerians" themselves or among nonphilosophers who concern themselves with "sexual politics." The complaint is of course not without justification. One looks in vain for the German equivalents of the words *erotic* and *sexual,* or even *male* and *female,* in Heidegger's magnum opus, *Being and Time.* And even if "birth" becomes an important theme there, natality rather than or in addition to fatality (SZ 372–74), it turns out that it is not a woman but a *Dasein* that gives birth.[1] What can one therefore make of Heidegger's silence concerning sex and the sexes—doubtless one of his several notorious silences? Derrida notes that neither "sexuality" nor "politics" are major items in Heidegger's vocabulary, so that it is not surprising that "sexual politics" is clearly beneath him (Ps 397/9).[2] Yet Derrida is not in a hurry to correct Heidegger's oversights or to fill his silences. His concern is to think through "the ontological difference" in Heidegger's thought, especially as he develops it during the years 1927–28, and to bring a number of questions surrounding "sexual difference" into rapport with the ontological.

The exemplary being for the existential analysis of *Being and Time*, which is to prepare the way for the question of the meaning of being in general, is *Dasein*. The *Da-* of *Dasein* does not manifest sexual difference, at least in any obvious way. Such a difference, along with all the adventures, joys, and calamities that accompany it, Heidegger would presumably relegate to some regional ontology or to one or other constellation of the "sciences of man," to biology or anthropology, sociology or psychology, or perhaps even religion. Or would he? *Could* he? What about that extraordinary discovery of Heidegger's called *Befindlichkeit*, which is the initial yet global disclosure of the being of Dasein, the disclosure by which Dasein "finds itself to be"? True, we translate *Befindlichkeit* hopelessly and helplessly into English as "state of mind" or "disposition," even though it is clear that Heidegger means something quite different and much more fundamental. If we stay with the awkward expression, how-we-find-ourselves-to-be, is it entirely clear that not merely at first and for the most part but fundamentally such "finding ourselves" has nothing to do with our sexual being, our sexual relations, and our sexual confusions? Do our moods and attunements to the world, our *Stimmungen*, in all their astonishing variety and intensity, have nothing to do with our being sexed and gendered creatures? Does that famous hormonal spectrum we learned about long ago display no rainbow hues of sexuality? Or does the word *spectrum* imply that the sliding scale of hormones flattens sexuality and sexual difference out, as it were, to sheer indifference? In any case, can we

---

1. SZ refers to Martin Heidegger, *Sein und Zeit*, 12th ed. (Tübingen: M. Niemeyer, 1972), a reprint of the seventh edition, released in 1953; the first edition was published in 1927. I refer to the 12th edition by page (as here) or section number throughout.

2. In the body of my text I will refer to the articles in the *Geschlecht* series, at least when the particular source is clear, merely by a page reference to the French and English editions.

truly conceive of a *Mitsein* and a *Mitdasein*, that is, a being with others, other Daseins, that would not be at least influenced by the gender and genital identities, perplexities, boondoggles, and dreams of every Dasein we have ever met? And what about that *Berühren*, that "touching" which no chair can do to a wall but which the French *chair*, that is, the flesh, does every day and every night? Are the disclosures of touch ever slack? Does the erotic tension ever diminish to the zero point? Is such tension unrelated to those mighty magnetisms, those famous reasons of the heart, that do not yield so quickly to our understanding? Are we entirely clear that these mighty lodestones have nothing to do with fundamental differences, with the multiple and proliferating *existentials*—for are not sex and gender differences a prime case of the *daseinsmäßig*, that is, of qualities that are "of the measure of Dasein" and that will not yield to categories? Why else would all the world be so terrified of them and fling labels over them so desperately and pass civil and religious laws concerning them and, if the laws will not stop them, how about mobs? Finally, can Heidegger be certain that the ontological difference, namely, the difference that opens up in the clearing of being in order to let beings show themselves *as* themselves, has nothing to do with gender and sexual differences? Derrida does not spell out all of these questions as I have done here, but I suspect that such issues as *Befindlichkeit*, *Berühren*, and *Mitdasein* prompt and prod his desire to juxtapose sexual and ontological differences. Yet let me rein in my wild steed, whether stallion or mare I cannot tell, and return to Derrida's and Heidegger's texts.

Ontological difference, or perhaps the pre-ontological difference (SZ 13, 16–17, 65), is marked by the capacity of a being to ask questions, including the question of the meaning of being. For Heidegger, such a capacity has the highest possible value—it is the difference of all differences, the difference that makes all the difference when speaking of being. Thus "sexual" difference does not seem to occupy the same "height," *hauteur* (396/8), as ontological difference. "Sexual" difference is perhaps *ontic* difference, difference with an *existentiel* import, but with no *existential* significance. Yet it is not as though human sexuality invites commentary only from the hacks who write for the illustrated weeklies that pile up in slovenly stacks at hair studios. Would philosophy consist of footnotes to Plato if Plato had not had his beloved Socrates, who in turn "loved what is most alive"? And what of "solider" Aristotle, the doctor's son? And in modernity, what could ever relieve the laboriousness of bachelor Kant if not his incisive pragmatic discourse on the wiles of womanhood? What tempts Schelling to sail off to the ancient isle of Samothrace, there to seek the pristine deity in Demeter and Persephone, while his friend Hegel, thinking of Schlegel's *Lucinde*, grows grim about the mouth and drops dialectic for vitriol? What forces Nietzsche to admit that, after all, these jibes of his at *das Weib* are merely "his" truths? Where would philosophy and philology be without the spark of Eros? Does that spark not attain to the heights of questioning? Has Heidegger merely *silenced* sex? And has he done so merely by chance? That seems unlikely. Derrida wagers that such silence and such a silencing are worth investigating.

Heidegger is unwilling, in his fundamental ontology of Dasein, to visit the parlous realms of gender and sexuality; it is as though sexual difference is neither here nor there for the "here" and "there," the *Da-*, of *Da-sein*. In spite of what we have said above concerning the existential structure of *Befindlichkeit*, a Heideggerian of the strict persuasion could certainly argue that sexuality as such offers no royal road to the structures of being-in-the-world, care, temporality, and so on, although "everydayness" has a much better chance. Yet Heidegger himself revisits—or confronts for the first time—the question of sexual difference soon after the publication of *Being and Time*, in section 10 of his 1928 lecture course, "The Metaphysical Underpinnings of Logic, with Leibniz as Point of Departure."[3] Here, in sections 10 and 11, Heidegger offers some "guidelines" concerning the problem of the "transcendence" of Dasein in *Being and Time*. He confirms what he says peremptorily in that book: for the purposes of the question of being, the exemplary being is the one that *questions*. That interrogating, interrogative being "we grasp terminologically as Dasein" (SZ 12; Ps, 399/11). In the 1928 course Heidegger explains that it is the *neutrality* of the neuter-gendered term *das Dasein* that justifies its use for ontology. The neutrality of Dasein is clearly quite general in its scope: Heidegger means to exclude all "ontic" relations, such as race, nationality, age, personality type, intelligence, education, health, sex, gender, sexual preference, and all matters of lifestyle and personal taste. These facets of existence might pertain to a philosophical anthropology or an ethics; they might even be discussed in what Heidegger calls—quite mysteriously—a "metaphysics of Dasein." Yet they play no role in fundamental ontology, which is the ontology of neutral Dasein. Dasein is, as it were, the

---

3. Published as Martin Heidegger, *Metaphysische Anfangsgründe der Logik im Ausgang von Leibniz*, Gesamtausgabe vol. 26 (Frankfurt am Main: V. Klostermann, 1978). Section 10 offers some "guidelines" for the interpretation of *Being and Time*; section 11 deals with the problem of *transcendence* in that work. For a detailed discussion, see IM, ch. 2, and DL, chs. 5, 7, and 8, esp. 184–89, 248–51, and 252–65.

text from which the meaning of being can be read or deciphered (SZ 7). Here Derrida repeats the point he makes in virtually every prior text of his on Heidegger: even though the existential-ontological self-examination of the *questioner* appears to guarantee the *proximity* of the research(er) to its object, with the questioner questioning the (existence of) the questioner him- or herself, Derrida—perhaps recalling the traditional definition of thought-thinking-itself in Aristotle and Hegel—raises a suspicion. Even if Heidegger is careful to cite repeatedly the problem of phenomenological *access* to the matter in question, is there not something axiomatic and even peremptory in this initial decision? It is a decision to *name*, to give a *neutral, neuter name*, to the questioner: "This being that we ourselves in each case are and that, among other things, has the ontological possibility of questioning, we grasp terminologically as *Dasein*" (ibid.). If such "grasping," *fassen*, seems peremptory—Derrida does not shy from calling it elliptical and even brutal (399/11)—Heidegger takes pains in his 1928 lecture course to justify that decision. The very first justification, in the form of a "guideline," involves the choice of a *neuter* word, *das Dasein*, rather than the masculine *der Mensch*. The neuter word means to neutralize all aspects of the being of the questioner except this one, to wit, questioning. Neuter and neutral Dasein is not indifferent to its being, to be sure. Neuter and neutral Dasein is *the questioner*—and otherwise, in the purview of ontology, *nothing*.

The elimination of all ontic characterizations of Dasein, its sex, ethnic origin, place and date of birth, and so on, is surely bound up with the ontological priority that modern philosophy gives to the *thinking* subject, the Cartesian *cogito*. Derrida himself describes Heidegger's reduction of Dasein to the *questioner* as *le trait nu de ce rapport à soi* (Ps 399). In my first letter to him, dated January 3, 1983, which was in response to the *typescript* of this first *Geschlecht*, I agreed that the "terminological" decision in *Sein und Zeit* appears to be "already framed in metaphysical subjectivity." However, I asked whether the emphasis on *Mitsein* in the 1928 lectures (the emphasis on at least *two* in the *Da-* of *Da-sein*) did not "help to de-center the *Selbstsein* of Dasein." I suggested that there is, at least by 1928, something like a profound and primordial *Mitsein*, and that Derrida himself might wish to highlight—and even radicalize—his treatment of *Mitsein* in this first *Geschlecht*.[4]

---

4. The correspondence with Derrida is available at the IMEC Archive in Caen.

And yet, whatever one may say of *Dasein* as *Mitsein,* the only neutrality Heidegger discusses or even mentions, as though leaping ahead into uncharted territory, which is the territory into which his *second* guideline leads us, is that of a neither-nor with regard to sexual difference. Neutral Dasein is marked (preeminently?) by *Geschlechtslosigkeit,* "sexlessness," "asexuality." One is surprised by this leap ahead, and, although Derrida does not venture such an absurdity, one may in the confusion of the moment be tempted to translate *Neutralität* quite falsely as "neutered." Dasein is "also," and Derrida underscores Heidegger's "also," "neither of the two sexes." Heidegger thus appears to be certain that there are only two, but he does not ask whether this duality is an ontic-existentiel happenstance or an ontological desideratum. The being that or who *we* are, viewed ontologically, is neither female nor male. In "our" factical concretion, "we" may presumably be one or the other; as those who are involved in their being, however, we are neither. Yet why neutralize sexuality first of all, and not only first of all but exclusively, since no other ontic quality or characteristic is mentioned? And why confirm the duality of the sexes by this very neutralization? From the outset, one must say, Derrida is gripped by this *keines von beiden,* "neither of the two," of Heidegger's proclamation, *keines von beiden Geschlechtern ist.*

At this point in his exposition Derrida himself leaps ahead. He notes that almost thirty years later Heidegger will engage the issue of *"Geschlecht"* in all its multifarious senses. Derrida does not yet mention the title of the relevant essay by Heidegger, but he is clearly referring to the second essay on Georg Trakl in *Unterwegs zur Sprache,* "Die Sprache im Gedicht: Eine Erörterung von Georg Trakls Gedicht." This is the text that "magnetizes" the entire *Geschlecht* series—especially its third, unpublished, generation. To repeat, only in the sense of "sex" will Heidegger be certain that there are but two *Geschlechter,* and he denies that this has simply to do with the grammar of the word. To be fair, one might object that it may have to do with the word itself: *die Geschlechter* could of course refer to manifold generations, tribes, and coinages, and yet the most "natural" translation of the plural will always be "the two sexes." Yet Derrida would surely reply, and rightly reply: From what nature does this "natural" translation derive? And would grammar alone account for Heidegger's singling out the *duality* of the *Geschlechter,* neither of which marks the questioner as such? At all events, whether singular or plural, what is this thing called *Geschlecht* all about? And why must it be excluded from fundamental ontology first of all?

Derrida's opening statement concerning this first generation of *Geschlecht,* footnoted in *Psyché,* merits extended quotation, in part because it is clear about the "magnetism" of Heidegger's Trakl essay, but also in part because it mirrors the gesture of Heidegger's "placement" or "situating" of Trakl—as Heidegger situates Trakl, so Derrida wishes to situate *"Geschlecht"* in Heidegger:

> This essay, like the following one ("The Hand of Heidegger: *Geschlecht II*") . . . will have to content itself with sketching in a preliminary fashion an interpretation to come by which I would like to situate *Geschlecht* in Heidegger's path of thought. In the path of his writing as well—and the impression, or inscription, marked by the word *Geschlecht* will not have been there for nothing. I will leave this word in its own language for reasons that should impose themselves on us in the course of the reading. And it certainly is a matter of *"Geschlecht"* (the *word* for sex, race, family, generation, lineage, species, genre), and not of *Geschlecht* as such: one will not so easily clear away the mark of the word (*"Geschlecht"*) that blocks our access to the thing itself (the *Geschlecht*); in that word, Heidegger will much later descry the imprint of a blow or a stroke *(Schlag)*. He will do so in a text we will not speak of here but toward which this reading is heading, and by which, in truth, I know it is already being drawn as toward a magnet: *Die Sprache im Gedicht*. (Ps 395/7)

Much could be made of this being magnetized, *aimanté(e)*, a word so close to *aimer*, "to love," and to the *amant(e)*, "the lover," a figure that occupies Derrida as much as it does Georg Trakl. Could it possibly have occupied Heidegger? He too would have been fascinated by this word *aimanté*, even if it belongs to the French language, inasmuch as its roots go back to the earliest Greek thinkers. The *Petit Robert*, which is anything but petite, has several listings for this word. The masculine noun *aimant* appears to be a transmogrified *diamant*, our *diamond* or *adamantine* substance, and it means a magnetized stone. Yet the homomorphic adjective *aimant*, from the verb *aimer*, means "naturally inclined to love," tender and affectionate. *Aimanté(e)*, "magnetized," would therefore be a word beloved of both Eryximachos the physician and Ion the rhapsode (of Plato's *Symposium* and *Ion*, respectively); it would be a word also for the omni-magnetized Lucretius, who offers us a vision of the power of an *inverted* magnet (*exultare etiam Samothracia ferrea vidi / et ramenta simul ferri furere intus ahenis / in scaphiis, lapis hic Magnes cum subditus esset: / usque adeo fugere a saxo gestire videtur,* "I have even seen Samothracian iron dance, and at the same time iron fillings go mad in a bronze bowl, when this magnet stone was applied underneath: so eager seems the iron to escape from the stone!"—*De rer. nat.* 6:1044–46); finally, to truncate the litany, it would be a word for both Empedocles of Acragas and the greatest of contemporary neo-Empedocleans, Sigmund Freud (SA *Ergänzungsband,* 384–86); it would be one of those macro-microcosmic secret words that joins—by magnetism—human beings to the larger world. "Magnetism," it may be recalled, is the principal category for Schelling's nature philosophy of the 1790s, which seeks the principle that unites the organic and anorganic realms of the universe. A very dramatic word for Derrida to use, no doubt, as though a mere poet, Georg Trakl, had the power to draw a philosophical project entirely to himself. It is above all in the third, unpublished *Geschlecht* that Derrida was to take up Heidegger's 1953 Trakl essay in detail. The fact that precisely this generation of *Geschlecht* is missing is therefore decisive for the "situation" of the entire series. Initially, one may put the question negatively: Where can the entire series be heading if it is missing its second pole, the one to which a certain magnetism draws it? As for the missing generation, only one thing is certain: it is headed toward that blow or stroke, the *coup* or *frappe,* the *Schlag* that is the very root of *Geschlecht.*

Astonishingly, yet perhaps also quite fittingly, it may have been Jean Genet who gives Derrida the word *aimanter, aimantation,* or gives it *back* to him, as it were. In his homage to Derrida, published by Jean Ristat in a special issue of *Les Lettres françaises* in the spring of 1972, Genet cites the opening lines of Derrida's then recently published *La Pharmacie de Platon.* He compares these lines to the opening lines of Proust's *À l'ombre des jeunes filles en fleurs.* The "attack" of Derrida's lines, in the musical sense of an instrumentalist's attack, is absolutely singular, according to Genet. Not the usual coarse dynamism of academic prose but a "gentle trembling" leads each phrase to the next one. The *sens* of Derrida's lines, in the sense of both their meaning and their direction, is guided by something entirely new. Genet calls it "a very subtle magnetism [*aimantation*] which would be found, not in the words, but beneath them, almost beneath the page" (cited at BP 293).

Let us return to the "guidelines" of Heidegger's 1928 lecture course, especially the guideline concerning "sexlessness." It is not Heidegger's silence about sex but his precipitation toward it that fascinates Derrida. Neutrality "also" means that Dasein is at least in some sense sexless; in spite of the "also," however, sexual difference is, to repeat, precisely where the examples both begin and end. Perhaps the neither-nor structure of the word *Neutralität,* the *ne-uter* indicating yet also negating binary opposition, leads automatically to the exemplary example of the duality of the sexes. Dasein is not human being, not *der Mensch,* and is thus a fortiori neither man nor woman, neither *Mann* nor *Frau,* and not even the neuter *das Weib.* Leads *automatically,* did we say? Whence the automatism? Whence the precipitation? Whence the exemplarity? Perhaps sex is all the students are interested in, and Heidegger is merely drawn to that example, automatically, by the circumstances of the lecture hall? Here Derrida remains discreet, practicing a silence of his own.

Derrida notes that to pass from the masculine and the feminine to the neuter is clearly, for Heidegger, to pass toward the transcendental, that is, toward a meditation on the conditions of the possibility of the *being* of Dasein. *Sein* is, without any sort of qualification or reservation, that which transcends, *das Transcendens schlechthin* (SZ 38; Ps 400/12). *Sein* also lies beyond any genus or species, and therefore a fortiori beyond anything like male or female. Yet transcendence transcends many things, and so, again, why stress sexlessness? One might think to explain it once again in terms of the duality expressed in the neuter itself, as the twofold *ne-uter,* "neither-nor." If Dasein is not *der Mensch,* then a fortiori it can be *ne* male *uter* female. Obviously. So patently obvious is this that one must ask why Heidegger needs to mention the fact. If fundamental ontology and the existential analytic of Dasein have nothing to do with anthropology and biology, does the special mention of sexual difference suggest that such a difference may be "beyond" biology? And, for that matter, beyond anthropology and even "ethics"? *Beyond* in the sense that sexual difference may have an import and an impact to which none of the "ontic" discourses is equal? Perhaps sexual difference is not a matter of course, not a matter that goes without saying, precisely in an ontology of difference?

Sexlessness, neutrality: apparently the negative is emphasized. And yet. In section 10 of the 1928 Leibniz-logic course Heidegger argues that the neutrality of Dasein with regard to sexuality is anything but impotence. Rather, such neutrality guarantees an "original positivity" and a "might of essence" (*ursprüngliche Positivität, Mächtigkeit des Wesens*) in Dasein. Indeed, Heidegger uses even stronger language—the language of being as such—in order to characterize such mightiness: "Only on the basis of the essence of 'being' ['*Sein*'] and transcendence, only within and on the basis of the full bestrewal [*Streuung*] that pertains to the essence of transcendence (cf. §10, guiding statement no. 6), can this idea of being as plenipotence [*Übermacht*] be understood; yet not by interpreting it in the direction of an absolute Thou, nor as the good, nor as value, nor as the eternal" (26:211 n. 3).[5] Derrida takes Heidegger at his word—and the generosity of his reading is nothing less than astonishing:

> By means of such manifestly negative predicates, one must be able to read what Heidegger does not hesitate to call a "positivity [*Positivität*]," a richness, and even, in a heavily charged code, a "potency [*Mächtigkeit*]." This clarification suggests that sexless neutrality does not desexualize; on the contrary, its *ontological* negativity is not deployed with respect to *sexuality itself* (which it would instead liberate), but with respect to the marks of difference, or more precisely to *sexual duality*. There would be no *Geschlechtslosigkeit* except with respect to the "two"; sexlessness would be determined as such only to the degree that sexuality is immediately understood as binarity or sexual division. "But here sexlessness is not the indifference of an empty void [*die Indifferenz des leeren Nichtigen*], the weak negativity of an indifferent ontic nothing. In its neutrality Dasein is not the indifferent nobody and everybody, but the primordial positivity [*ursprüngliche Positivität*] and potency of being (or of essence [*Mächtigkeit des Wesens*]). (402/14)[6]

It may be that Heidegger is contemplating an as yet unheard-of sexuality, a sexuality that is "pre-dual," "pre-differential," and in some

---

5. In his review of the second volume of Ernst Cassirer's *Philosophy of Symbolic Forms,* Heidegger does not hesitate to describe "plenipotence" as the *mana* of so-called primitive belief systems. He writes: "The thrownness of Dasein implies a being delivered over to the world in such a way that being in the world is overwhelmed by that to which it is transposed. Plenipotence can announce itself as such and in general only to a being that is delivered over. . . . In its dependence on the overpowering, Dasein is benumbed by it; only as akin to such a reality, only by belonging to it, can Dasein experience itself. Accordingly, in thrownness every being that is in any way unveiled possesses the ontological trait of plenipotence (mana)." Heidegger's quite extraordinary review of Cassirer's *Mythical Thought* appears in the *Deutsche Literaturzeitung* 49, no. 21 (1928): 999–1012; the quotation appears at 1009–10. On the "benumbment" or *Benommenheit* of Dasein, see now the discussion in chapter 4 of Krell, *Derrida and Our Animal Others.*

6. The second point I raised in my letter of January 3, 1983, was to object to the translation of *Mächtigkeit des Wesens* as *la puissance de l'être.* I suggested that *Wesen* and *Sein* not be conflated. The text as it appears in *Psyché* (402) now reads: "la puissance de l'être (ou de l'essence, *Mächtigkeit des Wesens*)." A small point—except for the fact that every aspect of Heidegger's attempted metontology of 1928 appears to be large.

sense prior to all binary oppositions. If the duel between the sexes arises from the dual itself, if the war between the sexes arises from such binary opposition, it may be that Heidegger is dreaming of a sexuality that flourishes—and mightily—precisely by escaping the dominion of oppositional struggles for power and the resulting violence. In other words, Derrida suggests, the privation of sexual difference with respect to Dasein may function in the way the privative-alpha of ἀ-λήθεια functions, which is to say, not as a privation at all but as a liberation, emancipation, and upsurgence of the truth of being—ontological difference and transcendence as such. To elaborate a bit: the "concealment" and "hiddenness" inherent in the word *Unverborgenheit*, "unconcealment," is in Heidegger's view not negative or pejorative. Rather, *Geborgenheit* suggests a being taken into protection, under wing, as it were; revealing does not tear what is hidden out of concealment. To unveil or uncover is thus to safeguard the things. Hölderlin remarks that "love is happy to uncover tenderly" (CHV 2:60), and Heidegger would concur that such gentle discovery is what he understands unconcealing to be. The implication would be that sexual difference, as we know it, namely, as binary opposition, obscures both the ontological difference between being and beings and the pre-ontological difference between Dasein and being; if by means of a metaphysics of Dasein or a metontology we can succeed in remembering the ontological and pre-ontological differences, the oppositional and conflictual traits of sexual difference may vanish. Or, inverting the proposition, if we can envisage the mightiness of essence and original positivity of neutrality in Dasein, we may be able to think ontological and pre-ontological difference more incisively. It is almost as though—Derrida does not go so far, at least not explicitly—Heidegger is joining Freud in the search for a sexual energy, a libido, or an Eros that would be unitary, and in that sense sexless; almost as though Heidegger is joining Lacan in the search for a singular signifier, a phallus that wields the power of essence only by disappearing, either in *pudeur* or repression or even in that feminine flaunting which we recognize in the cock of the walk. This would mean, not that the signifier would have nothing to do with desire and drive, but quite to the contrary, that it would be shared equally by men and women and all third + 1 kinds, indeed, shared as the fundamental source of the upsurgence of being, the fecundity of essence, the transcendence of Dasein.

Yet this would mean that sexual difference as we know it is *both* the cause of a certain dispersion or fragmentation of Dasein into the public realm—one is sexual the way "they" say one is to be sexual, whether the "they" in question is wretchedly conservative or wildly liberated—*and* the secret resource for a more original fecundity in Dasein. In other words, "by some strange yet very necessary displacement, sexual division itself leads us to negativity; and neutralization is *at once* the effect of such negativity and the erasure to which a thinking must submit this negativity so that an originary positivity can appear" (402/14–15). Derrida is already wondering whether for Heidegger there could be *two* strokes or blows delivered by sexual difference, a more primordial and even transcendental stroke yielding power to Dasein and a second blow driving Dasein into discord, dissension, and vacuous dispersion. If our *Geschlecht* has been subjected to two *Schläge*, how are these two strokes or blows to be envisaged? Which coinage or blow comes first, the neutral duality or the quarrelsome pair? Does one follow upon the other of necessity? And if the deleterious stroke comes second, but comes of necessity, is there any hope of restoration or recovery?

Derrida does note how enigmatic Heidegger's "guidelines" are, and we may want to pause a moment over the enigma. A metaphysics of Dasein seems to be in search of a certain puissance of essence that hides within the neuter term. What would be our access to it? Existential analytic must be concrete, its descriptions factical and precise, its analyses in no case derived from some unexamined and traditionally inherited and accepted "ideal." In *Being and Time* these descriptions and analyses seem to culminate in a sense that Dasein is not *mächtig*, is not equal to the thrownness of its existence, in spite of all the talk about resoluteness. Whence, concretely, the appearance of a *mighty* Dasein? In his 1928 lectures, Heidegger refers to an *Ursprung* and even an *Urquell*, an "origin" and "primal font" of existence, without letting us know where such a source may be found. Derrida notes that in the long essay *Vom Wesen des Grundes,* from the same year, Heidegger broaches a similar possibility for neutral, "sexless" Dasein. The issue here is that of "selfhood," *Selbstheit*, one of the most problematic concepts of the second division of *Being and Time.* Why problematic? Simply because the "occurring" or "happening" of Dasein, stretched and ecstatically self-stretching between birth and death, does not allow us to conceive of the "self" in any traditional way, as subject, ego, person, consciousness, and so on. In the same way that the interpretation of ecstatic temporality causes all prior interpretations of the "dimensions" of time to tremble, so does the standing-out of Dasein as *Existenz* (or *ek-sistence*) make it difficult to understand why and how Heidegger's appeal to a "self" is either necessary or possible. To be sure, it has to do with the individuating of Dasein, *die Vereinzelung,* yet whether the radically individuated Dasein can be called a "self" is unclear.

The problem of the "selfhood" of Dasein continues to trouble Heidegger in the 1928-29 essay—really a small monograph—*Vom Wesen des Grundes.* Derrida locates in this piece one of the rare references to sexuality, or *Geschlechtlichkeit,* once again in terms of *Neutralität.* Heidegger notes that the principal relation of Dasein to world is expressed in the formula, *Das Dasein existiert umwillen seiner,* "Dasein exists for the sake of itself" (W 53). He takes pains, however, to deny that such individuation has anything to do with egotism or "blind self-love." Neither isolation nor self-aggrandizement is meant, neither selfishness nor altruism, but rather something that lies behind the possibility of all these. Again the founding and grounding language of *Being and Time* appears—what Derrida would call "the order of implication":

> Only because Dasein as such is determined by selfhood can an ego-self relate itself to a thou-self. Selfhood is the presupposition for the possibility of the ego, which only ever discloses itself in the thou. Yet selfhood is never related to the thou; rather, because selfhood first of all makes all these things possible, it is neutral toward I-being and Thou-being and all the more so toward, say, "sexuality." (W 54)

At least two things are very odd in this passage, and Derrida notes one of them. Why does Heidegger emphasize sexuality here? Why *und erst recht . . .*? This is an a fortiori, to be sure, an "all the more so." I and Thou *and all the more so sexuality* are neutral in selfhood. Yet the phrase is even stronger than this in colloquial German. It suggests: "To say nothing of . . . ," "And what *really first of all* applies here . . . ." In other words, sexuality—if *Geschlechtlichkeit* may be Latinized—would be the prime case of neutrality, the very first item that would have to be neutralized. As in the Leibniz course, no other ontic feature of selfhood is mentioned, neither race nor ethnic origin nor family nor generation, even though *Geschlecht* could mean all of these. Strangest of all, however, is the "say," *etwa,* on which Derrida does not comment. It translates the Latin *aliquando,* "sometime," which also comes to mean "somewhere" and even "somehow" or "in some sense, say. . . ." Its gesture is one of uncertainty and indeterminacy, amounting to a "for example, perhaps"; it is often invoked in conditional clauses, expressing something that may or may not prove to be appropriate. It is as though Heidegger were casting about for a convenient example, perhaps looking up in the air and moving his hand in rapid circles, seeking an object as yet unascertained, waiting for something to occur to him. As in the Leibniz course, however, sexuality is all he can come up with.

Another very odd thing about the passage is Heidegger's asserting, very much in passing, that the ego can disclose itself only in the Thou: "Selfhood is the presupposition for the possibility of an ego, which only ever discloses itself in the thou." Whether Heidegger means the presupposed selfhood as such or the derivative possibility of the ego is difficult to say; what seems clear is that something very close to "me" only ever discloses itself (*sich erschließt*) in the Thou (*immer nur im Du*). It is almost as though he has heard the ego-psychologists assert that the infant swallows his or her identity with the mother's milk, that is, swallows the mother *with* her milk, such that identity is always of the (m)other. Almost—although any communication between Heidegger and ego psychology seems highly unlikely. By contrast, Heidegger is clearly aware of Martin Buber's *I and Thou*, published four years earlier. And it almost seems as though there is a surreptitious reference to the voice of the "friend" that Dasein, when it comes to the disclosure of its ownmost possibilities, "always carries with itself"—the very theme that will dominate the fourth generation of Derrida's *Geschlecht*. If this seems too fanciful, consider the final sentence of Heidegger's small monograph on the essence of ground: "And only by our being able to listen into the remoteness does there temporalize for Dasein as a self the incipient answer that arises from our Dasein-with, from our being-with-others, such that the ego can apply itself to the task of achieving for itself a proper self" (W 71). Periphrastically remote though he or she may be, the approaching friend alone extends to "me" the possibility of selfhood. This is one of the passages I would love to have discussed with Derrida. For it would take *Mitsein* in a new direction, perhaps toward that *Urquell*, introducing *Mitsein* to a dimension in which the "with" pertains to *Sein* as such. Much later in his life, Derrida writes the strange sentence, "The animals are not alone," *Les bêtes ne sont pas seules*, which might also be rendered, "Animals are not solitary" (B2 27; AO 38). It is as though after reading Heidegger's "On the Essence of Ground," along with his 1928 lecture course, one could write the even odder sentence, a sentence that might expand into an entire novel, "Being is not alone."

The uncanniness of a sexuality that pops up whenever ontological, metaphysical, and even transcendental matters are under discussion reappears during Heidegger's 1928–29 "Introduction to Philosophy," a course that demonstrates how demanding Heidegger is on students at the "introductory" level—taking up for discussion the most obstreperous problems of his own not yet fully formed fundamental ontology.[7] In the present "introduction," he is discussing the ontological basis of community, *Gemeinschaft*, arguing that it is to be found, not in the altruism of an I-Thou relationship, but in a more primordial being-with-one-another (*das Miteinander*). Yet once again sexual (or gender) difference announces itself as soon as the neutrality of Dasein (the word and the "thing") is invoked:

> In its essence, the being that we in each case are, human being [*der Mensch*], is something neutral [*ein Neutrum*]. We designate this being as *das Dasein*. Yet it pertains to this neutral essence that, inasmuch as it exists factically in each case, it has necessarily broken its neutrality [*notwendig seine Neutralität gebrochen hat*, that is, "broken," "broken with," or perhaps "refracted," in the sense that sexuality "refracts" the beam of light that passes through a prism, so that sexuality as such would be "refractory"—D. F. K.]; that is to say, Dasein, as factical, is in each case either masculine or feminine; it is a sexual essence [*ein Geschlechtswesen*, perhaps a "sexed creature," although Heidegger normally uses *Wesen* in the sense of an essence or an "essential unfolding"—D. F. K.]; this implies a quite determinate being-with and being-toward one another [*ein ganz bestimmtes Mit- und Zueinander*]. The limit and the scope of the impact of this characteristic is factically different in each case; one can only show which possibilities of human existence are not necessarily determined by the sexual relation [*das Geschlechtsverhältnis*]. Precisely this sexual relation is possible, however, only because Dasein in its metaphysical neutrality is already determined by the with-one-another. If every Dasein, which in each case is factically either male or female, were not already in essence with-one-another, the sexual relation as a human relation would be simply impossible. (27:146)

---

7. I am grateful to William C. McNeill for this reference to Heidegger's 1928–29 *Einleitung in die Philosophie* and for our discussions about it. Derrida had no access to this course.

To be sure, one must ask: If a neutral Dasein is always already refracted into sexuality, that is, if its neutrality with regard to the sexes is factically and in fact broken a priori, whence the metaphysical puissance or plenipotence of that neutrality? What do we who dwell under the multicolored dome of eternity know of white light? Furthermore, what is the status of the (empirical? transcendental?) claim that sexuality is "entirely determined" as an either/or, either masculine or feminine? What if the prism itself were a hormonal *spectrum*, rather than an either/or?

Heidegger's obvious scorn for the altruistic I-Thou, a scorn much more pronounced here than in Vom Wesen des Grundes, leads him to launch a polemic against "coarse materialism" in general. Only a Feuerbach or a Freud (the second not mentioned by name) would stoop so low as to mock the essential neutrality of Dasein. The polemic against coarse materialism in turn leads Heidegger to contrast sexual relations with "genuine and grand" *friendship*. Friends, such as Goethe and Schiller, are comrades in the good fight, passionate for whatever the object of that fight may be. Friends, presumably unlike lovers, do not "exchange sentimental gazes [einander rührselig anschauen]," and they do not "entertain" one another with "the insignificant exigencies of their psyches [ihren belanglosen Seelennöten]" (27:147).

It is important to state the conclusion to which Derrida is drawn by these strange discussions in Vom Wesen des Grundes, discussions that are even more unsettling in the 1928–29 Einleitung in die Philosophie. It may be that in these discussions of a metaphysical neutrality for Dasein Heidegger merely stumbles across the example of sexuality, perhaps because (*etwa*) his students are more than mildly interested in it; but so also is his *reading* audience interested in it, and this is an audience one would have expected to be immensely learned and hence above all that sort of thing. The logic of Heideggerian "selfhood" and of the "being-with" that is inherent in such selfhood is ultimately quite strange. Derrida notes that the *erst recht* or a fortiori is "irreproachable" only on one condition, namely, "on condition that the said 'sexuality' (in quotation marks) be the certain predicate of whatever is made possible by or from ipseity, here, for example, the structures of 'me' and 'you,' yet that it not belong, as 'sexuality,' to the structure of ipseity, of an ipseity not as yet determined as human being, me or you, conscious or unconscious subject, man or woman" (404/16).

The problem is reminiscent of the conundrum that hounded Schelling (7:406–408; cf. 8:279–315): if difference may be traced back to an earlier identity, that identity—if indeed it comes to differentiate itself—must contain the seed of difference, and that seed must already in some sense be bifurcated. There must already be the dotted line along which one tears. For example, if (1) good and evil are different from one another, yet (2) both partake of the "essence," at least if (3) that essence be human, which however (4) is said to derive from nothing other than the divine, then the essence itself must itself be predisposed to divorce the two—there must be a tendency toward what Schelling calls *Scheidung*, the "scission" or "separation" always already at work in both the human and the divine. Essence is therefore riven. Or, to take the reverse as our example, body and soul would never have been joined in the human identity if they themselves were not at some point identical. Essence is therefore uniform. If selfhood and its with-one-another are neutral, and yet if *ab ovo* they separate out into either male or female, and if such a separation, *horribile dictu*, results not only in sexual congress but also in sexual conflict, what is it about this "selfhood" and its "with-one-another" that so compel separation and strife? Is this not the classic metaphysical problem, namely, the attempt to ground negativity and dispersion on what ought to have been purely positive and unified? Is Heidegger not yet ready to surrender this kind of thinking?

It may be that a certain suspicion weighs on Heidegger, one that he would love to banish but cannot. In Derrida's words, "What if 'sexuality' already marked the most originary *Selbstheit*? What if it were an ontological structure of ipseity? What if the *Da* of *Dasein* were already 'sexual'?" (404/17). To be sure, such a *Geschlechtlichkeit* would be quite different from the dual sexuality that begs to be neutralized or neutered. Is Heidegger trying nonetheless to envisage it? What if something *like* "sexuality" were to mark (*etwa*) the very "selfhood" of Dasein, the "selfhood" and the individuation, the "in each case mineness," on which fundamental ontology bases its entire analysis? What if the analysis of those beings that are of the measure of Dasein, *daseinsmäßiges Seiendes*, Dasein as *Mitsein* and *Miteinandersein*, and perhaps even of those beings that are not of that measure, *nicht daseinsmäßig*, along with the analyses of appropriateness and inappropriateness, or authenticity and inauthenticity, *Eigentlichkeit* and *Uneigentlichkeit*, were ineluctably bound up with something like Eros? What if something like "sexuality" were a primordial ontological and transcendental structure of ipseity, of remoteness and nearness? What if sexual difference "were already marked in the opening to the question of the meaning of being and to ontological difference, so that, by that very fact, neutralization would be a violent operation?" (ibid.). The suggestion may even be broached as to whether the clearing of being, that is, Heidegger's *Lichtung des Seins,* along with the very granting of time and being, the themes that occupy Heidegger toward the end of his life, may have to do with something other than *Mensch*. If that word too has to be crossed out, so that only the *Da-* of *Da-sein* is left, would thoughtful *questioning* in and of itself reveal the survival of differences, multiple and protean differences, subtle yet unmistakable differences, that call for a rethinking of sexuality? The only possible answer to such a question, in Derrida's view, lies in the hope that both the word and the thing called *Geschlecht* can come to mean something other than the dual sexuality and the two genders as we know them, or believe we know them. Derrida leaves in suspense—as though it were a question for a missing generation—the possibility that "another *Geschlecht* will come to inscribe itself in ipseity, or will come to derange the order of all derivations, for example, that of a more originary *Selbstheit,* one that would make possible the emergence of the ego and of the you" (ibid.).

The key to an answer, if there is one, lies in the words *Streuung* and *Zerstreuung*. The first means a scattering of seed, a sowing, strewing, or *bestrewal*. The second, which merely adds the emphatic prefix *Zer-* to the word, means something like a being scattered to the winds, a chaotic dispersion and the resulting distraction. In Latinate languages, we often translate the *Zer-* as *dis-*, the problem being that the Greek διά, from which the *dis-* derives, may be taken in either a strongly pejorative or a quite neutral sense. The διά of "difference," for example, simply means that something has been "carried through" or "borne out," and that need not be bad. When and how does the *through,* the French *parcours,* become the *dis-* of I can't get no satisfaction? Even though Heidegger consistently denies the negative impact of the words that arise from his worst nightmares, *Zerstreuung, Zerstreutheit, Zerstörung, Zersplitterung, Zerspaltung,* scattering, distraction, destruction, fragmentation, bifurcation, these are the words that he uses when he wishes things were otherwise. Yet the problem is not merely with the words. Dasein itself is strewn into radical individuality, and the most serious task of fundamental ontology is to help Dasein confront its radical individuation. When the "mightiness of essence" strews Dasein, which is in each case my own, radically individualized, why is such bestrewal more acceptable and even desirable than that more emphatic dispersion that makes of me a sexual token? What can the positive neutrality of Dasein have been thinking when it allowed itself to be sundered and scattered? Derrida returns to the 1928 logic course in order to note how recalcitrant the problem of bestrewal is.[8]

Heidegger notes that Dasein contains within itself the tendency toward a *Mannigfaltigung* or *Vermannigfaltigung,* that is, a tendency toward the "manifold," literally, toward "multiple folds" of "development." Such "manifolding" or "proliferating" pertains to the might and positivity of the essence that propels it. The mightiness of essence, unfolding itself positively, produces "a factical dispersion" (*faktische Zerstreuung*) into "corporality" (*in die Leiblichkeit*). "And," Heidegger now adds (26:173), "thereby into sexuality" (*und damit in die Geschlechtlichkeit*). The "thereby," or "with that," or "ipso facto," conceals the problem. A first scattering or sowing of seed reflects the mightiness of essence; it is what makes Dasein *concrete* and *embodied,* "growing together" in itself. A second scattering, when the wind comes up, produces what everyone has to admit is a boondoggle. Even Kant called the division of humankind into the sexes an "abyss" that pure reason will never plumb. Yet worse is to come. For Dasein is not merely dispersed in sexual difference but always falls on one side of the line of that dispersion, so that one must say that each individualized Dasein is *zersplittert,* "split" or "fragmented," and *zwiespältig,* "riven" in a particular, determined sexuality (*in eine bestimmte Geschlechtlichkeit*). Hegel too complained of this split in his 1805–06 Jena lectures on genital difference: human beings never achieve the genus of their humanity, inasmuch as the products of their mating forever fall on one side of the gender line. Such endlessly one-sided repetition is what he will later call "bad infinity." Derrida uses the word *morcellement* to translate this *Zersplitterung,* and this reminds us of Lacan's use of the word "morcelized" (*d'une image morcelée, ce corps morcelé*) in his famous mirror-phase essay (És 97). The infant or small child takes delight in its

---

8. The problem of a not merely neutral but positive and powerful *Streuung* ("bestrewal"), which when emphasized as *Zer-streuung* ("dispersion," "distraction") becomes essentially negative and pejorative, elicited my longest comment in the letter of January 3, 1983. I hope to be forgiven the self-quotation, if only because the issue is so important and so baffling: "Yes, *Zer-* suggests *auseinander* [a driving apart], and so is related to *dis-,* 'two-fold, dual.' But nowadays *Zer-* seems to be a form of emphasis or intensification: cf. *stören, zerstören* [disturb, destroy], *drücken, zerdrücken* [press, squash]. Not so much a driving apart as driving to an ultimate or extreme point. This is important because it indicates what you are calling 'the order of implications.' Perhaps it is crucial in the order of *Streuung* (dissemination) and *Zerstreuung* (dispersion)? *Streuung* belongs to the order of *Sein, Zer-streuung* to the order of *Dasein.* The question of the *Zer-* is the question of implication as such! *Da-Sein ist Zer-Sein!!* Etc."

image, yet is already struck by the contrast between its apparent completeness of figure—a body nicely outlined and silhouetted in the glass—and the chaos of its uncontrolled movements and the hunger raging inside. All its life will be spent trying to satisfy that image of completeness, trying like Alfred Hitchcock to walk into its silhouette and fill it out, whether that image be of itself or conjured in the alluring figure of an other, *etwa* in the Thou of selfhood. Derrida makes no reference to Lacan here, nor does he comment on the technologies by which we might hope to do battle against gender *Zersplitterung*. Surely, by means of multiple surgeries (stopping just short of apotemnophiliac amputations) and delicately mixed hormonal cocktails we can exchange one morsel for another? The only thing that is missing, apparently, is the technology that will make us happy under our skin—although I read that the psychopharmaceutical firms have promised that this cocktail too is right around the corner. For the moment, however, morcelization. That too cannot be good.

Yet precisely this "cannot be good" is what Heidegger denies. None of these emphatic *Zer-* words, he insists, is meant pejoratively. While rejecting the Aristophanic solution that so attracted Freud (SA 3:266 n. 2), namely, the fantasy of a lunar sex of which today's males and females are the sundered parts, each part mad for its other, Heidegger affirms the multiplication or manifolding of corporality, which, Heidegger says, serves as an "organizational factor" for sexuality. The metonology of Dasein, it seems, does not shy from euphemism.[9]

Whatever appears to be the result of scattering and dispersion, *Zerstreuung*, derives from "an original dissemination," or "an original bestrewal" (*eine ursprüngliche Streuung*), which, while not exaggerated, is mighty. (Derrida says that the word *Streuung* appears only once in these Heidegger texts, yet it appears three times, each time trying desperately to distinguish between a fecund multiplication and a sterile scattering.) As Derrida notes, understating the matter somewhat, the distinction is difficult to maintain. "Yet, even if not rigorously legitimate, it is difficult to avoid a certain contamination by negativity, that is, by ethico-religious

---

9. It is difficult to follow Heidegger's sense here—of what serves as an "organizational factor" for what. Derrida's typescript originally had it as follows: "cette multiplication qui représente pour le corps propre du Dasein un 'facteur d'organisation.'" In my letter of January 3, 1983, I suggested that Heidegger's text had to be translated differently: "cette multiplication pour qui le corps propre du Dasein représente un 'facteur d'organisation.'" In the version that appears in *Psyché* (407), Derrida corrected my grammar, replacing my *qui* with *laquelle*. Yet he seemed to accept my exclamation at the end of the note, "This subordination of the body is very, very important!!"

associations that would come to align this dispersion with a fall or some sort of corruption of the pure, originary possibility (*Streuung*), which would seem to be affected by some sort of supplementary turn" (407/19). As readers of Derrida's *Grammatology* will remember, the "logic of the supplement" always entails a certain fatality: what one wants to celebrate as a neutral or perhaps even positive and mighty development always winds up tilting the axis of the earth, so that the planet reels; what the system requires but wants and needs to exclude will someday (*etwa*) strike it with the full force of *Melancholia*. So it is with *Streuung*.

Perhaps one further glimpse at the 1928–29 "Introduction to Philosophy" will confirm the strangeness of *Streuung* and *Zerstreuung*, that is, of a bestrewal that seems to slide from the heights of the transcendental to the pits of the empirical—even if Heidegger often denies the negativity implied in the word *Zerstreuung*, "dispersion" or "distraction." In his introductory course Heidegger tightens the knot of *Zer-streuung* by stressing the positive nature of negativity itself for finite Dasein: "The not-character is thus precisely the authentic force of the existence of Dasein" (27:333). Dasein, in its thrownness, its being a self, and its being with others, "is be-strewn [*zer-streut*] into the manifoldness of these relations" (ibid.).

> However, this dispersion [*Zerstreuung*] is not at all a dissolution of Dasein into parts that fall to pieces. Rather, the reverse is true: in this dis-persion [*Zer-streuung*, be-strewal] Dasein attains and possesses the original, entire unity that is proper to it. We therefore speak primarily not of a dispersion into these relations but of an original bestrewal [*Streuung*]. Such bestrewal is first of all the condition of the possibility of a dis-persion [*Zer-streuung*] in the sense that Dasein in each case can devote its energies preeminently to one of these relations, but always at the cost of its being unable to exist in the others. (Ibid.)

The result is that existence is always "compromised." The power that projects it into multiple possibilities is the power of a negativity, a finitude, that requires choices and decisions that themselves require compromises. A radically individualized Dasein must try to gain a foothold in the stream of bestrewal and in the winds of dispersion. Before too long Heidegger is invoking the most entangling forms of *nullity* and *untruth*, "dissimulation," "mere appearance," "blindness," and, of all things, *Benommenheit*, "benumbment," "bedazzlement" (27:335). It is almost as though dispersion is both the truth and the untruth of bestrewal, which itself is empowered by the nothing and nullity.

The emphatic form of *Streuung*, namely, *Zerstreuung*, belongs to Heidegger's vocabulary for a considerable period of time—from the Marburg period up to the very end of his career. It may be useful—although Derrida does not do this—to examine a much earlier lecture course in which the profound ambiguity of emphatic bestrewal, as dispersion and dissemination, becomes somewhat clearer.[10]

In his 1921–22 lecture course, "Phenomenological Interpretations of Aristotle: An Introduction to Phenomenological Research," Heidegger elaborates on dispersion (*Zerstreuung*) as the category pertaining to a movement in what at that point he is calling "factical life," a movement one might call inclination or proclivity (*Neigung*). Such an inclining dispersion in factical life already has two consequences: first, life disperses itself in the world, in this way "prestructuring" its possibilities; second, life returns to itself only in the reflected and refracted light of these dispersed possibilities, coming back to itself as "relucence." The first dispersion is enabling, the second crippling. "Self-dispersing life encounters its world as 'dispersion,' as dispersing, manifold, replete, preoccupying, vacuous, monotonous" (61:120). Indeed, the nascent structures of ecstatic temporality can be seen through the fog of such duplicitous dispersion, which is both "manifold" and "monotonous": when life inclines to this or that possibility, it moves (toward) itself, *auf sich zu*, the prepositions that in *Being and Time* mark the future ecstasis. When life takes care or trouble concerning the things that are closest to it at present, it radiates back upon itself, *auf sich selbst zurück*, the prepositions that mark the ecstasis of having-been. Thus the animatedness of inclination is both the seedbed of ecstatic temporality proper and the quagmire of dispersion, distraction, and sheer diversion. In the margin of his lecture notes Heidegger writes: "The specific larvance [that is, mask and masquerade] in the ambiguity of the linguistic expressions of the categories of facticity is not accidental. *Zerstreuung*: (1) dispersing itself (prestructuring); (2) the dispersal (relucent)" (ibid.). The implication is that relucent dispersal is the unavoidable effect exerted on factical life by things in the world, whereas the reflexive *sich zerstreuen* functions as an inevitable, necessary, and a priori structure, a transcendental prestructuring, *Praestruktion*. A tension remains between the prior, potent, enabling "prestructuring" dis-

---

10. The following account is based on DL, 185–86, with apologies for the repetition.

persal or "bestrewal" of factical life in its concerns and the subsequent reactive, structurally posterior dispersion, distraction, and scatteredness of that same life. Factical life thus sows the seeds of its own dissipation and ruin. The "fundamental peculiarity of life's animatedness," says Heidegger, is "ruinance, petrifaction" (ibid.). And yet, as life locks itself away from itself, incarcerates itself in the prison of an endlessly distracting world, it experiences an inchoate form of transcendence: factical life, precisely by means of its duplicitous dispersion, is *"away from itself," "outside itself"* (61:123: "Von-sich-weg," "Aus-sich-hinaus"). Such nascent transcendence, which Heidegger will later call *ecstatic,* is mighty. "The mightiness of relucence in the very movement of incarceration . . . wins from this flight from itself the modes in which it occupies itself with the world and with itself" (ibid.). Thus the seeds of ruin turn out to be the seeds strewn by the primal, abyssal ground of existence, by factical life itself. The ontic germinates, burgeons, and blossoms into ontology.

Note the alteration in both the *ratio cognoscendi* and *ratio essendi* of the earlier (1921) and the later (1928) interpretations of *Zerstreuung.* In 1921 we learn of "prestructuring" only after following the inclination of taking flight from ourselves and locking ourselves away, and even then we learn of the positive (or at least neutral) mode of dispersion only in the reflected light of the world. Here it is *Reluzenz* that is "mighty." Vacuity itself reveals the prestructuring in its reflected light. In 1928, by contrast, Heidegger tries to protect the mightiness of essence, which is the might of being, from the emphatic dispersion that can only result in sheer distraction. *Sein,* rather than ruinous, will be the granting. The 1928–29 "Introduction to Philosophy" seems to be somewhere between these two versions of *Zer-streuung.* But to return now to Derrida's reading of the 1928 text(s) and, underpinning them, the text of *Being and Time.*

The suspicion obtrudes that the entire effort in *Being and Time* to deny the negativity of structures such as *Geworfenheit, Bewegtheit, Uneigentlichkeit, Alltäglichkeit,* and *Verfallen,* along with *Zerstreuung,* that is, the effort to assert the positivity or at least modal neutrality (for existential analysis) of thrownness, "movedness," inappropriate existence, everydayness, falling prey or ensnarement, and virtually every form of dispersion and distraction, undercuts the very project of a dismantling or deconstruction of the history of ontology. And when in the 1928 logic course Heidegger tries to avoid the negativity implied in sexual bifurcation by insisting that there is a "generic striving for unity" in the sexes, *ein gattungshaftes Zusammenstreben,* Hegel's philosophy of nature—taken over uncritically, without anything approaching a deconstruction—is immediately there to confirm it. In other words, the alteration in Heidegger's *ratio cognoscendi,* endeavoring to prove to itself that it mirrors the *ratio essendi* of being and the might of essence, collapses back into the most classical formulations of Platonic-Christian ontotheology and metaphysics. Moreover, Heidegger's effort to deny the analysis any ethical intent, and his desire to expunge every pseudo-Christian theme there, runs against the grain of his own powerfully felt need to resist the inertia of the tradition. His own desire to "dequotidianize" existential analysis— Heidegger speaks of an *Entgegenwärtigung des Heute,* "a de-presentifying of our today" (SZ 391, 397), as an essential hermeneutical process, one that strips everydayness from our understanding of our own history—suggests that there *is* something negative about the way one philosophizes today, indeed, something distracted and dispersed, something *ruinous.* Not for nothing is *Ruinanz* the favorite word of the early Marburg lectures, replete as they are with imprecations against the ruinous dispersion and distractedness of contemporary humanity, including its philosophers. As we shall see, the missing third *Geschlecht* will be concerned above all with the fatality of an inevitable contamination of the mighty essence, the fatality of a supplemental turn that proliferation takes into a conflictual-sexual catastrophe. Already here in the first, however, and certainly by the time of the third, it becomes increasingly difficult to accept Heidegger's insistence that there is nothing of Platonism and nothing of Christianity in his ruing of the ruinous fall, of our dispersion in the "they," of the oblivion of being precisely in our philosophers, and of the second blow—the *Schlag* or curse of discord and dispersion in *Geschlecht.* Sexuality and discord? How very much like the apple of Paris, "the apple of Discord," or the *dudaim* (that is, the Mandragora) of Jacob and all his wives, the "forbidden fruit" of Eve and Adam. If Dasein, as analyzed in section 12 of *Being and Time,* is dispersed and even fragmented (*zerstreut, zersplittert*); if Dasein is bemused and benumbed by its idle curiosity (section 36); if there is inevitable alienation from its ownmost possibility of being; if there is falling prey and ruination and even crashing (*Absturz*), then it will become increasingly difficult for Heidegger to distinguish between the falling of Dasein and Hegelian spirit's plunge into time. "Much later," writes Derrida, once again alluding to the second Trakl essay, "Heidegger will interpret the decomposition of the human *Geschlecht* as a disessencing, or loss of essence, that occurred eons ago, *Verwesung* taken literally as a *Ver-wesen* of the figure of man" (413/25).

Yet even the most "innocent" structures of the analytic of Dasein, those that do not seem to portend a fall, appear to be marked by a kind of disessencing. If Dasein at first and for the most part is dispersed in a world, a world that reflects back on it and causes it to misinterpret itself—again, the phenomenon of *Reluzenz*—and if Dasein at first and for the most part confronts not a single object but is dispersed among a totality of object-clusters—the phenomenon of the *Bewandtnisganzheit*—then dissemination appears to be its very fate. If Dasein is "stretched" and "self-stretching" between birth and death, such stretching is not a mere Cartesian "extension" of Dasein into space but what Derrida calls *espacement*, "spacing," such that Dasein may be said to be a mere interval between its birth and death. And if, moved and even "thrown" forward and back by ecstatic temporality, Dasein "stands out" in the world, there may be a sense in which it sticks out like a sore thumb, and Heidegger is perhaps never far from what Hegel calls "unhappy consciousness." Dasein "happens," and its "occurrence," *Geschehen*, is its sole history, its *Geschichte*. Perhaps something of the collectivity, the *Ge-* of both *Geschichte* and *Geschlecht*, is marked in the very being of every radically individuated Dasein. If Dasein is the in-between, then difference and dispersion seem to pertain to it essentially. Heidegger himself, especially in 1928, stresses that *Mitsein* or the *Miteinander*, our being with others, is a result of transcendental dispersion. Yet how often Dasein experiences its being-with as a scattering of forces and a distraction! "Here I am," as the song says, "stuck in the middle with you." Yet Heidegger once again refuses to accept sexual difference as original and inevitable: Dasein, as *Mitsein*, "cannot be explained in terms of a generic being that claims to be original," such that its peculiar embodiment derives from some "sexually sundered corporeal essence," *geschlechtlich gespaltenen leiblichen Wesen*. If we ask what the original might and positivity of essence are, and from whence they derive, Heidegger does not hesitate to reply that they are of being, *Sein*. There is, then, a "transcendental dispersion" in the very being of Dasein that, far from being neutral, seems to derive from what Hegel calls "the monstrous power of the negative." The nothing, as we know, is also mighty in Heidegger's existential analytic, and it does not lose its power in the later thinking of *Ereignis*.

For Heidegger, however, the essential *neutrality* of these descriptions is to be preserved. It therefore once again seems that there are *two kinds* of falling and dispersion, or, better, that falling and dispersion are marked *twice* in Heidegger's analyses, first as a general structure of Dasein, altogether appropriate or at least modally neutral, and second, derivatively, as a mode of inappropriateness. Derrida wants to inquire into the order of implications by which the first coinage, the felicitous or at least neutral one, the mighty one, seems to make the second coinage—the sad birthmark on the brow of man, as Melville calls it—inevitable. And Derrida does not doubt that the sad birthmark, in spite of Heidegger's denials, has at least something to do with the tradition Heidegger himself will deride as "Platonic" and "Christian."

In the final pages of the first *Geschlecht,* Derrida broadens the scope of his inquiry. It is now the "privative" interpretation (in sections 10 and 12 of *Being and Time*) of life in general, *nur-noch-Leben,* "just plain life," that troubles him. Because a fundamental ontology of Dasein alone can display the possible projects of Dasein, and because the inquiries into life by biology, psychology, and anthropology are merely some among the many such possible projects, fundamental ontology asserts its priority. Yet this priority translates into a method of privative interpretation that proceeds by subtraction. What about life forms that are neither of the measure of Dasein nor entirely "at hand" as things? Neither "existentials" nor "categories" would appear to save their appearances. Just-plain-life is perhaps a key instance in which distortions and obfuscations are bound to occur. A certain methodological "negativity" is especially apparent here, and yet, Heidegger would insist, that negativity is not the result of some contingent lapse or mishap of interpretation. Heidegger is anxious to preserve the "neutrality" of such negative appearances, as when he says in section 12, "The being-in-the-world of Dasein, with its facticity, has always already been dispersed [*zerstreut*] in determinate ways or even fragmented [*zersplittert*]" (SZ 56; Ps 412/25). One finds a dozen places in *Being and Time* where dispersion *seems* to have a strongly pejorative sense, but only one where the sense is positive, that one referring to the call of conscience that "disperses" all our fleeting distractions and dispersions (SZ 273). Ironically, if the neutrality of the neuter form *das Dasein* rescues existence from the negative effects of dispersion, the neuter form of the "they," *das Man,* does not do so. (Note that in section 27 Heidegger specifically refers to the *Neutrum* of "the they.") Nor does any form of neuter *Gerede* rescue us.

Yet Derrida does not close the first *Geschlecht* with these doubts. He concludes instead by reinvoking the hope that "the retreat of the dyad" in Heidegger's strange treatment of sexuality (or, in *Being and Time,* his nontreatment) will open the possibility of a more original, more positive, and more powerful sexuality. Such a hope will in fact sustain Derrida's interest in the ostensibly nonexistent theme of "Heidegger and sexuality," sustain it throughout the decade of the 1980s and even beyond.

Let us now, by way of summary and conclusion, point to the seven specific places where themes that will be central to the unpublished and incomplete *Geschlecht III* are introduced already in the first *Geschlecht*.

First, the difficulty of deciding whether sexual division and duality, along with the imputed neutrality and sexlessness of Dasein, are problems or solutions, will be at the center of *Geschlecht III*. For the question as to whether in the realm of sexual difference(s) negativity and privation or positivity and might of essence are to be stressed prefigures the problem of the two strokes (*Schläge*) of *Geschlecht* in Heidegger's Trakl interpretation. To anticipate, we may say that one of these strokes will be beneficial or at least neutral, whereas the other will turn out to be the very essence of evil.

Second, Derrida emphasizes throughout this first generation of *Geschlecht* issues of idiom and language, including Heidegger's tendency to reserve all positivity for German words, employing Latinate expressions only by way of pejoration. *Geschlecht* is one thing, *sexus* another, so that the usual distinction between word and thing does not apply here. At a certain point in his first *Geschlecht* essay Derrida asserts that "we will even come to see that the thinking of *Geschlecht* and the thinking of translation are essentially the same" (405/17).

Third, Derrida invokes what we might readily take to be a utopian hope, namely, that an "other" form of sexuality, a nondual, nonbinary sexuality, may be seen as permeating what Heidegger calls the selfhood (*die Selbstheit*) of Dasein.

Fourth, the difficulty in understanding the negativity and positivity of bestrewal, dissemination, dispersion, and distraction (*die Streuung, die Zerstreuung, die Zerstreutheit*) will continue to play an important role in the third generation. In this regard, Heidegger's inheritance of certain negative valuations, stemming (Derrida will argue) from unacknowledged ethico-religious sources, will have effects that Heidegger very much wants to deny. Here the theme of *contamination*, central to deconstruction generally, will become important.

Fifth, and closely related to the foregoing, the question as to whether some sort of "fall" from a prior state of relative perfection, a lapse from being, characterizes Heidegger's thinking—again, in spite of his energetic denials—will dominate much of the later discussion.

Sixth, one of the few specific references to Heidegger's 1953 Trakl interpretation occurs when Derrida, countering Heidegger's denial of the negativity implied in dispersion, distraction, the "they," craving the new, falling prey, plummeting and crashing, focuses on Heidegger's acceptance of Trakl's "accursed *Geschlecht*," that is, Heidegger's reading of the curse in terms of decomposition and disessencing (*Verwesung*). Derrida will affirm that it is difficult to discern the positivity and potency—to say nothing of *plenipotence*—of such decomposition and curse.

Finally, seventh, Derrida notes that for Heidegger the dispersion or dissemination of Dasein seems to occur *twice:* first as a putatively neutral dispersion or even fragmentation (*Zerstreuung, Zersplitterung*) into manifold possibilities of being-in, but then as the deficient modes of everydayness and inappropriateness. The *twofold* stroke of bestrewal and dispersion—doubtless in an altered form, a form having less to do with the fundamental ontology of Dasein and more to do with Heidegger's conversation with *poetry*—will be a central theme of the third generation of *Geschlecht*.

2

# *Geschlecht II*

## Heidegger's Singular Hand

In a note added to the end of *Geschlecht I* as it appears in the 1987 *Psyché,* Derrida directs his readers to the simultaneously published *Of Spirit,* but also to his brief proleptic discussion of the missing third *Geschlecht* in "Heidegger's Hand (Geschlecht II)," to which we must now turn. Like the first in the series, the second, itself divided into two major sections, arises from the series of seminars Derrida held in Paris on "Philosophical Nationality and Nationalism." It would be controversial to say—yet I will say it—that this second *Geschlecht* is far more strongly marked by its context than the first. Moreover, the focus on philosophical nationality and nationalism will alter the remaining generations as well, shifting their emphasis toward questions of nationality and away from the possibility of a nonbinary sexuality. Derrida never stops dreaming of this possibility, but the political urgency of "the national" and "the nationalistic" interrupts that dream and propels it in new directions.

"Heidegger's Hand (Geschlecht II)," composed of two parts, is written with both hands, as it were, and is thus reminiscent of the magic writing pad of Derrida's 1967 "Freud and the Scene of Writing" (ED 293–340). One of the two hands, as it turns out, must always erase the assertions of the other, especially when more than one language or idiom is involved and the ever-present problem of translation intensifies. Derrida begins with an analysis of the seventh of Fichte's *Reden an die Deutsche Nation,* which appeals to "the spirituality of our race," *die Geistigkeit unsers Geschlechts,* presupposing that "race" can adequately translate the word *Geschlecht* and that "spirituality" can adequately translate the word *Geistigkeit,* which of course is true in neither case. Yet the question of *Geschlecht* touches on these differences of national idiom throughout— even when the discourse, as in Fichte's case, promises to open the hands and arms of the German people to all intellectual-spiritual persons across the globe, all "like-minded," as we speakers of English love to say. Such openness, such hospitality, is doubtless Fichte's intent. Yet how wide can those hands and arms open? Do they open wide enough to embrace (or as Heidegger would say, gather, *versammeln*) all races, ethnic groups, sexes, and life forms—provided we and they can all agree on the gist of *Geist* and *Geistigkeit*? Fichte employs a particular idiom on which Derrida does not comment, one that seems particularly striking to me. "Whatever" believes in such "spirituality" or "intellectuality," writes Fichte, and it is odd that he avoids the "who," as though the selection will not be reduced to some subjective or personal whim, "whatever" believes, he says, "belongs to us and *will join us*" (416). This "will join us," *wird sich zu uns thun*, strikes a note of conviviality and commitment that is hard to capture in any other idiom. If a friend—or even a stranger—enters a tent at a local wine or music festival in Germany, he or she may be invited to "do themselves to" a table of hospitable folk. *Sich tun* suggests (at least to my ear) a kind of intimacy, camaraderie, and conviviality that "to join" cannot capture. "To lie or to place somewhere" is the basic meaning, according to Hermann Paul's long article on the word (HP 679–81); Paul cites a negative yet telling example from Martin Luther: *Niemand soll sich zu seiner nächsten Blutsfreundin tun*, "No one should *sich tun zu* his closest blood-relation of the female sort." Luther may be referring to the seating order at the table, but he appears to be worried about something else.

At stake in the expression *ist unsers Geschlechts*, as Derrida rightly indicates, is the very humanity of a human being. If one is invited to the table, it is in acknowledgment of something profoundly shared; if one may say so, in acknowledgment of the shared *Geschlecht*. What happens when this conviviality goes missing? Recall the sense of lament that runs through Roberto Calasso's extraordinary book, *The Marriage of Cadmus and Harmony*, namely, the plaint that human beings no longer dare to invite the gods to sit at their table. Ever since the splendid yet rather raucous night of the marriage feast of Cadmus and Harmony, for reasons that never become clear, the gods are our foes; we know this because when we try to enter their space they never say, never even dream of saying, *Tun sie sich aber zu uns*. "After that remote time when gods and men had been on familiar terms," writes Calasso, "to invite the gods to one's house became the most dangerous thing one could do. . . . To invite the gods ruins our relationship with them but sets history in motion" (RC 387). And, just as the gods banish us from their table, as though we had served them a tantalizing stew of godly Pelops, so do we humans banish the animals—the *other* animals—from ours, unless those animals be our meal. Such banishment is always pronounced in "our" idiom, a language that the excluded others do not share, and with such exclusions, as Calasso notes and as Stephen Dedalus would concur, the nightmare of history commences. Fichte (followed in this respect by Heidegger) eschews the Latinate words for *Menschheit* and *Menschlichkeit*, principally the word *Humanität*, which offends the German ear and insults the mother tongue; furthermore, as Fichte adds, it even threatens the German nation's "ethical [or at least its customary and proper] way of thinking," its *sittliche Denkart* (419/29). It is as though the lessons learned from Gibbon's *History of the Decline and Fall of the Roman Empire*, if not from an endless string of Hollywood epics, are always already in place: no one should *sich tun zu* a decadent Roman feast and its wayward Latin. As the very word *animal* suggests, these southerly peoples have no *Seele* and no *Geist* to speak of. Thus, in Fichte's discourse everyone is invited to the table, all the like-minded from all across the globe, but the invited dare not neglect to read the fine print on the invitation, which contains something like an RSVP, "Do please respond," but always and inevitably *in unserer Sprache, bitte schön*.

For its part, the skilled and hospitably extended hand—in the singular—is one of the classic signs of the metaphysically conceived *Geschlecht* we call *humanity*, especially the humanity that is eager to oppose itself to animality. The opposable thumb we take to be in opposition to everything else that lives.

Derrida offers a close reading of Heidegger's complacent and sometimes mystifying remarks concerning the hand in *Was heisst Denken?* This was the first lecture course taught by Heidegger after the prohibition instituted by the French occupying powers in 1945 was lifted. Precisely at that time Heidegger was defending himself against the charge of Nazism by arguing that he opposed as strongly as he could the *biologism* of National Socialist ideology. Derrida both accepts that plea and poses critical questions concerning Heidegger's care and concern where matters "biological" are concerned—for example, in his view of the hand, the hand of man. The hand is crucial to Heidegger's thought throughout his career, from the *Zuhandenheit* and *Vorhandenheit* of *Being and Time* to the hand of handicraft in *What Is Called Thinking?* In the second part of *Geschlecht II*, Derrida takes up some familiar themes of *the* hand: *the* hand, here cited always (with but one exception) in the singular, as though the left and the right were one, is wielded as an amulet against dispersion above all, including "organic dispersion." The singular hand serves as the giver of signs (*Zeichen*); that hand is demonstrative, sometimes remonstrative. The potential *monstrosity* of the hand is originally a monstration, a pointing and showing. The hand essentially enacts a *giving* rather than a *taking*: if the *two* hands seize and grasp (*greifen, begreifen, Begriff*) after the manner of Hegel, the hand of Heidegger is that which shows and grants. As the clouds are the clouds of the sky, so the hand is the hand of being. The hand gives the sign of human exceptionalism. Even if the sign is unread, *deutungslos,* as Hölderlin says in one version of a late poem called among other things "Mnemosyne" (CHV 1:436), the hand signals and thus gives us to know. One hand reaches out to grasp another in salutation, adds Heidegger. And even when I am solitary my two hands (here is the exception) may fold together into one in order to join the great unifold. The way two hands fold into one, as in Dürer's famous drawing of praying hands, suggests the onefold as such: Heidegger's Trakl essay of 1953 will soon speak of the first stroke of sexuality, the felicitous coinage of man and woman, as *die einfältige Zwiefalt,* the unified or onefold twofold, or the twofold that is always folding back into one. In that particular phrase, *einfältig* will not have the usual colloquial sense of "simple" or even "simpleminded," but will refer to the gathering into a unity that the first stroke of *Geschlecht* promises even as it creates the twofold. The sign of such a promise would be the folded hand(s). The family that prays together stays together.

Yet does one make love with one hand or with two? A jejune and wayward question, perhaps. Derrida raises it more than once with a view to the guiding question of his initial *Geschlecht*. Why, if the hand is the giver, does Heidegger fail to mention the giving of *Hingabe* or *Hingebung,* the way one gives oneself over in love? Hands and feet and blood and ouns all given over in *Hingebung*—why does Heidegger not mention lovemaking or sexual difference at all with regard to the hand(s)? Would differences among the hands, notably among the caressing hands of men and women, be merely ontic contingencies having no ontological import, and demonstrably so? Would such differences never attain to, never even graze, the ontological realm, which is the ostensible, ostensive realm of "the" hand? Are the two hands omitted because they might be reminiscent of the two feet? Yet why should Heidegger, the thinker of the way or the path of thinking, scorn the feet? These are some of the questions raised by this second generation of *Geschlecht*. The question of the *loving* hands, and of their absence from Heidegger's Trakl essay, will become a crucial question for Derrida.

Heidegger's privileging of the singular hand of man is entirely in sympathy with a long metaphysical tradition. For example, Thomas Aquinas says of man that "he has reason and the hand," the latter defined by Aristotle as the "tool of tools."[1] The erect posture of the human being, which is how the Creator made him, in his own erect and alert image, as it were, liberates the hand from the position of the forepaws of animals. If human beings were prone and walked on all fours, their hands would long ago have become pedestrian and the *utilitas manuum*, here in the plural, would have been lost. If the hands were mere forepaws, the human being would have to seize its food with its mouth. The human head, as a consequence, would be oblong in shape along the horizontal axis, with its snout extended for convenient foraging, as with dogs and pigs. The lips and tongue would be coarse, "lest they be wounded by the world outside." This coarsening of lips and tongue would in turn impede speech. And speech is, as Aquinas assures us, "the proper work of reason." Without entering into the details of this Aristotelian-Scholastic account of the hand of man and all its consequences for speech and thought, Derrida demonstrates quite clearly the unity—within metaphysical thinking—of gesturing hand, speaking mouth, and reasoning brain. Speech and thought require the singular hand(s) of man. One recalls the detailed analyses of the writing hand in the second half of the *Grammatology* (II 4), the writing hand of the erstwhile boustrophedonic scrivener who, agreeing to the compromise of hand and eye, records traces of a voice that hears and understands itself while speaking.

Derrida pays special attention to the *writing* hand of Heidegger, often displayed in photographs of the Schwarzwald thinker, or the hand that holds the walking stick, itself not so much an aid to the feet as a pointer, or the hand that carries a pail of water from the nearby trough to the *Hütte*. The hand, tool of tools, is the organ of the artisan, of the *Schreiner* or cabinetmaker, says Heidegger in *What Is Called Thinking?* The handworker, *der Handwerker*, is a craftsman to the extent that he responds to shapes and forces that are already sleeping in the wood; the handworker ministers to those shapes, responds in his every maneuvering to those forces, and such ministration is the model for all *thinking*. The model is apt, at least if *thinking* is a cultivating, and cultivating a prerequisite of

---

1. Thomas Aquinas, *Summa theologiae, prima pars*, q. 91, a. 3. See my discussion in chapter 4 of AT, esp. 149–53.

the *dwelling* of mortals—*Bauen Wohnen Denken,* without punctuation, as though forming one word, the gesture of a single hand. To be sure, the hand belongs to a body, a human body, so that the question of *Geschlecht* is never remote from the matters under discussion. Yet Heidegger's body is that of a thinker and a writer, the body of an authorial artisan who harks back to a time prior to the contaminations of the hand introduced by technology and capital.

Heidegger, the declared enemy of *biologism,* is nonetheless quick to deny such a hand to the apes. What disturbs Derrida in this regard is the way Heidegger elevates his ignorance of all things touching the primates into a calm, self-assured claim about who has hands and who does not. This *non-savoir érigé en savoir tranquille* (428/41) is reminiscent—although Derrida does not say so—of Kant's transcendently bizarre empirical observations (all of them secondhand) concerning race in his lessons on *Geography.* Heidegger is prepared to keep the ontic preoccupations of the natural sciences at bay, if only because the sciences are in service to the tyrannical essence of technology, and yet he feels confident that he can make a "commonsensical" assertion about the "organs for grasping" that distinguish the ape from a handy *homo sapiens sapiens.* No doubt, somewhere along the way, our *Gymanasium* or high school teachers offered a convincing demonstration of that opposable thumb cited a while back. One wonders nevertheless whether the capacity of the ape to grasp branches with its feet, which enables it to be so secure in its network of trees, as though its feet were a second set of dexterous and adroit hands, is what causes the human being to be so envious. Birds have wings, while apes have hands *and* feet that enable them to fly among the trees. And we grounded ones? We grasp the pen with our prehensile organ, left or right, and, without thinking overmuch, take our revenge.

Before we turn to Derrida's account of Heidegger's spirited defense of handwriting, as opposed to typewriting, or what we today call, impossibly, horrendously, "keyboarding," I want to enter a personal remark or two, begging the reader's forbearance. I myself, when writing about my work sessions with Heidegger in the early 1970s, paid special attention to his hands, and especially his writing hand, the right. If I remember well, I admired him—at age eighty-five—for both his handwriting and his writing posture.[2] Derrida's analysis of Heidegger's fetishism of the

---

2. See "Work Sessions with Martin Heidegger," *Philosophy Today* XXVI, no. 2 (Summer 1982): 126–38. I also confess to having paid close attention to Derrida's hands. See Krell, "The Hands of the Man," *The Oxford Literary Review,* "A Decade After Derrida," 36:2 (2014), 223–25.

pen (he does not call it that, but he comes close) is an embarrassment to me, especially since everything I have ever written, with the exception of memos to deans, has first been written by hand. Especially in the writing of fiction I find that the heel of my hand, the right, alone can tell the story in the way and at the speed it wants to be told. Even the translations I have done, which amount to several thousand pages of text, were handwritten; they went through at least three stages of emendation and correction before I typed or "keyboarded" them onto a machine. Perhaps I never got over Gore Vidal's slighting remark concerning Norman Mailer, "Norman doesn't write; he types." (This is the sort of remark that earned Vidal a black eye, and precisely at the singular hand, or fist, of Norman Mailer. Vidal's comment to reporters concerning the incident: "You have to understand, it is so difficult to be Norman.") It is a wonder to me that Derrida writes so well, inasmuch as only his postcards and letters, to the chagrin of the recipients, were handwritten. And yet as the *Envois* of *La Carte postale* confess, the writer's love of the voice and of the intimate presence promised by the voice, is hardly absent in Derrida. Perhaps, then, he is not all that remote from a secret love of handwriting. After all, it is difficult to *type* postcards from Socrates to Freud and beyond. Enough. Back to the business of the singular hand.³

After learning from John Sallis of Heidegger's remarks in his Parmenides lecture course of 1942–43 concerning the virtues of handwriting, as opposed to typing, Derrida lends his incomparable skills to an analysis of these remarks. Heidegger's passionate asseverations are somewhat surprising, and somewhat Luddite, in view of the fact that one still uses one's hands when typing or keyboarding. Perhaps the problem is that one uses *both* left and right, again as though they were feet? In any case, it is difficult to see why Heidegger should object to the typewriter or computer as one aspect of what *Being and Time* calls *Zeug*, indeed, *Schreibzeug* (SZ 68). One would have thought that the typewriter could serve as an eminent example of *Zuhandenheit*, one that resists the shift to *Vorhandenheit*, at least until the scientist's or philosopher's machine

---

3. Benoît Peeters reveals what I secretly always knew, of course, even though Derrida never admitted it to me, which is that at least in his early days he wrote by hand. During the early 1960s, Peeters tells us, writing was an affair of great gravity for Derrida, and it had to be done by hand. Not only that. Peeters cites Derrida's confession (PM 152–53) that not even a ballpoint sufficed; no, it had to be a fountain pen, perhaps of the kind we see in the photos of Heidegger, or even a calligraphic pen, well-nigh a *plume* or quill, which Derrida dipped in ink, sketching endless versions of a text before committing a version of it to his "little Olivetti." See BP 169.

breaks down, or until Claes Oldenburg creates his hysteria-inducing "Soft Typewriter." Derrida mentions that Nietzsche was the first philosopher to type, but he neglects to mention that Nietzsche too hated the typewriter: the keys kept on sticking, the thing never worked properly, and no one was ever able to repair it to his satisfaction. Yet a sticky key is not Heidegger's problem. Heidegger's problem may indeed have to do with the two "hands" as opposed to "the" hand. Derrida cites (434/46) a phrase from the Parmenides lectures (54:118) that is quite telling: "The human being does not 'have' hands; rather, the hand retains [*hat . . . inne*] the essence of the human being." Heidegger goes on to say that the spoken word *shows* beings (*zeigt*), while the written word inscribes (*einzeichnet*) the showing. Yet it does so as *hand*writing, *Handschrift*. Saying, showing, and *hand*writing are therefore intimately related. What is happening today, says Heidegger, with the prevalence of all sorts of procedures for mechanical reproduction (Heidegger does not mention Benjamin), is that the art of handwriting is dying. Indeed, we live in a time of "the destruction of the word" (54:119). *Ceci tuera cela*, Heidegger would say, if only in German, as he points to the typed word as opposed to the handwritten text. Using fairly violent language, Heidegger asserts that the typewriter "tears writing away from the essential domain of the hand, that is, from the word and speech" (ibid.) The writing machine therefore "degrades" word and speech, as any metaphysician, such as Thomas Aquinas or Fichte, would have been able to see. When everything is typewritten, all human beings become an indistinguishable and undistinguished mass. The only thing that could restore their individuality would be the hand, the singular writing hand, which, and here one must cite Heidegger's text as Derrida does, *"zeigt und zeigend zeichnet und zeichnend die zeigenden Zeichen zu Gebilden bildet,"* "[the hand] shows and, showing, draws and, drawing, forms into forms the signs that show," or "shapes the signs that show into images" (54:126; Ps 435/47). These drawn forms or images, he adds, in words that have to strike a chord with the author of *De la grammatologie*, "are called, in accord with the '*Verbum*' γράφειν, the γράμματα" (ibid.). Thus writing is essentially *hand*writing, the inscription of a grammatological voice, even presumably when a Greek architect, using both hands, chisels a name onto a lintel. Derrida, without reverting in any detail to the analyses of the second half of the *Grammatology*, notes that what Heidegger is saying here is true only of the system of *phonetic* writing: the proximity of word, monstration, inscription, and the shaped letter has its home in the voice that hears and understands itself while speaking. Heidegger of course does not breathe a word of this.

Otherwise, the intimacy of silent voice, hand, showing, and (the writing of) the revealing of being would be disturbed once and for all. And yet, as Derrida indicates, Heidegger's apparent appreciation of writing fits in perfectly well with the tradition Derrida has called *logocentric* and *phonocentric*. The apparent celebration of manuscripture has to be seen in the light of what Heidegger will say later in *What Is Called Thinking?* concerning "pure" thinking: Socrates is the purest thinker of the West because he wrote nothing, that is, because he held out in the stormwind of thinking and did not, like Plato and countless others to come, resort to "literature" (WhD? 5, 52). The essential *gathering* performed by the hand occurs not as a gleaning and gathering in the sense of *writing*; rather, it occurs as the *Brauch* about which Heidegger writes in "The Anaximander Fragment." If *Brauch* may translate τὸ χρεών, "Necessity," the Greek word itself having been formed from ἡ χείρ, "the hand," that is because *Brauch* is the "need" and "usage" that Heidegger always and everywhere calls *Versammlung*, "gathering." Such necessitous "gathering" of the hand, which occurs in and as *thinking*, thinking and *questioning*, and not as what Heidegger derides as *Geschreibe*, "scribbling," is at the critical center of the entire *Geschlecht* series.

I cannot retire from the field of "the hand," however, without noting an oversight of Derrida's, which is also an oversight of my own. He says, in both the second and third *Geschlecht* articles and elsewhere as well, that Heidegger fails in any of his works to make "the barest allusion" to the two hands of human beings. This is, of course, not the case, as William McNeill has demonstrated.[4] An early reference, in section 25 of Heidegger's *Prolegomena to the History of the Concept of Time* (20:319–20), is itself quite remarkable. There Heidegger states, "There is no hand in general [*keine Hand überhaupt*]," but only either the left or the right, both hands always already oriented and essentially kinesthetic. The other reference, in *Being and Time*, section 23, "The Spatiality of Being-in-the-world," is

---

4. See William McNeill, "Spirit's Living Hand," in *Of Derrida, Heidegger, and Spirit*, ed. David Wood (Evanston: Northwestern University Press, 1993), ch. 7. See also DL, 255–56, 327n. 19, and 345n. 1. In the typescript that serves as the initial basis for *Geschlecht III*, Derrida asserts once again that Heidegger makes no reference to the two hands, or to the two gloves of Kant's "orientation" essay. At that point in the margins I wrote, "But of course he has: see section 23 of *Sein und Zeit* on 'Sich orientieren im Denken.'" But this note is in red ink in my photocopy, indicating that I had sent the copy to Derrida without the indication—a double fault on my part: (1) I failed to warn Derrida about the oversight, and (2) I myself was guilty of the same oversight until Will McNeill informed me of it.

one that Derrida must have known about at some point, inasmuch as he cites from this section the italicized phrase, *"In Dasein there lies an essential tendency toward nearness"* (SZ 105). As familiar as he was with Heidegger's notion of "un-distancing," and as critical as he was concerning all such instances of "proximity" in Heidegger, and as familiar as he also was with Kant's essay on "orientation" in thinking, Derrida nevertheless neglects Heidegger's discussion of the two hands, left and right, and Kant's treatment of those hands. The first aspect of section 23 that catches our attention is Heidegger's insistence that remoteness and nearness are measured—at least in our everyday dealings with things or items of equipment—not on the basis of a Cartesian or Galilean grid; rather, he says, "what is 'closest' lies at a distance determined by the average scope of our seeing, reaching, and grasping [*in einer durchschnittlichen Reich-, Greif- und Blickweite*]" (SZ 107). Apparently the Dasein that espies things, then reaches out and grasps things, does have organs that can extend and take hold. *Greifweite* could surely be said to have existential significance, even for one who spends a great deal of time seated at a writing table. Furthermore, Heidegger's description of the spatiality of Dasein lends itself to a much wider clientele than the human: primates certainly view, reach out, and grasp; mice may learn that cats too have an amazing capacity in this regard; even the ants that find their way to my improperly closed honey jar seem to know about *Ent-fernung*. As is so often the case with existential structures, the spatiality of Dasein does not appear to be the exclusive property of humankind. Would it not be a revelation if we were to base our biological research into various forms of animal movement and behavior precisely on the "existentials" elaborated by Heidegger? It simply does not matter that he would rend his garments upon learning of this. He would in any case have to use both hands in order to do so.

Virtually every example of "closeness," for example, the proximity of the glasses that sit on our nose but which are so far away from our viewing that we often lose sight of them, and indeed lose them altogether, precisely because they are as close as the nose on our face, begs for an expansion of the scope of the example. One must always heed the differences, of course, and not put sunglasses on the poochie so that we can take a derisory snapshot. We walk down the street, says Heidegger, and what could be "closer" than the pavement under our footsoles? Yet the neighbor who is twenty paces ahead is "closer" to Dasein than the pavement. Philosophers, says Heidegger, must cease thinking of human beings' orienting themselves as "ego-things trapped in a body." Yet is it not equally important to stop regarding other life forms as bodies trapped in the mind-games of the researcher? To the possum who descends from the trees the neighbor is also closer than the pavement under the pads of its feet.

The fundamental point of section 23 of *Being and Time* is that our orientation in the world has to do with our *projects*, not with a geometric grid of distances we have to "cross." Heidegger concedes that our "embodiment," or *"Leiblichkeit,"* is essential to orientation, as long as those scare quotes remind us that the body is no *Körperding*, no "bodything," but *an existence*. Yet discussion of the spatiality of the human body is not germane to the fundamental ontology of Dasein, Heidegger says (SZ 108), even if it does "conceal" a problematic all its own. Our embodiment requires that handy items used by and for the body, "such as, for example, gloves," which are meant to be "coordinated with the movements performed by the hands [*das die Bewegungen der Hände mitmachen soll*], are oriented according to left and right" (ibid.). Most tools, says Heidegger, forgetting for the moment about scissors (at least of the old-fashioned design), do not have to be oriented in such a way, even though they are meant to be handy. It is here that Heidegger takes up Kant's "Was heisst: Sich im Denken orientieren?" His response to Kant (SZ 109–10) need not detain us here, although it is interesting to note that Heidegger grants Kant's insight into the *possibility* of orientation as an *ontological* problem—even though Kant himself soon collapses the ontological into a psychological problem, that of the "subjective principle" of memory. What needs to detain us, as it detains Derrida, is the possibility that the spatiality, un-distancing, and orientation of an embodied Dasein in the world may not be so readily restricted to the being that Heidegger wants to privilege. There is a *homo habilis* that survives in every child born and in every adult—even in adults who carry pails of water or point with canes or instruct others with their pens. One more word about those gloves, the left and the right: in German they are called *Handschuhe*—shoes for the hand. Or, better, for the *hands*.

As we turn to the second of the two divisions of *Geschlecht II*, we find ourselves prepared to forgive Derrida's oversight, especially because it is a shared oversight. For, indeed, the Heidegger of *Was heisst Denken?* and many other texts is demonstrably singlehanded. Derrida begins this section by stressing the gendered nature—in both French and German—of the hand of man, *la main de l'homme*. Such gendering is a matter that he will stress also during the first year of his final seminar, *La bête et le souverain,* in which we hear him opening the very first session with a kind of singsong repetition of the definite articles, *la* and *le*—as though that were love's old sweet song, singing of the beast (feminine) and the sovereign (masculine). In the present instance it is a matter of *la main de l'homme*, once again *la, le*, with the *singularity* of the hand (feminine) hoping perhaps to accent this essential mark of the human, *des Menschen* (masculine). *Die Hand* is the feminine noun that makes the man, provided "man" be the collective noun. Derrida continues:

> [Y]ou will certainly have noticed that Heidegger not only thinks the hand as a very singular thing that rightfully belongs only to man. He also always thinks the hand *in the singular*, as if man did not have two hands but, this monster, a single hand. Not a single organ in the middle of his body, like the Cyclops who had a single eye in the middle of his forehead, although this representation, which leaves something to be desired, also gives one to think. (Ps 438/49–50)

The Cyclopic eye and hand, in the singular, would be de*monstra*tive, hence monstrous, and would leave one more hand—presumably, the *caressing* hand—to be desired. If the two hands make love, two or four, the singular hand sometimes seems to come down hard. One thinks of the raised right hand of the Judge, Pantocrator, in Michelangelo's *Last Judgment*, the hand feared as much by the Blessed as by the Damned. One thinks too of that astonishing sculptured fountain tucked into a corner of the Luxembourg Gardens where lovers try to hide, which has as its theme Polyphemus spying on Galatea.[5]

Derrida now presents the two poles of the magnetic field that will dominate this particular *Geschlecht*, that of the "organic dispersion" into two hands, which Heidegger seems to fear, and the folding of two hands into one, that is, into the gestures of pointing, signifying, praying, and gathering. What Heidegger appears to be avoiding are the hands that

---

5. Auguste Ottin designed two different sculptures, the marble group of the lovers Acis and Galatée, haunted by a menacing Polyphème in bronze overhead. On the same theme, see the beautifully designed cover of Jonathan F. Krell, *The Ogre's Progress: Images of the Ogre in Modern and Contemporary French Fiction* (Newark: University of Delaware Press, 2009), which reproduces Gustave Moreau's "Galatea." Moreau grants Polyphemus three eyes, two brooding "human" eyes and one gaping monstrous one. The giant ogre rests his brooding head on one hand as that singular eye gapes. See also, within the covers, Jonathan Krell's discussion of Michel Tournier's Tiffauges (85), the hero of *Le roi des aulnes*, who identifies himself (as "deep-eyed," *tiefäugig*) through the Polyphemic single eye of his single reflex camera, which roams wherever and devours whomever it will.

desire and that might caress, the hands that one might have thought essential to our *Geschlecht*.

Two explicit references to *Geschlecht III* appear in the second part of *Geschlecht II*, with which we are now engaged. The second occurs very near the end of the essay, and we will examine it later. In the first reference, appearing within square brackets on pages 439–40/51 of *Psyché*, Derrida notes that his question concerning the (missing) caress of lovemaking, of the desiring hands, as it were, ought to guide him toward the word *Geschlecht*, which he promises to take up in another text. Derrida says, "I will not give this part of my lecture, which should have been entitled *Geschlecht* III, and whose (typed) manuscript has been *photocopied* and distributed to some of you so that a discussion of it might be possible. I will confine myself then to a cursory sketch of it." We may expect, therefore, that the following paragraphs of *Geschlecht II* ought to contain much of the substance of *Geschlecht III*, or at least of those thirty-three typed, photocopied, and distributed pages. We will take up these anticipations of or expectations concerning the third generation of *Geschlecht* in later chapters (namely, 5 and 6) of the present book; here we will merely observe, by way of introduction, that the themes that magnetize Derrida are (1) the problem of the "site" of Heidegger's "placement" of Trakl's poetry, the *Ort* and *Ortschaft* of his *Erörterung*, and (2) the problem of the *Schlag*, better, the two *Schläge*, that form the root of the word *Geschlecht*, the first guaranteeing a more gentle unifold for the twofold of the sexes, the second (albeit not necessarily "chronologically" second) introducing discord and dissension—*die Zwietracht*, as opposed to *das Zwiefache*—into binary sexuality. In Heidegger's view, there is in Trakl's poem—he has but one, says Heidegger, his poem being as singular as his writing hand, even if that poem seems to disperse into multiple poems—something that promises to restore unity and accord to the sexes, so that the two discordant sexes will become an emphatic "*one* Geschlecht," the "*Ein* Geschlecht" of Trakl's "Western Song," *Abendländisches Lied*. (See Appendix A.)

Perhaps the very first aspect of Derrida's reading of Heidegger's interpretation of Trakl that has to be mentioned is Derrida's appreciation of *idiom*, that is to say, of the difficulty—if not impossibility—of discussing Heidegger's reading in French or in English. *Geschlecht II*, to repeat, was first presented as a lecture in Chicago, although the text had been written in French before it was rendered (by John P. Leavey Jr.) into American English. As we shall see, Derrida shows that, on the one hand, Heidegger's perpetual appeal to "our language," which usually means Old or Middle

High German, tends to limit his perspective in troubling ways, while, on the other hand, there seem to be many things—*Geschlecht* among them—that absolutely resist translation into any other national idiom. The result is a genuine predicament: "I knew I would have to speak in English the text I was writing in French on another I was reading in German," confesses Derrida (441/302). Nowhere, however, will either Derrida or Heidegger mention a national difference that should not be forgotten: Trakl was not German at all but Austrian, a contemporary of Karl Kraus and Robert Musil, and like them he was anything but a pan-Germanist. Only the *Germanist* gifted with the finest set of ears will be able to hear the Austrian idiom in Trakl, no doubt, and yet it would be incautious to suppose that the idiom is not there. After 1939, it would be, politically speaking, a reprehensible ignorance. In any case, Derrida and I, and now the reader, will have enough to worry about with English, French, and all the phases and places of High German.

The principal worry for Derrida involves the issue of polysemy, or what Heidegger calls *Mehrdeutigkeit,* not "ambiguity" but the multiple meanings of words. In *Was heisst Denken?* Heidegger cites as the principal danger for thinking in our time what he calls *Eingleisdenken,* "one-track thinking." He associates this with the predominance of technology and calculative thinking in our time, and he would be chagrined to find himself accused of it. Derrida comes close to making such an accusation, for it seems to him that Heidegger always manages to *gather* the multiple meanings of Trakl's expressions so that they seem to yield a univocal sense. Indeed, Heidegger equates the opposite of gathering, namely, what Derrida would call *dissemination,* with bad poetry; the rhymes of a "poetaster," and all mere "versifying," are something no *great* poet would ever do. Yet at what point does the gathering of multiple meanings into one become one-track thinking? Might not *Versammlung,* gathering, itself be the name of a single-track *chemin de fer heideggerien*?

In this first explicit reference to a third *Geschlecht,* Derrida introduces two passages from Heidegger's "Die Sprache im Gedicht," from which he will derive five "foci" or *foyers* for his questions. These passages appear at pages 49 and 78 of *Unterwegs zur Sprache,* and even though we will be dealing with them in detail later in the book, it would perhaps behoove us to present them here, first in German, then in an English rendering, setting aside for the moment all of Derrida's questions and comments. The first passage, beginning with a reference to Trakl's "Autumn Soul," refers to the poet's abandonment of the persons he loves, "the others." Heidegger identifies—problematically, as we will see—these "others" with what he calls *der Schlag der verwesten Gestalt des Menschen,* "the coinage of the decomposed figure of man." Heidegger continues, introducing for the first time the word *Geschlecht* into his essay (US 49–50):

> Unsere Sprache nennt das aus einem Schlag geprägte und in diesen Schlag verschlagene Menschenwesen das "Geschlecht." Das Wort bedeutet sowohl das Menschengeschlecht im Sinne der Menschheit, als auch die Geschlechter im Sinne der Stämme, Sippen und Familien, dies alles wiederum geprägt in das Zwiefache der Geschlechter. Das Geschlecht der "verwesten Gestalt" des Menschen nennt der Dichter das "verwesende" Geschlecht. Es ist aus der Art seines Wesens herausgesetzt und darum das "entsetzte" Geschlecht.
>
> Womit ist dieses Geschlecht geschlagen, d. h. verflucht? Fluch heißt griechisch πλήγη, unser Wort "Schlag." Der Fluch des verwesenden Geschlechtes besteht darin, daß dieses alte Geschlecht in die Zwietracht der Geschlechter auseinandergeschlagen ist. Aus ihr trachtet jedes der Geschlechter in den losgelassenen Aufruhr der je vereinzelten und bloßen Wildheit des Wildes. Nicht das Zwiefache als solches, sondern die Zwietracht ist der Fluch. Sie trägt aus dem Aufruhr der blinden Wildheit das Geschlecht in die Entzweiung und verschlägt es so in die losgelassene Vereinzelung. Also entzweit und zerschlagen vermag das "verfallene Geschlecht" von sich aus nicht mehr in den rechten Schlag zu finden. Den rechten Schlag aber hat es nur mit jenem Geschlecht, dessen Zwiefaches aus der Zwietracht weg in die Sanftmut einer einfältigen Zwiefalt vorauswandert, d. h. ein "Fremdes" ist und dabei dem Fremdling folgt.

Our language names the essence of the human being, which is struck in a certain coinage and is stamped in this coinage, the *"Geschlecht."* This word means the human race, in the sense of humankind, and also the *Geschlechter,* in the sense of tribes, clans, and families, all of this being coined in its turn by the twofold of the *Geschlechter.* The *Geschlecht* of the "decomposed figure" of human beings is called by the poet the "decomposing" *Geschlecht.* It is the kind of *Geschlecht* that has been expelled from its essence and is therefore the "horrified" *Geschlecht.*

By what has this *Geschlecht* been struck, i.e., cursed? *Curse,* in Greek, is πλήγη, our word "stroke." The curse of the decomposing *Geschlecht* consists in the fact that this old *Geschlecht* has been severed into the discord of the *Geschlechter*. As a result of this discord, each of the *Geschlechter* struggles within the unbridled tumult of the wildness of the animal, individualized and savage. Not the twofold as such, but discord is the curse. As a result of the tumult of blind savagery, discord transports the *Geschlecht* into bifurcation and so banishes it to unbridled individuation. Thus bifurcated and battered, the "fallen *Geschlecht*" can on its own no longer find the way toward its proper coinage. Yet the only *Geschlecht* that would attain its proper coinage would be the one whose twofold wanders ahead, on its way out of discord into the gentleness of a onefold twofold; that means it is something "strange," and it thereby follows the stranger.

Heidegger is not known for straightforward and transparent statements. Yet is there any Heideggerian text as strange as this one? It *is* strange, and it follows the stranger of Trakl's poetry. Virtually every aspect of it is uncanny, at once grandiose and bizarre. In the present context of *Geschlecht II,* Derrida merely lists some of those aspects that he would like to pursue elsewhere: *Schlag* and *Geschlecht,* the "stroke" or "coinage" of the human race, its generations, clans, and families, all of these "in turn" coined or struck by the two *Geschlechter,* which no translator, whether French or English, can translate otherwise than as "the two sexes"; *die verweste Gestalt des Menschen,* the "decomposed" or, more literally, "disessenced" figure of humankind; and perhaps most mysterious of all, the curse of discord between those two *Geschlechter* whom we can scarcely avoid calling the two sexes, the discord that stems not from the twofold as such but from a more mysterious stroke or blow that drives each of them into unbridled savagery. The only hope, and this hope is the uncanniest aspect of all, is that a disessenced humankind may wander ahead, or perhaps *back,* to a more gentle twofold, a twosome that folds back into one. Above all, Derrida will want to know why and how, by what mightiness of essence, the twofold was originally coined, and when and why an accursed second stroke botched the coinage; most of all, he will want to know how a "placement" of Georg Trakl's poem will help the botched human race to find its way ahead, or back, to a greater tenderness.

One word more, by way of anticipation, about the onefold twofold, the two folding back into one. Earlier we referred to Dürer's hands folded in prayer and the "great onefold" invoked by Heidegger in *What*

*Is Called Thinking?* Trakl appears to invoke such hands in the last of his "Rosary Hymns," titled "Amen" (see Appendix B). Perhaps these are the hands of the surviving members of his family during his father's funeral. However, he never speaks of the two hands becoming one; instead, the hands *wölben sich,* they form a "vault," and they do so cryptically, one must say. Although Derrida does not take pains to note it here, the "fold" of Heidegger's onefold twofold, *le pli,* will intrigue him throughout the seminar that ought to have become *Geschlecht III.* For the *pli,* in Derrida's view, is anything but a figure of gathering. Rather, it is a figure of the vault or crypt. As we will see in chapter 6, it is an eminent figure of *dissémination,* a figure that stands very much in contrast to Heidegger's *Mehrdeutigkeit* or polysemy.

The second passage comes from the third and final part of Heidegger's triptych (US 78). Here Heidegger is reading Trakl's "Western Song" and interpreting Trakl's emphasis there on the *one* of *one Geschlecht.* It is a *one* that in Heidegger's view promises a "gathering" of the *Geschlechter* "into the onefold of a more gentle twofold":

Das *"Ein"* im Wort *"Ein* Geschlecht" meint nicht "eins" statt "zwei." Das "Ein" bedeutet auch nicht das Einerlei einer faden Gleichheit. Das Wort *"Ein* Geschlecht" nennt hier überhaupt keinen biologischen Tatbestand, weder die "Eingeschlechtlichkeit," noch die "Gleichgeschlechtlichkeit." In dem betonten *"Ein* Geschlecht" verbirgt sich jenes Einende, das aus der versammelnden Bläue der geistlichen Nacht einigt. Das Wort spricht aus dem Lied, worin das Land des Abends gesungen wird. Demgemäß behält hier das Wort "Geschlecht" seine volle bereits genannte mehrfältige Bedeutung. Es nennt einmal das geschichtliche Geschlecht des Menschen, die Menschheit, im Unterschied zum übrigen Lebendigen (Pflanze und Tier). Das Wort "Geschlecht" nennt sodann die Geschlechter, Stämme, Sippen, Familien dieses Menschengeschlechtes. Das Wort "Geschlecht" nennt zugleich überall die Zwiefalt der Geschlechter.

The *"one"* in the phrase *"one Geschlecht"* does not mean "one" instead of "two." Nor does the "one" signify a bundle of things that share some insipid identity. The phrase *"one Geschlecht"* here does not mean any kind of biological state of affairs, whether "having only one sex" or "being of the same sex." In the emphatic *"one Geschlecht"* there lies concealed the unifying that unites on the basis of the gathering azure of the spiriting night. The phrase speaks within the song in which the Land of Evening is sung. Accordingly, the word *Geschlecht* here contains the full range of the manifold significance we have indicated. For one thing, it names the historical *Geschlecht* of human beings, humankind, in distinction from other life forms (plant and animal). The word *Geschlecht* then goes on to name the generations [*Geschlechter*], tribes, clans, and families of this human *Geschlecht*. At the same time, the word *Geschlecht* everywhere names the twofold of the *Geschlechter*.

Heidegger's account here differs from the earlier one in several respects. This second account begins and ends with references to the plural *Geschlechter* in the sense of the twosome, the two genders or sexes, presumably, which when they are unified in Trakl's sense cannot be merely "unisex." To repeat, it is difficult if not impossible to read the expression *Zwiefalt der Geschlechter* in any way other than "the twofold of the sexes," except perhaps in the line that refers to tribes and clans, where the plural seems to designate multiple "generations." And so I have translated it here, *Geschlechter* as "generations," indicating the German word in square brackets. Otherwise, the plural *Geschlechter* usually, that is to say, in the common parlance of "our language," means the sexes. Certainly the words *Eingeschlechtlichkeit* and *Gleichgeschlechtlichkeit* do not refer to one's belonging to a single identical "generation." Derrida indicates (444/55) that the French translation wavers between two translations of *Geschlechter* in the sense of the sexes, the first, *dualité générique des sexes*, explicitly citing the sexes, the second, *dédoublement générique*, cautiously avoiding specific mention of them while making it plain that they are meant. Along the same lines, in the present passage Heidegger is careful to exclude "biology," as he has always done ever since *Being and Time*. Here it is a matter of a gathering, *Versammlung*, portrayed in terms borrowed from Trakl's poetry: a blueness or azure, *Bläue*, that appears at eventide in the Land of Evening, *das Abendland*, which is the West, the Occident. The gathering azure, says Heidegger, unites and unifies. Moreover, Heidegger here alters the reference to "humankind" by identifying it as "historical." What is the relation between "humankind," considered beyond all "biology," yet in terms of the history of the West? Can these two matters, humanity and the Occident, be conflated? A number of nations and cultures across the globe would object. And the night that is "spiriting," *geistlich*, means what? Heidegger will peremptorily distinguish *geistlich* from *geistig*, insisting that Trakl uses the former word in a way that bears no relation to either Platonistic "intelligibility" or Christian "spirituality." Derrida will wonder why Heidegger insists on this so strongly, and he will ask whether Heidegger's insistence is in any way convincing. Furthermore, even after biology has been banished from Heidegger's reading of Trakl, why the reference to other life forms, vegetable and animal, if only to exclude them? What lies behind all these denials and efforts to exclude? Here the multiple meanings of *Geschlecht* are emphasized once again, even though a "uniting" and "unifying" appear to promise some ultimate, univocal sense for the word. True, in the penultimate line of the poem *Abendländisches Lied* Trakl writes the words, "O n e Geschlecht." Yet by what method, or along what path of thinking, or from what place or situation, are we to read and hear these words?

The second of Derrida's two explicit references to *Geschlecht III*, with which *Geschlecht II* in fact comes to a close (446–51), mentions "some one hundred pages," *les quelque cent pages*, that Derrida elsewhere (that is, in the seminar on "The Phantom of the Other") has devoted to Heidegger's Trakl essay. In Heidegger's conversation with the poet, which wants to be a *Zwiegespräch*, the talk of a twosome about the twofold *Geschlecht*, Derrida isolates five areas of "focus," five *foyers*, for his own reading of Heidegger's reading. The fourth of these "foci," involving the idiomatic nature of particular German words, is subdivided into yet another five, labeled "a" to "e." Derrida remarks that, in spite of what was argued earlier, Heidegger in fact always writes, whether wittingly or not, with two hands, so that it is not a matter of "criticizing" his reading; it is always and everywhere, Derrida insists, an effort to see whether the "place" of Trakl's poetry can be located with any degree of assurance. The five general areas of Derrida's inquiry—an inquiry he promises to pursue in what will be the *third* of his own *Geschlechter*, are, briefly stated, (1) the problem of humanity and animality, viewed not "biologically" but in terms of Trakl's repeated mention of "blue game," *ein blaues Wild*, along with Heidegger's unquenchable desire to identify a humankind that leaves behind all reference to animality; (2) good polysemy, or multiplicity of meaning, which Heidegger clearly affirms in his conversations with poetry, versus bad dispersion or dissemination of meaning; (3) the methodology by which Heidegger wants to *situate* or *place* Trakl's "unspoken" poem, and the apparent circularity or alternation (*Wechselbezug*) of commentary (*Erläuterung*) on particular poems or specific verses and placement (*Erörterung*) of the unspoken single poem, inasmuch as the latter without the former is arbitrary, the former without the latter blind; (4) Heidegger's *manner* or *maneuvers* (derived from *les mains*, and their way of "handling" a text) when it comes to discussing the meaning of particular words, his recourse always and everywhere to the concealed history of "our" language, meaning German, especially Old High German, when it comes to essential words in Trakl's printed poems, words such as (a) *Schlag* and *Geschlecht* as such, "stroke," "blow," "coinage," or perhaps also "beat," and all the sundry senses of *Geschlecht* that have already been mentioned, (b) the *Ort* of *Erörterung*, the site, or the "point of the spear," where all multiplicities and manifolds, including the twofold, presumably gather into one, (c) the subtle opposition that Heidegger insists on between *geistig* and *geistlich*, which putatively enables him (and "his" Trakl) to avoid the Platonic-Christian distinctions between mind and matter, eternity and time, good and evil, and so on, all the while alluding to them, both *geistig* and *geistlich* deriving from *gheis*, which means or at least suggests "flame," (d) *fremd*, derived from *fram*, meaning not "foreign" but "under way toward," heading not away from but toward a certain destination and thus avoiding dispersion into the foreign, and (e) *Wahnsinn*, which means, when viewed in terms of the medieval roots *wana* and *sinnan*, avoiding the usual paths and striking out on new ways, although once again not into the foreign; and finally, in order to end the larger list of general areas or *foyers*, (5) *die Verwesung*, the decomposition or disessencing of (Western) humanity as the result of a second stroke or blow that introduces discord, dissension, and indeed savagery and bestiality, perhaps even incest, into the twofold of the sexes, such that humanity is disfigured—a disessencing that once again compels Heidegger to repeat in classic gestures the very language and conceptuality of Platonism and Christianity all the while denying that either he or Trakl is doing so.

With that cascade of issues and problems, *Geschlecht II* comes to its *chute*, its precipitous conclusion, intended to serve as an *envoi* to Derrida's listeners. We will take up that *envoi* or "sending" in chapters 5 and 6 of the present book, but not before examining a text that at least appears to interrupt the *Geschlecht* series, namely, the 1987 *Of Spirit: Heidegger and the Question*. And in a move that is more controversial, we will even consider the 1989 *Geschlecht IV* before turning back to the typescript of *Geschlecht III* and the 1984–85 seminar in Paris, *Le fantôme de l'autre*, on which the typescript is based. The reason? Principally because in the book that appears in the midst of the *Geschlecht* series, as well as in *Geschlecht IV* itself, the second magnetic pole of the series, namely, the poetry of Georg Trakl and its emphatic "*Ein* Geschlecht," receives very little attention, whereas it is at the core of the typescript and the 1984–85 seminar. And the less visible reason? The fact that the material in both the typescript and seminar notes is more thought provoking today than ever before and therefore merits greater exposure and discussion.

3

# Of Spirit

### Ecce homo

> Yes! I know from whence I came!
> Insatiable am I, just like the flame;
> I shine and then consume the same.
> All things glow beneath my hand,
> All becomes ash beneath my brand:
> Flame, flame is surely what I am.
>
> —Friedrich Nietzsche

I wonder if it is too much to say that this book, *Of Spirit: Heidegger and the Question,* which is the somewhat expanded version of Derrida's 1987 address to a colloquium dedicated to "open questions" concerning Heidegger, changed virtually everything about Heidegger studies. For Derrida was able to show that every variety of Heidegger scholar—from the Holy Heideggerians to the Heretical Heideggerians, and from the milder variety of Anti-Heideggerians to the Heideggerophobes of all stripes— had thoroughly ignored the strange case of *Geist, geistig,* and *geistlich* in Heidegger. In *Being and Time,* the phenomenologist instructs himself and us to "avoid" these words, and total avoidance likewise characterizes the reception of Heidegger's work in this regard. Including my own reception of it.

Yet especially during the years 1933 to 1935 Heidegger speaks not only *of* spirit but *in the name of* spirit, *for* spirit, as it were, and precisely in the most frightening political circumstances. He then, after the war, in his second Trakl essay (1953) tries to distinguish between *geistig* and *geistlich* in a manner that is both entirely unconvincing and highly significant.

Significant of what? The word *geistig,* says Heidegger in 1953, encapsulates all that is corrupt in the Platonic-Christian tradition, its intellectualism and its spiritualism. *Geistig,* however, is the word that appears over and over again in Heidegger's texts of the 1930s, not merely mentioned but used and advocated. Only in 1953 will *Geist* and *geistlich* prove to be furious words, that is, words having to do with fire. As such they will show us a Heidegger who wants to resist the force of the *pneumatic* tradition of spirit in order to commence an "other" thinking of Heraclitus's πῦρ ἀείζωον, "everliving fire." *Geist* will, toward the end of Heidegger's career, appear in the form of flame. Ironically, this would be one of the very few words that are identical in the Gallo-Latin and Germanic language groups: flame, *la flamme, die Flamme.*

At the outset of his *De l'esprit,* Derrida comments on the Ciceronian character of the title, itself borrowed from Helvétius's *De l'esprit,* a book that was condemned and consigned to flames on the grand stairway of the Palais de Justice on February 10, 1759. Even Rousseau hated the book, although he consigned his own polemical pages on it to the flames when he learned that Helvétius was being persecuted on account of his book. An important aspect of Derrida's effort in *Of Spirit* is to bring both the Latin and the German languages and cultural heritages to center stage, in order to ask whether *Geist, geistig,* and *geistlich* are at all *de l'esprit,* and whether translation does not here confront an absolute aporia. Such an aporia finds us in an *Ort* or *Ortschaft,* a "place," in which discussion or "placement" (*Erörterung*) is both demanded and made precarious, perhaps even impossible; it would be an intersection marked by a dizzying array of signs, among them "what one calls history, language, nation, *Geschlecht,* the Greek or the German" (DE 18/5). In short, "spirit" initially appears to be irrelevant to Heidegger's thinking, or at least not to be a rubric that Heidegger himself advertises. And yet, says Derrida, words that we would inevitably translate in terms of the "spiritual" seem to *magnetize* Heidegger's thinking from beginning to end, not only in his infamous political texts of the 1930s but also in his lectures and essays on Hölderlin, Schelling, Nietzsche, and, years later, Trakl. As bizarre as such a claim may seem, Heidegger's work as a whole, says Derrida, *se laisse pourtant aimanter* by *Geist* (DE 16/3). *Aimanter,* we recall, is the word that Derrida selects to characterize his own fascination with the 1953 Trakl essay.

The second chapter of *De l'esprit* presents the four "open questions" that are Derrida's own; questions, he says, where his hesitation and uncertainty concerning Heidegger are greatest. It is fair to say that each of these four "threads" has both an exoteric and an esoteric twist—that is to say, they are immediately understandable and yet require a long and difficult exegesis. These four threads, which Derrida sees forming a knot or tangle, and perhaps even a weft or tapestry (this time not a *Geschlecht* but a *Geflecht*), may be described briefly as follows.[1]

1. Questioning, *Fragen*, is the piety of thinking, says Heidegger at the end of "The Question Concerning Technology" (VA 44; BW 317). In *Being and Time* he identifies Dasein as the exemplary questioner, the only being that can interrogate—although it has not yet interrogated—being as such. The questioning of being, and not some property or quality of "spirit," serves Heidegger as the appropriate starting point for an analysis of human being. It is not until very late in the day, in "The Essence of Language" (US 157–216), from the year 1958, that Heidegger challenges the supreme dignity of the question by asserting the preeminence of the "address" and "assent" (*Zuspruch, Zusage*) of and to language over all explicit questioning. (The long note dedicated to Françoise Dastur, in chapter 9 of *De l'esprit*, based on a long discussion between Derrida and Dastur at the University of Essex in 1986, is essential in this respect.) Here Derrida joins Heidegger's thinking with perhaps the greatest sympathy and engagement, reflecting on the *promise* that the call of thinking enjoins. For Derrida, that promise involves a double affirmation, a double *yes* that evokes and engages questioning. As the subtitle of *De l'esprit* betrays, this first guiding thread is also the most persistent in Derrida's text. "Thus I shall try to show," writes Derrida (DE 25–26/10), "that *Geist* is perhaps the name that Heidegger gives, beyond every other name, to this unquestioned possibility of the question."

A perhaps more esoteric approach to the question of the question would involve our acknowledging that questioning is not the only relation to being that Heidegger discusses in the opening pages of *Sein und Zeit*. There he stresses that Dasein is "involved" in its being, that its being "matters" to it. Dasein *geht um* its own being. This apparently simple *Umgang*, the familiar involvement with both the word and the "thing" called *being*, is there long before any question arises. Indeed, Heidegger stresses that the question has today been forgotten, that a

---

1. I will borrow from my discussion (in chapter 8 of *Daimon Life*) of these four threads (see esp. DL, 266–68), once again with apologies for the repetition.

needlessness and heedlessness characterizes the question. For that reason, something like a sense or sensibility for the question has to be awakened. Furthermore, says Heidegger, we *live* in a pre-ontological understanding of being. This means that the entire issue of "life," including animal life, which Derrida will take up as his third thread, is crucial for fundamental ontology from the very start. It may seem far-fetched to want to connect Dasein's *Umgang* with being, or its *living within* some sort of understanding of its being, with the *Zuspruch* and *Zusage* of Heidegger's later thinking, yet the effort might prove to be worthwhile. It may prove that even the simplest of "understandings," here understood in terms of *possibility-being,* and even the least reflective modes of our *living* involve something like the affirmation of a double-yes. Derrida does not venture here such a thinking, which no doubt would have to face the charge of being esoteric.

2. The *essence* of technology is nothing technical, says Heidegger in that same essay, "The Question Concerning Technology." This is a recurrent strategy of his, one that would preserve the realm of essences (in the science of ontology as well as in poetizing thinking) from the merely contingent, the ontic, the prosaic. Indeed, Derrida is less concerned with the issue of technology than with that of essence, *Wesen*. Heidegger tries to think the essence verbally, as "essential unfolding" or even "coming to presence," and yet even the verbal essence has its problems. For one thing, "presence" marks the meaning of being for metaphysics. How could Heidegger's thought of *Wesen* as *An-wesen,* "coming to presence," avoid the contamination of the metaphysical heritage? More generally, there is always in Heidegger's texts a hidden appeal to the authority of such a metaphysics. When Heidegger says that *Wesen* is the verbal "unfolding," rather than the traditional *essentia,* he makes a suppressed appeal to the *essentia* of *Wesen*. And although Heidegger rarely refers to it, the initial sense of the verbal *wesen* is to "haunt." For Derrida's *Of Spirit,* this would have been a delicious discovery: the essential unfolding of being in the history of metaphysics is all about ghosts, all about spirits. And spirits are known to *return* as *revenants,* especially when we try to lay them to rest. At a certain point in his academic career, in the early- to mid-1930s, Heidegger is keen to rescue *Geist* from a certain destitution or disenfranchisement, a certain decrepitude or disempowerment, *Entmachtung des Geistes.* Moreover, he tries to rescue it by force of an "essential will" or "will to essence," *Wesenwille,* which itself is a fateful inheritance from metaphysics. Nor will he shy from raising the decisive issue for metaphysics and morals, namely, the distinction between good and evil, as a matter of *Geist.* The

desire to preserve spirit from "disessencing" or decomposition, *Verwesung,* propels Heidegger's 1953 Trakl essay, so that the long career of *Wesen* in Heidegger's thought remains one of the "open" questions.

3. The discourse on animality in which Heidegger participates but which he by no means masters is perhaps the second most visible thread in *Of Spirit.* How could it be otherwise, if "spirit" is traditionally defined in opposition to nature, materiality, and bestiality; or if, as "On the Essence and Concept of Φύσις" (W 309) indicates, *Geist* is aligned with "grace," the "supernatural," "art," and "history"? However much the animality of "mere life," "just-plain-life," *nur-noch-Leben,* appears to be excluded from the purview of fundamental ontology, and however much life too appears to be a matter that necessitates avoidance (precisely because life is neither Dasein nor what is handy nor what is at hand), animality remains a problem that returns again and again to haunt Heidegger's thought, haunt it to the point where the ontological difference itself is made to tremble. At least, this is what Derrida will argue in the very last seminar of his own life. For even in later texts such as *What Is Called Thinking?* Heidegger's discourse on man and animality surrenders to a rhetoric so "peremptory and authoritarian" that it appears actually to be a "dissimulation in the face of an impasse" (DE 28/11). That impasse becomes most visible in the 1929–30 lectures on *The Fundamental Concepts of Metaphysics: World—Finitude—Solitude,* in which Heidegger tries to compare the world-relations of stone, animal, and Dasein. If the stone is worldless, and humanity world-shaping, animality is in some enigmatic sense both *with* and *without* world. In a word, and an embarrassing word it is, animality is "poor in world," which of course sounds like one of the Beatitudes. Such "world poverty," less beatific when translated this way, is no doubt bound up with the animal's lack of essential "technique," which is a lack of "know-how," bound up too with its inability to pose questions and to confront its dying *as such:* thus, the first three threads—the question of the question, the question of the essence, and the question of life—begin to twist and knot themselves, as it were. Because they *always* have done so in our history, viewed as the history of being, they point to the fourth and final thread.[2]

4. The "epochality" of Heidegger's history of being, especially his understanding of the history of metaphysics or of "beyng" as essentially

---

2. On the third thread, see the remarkable late texts by Derrida, *The Animal That Therefore I Am,* and the two volumes of his final seminar, *The Beast and the Sovereign.* For a discussion of these texts, see D. F. Krell, *Derrida and Our Animal Others* (AO).

*one* epoch, preserves traces of an ontotheological and teleological thinking, particularly in what it forecloses for thinking and excludes from the history of being. Derrida sees such foreclosure at work in Heidegger's interpretation of the Platonic χώρα as a "preparation" for the Cartesian interpretation of objects in space as *extensio*. He sees it also in Heidegger's tendency to exclude recalcitrant figures from his critique of modern subjectivity, figures such as Spinoza, who cannot be so readily subsumed under the rubric of subjectivity. The *telos* of Derrida's own book—if it is fair and accurate to apply the same word to his endeavors—is to put in question and even to suspend Heidegger's rejection of the entire Platonic-Christian tradition (as though in its "entirety" it were *one*). Precisely here is where *Of Spirit* comes closest to the *Geschlecht* series, and especially to the unpublished *Geschlecht III*. For what Derrida objects to here is Heidegger's effort to acknowledge the word *geistlich* (but not *geistig*, affirmed and used in 1933 and 1935 but spurned twenty years later) in Trakl's poetry. As we will see, the final sessions of Derrida's 1984–85 seminar, "The Phantom of the Other," resist Heidegger's effort strenuously—not in order to affirm either the "Platonism" or the "Christianity" of Trakl's poetry but to show how peremptory and authoritarian such "epochal" reductions and exclusions are.

That the word and the things called variously *Geist, geistig, geistlich* knot these four threads Derrida claims to know "ahead of time," *comme par avance* (24/19). The word *hypothesis* is there merely out of courtesy. Yet if Derrida knows *Geist* to be the truth of being, that is, the gathering of both Heidegger's and his own thought, at least on the present occasion, the result of such knowledge is as ominous as it is paradoxical. For Derrida's only surety is a "negative certitude," and the thesis concerning the importance of *Geist* for Heidegger *remains* his, Derrida's, hypothesis: the only thing that Derrida is perfectly sure of is that he does not understand very well "what ultimately regulates the *spiritual* idiom in Heidegger"; equally uncertain, however, is his hypothesis that a figure of excessive clarity, "the ambiguous clarity of the flame," will illuminate the tangle of these four threads (DE 29–30/12–13).

The third and fourth chapters of *De l'esprit* offer a close reading of the word *Geist*, mentioned mostly by way of avoidance, in *Sein und Zeit*. Heidegger does not try to define *Geist*, whether he is avoiding it, mentioning it, or using it. He employs the word, Derrida says, axiomatically. Yet whenever Heidegger does appeal to the word the results are dramatic. Why dramatic? Because the word and the "thing" called *Geist*, so central to the tradition that calls for *Destruktion* and *Abbau*, or "deconstruction," appears to escape from or lie beyond all critical dismantling. It seems to be a part of that "inheritance," *Erbe*, that Heidegger cites in section 74, a "heritage" that apparently suffers no *Destruktion*. In *Being and Time* it is, to repeat, principally a matter of avoiding *Geist*. The word belongs to the ontotheological tradition, however, and to that extent would have to undergo *Destruktion*; it pertains particularly to the Cartesian *res cogitans*, whose *being*, namely, the being of the *sum*, has suffered neglect. Derrida works carefully through section 10, "Delimiting Dasein from Anthropology, Psychology, and Biology," in which Heidegger emphasizes the complacency or ostensible needlessness (*Bedürfnislosigkeit*) that has characterized the question of "the *being* of the subject, of the soul, of consciousness, of spirit [*des Geistes*], of the person" (SZ 46). Even when Heidegger uses the word *Geist* without quotation marks, he is mentioning it only in order to enforce avoidance of it. Even if what it means is altogether unclear, or, rather, precisely on account of its lack of clear meaning, *Geist* is to be shunned. Dasein, and not spirit, raises the question of being. Dasein, and not some dogmatically asserted "spirit," is to be the concrete starting point for fundamental ontology.

Here Derrida reverts to a suspicion he has entertained at least since the 1968 "Ends of Man," which we examined briefly in the Introduction. Concerning Heidegger's peremptory assertion of *Dasein* as the privileged *questioner* of *Sein*, Derrida writes: "This exemplarity can become, or can remain, problematic" (MA 36/17). Such a suspicion cannot itself readily become a question, as Heidegger would wish, inasmuch as a kind of "reflexivity" of questioning is in play here. How *question* the structure of *Fragen* without on the one hand confirming its power and on the other begging the question? Precisely what students have always found most compelling about *Being and Time*, to wit, the fact that the fundamental ontologist begins by thinking about what he or she is doing and so engages phenomenology to factical life, can also become terribly disquieting. How could one possibly test the "legitimacy or axiomatic necessity" of this point of departure (DE 37/18)? A questioning of being-able-to-question: Would not such a reflexivity undermine the very order of existential analysis and all its demonstrations, derivations, orderings, hierarchies, groundings, implications, and descriptions? Derrida is right to remind us that this issue of the proper starting point, which Heidegger calls *den rechten Ansatz*, and of the appropriate access, *angemessenen Zugang*, obsesses Heidegger before, during, and after the Marburg years in which *Being and Time* has its genesis. It dominates the 1921–22 analysis of factical life and the 1929–30 lectures on the animal world as much as it does

*Being and Time*. Yet the more "esoteric" interpretation of the "question" has to be recalled here. The very "needlessness" of Dasein when it comes to an explicit questioning of being is what Heidegger wants to stress: Dasein "lives within" and is somehow "involved in" an understanding of its being, no matter how vague and imprecise that understanding may be. The apparent reflexivity of the "question of the question" would be broken if we could get closer to our *Umgang* and perhaps even our *Leben*. How difficult this was for Heidegger himself becomes clear when we remember his earlier analyses of "factical life" in the Marburg lecture courses. In the 1921–22 lectures, which we will take a brief look at in just a moment, Heidegger stresses the thoroughgoing *Ruinanz* of factical life, which takes it easy and locks itself away from an examination of its life. What Heidegger is never able to explain, however, is what he calls *Gegenruinanz*, namely, the impulse that counters the forces of inertia and complacency, thus making philosophical inquiry possible.

The principal issue elaborated by Derrida in this third section is the problem of three different kinds of indifference (*Gleichgültigkeit*, but also *Indifferenz*) with respect to the question of being: (1) the indifference of every being at hand toward its own being, (2) the indifference (*Indifferenz*) that belongs to Dasein structurally and is essential to the *modal* nature of existential analysis, and (3) complete indifference (*Bedürfnislosigkeit*) vis-à-vis the question of the meaning of being. Indifference in these three senses causes *Geist* (along with consciousness, subjectivity, person, and so on) to be interpreted as some thing at hand. Perhaps existential-ontological analysis as a whole can be viewed after all as an effort to deconstruct *Geist,* precisely by removing it from handy assertions about things at hand and rerouting it in the direction of *Gemüt* (a remarkably untranslatable term, whether into French *or* English, but suggesting something like one's "heart of hearts" or "innermost core"), and *Gemüt* in turn in the direction of *Existenz:* "The apparently new beginning of philosophizing [in Descartes] reveals itself to be the sowing of a fatal prejudice, as a result of which succeeding ages neglected a thematic ontological analysis of '*Gemüt*' along the guidelines of the question of being and also as a critical confrontation with the ontology inherited from antiquity" (SZ 25). Using yet another metaphysical word that by rights ought to be avoided, Heidegger concludes: "The 'substance' of human being is not spirit, as the synthesis of soul and body, but *existence*" (SZ 117). Here one can readily see how the issues of *essence* and of the *question* implicate the third thread, animality and, in general, the question of life, as well as the fourth, namely, epochality. It is also clear that the shift from *Geist* to *Gemüt*, the latter being even less translatable than the former, if only because it is more fraught with melancholy (*Schwermut*), leads us to suspect that the matter of "spirit" in *Being and Time* is, as it were, a closed book. Spirit? And *Heidegger*? Has Derrida simply confused him with Hegel?

Yet spirit does return to haunt. Although Heidegger begins by avoiding the word, it becomes clear that "something of spirit can be subtracted from the Cartesian-Hegelian metaphysics of subjectivity, something that points in the direction of [*faire signe vers*] the *Gemüt*" (DE 44/23). Surprisingly, spirit's return occurs not only after *Being and Time* but also within it. For example, when Heidegger refers to the "spiritual" nature of Dasein's spatiality after having insisted that Dasein is not a *Geistding* encapsulated in a *Körperding* (SZ 56). In section 70, Heidegger writes: "Rather, because it is 'spiritual' ['*geistig*,' still in quotation marks, to be sure], *and only for that reason,* Dasein can be spatial in a way that remains essentially impossible for an extended corporeal thing" (SZ 368). Heidegger himself emphasizes the words "and only for that reason," as though the word *geistig* has enough residual sense for the fundamental ontologist, and as though the word can be used precisely in order to resist the Cartesian *esprit*.

Spirit returns even more powerfully as the epitome of the vulgar understanding of time. That is to say, *Geist* returns in section 82 under the aegis of Hegel. In Heidegger's view, Hegelian spirit merely "falls" into time, as Hegel himself admits, "falling" as one thing at hand into time as another such thing. Quotation marks continue to constrain *Geist* here, yet the privileged horizon of *time* in Heidegger's project requires that the position of spirit and "time" not be symmetrical with that of the "*geistigen*" nature of the spatiality of Dasein. Heidegger writes, near the conclusion of section 82 (SZ 436): " 'Spirit' does not first of all [*nicht erst*] fall into time, but *exists as* the original *temporalizing* of temporality." *Geist* appears in quotation marks once again, this time as an indication that it is Hegel's word. Yet something apparently can be translated from the latter's superlatively metaphysical text into Heidegger's own analysis of the temporalizing (*Zeitigung*) of Dasein; something can be subtracted from the vulgar conception of a plummeting spirit-thing falling into time and so saved for an existential analysis of the temporal ecstasis of the present as falling prey, entanglement, or lapse, *Verfallen*. Whether and how such "subtraction" can be thought without the most rigorous and painstaking efforts of deconstruction remains one of those open questions. At all events, Heidegger concludes: " 'Spirit' does not fall *into* time; rather, factical existence 'falls' as lapsing [*verfallende*] *from* original, appropriate temporality." The fall is, as Derrida notes, "displaced," becoming a lapsus from one mode of temporalizing to another, although whether Heidegger will ultimately be able to sustain *two* modes of temporalizing is doubtful, to say the least. (Recall the extended analyses of so-called vulgar time in "Ousia and Grammè," as of the "horizon of presence" in Heidegger.) In any case, for Heidegger, all reverts to the ecstatic interpretation as opposed to the vulgar understanding of time, just as much later, in 1953, both good and evil will revert to the *flame* of spirit (a "spirit" that by that time is fully divested of its "scare quotes").

It is precisely here that a close reading of Heidegger's 1921–22 lecture course ("Phenomenological Interpretations of Aristotle: An Introduction to Phenomenological Research," examined briefly in chapter 1) supports Derrida's reading of *Sein und Zeit* in *Of Spirit*. Factical life is *animated* as falling; its very *Bewegtheit* or κίνησις is *Ruinanz*, "ruination" or "ruinance." Mirrored in the world by a kind of reflected light or *Reluzenz*, seduced by the carnival and masked ball of what in *Being and Time* Heidegger will call inappropriate everyday existence but here *Larvanz*, life plunges into the nothing, *"the nothing of factical life."* The mystery and even miracle in such a fallen and falling world is that a counterthrust against or resistance to ruinance, *Gegenruinanz*, can occur. It transpires, says Heidegger, in philosophy's tendency to seek illumination, *Erhellung*. As a result of some indescribable "gnawing" at the philosopher's innards, factical life becomes aware of its failings and its lacks, its *Darbung*, and struggles against the plunge. (The baroque and even gothic language of these early analyses of factical life—*Ruinanz, Reluzenz, Larvanz, Darbung, Abriegelung*, and so on—merits an analysis of its own.) If *Geist* remains unnamed in such a scenario, the *Erhellungstendenz* of knowing and philosophizing, so close to the tradition of a luminous "spirit," remains the only force by which total distraction, dispersion, and diffusion (*Zerstreuung*) can be countered. Significantly, spirit *does* appear in this early lecture course when it is a question of "the problem of leadership" (*das Führerproblem*) in the university, or a matter of the "spiritual-intellectual preparation" of students, as opposed to the fatuous wit of mere *"Geistigkeit."* The latter appears in quotation marks, surely inasmuch as *Geistigkeit* in this case is a translation of *esprit*, the mere wit of a *belle-lettrist* who almost certainly lives on the other side of the Rhine. One does not have to wait until 1933 to hear Heidegger complain about the "spiritual condition we find ourselves in," or about "the corruptors of spiritual life," who abuse philosophy (61:70, 117–18).

Derrida's fifth chapter does bring us to 1933, where "the law of quotation-marks" is rescinded. Here the book *Of Spirit* takes one of its most dramatic turns. The usage of quotation marks—a usage that has long preoccupied deconstruction, which embraces "paleonymy" and inaugurates the "epochal regime of scare quotes"—reaches a kind of crisis. For in the 1933 rectorate address, *The Self-Assertion of the German University*, of which this section is a close reading, Heidegger drops the scare quotes. Derrida pictures them as pins (" ") holding a curtain that is lowered before a stage: as the pins fall away, the curtain, which was always raised a crack, opens onto the political play "Of Spirit" itself. The stage is not designed for a presentation of the gigantesque, except perhaps for an academic's conception of the gigantesque. The curtain rises on a scene of academic-political solemnity: Spirit itself, in the person of the *spiritus rector* in procession, appears in mortarboard and ermine in order to confirm the self-affirmation of the German university. The prudence and methodological rigor of *Being and Time*, as well as its resistance to the rhetoric of "spirit," bow to the fervent rhetoric of the newly ordained spiritual leader of the University of Freiburg.

The spiritual mission of the German university under its new leadership (*Führung*) sanctions the end of those constraints that scare quotes clearly are, the constraints that bind the words *Geist* and *geistig* in *Being and Time*. Two decades after the *Rektoratsrede*, in the Trakl essay of 1953, Heidegger will counterpose Trakl's word *geistlich* to the term *geistig*, claiming that the latter remains embroiled in the Platonic-Christian ontotheological tradition, whereas the word *geistlich* ostensibly escapes from all contamination by that tradition. However, in 1933 Heidegger promulgates the word *geistig*, not *geistlich*, and he sets it, not in scare quotes, but in italics; he underlines and stresses it rather than pinning it with constraints; he ignores the word *geistlich* (which of course would be odd outside of a strictly clerical or ecclesiastical context), and he does not suggest that *geistig* has anything to do with a tradition that has to be deconstructed. *Geistige Führung*, which has more to do with inheritance than tradition, will not concern itself with such a *Destruktion*. At the core of the rectorate address, Heidegger defines *Geist* not in a Cartesian or Hegelian sense but in terms of the mission (*Auftrag*) of the German university as such. Derrida singles out four predicates contained in Heidegger's invocation of spirit, predicates that, in spite of the apparent distance of the rectorate address from *Being and Time*, stand in discomfiting proximity to it: (1) spirit *questions*, provided it is understood as a will to knowledge and a will to essence (*Fragen, Wissenschaft, Wesenswille*); (2) spirit expresses or reflects the *spiritual world* of the people (*geistige Welt*); (3) spirit is nourished by the forces or powers of earth and blood, even in the august, elevated, urban, and urbane German university (*erd- und bluthaften Kräfte als Macht*); (4) spirit is resolute openedness, or what one might in this new context translate as "resoluteness" or "resolve" (*Entschlossenheit,* one of the most important concepts of *Being and Time,* retained also, although Derrida does not mention it, in Heidegger's postwar *Gelassenheit* [G 19]).

Derrida cites a long passage from the rectorate address (SB 14), describing it as a celebration, exaltation, and kerygmatic proclamation of spirit. It is a text of superlatives, of singularities, of the essence, and of the utmost gravity: *Geist ist ursprünglich gestimmte, wissende Entschlossenheit zum Wesen des Seins.* "Spirit is originally attuned, cognizant resolute openedness to the essence of being." Yet also a text of the utmost violence and danger: *Und die* geistige Welt *eines Volkes . . . ist Macht der tiefsten Bewahrung seiner erd- und bluthaften Kräfte als Macht der innersten Erregung und weitesten Erschütterung seines Daseins.* "And the *spiritual world* of a people . . . is the power that most profoundly preserves a people's forces of earth and blood, the power that most intensely heightens and most extensively shatters its Dasein." Here Heidegger erects and exalts both "the highest," *le plus haut,* and the "deepest." Derrida therefore indicates the highs and lows that often dominate the rhetoric of Heidegger's discourse. In the *Rektoratsrede* of 1933 it is a matter of the elevated historic destiny and the *hauteur* of a people gathered in *dieser hohen Schule* that has its foundation ostensibly in the depths of Germanic earth-and-blood forces. Spirit here has nothing to do with metaphysical subjectivity, at least in Heidegger's own judgment. "No contradiction with *Being and Time* in this respect," remarks Derrida (DE 61/37). There remains of course the possibility that the new rector's "massive voluntarism" is embroiled precisely in the decisionism and will to election of modern metaphysical *Subiectität,* and that the union of *Geist* and *Geschichte* (*geistig-geschichtliches Dasein, geschichtlich-geistige Welt*) cannot so easily be disentangled from its Hegelian inheritance. Yet such an inheritance would be disastrous for both fundamental ontology and Heidegger's "other" thinking. For if *Dasein* and *Welt* are now unified in *Geist;* if the global phenomenon of being-in-the-world is nothing other than a willful spirit; if openedness to the essential unfolding of the truth of beyng is *Geist;* and if the history of being is the existence of spirit (*das Dasein des Geistes*); then Heidegger's thinking from beginning to end is no more than an epiphenomenal right-wing Hegelianism.

Derrida does not propose such a reduction. Not for nothing has he been a kind of "envoy," insisting that his French and American colleagues read and study Heidegger with the greatest care. And yet the entirety of

*De l'esprit* is haunted by the spectral return of a *Geist* that always means more than either Heidegger or Derrida himself can control. It is as though spirit were not a flame but a kind of fungus, a mushroom thrusting its head through pine needles on the Black Forest floor.

Spirit and history unite for Heidegger in *essential questioning*. The first and second threads of Derrida's hesitation and perplexity therefore return again in the terrifying entanglements of *The Self-Assertion of the German University*. Science is *das fragende Standhalten* in the midst of beings as a whole (SB 12). Science obligates the one who assumes spiritual leadership (*geistige Führung*) "to the essentiality and simplicity of questioning," *zur Wesentlichkeit und Einfachheit des Fragens* (SB 17). Such questioning understands itself as response, and response as acceptance of the call to responsibility. Once again, echoes of an ethico-religious discourse, echoes that will return in chapter 9 of *De l'esprit* when Derrida himself invokes—not without trepidation—the responsibility of political engagement.

*Heidegger's* discourse *of spirit* would legitimize National Socialism. One could therefore turn against Heidegger the charge he brings against Nietzsche in "Who Is Nietzsche's Zarathustra?" when he writes of Nietzsche's "supremely spiritualized spirit of revenge," *höchst vergeistigter Geist der Rache* (VA 117; Ni 2:228). And yet one must also acknowledge that in this very same gesture, to wit, Heidegger's acceptance—or arrogation—of spiritual leadership, he takes his distance from National Socialism, interrupts his commitment to what will prove to be anything but a *spiritualized* politics of "earth and blood." Derrida argues that ultimately one cannot isolate Heidegger's spiritualism from a reductive and racist biologism, no matter how vociferously Heidegger would object, and it is this *contamination* of the discourse of "freedom of the spirit," as well as the *complicity* in which all such discourses are inevitably caught, that haunts Derrida's *Of Spirit*. No doubt one must choose the least hazardous of such complicities and contaminations that one can, even though choice itself is the greatest hazard; to dream of escape from the necessity and the hazard of choice, however, would be to give up the ghost. And so the other ghost, the specter of spirit, always returns; doubling itself, it passes into its opposite and begins to ventriloquize. "Metaphysics returns," writes Derrida, "and I understand this as a returning-to-haunt; *Geist* is the most fatal figure of this haunting return" (DE 66/40). Even Heidegger, with all his apotropaic scare quotes, all his *Anführungszeichen* and *Gänsefüßchen*, cannot escape it: such equivocality, ambiguity, and even dispersion and dissemination appear to be of spirit, *de l'esprit*. The haunting of spirit, in both the subjective and objective genitives, returns almost immediately, in the 1935 lectures that offer an "introduction to metaphysics," and decades later, in the 1953 "Language in the Poem."

Spiritual *Führung* is in(tro)duction into metaphysics; it means to conduct us to an inquiry into the fundamental or grounding question, *Hineinführen in das Fragen der Grundfrage.* Heidegger's geopolitical analysis of spirit in 1935, an analysis conducted from the apparently sole possible vantage point of "the metaphysical nation" that Germany is (EM 29), oscillates between the despair-beyond-pessimism of "the darkening world" and the hope-beyond-optimism of "new historical-*spiritual* forces from the middle" of the Continent. Derrida continues his analysis of this text, *An Introduction to Metaphysics,* in chapter 7 of *De l'esprit.* Having cited Heidegger's "*Weltpolitik* of spirit" and his lament of *Weltverdüsterung,* or the "spiritual decline" of the world, Derrida now picks up another thread, the third, which asks how the spiritual world is related to the world of beings that are ostensibly unlike Dasein. Animals, for instance. *Other* animals.

In chapter 6 Derrida treats at some length the analyses of animality and the world-relation of animals as Heidegger develops them in his 1929–30 lecture course, *The Fundamental Concepts of Metaphysics: World—Finitude—Solitude.* He emphasizes Heidegger's hostility to *Lebensphilosophie,* without noting, however, that Heidegger's dissatisfaction with transcendental phenomenology and his advance through *Existenzphilosophie* to fundamental ontology has much to do with his conviction, dating from the early 1920s, that philosophy will flourish only by remaining close to "factical life." This is not to say that Heidegger is a *Lebensphilosoph,* a life-philosopher of the Bergsonian, Nietzschean, or Schelerian sort, much less a disciple of Oswald Spengler or Ludwig Klages. However, it does mean that Heidegger's polemic arises from a need and a frustration at the heart of his own thinking.

If at this point I may insert two critical comments, the first would be that Derrida's analysis does not do justice to the Diltheyan, Schelerian, and even Leibnizian background to the question of life, life-force, and animality; it thus misses something of the centrality of this particular thread, that of life-philosophy, in the tapestry. A second difficulty with Derrida's analysis here, in my view, is that it begins by anticipating the "raising of the curtain" on *Geist* in 1933–35. Derrida projects the proclamation from the year 1935, "*Welt ist* geistige *Welt. Das Tier hat keine Welt, auch keine Umwelt*" (EM 34), back onto the 1929–30 lectures. That the animal has no world, or has-it-in-not-having-it, or is poor in world, would according to Derrida amount to saying that the animal is poor in spirit. World-poverty would be spiritual poverty. While I believe that Heidegger's thought does betray this tendency, and am therefore wholly in accord with the essential thrust of the analysis, I believe it is essential not to confuse 1929 with 1935. The very poignancy of Heidegger's lectures on animal life derives from the fact that there he does *not* appeal to spirit. There, as in *Being and Time,* it is a matter of avoiding *Geist,* even when it seems most appropriate (from an ontotheological point of view) to introduce it. As far as I can see, Heidegger does not in 1929–30 introduce the word even negatively, in scare quotes; he opposes the use of the words *Seele* and *Bewußtsein* in his discussion of animality, but leaves *Geist* altogether out of account. Now, it is precisely Derrida who teaches us the importance of observing scrupulously the use or nonuse of the *geistigen* vocabulary, and such scrupulous care is called for especially here: when at the end of his 1929–30 course Heidegger tries to define the *human* relation to its world as *Weltbildung,* he engages in a long analysis of speech as apophantic discourse, of the "as" that introduces human beings to the realm of essences (the rock *as* rock, sunlight *as* sunlight, lizard *as* lizard); yet he never appeals to the *Geist* that in classical metaphysical discourse seemed to guarantee access to that realm. It is precisely in the *avoidance* of the word that one senses the hovering Hegelian spirit, not so much waiting in the wings as suspended in the machinery located above center stage, the machinery labeled *Gattung,* understood as either "genus" or "species." What Heidegger does introduce in the final part of his course are the following notions, each designed to specify the *human* relation to the world and to exclude the animal from it: freedom, openness to the world (*Weltoffenheit*) and the ruling sway of the world (*Walten der Welt*), the difference (*Unterschied*) between being and beings, the confrontation or encountering "hold" that is established between human beings and all other beings (*Entgegengehaltenheit*), and the project and projection (*Entwurf*) of being into beings that constitutes a human life. None of this appeals overtly to *Geist,* to either *geistigen* or *geistlichen* matters.

Not that Heidegger's analysis avoids all the pitfalls. If *Weltoffenheit* characterizes humanity, says Heidegger, *Weltoffensein* characterizes animality. Yet how does *-sein* differ from *-heit,* indeed in such a way that Heidegger can be assured that an "abyss of essence" separates human beings from animals? Precisely in this *non-naming* of *Geist* the spirit of metaphysics (once again, the objective and subjective genitive) returns. Heidegger tries to reduce the *Offensein* of animality to its enclosure within a ring of disinhibitions, an enclosure of passive subjections and preprogrammed responses (*Hingenommensein, Eingenommensein*), a closed circle of benumbed behavior (*Benommensein*). Yet the circle is continually undone, the ring repeatedly shattered, by something like *time*, and something very much like *death*. Derrida's case is made all the stronger if we insist on prolonging—as Heidegger does—the avoidance of spirit. Heidegger's effort to distinguish the world-relations of humanity and animality is fundamentally aporetic: it is, as Derrida says, and will repeat in his 1997–98 *The Animal That Therefore I Am*, "nonplussed" by the "vertiginous" question of world; the intention of Heidegger's "comparative" method is not to belittle stones and mock animals but to show that the concept of *world* is fundamentally obscure (A 212; AO 90). By reintroducing the notions of *lack* or *privation*, the very notions that he employed in order to subordinate the problem of "just-plain-life" (*Nur-noch-leben*) in *Being and Time* (SZ 50), Heidegger reverts willy-nilly to the standard of Dasein. Although Derrida does not state the matter as baldly as I will here, I believe he would agree that the very effort to define the *singular difference* between humanity and animality inevitably obfuscates the *proto-ontological* and *ontological differences*. I would stress far more than he does the fact that Heidegger uses the very same word to describe the world-relation of animals and the appropriate comportment toward being that characterizes Dasein: if the lizard sunning itself on a rock is benumbed (*benommen*), so is Dasein, not only when it succumbs to the world's distractions and goes sunbathing but also precisely when it confronts the uncanniness of its own mortal existence in anxiety. Appropriate Dasein, rapt to the ownmost possibility of its existence, is an animal.[3]

Here perhaps is where the ghost of metaphysics descends in order to haunt, not merely as a return of Hegelian spirit but as an epiphany of the spirit—dare one say *the daimon*?—that captivated Heidegger throughout his life. The *nothing* invades animal life and disrupts the ring. Death shatters that ring and signals the way in which time—or the *marking* of time—always bears a fundamental relation to the animal's life. The animal is thrown or cast into its life and is projected toward its death as no stone is ever thrown; the effects of that invasion, disruption, and shattering of the ring by (something like) the nothing are felt also at the center of the vital sphere of Dasein. That sphere and the ring of animality suddenly become coextensive, if only for a fleeting instant. If Heidegger returns

---

3. Allow me to refer the reader to chapter 4 of *Derrida and Our Animal Others*, which focuses on the uncanny aspects of Heidegger's treatment of *Benommenheit* (AO 107–109).

to his bugs and his bees, apparently confident that the world of humankind will prove to be essentially different, just as Hegel was confident that spirit would assume essentially higher forms; if, in other words, the "troubling affinities" between Heidegger and Hegel, or between Heidegger and the ontotheological tradition as a whole on the question of animality, continue to plague us, it remains the case that the daimonic, which Heidegger in 1928 identified as τὸ δαιμόνιον, combines for Heidegger in mysterious ways the matters of godhead, animality, factical life, embodiment, sexuality, and the abyss of anxiety. Derrida more than anyone else would want us to recall the note from the 1928 logic course (26:211n.) that weaves a complex tapestry with the themes of semination and dissemination (*Streuung, Zerstreuung*), the overpowering (*das Übermächtige*), the holy and divine (*Heiligkeit, das Göttliche*), the realm of the "daimonic," the nothing, and anxiety. Whereas Derrida stresses throughout *Of Spirit* that spirit is a gathering into a unifying one (*Versammlung*), the author of *Geschlecht I* would want us to acknowledge Heidegger's insight during the period 1928–30 that transcendence is, if not *dissemination,* then at least *bestrewal* into factical concretion, embodiment, spatiality, and (something like) sexuality (26:173). Semination and dissemination, bestrewal and distraction, *Streuung* and *Zer-streuung* alike, are therefore also "of spirit." Insofar as *Geist* is daimonic, it is no less disseminative than it is gathering. It flickers like a flame.

This emendation or qualification of mine does not cause *Of Spirit* to tremble, much less to shatter, but it does perhaps suggest that Derrida's *Geschlecht* project remains the more radical one, the project into which *Of Spirit* must be inserted. Hence my conviction—one of the few of which I am possessed in this regard—that Derrida's *Geschlecht* project must somehow continue. And it ought to continue, I believe, not only with an imagined dialogue between Heidegger and the theologians but also with the already initiated negotiations between sisters and brothers and among lovers. "Negotiations" is of course not the right word. A meditation both intense and tender, rather, on Georg Trakl's magnetizing poetry.

Toward the end of chapter 6, Derrida's threads twist together to form several very tight knots. The animal (thread 3) lacks both the experience and the language of the *as such*, the language of essence (thread 2); lacking language, the lizard poses no *questions* about the rock across which it stretches (thread 1); it is as though one must cross through (*durchstreichen*) the word *rock* for the lizard, just as the word *Sein* will have to be crossed through for "man," as one confronts the *epochality* of the granting in *Ereignis* or propriation (thread 4). These knots, tied even before 1933–35, will doubtless have profound *political* consequences; yet they will be utterly *equivocal* consequences. To distinguish Dasein from animality might of course be taken as the very best means of refuting the prevalent biologistic and racist ideologies, but that distinguishing, in Heidegger's case, is aimed at least as much against Rilke, who poetizes animality as an opening onto being. Such distinguishing rests in fact on the most traditional sorts of teleological humanisms, on hierarchizations and evaluations that are both humane and all too human. Derrida is therefore troubled by the complicity and the contamination that prevail between humanistic and racist discourses, "the terrifying mechanisms of this program, all the double constraints that structure it" (DE 87/56).

Yet this leads us to emphasize once again a particular point about chapter 6, the most important point with a view to *Geschlecht,* and one that will demand our attention in the later chapters of the present book. Derrida carefully notes what others would take to be a minor equivocation or inconsistency in Heidegger's vocabulary. He observes that from the outset of the rectorate address Heidegger stresses—that is, sets in italic type—the word *geistig.* That is the very word that in 1953 he will say is tainted by the Platonico-Christian tradition, the word that therefore Trakl bypasses, choosing instead the presumably uncontaminated word *geistlich.* Yet in 1933 it is the word *geistig* that is said to be *not* contaminated by "the later Christian theological interpretation of the world." Is this simply an inconsistency of vocabulary, not unlike the apparent confusion over the word *Benommenheit,* "benumbedness," in 1927 and 1929–30? Or is the confusion surrounding *geistig, geistlich,* and *Geist* what one might be tempted to call Heidegger's "unthought"?

After having looped back in time to the 1929–30 lectures on animality, Derrida returns in chapter 7 of *De l'esprit* to the political scene of 1933–35, the scene not of world-poverty but of world-darkening, *Weltverdüsterung.* He cites a long passage from *Introduction to Metaphysics* (EM 34–35) on the misinterpretation, debilitation, deposition, disempowerment, or disenfranchisement (*Entmachtung*) of *Geist.* In one of the most controversial developments of his text Derrida compares these famous pages with less well-known passages from other authors. He cites Husserl's attempt to define "European humanity" in terms of its "spiritual meaning": spiritual Europe includes the English Dominions and the United States, but excludes the Eskimos and other Native Americans, "who are on sideshow display at the fairs [*Indianer der Jahrmarktsmenagerien*]." A *Jahrmarkt* is a fair or traveling show, a *Menagerie* an animal or some sort of sideshow. Husserl also excludes "the gypsies who are constantly roving about Europe [*die dauernd in Europa herumvagabundieren*]." This "sinister passage," comments Derrida, appears in a public lecture delivered in Vienna in 1935, only a few years prior to the *Anschluss*. Derrida also cites at length Paul Valéry's *Variété* as an exemplary text for the era 1919–1939, in which discourses on "Europe" and "Spirit" abound. His purpose is not to reduce the differences in the situations of Husserl, Heidegger, Valéry, and the others. (One thinks of all the discourses on *Geist* in the Weimar years, commencing with those of the Mann brothers and the Stefan George Circle, culminating in the discourses of the *Jungkonservativen*, all of them represented so devastatingly well in Robert Musil's *Der Mann ohne Eigenschaften*). Yet in the end Derrida does not shy from posing the questions "Which is worse?" and "Where do we find the worst?" (DE 96 n. 2/122 n. 1).

It is difficult to do justice to these analyses, as rich and nuanced as they are provocative, inasmuch as the breadth of material on which they draw (materials assembled in and for the seminar on "Philosophical Nationality and Nationalism") stretches far beyond my competence or that of anyone I know. In particular, Derrida's insightful comparison of Heidegger, Husserl, and Valéry as three thinkers of the "European spirit" is (for me) an entire education. However, I do wish to add one complication to Derrida's discussion of "the demonic" in *Introduction to Metaphysics* (EM 35). It is not enough to contrast Heidegger's *das Dämonische* and *diese Dämonie* to the *malin génie* of Descartes, even though Derrida shows brilliantly that the Cartesian *cogito* and the hegemony of the *subiectum* in French rationalism and idealism are precisely the evil spirit in Heidegger's history of being. In my view, it would also be necessary to relate the demonic to the *daimonic* (of Heidegger's 1928 Marburg lecture course), of which, I suspect, it is a monstrous mutant. In other words, when Heidegger in the mid-1930s and early 1940s refers to the demonic in terms of Spengler's predator (*Raubtier*) or to the violence of intra-European conflict in the epoch of spirit's debility, this has direct implications for the questions of both animality and theology: *Dämonie/daimonion* may well be the royal road to *esprit* as *Geist* and *revenant*, spirit and ghoul alike. "Spirit" would then be the carrier of all that is most divine and most bestial in the human being, "bestial" of course having nothing to do with the animal, which is not capable of bestiality or evil of any kind. Derrida is right to recognize here traces of the problem of evil in Schelling's philosophy of the Indifferent, to which we will turn in a moment.

Derrida's trenchant analysis of the "four misinterpretations of spirit" in *An Introduction to Metaphysics* (EM 35–37; DE 103–105/64–65) merits careful reading, but here I will emphasize what seems to be the cardinal point. That the world is going to gloom and doom (*Weltverdüsterung*) and spirit to disempowerment (*Entmachtung des Geistes*) Heidegger takes to be demonstrated by four phenomena that he sees dominating everything "European," that is to say, all that is caught in the pincers of pragmatic-positivistic "America" and Bolshevik "Russia": first, *Geist* is reduced to *Verständigkeit,* the capacity to calculate by virtue of one's high IQ; second, IQ becomes a mere tool at the service of the material and social forces of production, a tool employed in education, aesthetic experience, competitive sports, popular culture, and so on; third, poetry and the fine arts, religion, science, and politics all submit to the realm of calculative planning; fourth, everything is reduced to a national "culture" and becomes material for propaganda. All that seems clear enough, dark enough. Yet Heidegger's lament concerning the "darkening of the world" and the "disempowering of spirit" is fundamentally ambiguous. For that very darkening and disempowering reveal that spirit as such is both powerful and impotent. Spirit is of supreme value—otherwise why the lament?—and yet is supremely vulnerable. Nothing can be weightier or more essential than spirit, and yet spirit allows itself to be disenfranchised and its world to be diminished or even devastated. Spirit is everything, but it comes to nothing. And this coming to nothing *appears to develop from within,* impelled by some unaccountable fifth column within spirit. The ambiguity or ambivalence of spirit, which seems to be haunted by the inevitability of its own demise, constitutes the entire drama of spirit, the raising of the curtain, the flash of blinding footlights, and the bright white spotlight on "the center of Europe," to wit, Germany: our nation, says Heidegger, will have to assume its historic mission as the midpoint of the West (EM 38: *Übernehmen der geschichtlichen Sendung unseres Volkes der abendländischen Mitte*). Derrida's analysis of that mission, the mission of "our people" and "our language," is one of the most powerful and subtle of *De l'esprit*. Most powerful because it displays the inexplicable mystery of a spirit that is both the power of all powers and the helpless victim of the vulgar forces that reduce its power to impotence. This is surely related to the paradox of a transcendentally powerful bestrewal—for example, into embodiment and sexuality—that results in dispersion, distraction, and perhaps even discord. Later on in his career Derrida will refer to such a mystery as *auto-immunity.* For the fatal "misinterpretation of spirit," to repeat, is performed by nothing other than spirit itself, which is both untouchable and eminently fragile. Valéry would say that Hamlet's ghost haunts all of Europe, and that the European spirit amounts to a heap of ashes. If spirit has demons and is capable, as Heidegger says, of "destructive malevolence" (EM 35), those demons are themselves *of spirit*. They would not be Descartes's *malin génie*, who is so readily overcome by a mere feint of faith, namely, trust in the goodness of an undeceiving Creator. Rather, they would be forces of terrible devastation, forces of *demonic* power. Yet as Lucifer is the brightest of the bright lights, so is the demonic essentially "spiritual," whatever that may portend. Spirit is haunted by the phantom of the "other," and yet spirit itself does the haunting. For this "other" is internal to it, "intestinal," as Derrida says.

It is at this point that we find in chapter 7 of *De l'esprit* some anticipations of, or perhaps reflections back upon, the Heidegger-Trakl dialogue of 1953. Derrida writes:

> When Heidegger names the demonic (EM 35), he specifies, in a brief parenthesis, demonic in the sense of destructive malignity (*im Sinne des zerstörerisch Bösartigen*). The spiritual essence of evil. Some of Heidegger's formulations here are literally Schellingian. We shall meet them again in the text on Trakl which includes at its center a thinking of evil as torment *of* spirit. The "spiritual night," or the "spiritual (*geistliche*) twilight" (expressions of Trakl's that Heidegger will want to remove from the metaphysics of *Geistigkeit* as well as from the Christian value of *Geistlichkeit*—a word that will itself thus find itself doubled) are not without their profound relationship with what is said twenty years earlier of the darkening of world and spirit. In the same way, the *Entmachtung* of spirit is not without relationship, in the *Introduction to Metaphysics*, with the decomposition of man, or rather—we shall come to this— with the *"verwesenden Geschlecht,"* the *O des Menschen verweste Gestalt* of Trakl as Heidegger will interpret it in *Unterwegs zur Sprache*. (DE 102/63)

Derrida here cites Heidegger's citation of Trakl's "Siebengesang des Todes" (see Appendix A). One can—and Heidegger certainly does—trace an entire range of such phrases in Trakl's poetry: in "Dream and Delusion" Trakl invokes "the curse of the degenerate *Geschlecht*," *der Fluch des entarteten Geschlechts;* the third section of that same prose poem begins with the apostrophe, *O des verfluchten Geschlechts*, "Oh, the accursed *Geschlecht*," and ends with the falling of night, *die Nacht das verfluchte Geschlecht verschlang*, "the night devoured the accursed *Geschlecht*"

(T 80–83). Crucial to Heidegger's analysis of the "curse," as we will see, is the very *Schlag* of *Geschlecht*, that is, the "stroke" or "blow" by which humanity is bifurcated into male and female—which, however, is merely a "coinage," merely a division into a "twofold," not itself a curse—and then a *second* stroke or blow by which the bifurcation becomes discord, dissension, war, and radical evil. This part of the drama unfolds in the 1953 Trakl interpretation, which is at the center of Derrida's *Geschlecht III*.

One last aspect of chapter 7 of *De l'esprit* merits our attention. If the center of Europe is dominated by "our nation," that is, Germany, and if the task of "our nation" is to resist the gloom and revivify the spirit, that can only happen in "our language." What will remain in force throughout Heidegger's career is his confidence that German and Greek are the two "spiritual" languages of the Occident, with German eventually given the edge. The proximity of the two cannot result simply from the grammar and syntax of German, which were formed during the period of classic humanism, the humanism of Erasmus, which turned to classical Latin and Greek for its models. It may simply be that Heidegger is convinced by the examples of Hölderlin and Schleiermacher—by Hölderlin's extraordinary "translations" of Pindar and Sophocles and by Schleiermacher's unsurpassed renderings of the Platonic dialogues—in whom and in which the similarity of word order and syntax in German and Greek does suggest that the two languages at least *can* be intimately related. Nor would Derrida wish to deny this. Yet what he shows is that several kinds of dissymmetry operate within Heidegger's confidence. First, Heidegger makes his claim in German; Sophocles would never have done so. Indeed, to say the obvious, it would have been difficult for him to do so. Heidegger, the thinker of epochality, would have to meditate on this obvious happenstance. Heidegger remarks to the editors of *Der Spiegel*, apparently in all seriousness and in all innocence, that when his French friends try to *think,* they confess to him, Heidegger, with whom they are surely speaking German, that they *must think in German.* Their French fails them, as it fails Heidegger, although for different reasons. Derrida remarks upon the witlessness of Heidegger's remark, its lack of *esprit,* and observes that the theme "of spirit" is at one and the same time terribly serious and quite droll: there are moments when one does not know whether to weep or laugh. Heidegger's is not merely a Eurocentrism but a Centro-Euro-Centrism. Of course, if *Geist, Sein,* and *Denken* are all untranslatable words—and much testifies to this—then every French philosopher will have to think them in German, at least some days of the week. Some difficult days of the week.

A second dissymmetry has to do with the Trakl interpretation. For, to repeat, in 1953 Heidegger will insist that Trakl's use of the word *geistlich*, rather than *geistig*, indicates that the latter word (which was the word he used consistently in the 1930s) cannot shake its Platonic-Christian heritage, whereas the word *geistlich* thinks spirit in an as yet unheard-of way. In the 1930s Heidegger denies that the word *geistig* is contaminated by the said tradition; in the 1950s it will have been so contaminated. At the center of this odd inconsistency is Heidegger's claim in the 1953 Trakl interpretation that *only the German, and not the Greek* language can point to a radically nontraditional sense of *Geist*. For "spirit," or, rather, *Geist*, is not the pneumatic, breath-like spirit of the Gospels and of the classical Greek ψυχή, but *flame*. Whereas in the 1930s German and Greek are the two "spiritual" languages, precisely because they are "not yet" contaminated by Platonism and Christianity, in the 1950s the Greek will have succumbed to contamination, leaving only German to harbor the flame of spirit.

It is fair to say that the negative thesis of Derrida's *Of Spirit*, to the effect that Heidegger cannot banish the Platonic-Christian spirit of either his or Trakl's oeuvre as decisively as he claims he can, even when he appeals to the word *geistlich*, is entirely convincing. All that needs to be done is to "flesh out" this negative thesis, and this is precisely what occurs in the 1984–85 "Phantom of the Other," which we will examine in chapter 6 of the present volume.

Chapter 8 of *De l'esprit* is particularly difficult to discuss or even summarize: here Derrida touches on Heidegger's readings of Nietzsche, Hölderlin, and Schelling—each of which could and should claim a chapter or a tome of its own. Derrida begins with the equivocal gesture by which Heidegger seeks to rescue Nietzsche from a biologism or racism that the current interpretations of the mid-1930s are happy to attribute to him. Derrida wonders whether Heidegger's insistence that Nietzsche eschews biologism, racism, and all forms of "naturalism" in order to develop a "metaphysical" interpretation of race is any less grave in its consequences than the things it avoids, namely, the "biologism" of race. He holds the question "in suspense," taking up a second aspect of Heidegger's Nietzsche interpretation. For Heidegger also emphasizes Nietzsche's ostensible adherence to metaphysics, precisely in his emphasis on the human body over spirit, the human body as the locus of will to power. At the end of the history of metaphysics, according to Heidegger, Nietzsche announces that *homo brutum bestiale est*, and that the last word for humanity is *brutalitas* (N II: 200; DE 118/73).

The relation of *Geist* to *Seele*, as discussed in Heidegger's *Nietzsche*, especially Heidegger's opposition to Ludwig Klages, leads Derrida to Heidegger's lecture course on Hölderlin's *Der Ister* in 1942. In the context of Hölderlin's *Stromdichtungen*, or "river poems," Heidegger (53:157) cites lines that define *Geist* as a "spirit" that "is at home / not in the beginning, not at the source." Whatever differences there may be between thinker and poet, Hölderlin the poet invokes (in Heidegger's view) the spirit of *gathering*, the gathering of a historical community. The reading of *Geist* in Hölderlin is thus continuous with Heidegger's 1936 lectures on Schelling's 1809 treatise *On Human Freedom*, in which Heidegger defines *Geist* as "originally unifying unity," a unity that encompasses the poles of existence and ground in the essence of God. "As such a unity, spirit is πνεῦμα" (SCH 154). In his Schelling lectures, Heidegger emphasizes the importance of Schelling's recognition that spirit as *pneuma* is not the highest; the highest, rather, is love, *die Liebe*, of which pneumatic spirit is the mere sigh, the sigh of yearning and languor, *Sehnsucht*. It is of course precisely this pneumatic interpretation of *Geist* that Heidegger will later oppose in his 1953 Trakl interpretation, which interprets spirit as flame. Derrida is drawn to this flame, as is Heidegger, precisely because of the promise and the menace: if the flame is *die Liebe*, such love will prove to have two coinages, two imprints, two sets of results—one of which might be called the promise of a more gentle twofold, the second the rage of unbridled malevolence.

Derrida himself is clear about the merely suggestive character of this eighth chapter, which has but two aims: first, to exhibit the profound continuity of Heidegger's own discourse with that of German Idealism, which is as much an invocation of fire and flame (in the form of love) as a thought of spirit; and second, to put into question the borderline that Heidegger wishes to draw between an ontotheological, Platonic-Christian tradition of πνεῦμα and *spiritus*, on the one hand, and a more originary thought of *Geist* as *Flamme*, "fire" or "flame," on the other. What principally concerns Derrida here is the *motif* or the "movement," the "trajectory" of Heidegger's thinking, in the direction of the Trakl interpretation.

Allow me to focus a moment longer on Heidegger's desire to remove Trakl from the "pneumatological" meaning of spirit in order to place him in the vicinity of *flame*. Here, to repeat, in the move from a pneumatological to a pyrological understanding of spirit, Schelling is the essential mediator: "What he [Heidegger] names then in *das Wehen* (a word which means breath but is never far from suffering or sighing, from the breathless or breathless-making 'spiration' of spirit) is only the breath (*Hauch*) or spiration of what properly unites in the most originary fashion: love" (DE 123/77). Derrida does not comment further on the meaning of *das Weh*, which is hurt or pain, and which indeed is never far from suffering, never far from both *Leid* and *Schmerz*. *Die Wehen* are the contractions or pangs of childbirth, or, as *Wehungen*, the swells and drifts of deep snow heaped by the winter wind. And when a parent warns a child, *Wehe dir, wenn du . . .* , there is a promise of punitive pain. When Derrida translates Schelling's *Sehnsucht* as mere "nostalgia" (DE 124–27/78–80), he fails to note sufficiently the radicality of pain and suffering—the *languor* and *languishing*—in the word.[4] Derrida does report the proper etymology of the *Sucht* in *Sehnsucht*, which has to do with sickness and epidemic, *Seuche*, rather than with *suchen*, "to search," even though Schelling himself commonly plays with the ambiguity in *Sucht* between seeking and succumbing to epidemic. Yet Derrida says little in *De l'esprit* about the pain and pangs of spirit in the sense of *Sehnsucht*. What in my view tends to rescue Heidegger's thinking of spirit as flame, and flame as both gentle ardor and consuming malignancy, from the history of metaphysics and morals—if one may speak of "rescue" here—is that sense of pain, *Schmerz*, toward which I was always "sending" Derrida.

Yet it is time to take up chapter 9 of *De l'esprit* in some detail, inasmuch as here Heidegger's Trakl interpretation is at center stage. In the margins of the Trakl chapter in my own copy of *De l'esprit*, a chapter that invokes the notion of promise—namely, the promise of a more matutinal dawn and of a more gentle confluence of the twofold—I find a second set of marginal notes. I scribbled them into the margins wherever and whenever Derrida "promises" to take up Heidegger's Trakl interpretation once again elsewhere "with greater patience," thereby "rendering greater justice" to the theme (DE 137, 178/86–87, 108). These marginalia of mine, reminders to myself about Derrida's promise, invariably refer to the *sister* or to "the femininity of the soul" in both Trakl's poetry and Heidegger's placement of it (DE 172/105).

By the ninth chapter, it becomes clear that, structurally speaking, *Of Spirit* exhibits the two magnetic poles that form the force field of the *Geschlecht* series as a whole. The pole of love and sexual difference is

---

4. See Krell, *The Tragic Absolute: German Idealism and the Languishing of God*, which was published more than a year after Derrida's death. There are many references to *Sehnsucht* there, especially with regard to Schelling, in chapters 3–6, and to *Leiden*, in Hölderlin's "Notes on Sophocles," discussed in chapters 9–11. See, above all, TA 136–38.

never entirely missing from Derrida's book, and the farther pole—Heidegger's interpretation of Trakl—remains the *terminus ad quem* of the whole. "What is spirit?" asks Derrida at the outset of chapter 9, repeating Heidegger's own question in "Die Sprache im Gedicht" (US 59). The being of spirit, according to Derrida, does not cease to occupy Heidegger after 1933, once the quotation marks have been removed from the word. Heidegger's final answer to the question, after twenty years have passed, years not untouched by fire, is that *Geist* is flame, immolation, conflagration. That final answer has more to do with commencements than with ends, however, when years themselves are spiriting, *geistliche Jahre*. If Derrida ends his chapter by citing Heidegger's text at length, it is merely to summarize the detailed reading that the chapter will already have developed. Perhaps it would serve to begin by citing this passage from "Language in the Poem" (US 59–60), adducing Derrida's inserted comments at the end. In the second part of his tripartite Trakl essay, Heidegger writes:

> Yet what is spirit? In his final poem, "Grodek," Trakl speaks of "the hot flame of spirit" (T 94). Spirit is enflaming, and perhaps only in this way is it an afflatus [*Der Geist ist das Flammende und erst als dieses vielleicht ein Wehendes*]. Trakl does not first of all understand spirit as pneuma, or as spiritual [*spirituell*]; rather, he understands it as flame that enflames, rouses, rages, discomposes. Flaming is ardent illumination. What enflames is outside-itself, clearing and bringing to shine, which however can eat away at things and devour them to the pallor of ash.
> 
> "Flame is brother to the most pallid [*Flamme ist des Bleichsten Bruder*]," says the poem "Metamorphosis of Evil" (T 55). Trakl sees "spirit" on the basis of the essence that is named in the original meaning of the word *Geist*: for *gheis* designates what is infuriated, outraged, outside itself [*aufgebracht, entsetzt, ausser sich sein*].

Derrida notes that *das Flammende* suggests both that spirit enflames, causing something else to burn, and is itself aflame, *l'esprit en flamme*. He notes further that the Latinate word *spirituell* is quite rare in Heidegger's works; it is surely one of those southerly words that he wishes to avoid. Why? Because it is preeminently understood as *das Wehende*, that which wafts, blowing in the wind of the pneumatic Platonic-Christian tradition. Concerning the "enflaming" (*Flamme, die entflammt*) of spirit Derrida notes that it is proper to spirit that it burn: flame is spontaneous and auto-affective combustion, needing nothing outside itself to give or take fire, to catch fire or pass it on to another. When we recall from *Geschlecht II* the singular hand that grants or gives, one might say that spirit is two-handed, both dispensing fire and claiming it for itself. Spirit is at all events ecstatic, and we might think back to the raptures of ecstatic temporality: spirit is the outside-itself in-and-for-itself (IM 54). It will therefore not be surprising to find Heidegger associating spirit with the passing of time and the diurnal journey of the sun—and Trakl's poetry will give many occasions to associate spirit and time in this way. Finally, Derrida comments on Heidegger's admission that flame burns for good or for ill. It lights and heats, but it also consumes, rages, calcinates. Spirit as flame starts or raises the animal out of its lair, it causes things to move, and it even outrages them, destroying all composure.

Derrida insists that the definition of spirit as flame is a pronouncement (*énoncé*) by Heidegger, an endorsement or signing by Heidegger himself, even if Trakl's verses should appear to induce the pronouncement. Twice in his discussion (DE 137/86–87, 178/108), Derrida explicitly promises to continue his study of the Trakl essay, and to return to it in later writings of his own. Because one wants to hold him to that promise, hold him to it even in the clear evidence of his absence, I present the earlier, more detailed pledge here:

> This *Erörterung* ["placement"] of Trakl's *Gedicht* is, it seems to me, one of Heidegger's richest texts: subtle, overdetermined, more untranslatable than ever. And of course one of the most problematic. With a violence I can neither dissimulate nor assume, I shall set about extracting from it the specter that responds to the names and attributes of spirit (*Geist, geistig, geistlich*). Because I shall continue to study this text elsewhere, with a patience that is more decent, I hope to be able one day to render justice to it (beyond the scope that this conference today allows me), by analyzing its gesture, its mode, or its status (if indeed it has one), its relation to philosophical discourse, hermeneutics, or poetics; but also by analyzing what it says about *Geschlecht,* about the word *Geschlecht,* and also about place (*Ort*), as well as animality. For the moment, I shall pursue only the passage of spirit [*le passage de l'esprit*].

It is Derrida's promise to return to Heidegger's Trakl essay that accounts for the structure of the present book, that is, the fact that

*Geschlecht III* is considered only after the *Geschlecht* series is brought to its apparent conclusion in *Of Spirit* and *Geschlecht IV*. Spirit is all about return to an origin prior to all origins, all about the *revenir* of the *revenant,* the phantom of the other.

One might object that not spirit but *soul* dominates Heidegger's Trakl essay, which responds to Trakl's line, *Es ist die Seele ein Fremdes auf Erden,* "Something strange is the soul on earth." Yet what arouses Derrida's suspicions most is Heidegger's effort is to resist the "Platonic-Christian" understanding of "soul" in terms of the "vale of tears" tradition: the "soul" of Trakl's "Springtime of the Soul" *seeks* the earth, says Heidegger, is under way *toward* it. Not only *Seele,* however, but also *Geist* is introduced in that same poem in the phrase *Geistlich dämmert,* dawn rises, or dusk descends (it is almost always impossible to say which) "spiritually," "spiritingly." It is such "spiriting" that fascinates Derrida. Heidegger refers to the "essential essential-unfolding" (US 47: *wesentlichen Wesens*) of this twilight. The doubling of *Wesen* recalls Derrida's second thread: Heidegger everywhere insists that his conversation with Trakl, however humble the thinker takes himself to be, touches on *the essentials*. In addition to the scene of twilight, whether as the dusk of evening or the dawn of day, *geistlich* is also attributed to two other moments, namely, "night" and "year." The latter is especially important for Heidegger's reading of Trakl: he traces the word *year* in the phrase *das geistliche Jahr* to *ier,* ἰέναι, *gehen:* to go or to pass, in the sense of passing by. Such passage (*gehen, Gang*) might well have reminded Derrida, himself the author of the heliotropic "White Mythology," of the passage of "the wandering sun" in *Being and Time,* a passage that is crucial for the *spacing* of time in Heidegger's existential analytic. The burning sun, which dispenses light and heat and divides the day from the night, wanders across the sky and so grants the four principal regions of space. Such wandering occurs precisely in a "nature" that is neither *daseinsmäßig* nor simply *vorhanden* but in an altogether exceptional way *zuhanden,* a way more than merely reminiscent of *animality* (SZ 70, 80, 103, 211, and 413), thus touching on the third of Derrida's threads.

Derrida refers briefly to his interpretation of the two "blows" or "strokes" of *Geschlecht,* namely, the stroke that coins humankind into (1) the *duality* and (2) the *discord* of the two sexes. He proceeds to the question of the dawn, *die Frühe,* the morning before all mornings, the *archi-origin* and essence of primal, primaveral time, which in Heidegger's view constitutes the *future* of humankind. Such time is in Heidegger's estimation *geistlich,* not in any ecclesiastical sense, but in the sense of a promise. It is a promise that seems to survive even death itself: Heidegger follows the "stranger" and "brother," Elis, Helian, and Sebastian, the uncanny figures that haunt Trakl's poetry, precisely as already dead or not yet born. Here Derrida takes up a theme that appears in all his work of the 1990s, namely, that of the double-yes or promise that in some sense precedes all questioning: precisely at the point where Heidegger attempts "a more originary thinking of time" than that broached in *Being and Time,* Derrida himself focuses on the "more promising" (*versprechender*) precedence that guides his own thinking. Here we find ourselves very close to the provocation, the regnant spirit or tutelary genius, of *De l'esprit,* "the promise that, opening all speech, renders possible even the question, . . . the asymmetry of an affirmation, of a *yes* prior to all opposition of *yes* and *no,* . . . prior to every question," the promise that would be "*une promesse* de l'esprit" (DE 147/94).

Derrida now inserts a remarkable footnote dedicated to Françoise Dastur, whose discussions with Derrida at the University of Essex in 1986 sparked the note. The long note, dominating eight pages of *De l'esprit,* is undeniably one of those footnotes that would merit close scrutiny, perhaps even a "note on a note." The note states the book's thesis and then goes on to identify a passage in *Underway to Language* that supports that thesis. Finally, it poses a number of challenges to Heidegger's thinking of language and of *propriation,* the recurrent themes of his later thought, and calls for nothing less than an entirely new reading of Heidegger. The note begins by commenting on the priority of the *Zusage* or *Zuspruch,* the assent, consent, affirmation, and address in all language, over and above all questioning:

> Well, then: prior to every question. It is precisely in this place that the "question of the question" vacillates, the question that has hounded us from the outset. It vacillates the instant it is no longer a question. Not that it is subtracted from the unlimited legitimacy of questioning; rather, it slips into the memory of a language, of an experience of language that is "older" than the question, always anterior and presupposed, so ancient that it never was present in an "experience" or an "act of language"—in the current sense of these words. This moment—which is not a moment—is *marked* in Heidegger's text. (DE 147 n. 1/129 n. 5)

An experience that is not an "experience," a moment that is no moment, a priority that is absolute, "the earliest without reservation or qualification," as Heidegger once said of the "ecstematic horizon" of temporality: *Geist* designates the return (*revenance*) to a birth that survives the death of the "corrupt" or "decomposing" *Geschlecht*. *Geist* prevails in an "earlier" that precedes all commencement. Such is Heidegger's thought of the granting, the *Es gibt*, developed in those pages of *Underway to Language* (US 174–76, 180–81) where the interrogation mark of questioning is suppressed or at least subordinated to the assent of and to language; the piety of thinking (as questioning) recedes in the face of what Heidegger calls the *Zusage* or *Zuspruch* of language. The questioning attitude depends on and responds to a prior address by language; it reflects a readiness on the part of the addressee to hear and affirm what is to be thought. Heidegger writes: "What do we experience when we consider the matter sufficiently? That questioning [*das Fragen*] is not the appropriate gesture of thinking [*nicht die eigentliche Gebärde des Denkens*]; rather, [the appropriate gesture is] hearing the consent of what is to come into question [*sondern—das Hören der Zusage dessen, was in die Frage kommen soll*]" (US 175). Interrogation is not the last word of language, even if in 1927 it was the character of Dasein as *questioner* that seemed to guarantee a proper starting point for fundamental ontology. The *Zusage* is in Derrida's view the double *yes* that engages us in questioning without necessarily being spoken aloud or written explicitly, although it always announces itself in a particular language; he calls it *le gage*, a forfeit, surety, guarantee, assurance, pledge, or promise that *engages* thought. The forfeit paid to language is not a prelinguistic or metalinguistic silence, however. Quite the reverse: it is engagement in language and responsibility to it. A singular event, more than simply reminiscent of the *singulare tantum* of *Ereignis*, the pledge is more like the earliest stirrings (*Regungen*) of propriation (*Ereignis*) in the telling silences of language, "an event the memory of which precedes all remembering [*dont la mémoire devance tout souvenir*] and to which we are bound by a faith that defies all telling [*une foi qui défie tout récit*]" (DE 149/130). No erasure, no crossing-through, is possible here. Here the guiding pulsion of deconstruction itself appears to be stilled at least for a spiriting moment. There is no getting back behind the forfeit to language. "*Aucune rature n'est pas possible pour un tel gage. Aucun retour en arrière*" (ibid).

I will not continue to comment on this remarkable note, which has only just begun and which goes on to discuss the "turning" (only in order to reject it as a strategy for interpreting Heidegger's path of thought) and a new topology for rereading Heidegger, a new series of tasks for thinking, indeed, "a new *order*," centering on issues of responsibility, indebtedness

(*Schuldigsein*), resolve, reliability, affirmation, promise, and propriation. Needless to say, there is a great deal of future in this note, the future of anyone who has ever read any of Heidegger's texts with any care.

As Derrida enters into the final phase of *De l'esprit*, the fourth of his threads of hesitation and perplexity, epochality, comes to predominate. Heidegger insists that Trakl's poetry stands outside the Platonic-Christian epoch, outside the χωρισμός or gap that ostensibly separates the intelligible from the sensible, beyond the decomposed *Geschlecht* of ontotheology. Derrida accuses Heidegger of a "massive and gross" reduction of that tradition (DE 55/95), and tries to restore the Heidegger-Trakl dialogue to the broader context of a conversation with representatives of the Judeo-Christian theological tradition(s). One can sense the necessity of such an attempt, and one marvels at Derrida's dexterity in fashioning such an imagined conversation. Yet one may ask whether Heidegger's compelling need to extract Trakl from ontotheology is as gross and as caricatural as Derrida suggests. In my earlier attempts to consider this question, in *Daimon Life* and in later articles, I was more confident than I am now about the nature of Heidegger's need. Earlier on, it seemed to me that Heidegger demands such extraction within a specific context of *Trakl-Rezeption*, which Derrida, for his part, ignores. Is not Heidegger responding to the religiously committed *Brenner*-circle, which is keen to gather Trakl into the Platonic-Christian fold? Is Heidegger a crass de-Christianizer of Trakl, precisely this same Heidegger who since his youth is so fatefully and fatally drawn to the flame of *Geist*? Or does he manage to gesture toward a figure beyond *Geist*, beyond *spiritus*, perhaps even beyond the Hebraic *ruah* these words may be trying to "translate," as Derrida says, a figure and a "haunting shadow" to which Derrida himself is drawn? Heidegger writes:

> Whether, to what extent, and in what sense Trakl's poetry speaks in a Christian way; in what manner the poet was a "Christian"; what "Christian," "Christianity," "Christendom," the "Christian character" mean here, or anywhere—all this encompasses essential questions. However, our situating them hangs suspended in empty space as long as the site of the poem has not been located thoughtfully. Furthermore, situating them demands a meditation for which neither the concepts of metaphysics nor those of Church theology are adequate.
>
> A judgment concerning the Christian character of Trakl's poem would above all have to consider his two final creations,

"Lament" and "Grodek." It would have to ask: Why does the poet here, in the uttermost need of his final saying, not call on God and Christ if he is such a decided Christian? Why instead does he designate "the haunting shadow of the sister," the sister as "the one who greets"? Why does the song end, not with the confident prospect of Christian redemption, but with an allusion to the "unborn grandchildren"? Why does the sister also appear in the other final poem, "Lament"? Why is "eternity" here called "the icy wave"? Is that thought in a Christian way? It is not even Christian despair. (US 75–76)

Is Heidegger here offering a caricature of Christianity? We must postpone the reply until we consider Derrida's 1984–85 seminar, "The Phantom of the Other." There Derrida engages in a rather harsh critique, but he also responds to the sister, to the lunar voice, and to ice in what he admits is Heidegger's subtlest and most challenging text. For the moment he is preoccupied by fire and *Geist*. At the end of chapter 9 he cites that long passage (US 59–60) with which we began, on spirit as flame, ecstatically outside itself, glowing and consuming at once, both a bright light and the white pallor of ashes. Here Heidegger moves boldly back behind the pneumatic tradition to that of fire, apparently not by turning to Empedocles or even to Heraclitus but by having recourse to the resources of the German language alone: *Geist* in its "original sense" is *gheis*, infuriated, enraged, beside- or outside-oneself.

Let us pause an instant over Heidegger's derivation of *Geist* from *gheis*. Neither the Brothers Grimm nor Hermann Paul's *Deutsches Wörterbuch* cite the form *gheis*. The Grimm *Deutsches Wörterbuch* cites the Old High German *keist* or *geist*. Paul mentions the Gothic *usgaisjan*, "to drive one outside oneself," and the Old Nordic *geisa*, "to rage" (HP 237–39). Yet I cannot find in either Grimm or Paul any direct attribution of fire or flame to *Geist*, whereas there are countless references to wind and storm. Paul confirms the sense of ecstasy in the early religious or shamanistic usages of *Geist* and notes the association of multiple *Geister* or "vital spirits" with the nervous system. Wherever *gheis* may ultimately hail from, one must wonder whether either it or these "Gothic" and "Old Nordic" words truly belong to *unserer Sprache*. In general, it needs to be said that the farther back one traces the etymology of any modern German word the more one is inevitably led to an entire family—indeed, an entire *Geschlecht*—of European languages. Ironically, it is the *Oxford English Dictionary* that cites *gheis* as a "root" of *Geist* and *ghost*, apparently pre-Teutonic in origin and related to the Sanskrit *hedas*, "anger," "fury," which might of course get us eventually to fire and flame. Yet we would get there precisely through the sort of cultural and linguistic anthropology that Heidegger is at pains to avoid.

One last word on the "epochality" of *Geist*, a recollection of something we have already noted more than once. Derrida several times insists on the continuity of Heidegger's fascination with that word after 1927, that is, once the scare quotes have been removed from the word and the curtain rises on 1933. When Heidegger in 1953 eschews *geistig* as a metaphysical, ontotheological term, he gives the impression that he himself would never use it. Yet in the "Rectorate Address" and in the 1935 *Introduction to Metaphysics,* as we have seen, Heidegger invokes *Geist* and does not shy from speaking in its name—precisely in order to escape from Platonic-Christian constraints. The inconsistency, perhaps the result of what Nietzsche calls "active forgetfulness," is nothing short of shocking. The only demur that needs to be entered is that Heidegger's invocation of *Geist* is not as continuous as Derrida claims. Derrida does not consider carefully enough Heidegger's continued *resistance* to "spirit," not only in his 1929–30 lectures, but also, for example, in the 1959 "The Way to Language" (US 239–68, esp. 246–49; BW 393–426, esp. 402–405). There Heidegger cites Wilhelm von Humboldt's introduction to the Kawi language of Java, an introduction that examines language in terms of *der geistigen Entwicklung des Menschengeschlechts,* "the spiritual [or intellectual, as the translator sometimes says] development of the human race." Heidegger goes to some lengths in his effort to think language as language, and not as something else, in particular not as one among the many aspects of humanity's "labor of spirit." Similarly, one does not find the words *Geist, geistig, geistlich* playing as crucial a role in the 1936–1940 Nietzsche lectures, which Derrida knows well and quite often cites, nor even in the 1935–36 *Origin of the Work of Art*. Furthermore, one finds scarcely a reference to *Geist* in the 1936–38 *Beiträge zur Philosophie: Vom Ereignis,* even in the contexts where one might well have expected to find it. To be sure, this last text became available only in 1989, so that it could not have played a role in the 1987 *Of Spirit*. Nevertheless, it is odd that Derrida ignores this text in his final inquiries into Heidegger, for example, in *Aporias* and *The Beast and the Sovereign*. Do the words *Geist, geistig, geistlich* in fact dominate Heidegger's thought after 1933? Is "spirit" the missing link that joins what the *Beiträge* call *Anklang* and *Zuspiel, Sprung* and *Gründung*? Do *Da-sein* and *die Wesung (bzw. Zerklüftung) des Seyns* prove to be "spiritual"? Do the "futural ones" who attend to the "passing of the last god" show themselves to be *geistlich*? The reply has to be in the negative: the drama of spirit-resurrected-from-quotation-marks will not be the exclusive drama to which we shall give the name "Heidegger."

And yet. The year 1953 does arrive, and it finds Heidegger invoking *Geist* and *geistlich* with what seems to be the full authority of his thought. Heidegger and spirit? Sometimes no, but sometimes yes.

In the tenth and final chapter of *De l'esprit,* Derrida draws attention to Heidegger's spiritual fires, as he elsewhere (especially in the 1974 *Glas*) draws attention to Hegel's. The German nation, for both Hegel and Heidegger, is the guardian of the sacred fire of philosophy, keeper of the ancestral hearth of thought, the very homeland and heartland of spirit, *Geist* itself in one privileged language: there is, from Hegel to Heidegger, a certain continuity of the pyric tradition in Europe's middle. Essential to that tradition is the understanding of *Geist* as *gas,* that is, as the vaporous exhalations of a fermentation. For Hegel, who accepts the spurious (or phantasmatic) etymology of the German *Gas* from the Dutch *geest,* spirit would be that which rises as an afflatus from the corruption and fermentation of matter, including the material human body as the corpse in decomposition. Such an afflatus needs only a final spark to reduce all of nature to an ultimate conflagration, a holocaust. All that would remain of nature would be the ashes of the Phoenix bird that is *Geist*. (J. B. van Helmont, the chemist who invented the word *gas* in the early seventeenth century, himself imagined a very different etymology: pronouncing the g as an aspirant, he took the word of his invention [*gas*] to be a child of χάος, Hesiodic "chaos," inasmuch as a gas, the most rarefied of all forms of matter, tends to fill all the space that is available to it.) Derrida, pressed for time, inasmuch as his lecture is entering into its fifth hour of the evening, neglects to cite the most heartwarming fire and the most scorching flame in Heidegger's oeuvre: he sets aside the theme of *der Herd* in the 1942 lectures on Hölderlin's hymn, "Der Ister" (53:134–43, 151), where the Romantic rhetoric of domesticity flickers and crackles in Heidegger's text; he also ignores the unnerving and even horrific juxtaposition of bread and Heraclitus in the baker's oven (55:6–9, 22–23; W 185–86). Yet Derrida succeeds in complicating Heidegger's picture of a spirit that, as *geistlich,* fiery rather than aspirant, has left the πνεῦμα of Platonic Christianity decisively behind. Derrida reveals that already in Aristotle πνεῦμα is not merely breath but also and preeminently a warm vapor or gas—an ardent, life-sustaining exhalation, whether of the breath or of sperm. Heidegger would have to concede, perhaps upon the urging of Eugen Fink, that πῦρ ἀείζωον, "ever-living fire," and the Homeric-Pindaric ζάπυρος, "exceedingly fiery," do not need to wait upon the German *Geist* as *geistlich*.

The larger point, in Derrida's view, is that Heidegger is locked into a "linguistico-historical triangle," the three apices or vertices of which are represented by the words πνεῦμα, *spiritus*, and *Geist*, a triangle that Heidegger himself wishes to be rigorously closed, and which in effect he forecloses. In the most daring move of the entire lecture, Derrida now asks: Yet what if these three words—at least, during and after the time of the Evangelists—are attempting to translate the Hebrew word *ruah*? Can the triangle be closed or foreclosed? What would one make of the ironic fact that the theme of *fire*, as *ruah*, is ubiquitous in Jewish prophetic texts and even in the Gospels' account of Pentecost? Heidegger alludes to the Pentecostal tongues of flame (US 203), but he leaves in silence the earlier prophetic texts; indeed, he leaves in silence everything that might have gone into the formation of πνεῦμα. Can Heidegger, whose position is ineluctably *inside* the triangle of the Greek, Latin, and German, decide anything about a thought of *Geist* that would transgress the boundaries of Europe and Asia, transforming the meaning of both Occident *and* Orient? Recall that this last claim is made in the 1936 "Anaximander Fragment," where the thought of the eschatology of being, the gathering into the "land of evening," *das Abendland*, is said to "overwhelm Occident and Orient alike" (H 300; EGT 17). It is as though Heidegger has forgotten Hölderlin's labors during the weeks when his translation of Sophocles's *Oedipus the Tyrant* and *Antigone* is drawing to a close, to "orientalize" his translation. It is as though he has forgotten Schelling's labors to interpret the Cabirian deities of Samothrace as Phoenician in origin. Such questions—the triangle of Greek-Latin-German, the Hebrew *ruah*, Occident and Orient—form nodes along that fourth thread of hesitation, perplexity, and suspense that Derrida calls "epochality."[5]

Derrida himself poses questions to Heidegger's indebtedness to Schelling with regard to the theme of good and evil in the solitary flame

---

5. Françoise Dastur adds a comment on *ruah* that brings it quite close to the themes of *Geschlecht*. She writes: "Another point that is also interesting for Derrida is the relation of spirit to the soul, which can be referred to the Christian opposition *pneuma-psychè* that can be found in St. Paul's first Epistle to the Corinthians, an opposition that is based again on the Hebraic distinction between *ruah* and *nepech*. This opposition has to do with the sexual difference and explains why the origin of evil can be understood as the discord between spirit and soul, the masculine and feminine." And in order to avoid *all* foreclosure, moving beyond the Jewish tradition, Dastur adds: "Such a thinking about fire and an identification of fire and spirit can however be found in Persian mazdeism, whose influence on Judaism and Christianity should not be underestimated, especially with respect to the opposition of a holy spirit and an evil spirit, which has been taken up again in Judaism and Christianity." See Françoise Dastur, "Heidegger and Derrida on Trakl," in *Phenomenology and Literature: Historical Perspectives and Systematic Accounts*, ed. Pol Vandevelde (Würzburg: Koenigshausen & Neumann, 2010), 43–57, esp. 55–56.

of spirit. Here the same gesture is repeated: Heidegger tries to remove Schelling's metaphysics from the site of Christian ontotheology, just as he seeks to rescue Trakl's poetry from it. While Derrida is surely right about the continuity of this "metaphysics of evil" in Heidegger's thought, which is continuous with the thought of Schelling, and while such continuities obviously jeopardize every notion of epochality, I am still uncertain about what to make of his point. Is there not some sense in which Schelling's thought of evil in the 1809 treatise *On Human Freedom* is indeed a *radical* one? Is it not very difficult to *place* Schelling's most radical thinking in any Christian context one can think of, no matter how differentiated or nuanced that context may be for us? Does not Schelling dislocate and displace that context, perhaps as Trakl's poetry displaces and dislocates the word *Christian*? When Schelling comes to give an account of the blow or stroke of evil as an "eternal deed" performed once and for all in a time before time, in a life before life, a deed—like creation itself—performed "in one magical stroke," *in Einem magischen Schlag* (7:386–87), would we not find it as bootless as Heidegger does to discuss Schelling in the context of "Christianity"? (It is that single *Schlag* in Schelling, incidentally, that ought to fascinate the thinker of *Geschlecht*—not two strokes in this case, but one; recall that the one magical stroke defines "the manner and quality of the human being's [*des Menschen*] corporization," but also the proclivity of the human essence to evil.) Neither here nor in the case of Trakl, it seems to me, should we be too quick to adjudge Heidegger's efforts to "de-Christianize" the site "crude," "gross," or "conventional." And yet, no matter how radical Schelling's thought, and no matter how unique Trakl's poems, can we really suppose that the thinking and the poetry bear no relation at all to Platonic or Christian traditions? We will have to labor over this question up to the very end of the present volume. And no doubt beyond it.

Derrida himself is never quick to judge, one must say. He acknowledges that *one* of Heidegger's paths—which may have to become *our own* path, whoever *we* may be—leads him to the thought of another beginning, another *Geschlecht*, one that is heterogeneous with regard to origins. That path, more original than any known origin, promises to lead us to the thought of "something altogether other," something "provocative, disruptive, irruptive" (DE 177/107). This would be the oddly circular path *aus der Frühe*, "out of" or "on the basis of" the dawn that is undecidably both behind and ahead of us—as our imprevisible but promised future. The path by which Heidegger would rescue Trakl from the malaise of Platonistic and Christianizing interpretations Derrida does find forced and even violent—in his words, "laborious," "caricatural," and even "conventional." Yet he is not prepared to give up the dream of something "altogether other," something like the dream of love, and so he feels compelled to see how far the theologians are willing to go, how far they can stretch. He concludes *Of Spirit* with that imagined dialogue between Heidegger and a group of aggrieved Christian theologians who find everywhere in Heidegger's presumably de-Christianized Trakl a vast array of religious symbols and theological themes: a promise that is *more* promising and more *telling* than any known promise, *versprechender* than the *saeculum*, an origin that is earlier than and different from all known origins, an apocalyptic or eschatological end to conclude all prior history, which is the history of a fallen and decomposing humankind, and the commencement of an unforeseeable history, that of a more gentle twofold, as though the human race could become childlike once again—if it ever was childlike, even back in its infancy. In short, a falling and a curse, a subsequent banishment from the garden, a descent into quarrel and dissension, but then a *Zuspruch* that Trakl places in the mouth of God, an affirmation that Heidegger himself cites: *Gott sprach eine sanfte Flamme zu seinem Herzen: O Mensch!* (T 54). "God spoke a gentle flame to his heart: Oh, Humanity!" A curse and a resurrection, then, a rescuing stroke, a writing of fire—all these traits constitute the stock in trade of the Christian theologian. The last trait, a writing of *ruah*, even elicits "a similar echo from my friend and coreligionist, the Messianic Jew" (DE 181/111).

The response that Derrida imagines for Heidegger, his response to these patiently impatient theologians, is by no means caricatural. One may characterize it as a strategic retreat, a retreat that one sees everywhere in Heidegger's work: its self-proclaimed modesty, its emphasis on withdrawal as protective concealment, hence on the need for letting-be. Heidegger would simply say that he is not at all seeking to overcome either Platonistic metaphysics or Christian theology, but leaving them to their own devices. Not *Überwindung* but *Verwindung* would be his last word. He is simply submitting himself utterly to the demands of a meditative *hearkening* to the poetic word. Such a word may well repeat words from the past, and in fact it must do so; yet the path of the poet would cross or intersect with the unutterable. Heidegger would perhaps even affirm the word that is dearest to Derrida, that of *le tout autre*. Whatever the poet may be pointing to as his path intersects with the path of the unspeakable, we may be certain only that it is "altogether other" than anything we have been thinking.

Derrida concludes his astonishing effort in *Of Spirit: Heidegger and the Question* by invoking once again "the path of the altogether other," a path that is fraught with danger. A particularly disarming passage in *Of Spirit* appears not quite at the very end but immediately preceding the imagined dialogue between Heidegger and the theologians. It raises the ghost of alterity in the form of power, *puissance,* even a terrifying violence, the unimaginable violence that marks and mars the seeming innocence of spirit. What does "spirit" involve, after all, with or without the quotation marks?

> It involves "events" past, present, and to come, a composition of forces and of discourses that seem to wage a war without mercy (for example from 1933 to our own day). It involves a program and a combinatory whose power remains abyssal. Such power allows none of these discourses to be innocent in any strict sense; discourses can only exchange their power. Such power leaves no site untouched, no site which might support a seat of judgment. Nazism was not born in the desert. We know it well, but it is always necessary to recall it. And even if, far from every desert, it had sprouted like a mushroom in the silence of a European forest, it would have done so in the shadow of great trees, in the shadow of their silence or their indifference, but in the same soil. I will not draw up the account of these trees which in Europe people an immense black forest. I will not count the varieties. For essential reasons, their presentation defies the space of a tableau. In their burgeoning taxonomy they would bear the names of religions, philosophies, political regimes, economic structures, religious or academic institutions. In short, what we also call, confusedly enough, culture or the world of spirit. (DE 179/109–10)

That immense black forest has by now been devastated, or so one must think. Yet it is still haunted by ghosts of the past, ghosts that never will, or certainly never should, be laid to rest.

4

## *Geschlecht IV*

### Heidegger's Philopolemological Ear

Whereas the French versions of the first two *Geschlechter* appear in *Psyché: Inventions de l'autre* (published in 1987 along with *De l'esprit: Heidegger et la question*), and whereas *Geschlecht III* never was published, the fourth *Geschlecht* is appended to *Politiques de l'amitié* ("Politics of Friendship"). Although the last-named text was published only in 1994, it derives from a seminar taught in Paris in 1988–89, which is to say, at the same time that "Heidegger's Ear" was written and presented. It is entirely fitting that *Geschlecht IV* appears where it does, not only because of chronology, but also because of its principal theme, namely, Heidegger's relationship to friendship or φιλεῖν, the Greek verb for "to love," and to πόλεμος, the Greek noun meaning "war," "struggle," or "conflict" in general.

Of the four long chapters of *Geschlecht IV*, which as a whole shifts the focus of the series from hand to ear, I can say very little here. The provocation for the entire piece is a remark—almost an aside—in *Being and Time* that was brought to Derrida's attention by Christopher Fynsk, Jean-Luc Nancy, and Jean-François Courtine. The remark appears in section 34, on "Da-sein and Speech; Language," and it has to do with hearing and listening. Hearing, for Heidegger, is not an aural matter; it does not have to do with acoustics. Hearing is, for Heidegger early and late, the very essence of speech and language. Indeed, it is much more than that. "Hearing even constitutes the primary and appropriate openness of Dasein for its ownmost ability to be [*sein eigenstes Seinkönnen*], as hearing the voice of the friend that every Dasein carries with itself [*als Hören der Stimme des Freundes, den jedes Dasein bei sich trägt*]" (SZ 163; PA 341). Derrida's reading of the remark or aside concerning "the voice of the friend," to which we referred in chapter 1 when considering the "thou" of selfhood as discussed in "On the Essence of Ground," proceeds word by word. That reading is relentless and insightful. Yet Heidegger's thought both before and after *Being and Time* is about not only friendship but also struggle, *Kampf.* Heraclitean πόλεμος, "war" or "conflict," discussed later in *Geschlecht IV,* proves to be a powerful force in Heidegger's thinking of the 1930s and 1940s, and even beyond. As though Derrida were reflecting on Freudian "lovehate," the word *Philopolemology* is the first rubric in the subtitle, followed by the parenthetical (*Geschlecht IV*).

Everything about this brief aside in section 34 of *Being and Time* is odd: there appears to be only one further reference to the "friend" in *Being and Time,* so that the friend who turns up in section 34 comes unannounced, as it were. That friend is associated with or represented by his or her *voice,* although not calling with the call of conscience and not saying anything we can identify with other aspects of Heidegger's magnum opus. Each Dasein, that is, Dasein as *jemeinig,* "in each case my own," but presumably also as *Mitsein* and *Mitdasein,* is constituted at least in part by such a friend—or, better, by such an internal *hearing* of the friend's voice. Hearing is a theme or a figure that Heidegger never abandons, or, better, a theme and figure that never stop speaking to him. And the friend? Where is this friend? The friend is carried with or within one's own Dasein, which *trägt* the friend. Derrida will focus on such *tragen* or carrying, both in *Being and Time* and in later essays that have to do with the *Austrag* of the ontological difference—one of the most abstruse of Heidegger's themes. "Carries with itself" or "within itself," or perhaps even "at home with itself," *bei sich,* is an odd expression, more reminiscent of Hegel than of Heidegger. True, the ecstasis of the present, which is particularly bound up with everydayness, has to do with the being-alongside or being-right-next-to (*sein-bei*) handy items in the world. Yet this *sein-bei* does not seem to apply here. The voice of the friend is hardly some handy item in the tool chest of our workaday world.

*Bei-sich-sein* is written countless times in *Hegel's* works, in order to designate a "concept" or a "grasp," *den Begriff,* that has made its way to both inside and outside, the concept that is therefore *absolute.* As such, it is also the life of a spirit, *Geist,* which after all its journeys is finally altogether at home in or with itself, *ganz bei sich.* Both the in-itself and the for-itself, *an-und-für sich,* shrink in importance next to the intimacy and intensity, *die Innigkeit,* of a spirit that is *bei-sich.* It is clear, of course, that for Hegel the *bei-sich* will command the verb "to be," or at least the verb "to arrive," *bei-sich-sein* or *bei-sich-ankommen* are the most common phrases. I do not know whether Hegel ever uses *tragen* in this context. (I should also note that I have seen the phrase *bei sich trägt* only in a German translation of Rousseau's *Émile*, at the point where Rousseau says that *freedom* is something that a well-wrought human being *bei sich trägt*. Otherwise, Heidegger's phrase seems to be rare in the philosophical literature, unless perhaps one thinks back to the συνουσία of the "friendship of equals" in Aristotle's famous treatise on friendship.) It is also clear that Heidegger, for his part, has no intention of invoking the absolute, either as concept or as spirit. And yet. The voice of the friend that Dasein in each case carries "with itself," if and when that voice is *heard*, constitutes "the primary and appropriate openness of Dasein for its ownmost ability-to-be."

The root *eigen-* appears here in two words, *eigentliche* and *eigenstes*, and we might pause over it even longer than Derrida does. Appearances of *eigenstes* in the first division of the first part of *Being and Time* are extremely rare, for it is the second division that is to focus on the "fundamental" possibility of Dasein, namely, its being-toward-the-end. It is a mark of the thoroughly informed reading of Heidegger by Christopher Fynsk, in *Heidegger, Thought and Historicity*, that it identifies the voice of the friend with death—as though *Being and Time* were a script by Ingmar Bergman.[1] Recall that the very first characteristic of the existential conception of death is that the possibility of my death is my *ownmost* possibility, *die eigenste Möglichkeit*, hence my *eigenstes Seinkönnen*. Yet, to repeat, this comes up only in the *second* division. In the first division, however, we find another reference to the "ownmost" possibilities of Dasein, one that Derrida does not refer to, but with which, given his work on "datability" in *Shibboleth*, he must have been familiar. In the course of his account of the spatiality of intramundane things, especially "handy" items, Heidegger mentions the sun. The reader will smile or frown, knowing that the solar disc is too hot to handle. Much later in *Being and Time* (SZ 413), Heidegger will distinguish the "day-after-day" (*tagtägliche*) experience of the sun's rising and setting from any notion of "everydayness" (*Alltäglichkeit*). There is something special about the sun's position in the sky, something that points to "fundamental" rather than merely "diurnal" or "quotidian" possibilities. Heidegger writes:

> Kirchen und Gräber zum Beispiel sind nach Aufgang und Niedergang der Sonne angelegt, die Gegenden von Leben

---

1. See Christopher Fynsk, *Heidegger, Thought and Historicity* (Ithaca: Cornell University Press, 1986), 42–43. Derrida cites Fynsk at PA 345/165 and 362/217.

und Tod, aus denen her das Dasein selbst hinsichtlich seiner *eigensten* Seinsmöglichkeiten in der Welt bestimmt ist. (SZ 104; emphasis mine)

Churches and graves, for example, are laid out according to the rising and the setting of the sun, the regions of life and death, on the basis of which Dasein itself is determined with a view to the *ownmost* possibilities of its being in the world.

While I can still affirm the interpretation of this passage that I offered decades ago in *Daimon Life* (DL 74–78), it is unfortunate that I did not try to connect—as bizarre as it may seem—these churches and graves with the voice of the friend. Each of these declarations involves a particular aspect of the analytic of Dasein in its average everydayness, the spatiality of being-in-the-world and the being-*with, Mitsein,* of Dasein; the one has to do with the worldhood or worldliness of the *world* of Dasein, the other with the *who?* of Dasein, Dasein as being-in. These two, the *world* and the *who?* as Heidegger reminds us constantly, are the two articulations of the *global* phenomenon that being-in-the-world *is*, and they need to be thought together. One of the remarks that Derrida makes in *Geschlecht IV*, as he stresses the indeterminacy of this "friend," is that he or she may be either living or dead. The voice of the dead may indeed open up for us the "ownmost" possibility of our own ability to be, or not to be, in the world. When Freud tells us that the ghost of the father is far more potent than the living father could ever be (SA 9:427), we might add that the voice of the dead friend may demand our hearkening and heeding more powerfully than voices of the living. I once heard Hélène Cixous say, while addressing a group of student playwrights, "In every play you write, you must bring the dead onto the stage—otherwise what chance have they got?" Yet I believe she would agree with me when I say that the dead always find their opportunity, will always have a chance with the living. Once the poison is introduced by Claudius into "the porches of mine ear," as Hamlet's father says, the ghost will commence its haunting. This is, of course, only one reading of the "voice of the friend," and there are doubtless countless others.[2]

---

2. More recently, during the autumn of 2013 at Brown University, I heard Hélène Cixous read a paper called "The Shout of Literature." The voice of her deceased friend, Jacques Derrida, sounded as an echo, haunting and intense, throughout her discreet "shout."

In each of these possible readings of the voice of the friend, however, it seems essential to retain the ambivalence and the sense of danger to which those "porches" of the ear are exposed. Heidegger no sooner introduces the friend than he assures us that "listening to one another" may mean "following" or "going along with" the other; but it may certainly also involve the "privative modes" of "not listening, opposing, spiting, and turning away" (SZ 163). This brings to mind the early description by Heidegger of "factical life" in terms of *Abständigkeit,* our taking a distance on one another, descriptions that survive in *Being and Time,* section 27. Derrida does not refer to them explicitly, yet a brief reference to them helps us to understand the ubiquity of spite. Factical life, says Heidegger (61:101–10), is for the most part consumed by its passion to *distance itself* from the others, boosting oneself beyond them or, if this is impossible, suppressing or subjugating them in some way. For the voice of the "friend" can also strike a mocking tone. Yet this distancing is precisely what all the others are doing with respect to me, this is what one (*das Man*) does, and so the effort to distance oneself from the others collapses into the insipid uniformity of the "They." When one recalls Heidegger's earlier accounts of "distantiality" and of "masquerade" (DL 40–49) in our "being-with" others, one must wonder *whence in all the world* the voice of the friend who does *not* mock? Indeed, what tone is struck by the friend, the friend who will never cease haunting?

The moments in *Geschlecht IV* when Derrida comes closest to the foci of *Geschlecht I* are those in which he stresses the apparent "sexlessness" of the friend, or, let us say more cautiously, the unannounced and unspecified sex and gender of the friend. The later Heidegger's fondness for the infinitive of the Greek verb "to love," φιλεῖν, as opposed to the noun φιλία, "love" or "friendship," speaks to the continuity of Heidegger's awareness of *Geschlecht*; yet everything about the "friend" that every Dasein carries with itself is "furtive and enigmatic" (PA 346/166). Heidegger seems to be making what others would call a poetic allusion, appealing to the "figure" of the friend, and it is true that one finds, or hears, *die Stimme des Freundes* in a poem by Karoline von Günderode, "Der Gefangene und der Sänger," or in German translations of Vergil's *Aeneid,* Book Six, or in Sophie LaRoche's *Rosalie,* and indeed in many other works of literature. Yet virtually everywhere the voice of the friend belongs to the friend who in fact is present in flesh and blood. Nor does Heidegger's expression seem to come from some German *Sprichwort* or folk tale, nor from some work in the philosophical canon—although who could perform an adequate search in this respect? Derrida is nonetheless right to say that something of a poetic figure—and of figurative language—is there.

It is perhaps relevant that one of Heidegger's most extended pronouncements on the *Austrag* or διαφορά, the "carrying out" or "settlement" or "carrying to term" of the *ontological difference,* that is, the difference between being and beings, occurs in the *first* Trakl essay of *Underway to Language,* namely, "Die Sprache." Heidegger there interprets Trakl's poem "A Winter Evening." Yet there the focus is on the interplay of world and thing, the "carrying to term" of world in the things, a carrying that is also a "gesturing." The old word *bern* is preserved in the words *gebären,* "to bear a child," "to give birth," and *gebärden,* "to gesture." Derrida is tempted to invent a translation, more *calembour* than translation, and so we in English might think of thing and world in terms of gesture and gestation as "gesturation." Yet the more earnest side of the *Austrag* is its dominion (*Walten,* a word that will occupy Derrida throughout his final seminar, in 2002–03) throughout the epoch of metaphysics. The ambivalence of such "dominion," itself crucial for the *Geschlecht* series, which tries to think together the *sexual* with the *ontological* difference, is that it holds sway over both the epoch of metaphysics, in which the difference comes to nothing, and the "other thinking" that Heidegger himself attempts to institute—in a word, the thinking of *Ereignis* and the granting of time and being. One of the most troubling aspects of this ambivalence in the *Austrag* is Heidegger's tendency to express the negative side always in terms of Latinization, of a Rome and a Christendom that obfuscate the Greco-German desire for being. And *desire* is the right word: philosophy *loves* being, loves and *mourns* it, as what has sunk into oblivion. Heidegger's attempt to leave philosophy on its own and to turn to a thinking of being as *Ereignis* will always and everywhere be a thinking of the gathering, *Versammlung,* and of the human capacity to think being *as such.* Yet it will be a gathering of something that has been lost, obfuscated, forgotten, abandoned. What human being can rise to such a challenge?

As always, "human" here is said in "our" language, so that it will always be a matter of a certain community, a certain "people." Struggle, *Kampf,* will therefore always be proximate to such thinking. Derrida recalls all those aspects of Heidegger's appeal, in section 74 of *Being and Time,* to a "heritage" or "inheritance" that Dasein is to appropriate, follow, or obey—*Hörigkeit,* "obedience," will turn out to be an inevitable component of one's response to the voice of the friend. It is odd that at this moment in his discussion (PA 360–61/177–78) Derrida does not mention Heidegger's use (at SZ 385) of *"Generation,"* the Latinate word that otherwise would be rendered as *Geschlecht.* The fact that Heidegger is using the word quite positively here is what is disturbing: one joins one's "generation" in order to "choose one's hero" and to engage in struggle on behalf of a community or nation—and soon one hears or remembers hearing "a column on the march" and the roar of motorcycles instead of the voice of the friend. And yet, as Derrida notes at the end of the first chapter of "Philopolemology," there is nothing in *Being and Time* that denies the possibility that the "friend" is a foreigner who speaks a language we do not understand. And if the voice of the friend speaks words we cannot understand, even though we can hear them, would we not be opened up in a very special way to the fragility of our being and its ownmost possibility? Furthermore, would not the struggle *against* such a foreign friend, turning a deaf ear to his or her wants and needs, indicate not open resolve but an attempted yet futile flight from one's ownmost ability to be?

The second of the four chapters of *Geschlecht IV* takes up the theme of struggle and war in Heidegger's "Rectorate Address" of 1933, his *Introduction to Metaphysics* and "The Origin of the Work of Art" of 1935, along with his lectures on Hölderlin and Heraclitus of the mid-1930s and mid-1940s, respectively, and his 1955 lecture, "What Is That—Philosophy?" All of these in the context of what Derrida calls "the politics of friendship." He begins with the 1955 essay's identification of Heraclitean λόγος with φιλεῖν, "to love," which Derrida translates as *aimance*—a clear reminder of what the *Geschlecht* series as a whole is about, and by what it is "magnetized." The lover of wisdom, the philosopher, says Heidegger, comes always too late with his or her "love of wisdom," inasmuch as the Heraclitean sense of φιλεῖν as *Gunst*, "favoring," has disappeared by the time Plato and Aristotle arrive on the scene. Philosophy is thus always nostalgic, perhaps even mournful; it yearns for the time when one could "say the same" as the λόγος, as Heraclitus commanded. Another name for such nostalgia is Ἔρως, a word that is quite rare in Heidegger's works, mentioned only briefly in the 1955 "Was ist das—die Philosophie?" It is mentioned just as fleetingly in the 1936–38 *Beiträge zur Philosophie* (65:210), there in the context of εὐδαιμονία, "happiness." To be sure, Ἔρως is a word that is not remote from "the question of *Geschlecht*" (PA 383/191). Derrida notes:

> The gravity of this elliptical allusion to Eros can be evaluated in myriad ways. Its implicit context is so rich. But in supposing a sort of pre-erotic moment of φιλεῖν, does not Heidegger point to a kind of *Lieben* or loving [*aimance*] that would still fall short not only of φιλία and of the different types of friendship distinguished by Aristotle (according to virtue, political interest, or pleasure), but also of the distinguishing mark [*insigne*] and

the enigmatic distinction between love and friendship, this last resembling perhaps in its canonical model, as I have tried to show elsewhere, the homo- or monosexual de-erotization or sublimation of fraternity, that is, of the virile duo. Where then, in this respect, is the voice of the friend placed, the friend that each *Dasein bei sich trägt*? Is this voice pre-erotic or not? What can that mean? What about its *Geschlecht* and its relation to fraternity? (PA 385/192)

Although Derrida does not go so far, we might wonder whether philosophy's loss of Heraclitean φιλεῖν, of the pre-erotic φιλεῖν, and the resulting mourning and nostalgia of philosophy, which is precisely the long-enduring epoch of a troubled and troubling Ἔρως, is the result of a second *coup* or *frappe* by which the Western world has been struck. To say the least, this would cause us to rethink the history of being (or of beyng): the abandonment by being of beings and the consequent oblivion of being throughout the epoch of metaphysics would be essentially an *erotic* disorder. Such a disorder would have to do preeminently with mourning and melancholy. Could such a thought be attributed to Heidegger? One is tempted to make such an attribution, and yet one shrinks from doing so. Such anxiety on our part, it seems, is an essential aspect of our erotic disorder, amounting to a kind of timid vice. Recall Nietzsche's observation in *Beyond Good and Evil*, no. 168: "Christendom administered a poison to Eros:—to be sure, he did not die on account of it, but he did degenerate to vice" (KSA 5:102). And yet, at the end of that long epoch of metaphysics, with the publication of *Being and Time*, would we still be participants in the epoch of a vicious Eros? Derrida, thinking back to the voice of the friend that every Dasein carries with itself, wonders whether *Being and Time*, "among all the books we have been given to read in this century," may have been "the most and the least erotic" (PA 386/193).

However that may be, in the 1955 "What Is That—Philosophy?" one cannot fail to see that Heidegger emphasizes above all else the uniting power of such philiac, if unerotic, favoring, the *gathering* power of love. Derrida, as though remembering the "politics of friendship" to which his essay is attached, asks whether "the democracy to come" will be able to reconcile such insistent unification and incessant gathering with the heterogeneities, dissymmetries, disproportions, and incommensurabilities with which our democracies will increasingly be confronted (PA 372/183). It seems undeniable that, for Heidegger, *all* is a matter of gathering, *Versammlung*, to which the "inner ear" is always alert. This is the same ear that Heidegger evokes in the 1957 *Der Satz vom Grund* (SG 87–88), and it is the ear that was already celebrated in the 1934–35 lectures on Hölderlin's "Der Rhein" as "the ear of the poet" (39:196–203). In the 1943–44 Heraclitus lecture course, Heidegger is not reluctant to refer to the noun φιλία, which he understands, to repeat, as *Gunst*, "favoring." Derrida is captivated for the moment by the favoring or granting of being, which Heidegger defines as follows: "Original favoring is the granting of what is owed the other, inasmuch as it belongs to the latter's essence, inasmuch as it bears the other's essence" (55:128). Being favors beings by granting them what it owes them, giving them what they essentially need, namely, their coming to the fore in presencing. A kind of generosity is thought here, one that carries and grants to the other what it does not have, but which it needs. Something of this generosity is felt also in the invocation of the granting of jointure, *Fug*, discussed by Heidegger in "The Anaximander Fragment," that jointure of order by which beings grant one another their time and place in being and do not insist recklessly on their own existing. And yet Derrida closes this chapter by noting the uncanny proximity of Ἔρως and Ἔρις, love and hate, Eros and Discord, in Heidegger's thinking of "gathering." For if after World War II Heidegger finds the λόγος to be a gathering in φιλεῖν, which is to say in peace and harmony, in the 1930s he sees the gathering storm of λόγος in terms of πόλεμος, "struggle," "war," and "combat." In "our" language, *Kampf*.

Chapter 3 continues to pursue the same set of issues in terms of what William Blake called the marriage of heaven and hell—the role of opposition and strife within friendship—with reference to Heidegger's 1933 correspondence with the National Socialist jurist Carl Schmitt, along with Heidegger's own "Rectorate Address." In the 1935 *Introduction to Metaphysics*, Heidegger identifies λόγος with struggle: "Πόλεμος and λόγος are selfsame" (EM 47). It is almost as though Heidegger is making two press releases, the first in 1935, the second in 1953, each in accord with the spirit of the times: after the war, "gathering" is all peace and love; before the war, and in collusion with the warriors, it is all struggle and combat.[3] Derrida's reading of Heidegger's political imbroglio

---

3. To be sure, the division suggested by such "press releases" is oversimplified. In his lecture course of 1928–29, Heidegger discusses the φιλία of philosophy in terms of "inclination" (*Neigung*), but an inclination that includes struggle (*Kampf*) or πόλεμος: "This inclination, this inner friendship with the things themselves, is what is designated by φιλία—a friendship which, like every genuine friendship, and in accord with the very essence of friendship, must fight for what it loves [*um das, was sie liebt, kämpft*]" (27:22).

of the 1930s is relentless, merciless; and yet it is balanced by the question as to whether in the "democracies" of today all that much has changed. When Heidegger calls upon his students to take up the three "tasks" of labor service, learning service, and military service, all of them services to the state, Derrida wonders whether anyone today can be so confident that these terrible "tasks" and "services" have been set aside. He enters a long parenthetical paragraph:

> (I would pose here, between parentheses, to whoever would be shocked in all good conscience by what Heidegger says of the originary and indissociable coordination of these three services or prescriptions, the following question: how and *according to what criteria* would you be able *in all rigor* to dissociate them in *our own* existence as citizens, and even as teachers, in the modern democracies of the industrial age, before or after the two world wars? Where, even in an industrial democracy, does the rigorous frontier pass between knowledge, armies, and productive labor in general? This parenthesis is not intended to minimize Heidegger's evident and serious engagement with Nazism. One must never do that. What the "Rectorate Discourse" says, *in this context*, about the three services, is compromising enough by itself. But if one does not forget that in our so-called democratic context no discourse—even were it to possess another tone—succeeds in *rigorously dissociating* the scientific, the military, and labor, whether skilled or industrial, or can praise the one without the others, then one measures things otherwise, one at least avoids good conscience or ridicule.) (PA 393/198)

This caution is in fact one of the things that distinguishes Derrida from the large contingent of Heidegger bashers and burners: Derrida is aware of how comforting it is to turn back to the past and wield the sword of righteous condemnation—it is perhaps the very best way to avoid one's responsibilities in the generally impenetrable and frustrating here-and-now and to don the mantle of the just.

If I may interject a remark, however, I am struck by the way in which the two guises of "gathering," in love and in hate, have always guided Heidegger's work. I am thinking of the endless *polemics* running through all of Heidegger's early Marburg lectures, even as Heidegger is seeking to develop there a new and entirely positive relation to phenomenology.

*Being and Time* itself bears traces of such a struggle—in Empedoclean terms, the struggle between Love and Hate within the one sphere, which is itself a sphere of struggle. What I mean is this: Heidegger's phenomenological training induces him to use the word *lassen*, "letting," the root of *Gelassenheit*, "letting-be" or "releasement," at key moments in his early project. One must "let" the things show themselves as they are, one must "let" them come to the fore on their own, without doing them violence. And yet one must also clear away obstacles, so that the things *can* appear; one must act like that desperate man in Pina Bausch's dance performance "Café Müller" (seen also in Alomodóvar's film *Habla con ella*) who clears away the clutter of chairs and desks so that the somnambulant woman will not come to grief against them. Allow me to present a few examples of this desperately polemical clearing-action by the phenomenologist (soon to be the thinker of *Gelassenheit* and of being as *Ereignis* and the granting) who wants nothing more than to be able to let-be. One must not seek to escape from the hermeneutic circle, says Heidegger (SZ 153); one must endeavor to step into it in the right way. Yet once one is in it, reading texts as a hermeneutician should, what one sees on the printed page tends to confirm all one's prejudices—they are all there, all one's prejudices, right there on the page, *unless* one has done oneself the terrible violence of stripping away the self-deceptions that enable and empower prejudice (SZ 150). Even our most prized convictions, the convictions we have inherited from the philosophical traditions we love, need to be radically dismantled and deconstructed (SZ 21). Furthermore, everything that fills our newspapers and screams at us from the television channels at airports needs to be stripped away: as we heard in chapter 1, Heidegger calls for *eine Entgegenwärtigung des Heute*, a "depresentifying of the today," a blotting out of the quotidian white noise that is meant to distract and disempower us (SZ 391, 397). Indeed, one is tempted to think Heidegger's phrase as *Entheutigung*, "de-todaying," as a kind of detoxification, and to hear *Entheutigung* as *Enthäutigung*, as though one had to "flay" oneself to get rid of such mundane influences. How powerful and omnipresent is the *Gerede* of our own public world—could Heidegger himself ever have dreamt how bad it would get (SZ 169)? That public world predigests everything for us, so that we do not know what to believe. Trapped in an ambiguity that will not abate, we do not know when to trust our own judgment: "Everything looks as though it were genuinely understood, grasped, and said, and yet at bottom it is not; or it looks as though it were not, and yet at bottom it is" (SZ 173). Our preachers still preach of "eternal truths," and yet they have not passed through eternity in order to garner such truths, have not really been anywhere (SZ 229). And our politicians? The clips our comedians play for us on their satirical "news" programs tell us all we need to know about the politicos. What we have to do is "twist free" of all this deception and ambiguity (SZ 197, 201), and that accounts for the occasional violence, *Gewaltsamkeit,* of our language (SZ 183). In fact, in order to let things be we have to snatch them out of the concealments that cover them up: "The truth (discoveredness) always has to be first of all wrested from [*abgerungen von*] beings. Beings have to be torn [*entrissen*] out of concealment. In each case, factical discoveredness is, as it were, always and everywhere, a *theft* [*ein* Raub]" (SZ 222). We wanted always to be humming Paul McCartney's "Let It Be," and now we are desperadoes and violators. No wonder, then, that genuine progress in our phenomenological voyages, which confront so many enigmas and challenges, is measured in terms of our capacity for shipwreck, *Scheitern* (SZ 148). In short, the phenomenologist *and* the thinker of being who wants to *let being be* will very often be driven to the most polemical sorts of attacks.

One further remark, if I may, concerning Heidegger's 1936–38 *Contributions to Philosophy,* where the polemical tendency reaches new heights, or depths. Here the mix of pious *Gelassenheit* and sardonic polemic in the language of the text is nothing short of disconcerting. Years ago I ventured to call it "paranoetic thinking," a thinking more desperate than paranoid thinking inasmuch as no particular being (*Seiendes*) menaces it, but only being (*das Sein*) itself and as such (DL 198–99). On the one hand, Heidegger's *Contributions* sustain the mood or fundamental attunement of "awe" and "reticence" (*Scheu, Verhaltenheit*); on the other hand, they are whipped by the winds of "terror" and "jubilation." One of the most hated objects of Heidegger's polemic is *Lebensphilosophie,* for which he has bottomless contempt: its sentimental and besotted discourse, the last gasp of a fatuous Neo-Kantianism and moribund Idealism, is a mere shadow of the positivism and the machinations of our time. It is as though Heidegger's compulsion to polemic, to the sarcastic and sardonic, intends to blow away the obstacles to his more docile moments of pious acceptance—the thinking of gentle response, releasement, and letting-be. The alternating current of polemic and piety seems to drive the text and energize the thinking as such. Such thinking is not paranoid, since there is, to repeat, no particular being that instigates the paranoid process of fixation, repression by means of reversal, the return of the repressed, and delusional reconstruction (formulated in Freud's language, from his "Schreber" case (SA 7:186–94), in the four statements, "I love him," "He loves me but I hate him," "He hates me and persecutes me," and "Such is my wretched universe"), although when one considers the objects of Heidegger's polemic, from Platonism to Ludwig Klages, and from modern subjectivity to technological gigantism, one sees how such objects and the wrath they incur could feed such a paranoetic process. What remains noteworthy is the bleakness of Heidegger's text, with its "shivering deities" struggling to be born from the dark declivity of the present age, a bleakness that readily translates to the expression, "Such is my wretched universe." The uncanny inflation of the language throughout the book, with its biblical storms and jubilations, its *Sturm* and *Jubel,* its verbal *Erzittern* and *Göttern* suggesting the troubled birth of tremulous gods, its sense of desperate embattlement—*Wir stehen in diesem Kampf um den letzten Gott,* "We stand in this battle for the last god" (65:412)—suggests the paranoetic nature of the thinking itself, a thinking to which no noematic correlate is equal and in which no νοεῖν can find its equilibrium in a self-thinking, autonoetic thought. To my knowledge, Derrida seldom if ever cites this bizarre volume, which was immediately hailed as Heidegger's second magnum opus, published in the very year that *Geschlecht IV* was presented. And yet this volume, perhaps more than any other in the Heidegger *Gesamtausgabe,* demonstrates the *gathering* forces of both letting-be and polemic, both love and war, the entire philopolemology. Whether the two hands (Robert Mitchum's two tattooed fists of "Love" and "Hate") strike with equal consistency, however, with love balancing hatred, we may have to doubt. The polemical rage suggests the preeminence here (the years are 1936–38) of Heraclitean πόλεμος and Empedoclean νεῖκος—if the names of the great Ephesian and Sicilian dare be attached to what is after all *Heideggerian* polemic.

Derrida, reading Heidegger's texts of 1933 and 1935, focuses on the word *Kampf,* perhaps overtranslated by the French word *combat,* inasmuch as any form of struggle, not only the military or pugilistic form, is evoked in the word *Kampf.* Derrida himself is aware of how difficult it is to assign a specific meaning to the term. In any case, it is impossible to deny that anyone in Germany during the early 1930s, when employing the word, is looking ahead to the late 1930s, sometimes in trepidation, sometimes with elation. More troubling still to Derrida is the term *Kampfgemeinschaft,* "embattled community," or "community of fighters," from the "Rectorate Address," reminiscent of the *Gemeinschaft* of *Being and Time* and its call to *Kampf.* When the "community" and the "generation" cited in section 74 of *Being and Time* conjoin with a view to struggle, or even battle, then the *gathering power* of the *logos* assumes a particularly disturbing form. Without citing Heidegger's commentary on the *colon* that precedes the expression *"E i n Geschlecht"* in Trakl's *Abendländisches Lied,* Derrida here takes special note of Heidegger's use of the colon in his "Rectorate Address" to *gather* the "essential wills" of both teachers and students to readiness for *Kampf* (PA 396/200). And here, Derrida insists, Heidegger is not far from Carl Schmitt, for it is difficult to conceive of the plea for "struggle" without the presence of a foe that confronts the *Kampfgemeinschaft*. True, Heidegger does not plead for the "real possibility" of "physically killing" the foe, as Schmitt does (see PA 108–109; 317); yet his "Address" and his actions advancing the *Gleichschaltung* of university teachers and students in line with the Nazi-dominated state falls just short of that. Derrida's question to Heidegger—his *philosophical* question—is whether the discord that is expressed in the word *Kampf* is being thought in genuine Heraclitean fashion, or whether it does not display something of the curse that derives from the "second stroke" cited by Heidegger two decades later in his second essay on Trakl. That is to say, does not the stress on *Kampf* and *Auseinandersetzung* ("confrontation") suggest that Heidegger is precisely a *philosopher,* one who loves wisdom nostalgically, mournfully, saturated as he is by a sense of loss? Loss of what? Of a sense for the meaning of being, of a sense for the meaning of the *question* of being, but also the loss of a sense of *community,* about which everyone today is still writing. Whether Heidegger's reading of πόλεμος in Heraclitus is "originary" or merely "philosophical" in the pejorative sense, says Derrida, is entirely equivocal—in the sense of an equivocation or an ambiguity that never is and never can be "formalized" by Heidegger himself. Identifying himself with the "few," the "only some of us" who can join the *Kampfgemeinschaft,* Heidegger succumbs to a voluntarism of the "essential will" of *Volk* and *Führer*. The "self" of the *Selbstbehauptung* of the university, the αὐτός identifying itself as the fundamental "spirit" of the Western world, will be the "self" that "we" wretched and mournful latecomers arrogate to "ourselves" in lieu of something better.

If I may insert yet another remark, this time on the relation of Heidegger's incipient reading(s) of Hölderlin's poetry during the 1930s to the discord of polemic and πόλεμος: it is disappointing, to say the least, that any reader of Hölderlin could affirm as enthusiastically as Heidegger does the *Kampfgemeinschaft*. Where is Heidegger's reading of *Hyperion,* whose hero laments that his own embattled community, which was supposed to liberate Greece from Ottoman domination, turns instead into a horde of "barbarians" plundering the Greek countryside (CHV 1:720)? Hyperion ridicules his own delusional project, "to sow my Elysium with a band of thieves" (ibid.). Nor is Hyperion alone in his lament: would not any reader of Kleist's *Michael Kohlhaas* have sensed the same danger? And if Heidegger also reads Hölderlin's *Der Tod des Empedokles,* how can he fail to see in the machinations of the three successive leaders of the Greek city-state the tyranny that has overwhelmed Germany? Even and especially if Heidegger determines to remain "in the provinces" of southern Germany, how can he confuse the ideals of Empedocles and Hölderlin with Berlin? And as for Heidegger's enduring philo-Germanism, how can he fail to have an ear, an open ear, an inner ear, for Hyperion's devastating evaluation of "the Germans"?

> And so I arrived among the Germans. I did not ask for much, and I was prepared to find less. Humbly I came, like the homeless and blind Oedipus to the gates of Athens, received by the sacred grove; and beautiful souls came out to meet him—
> How differently it went with me!
> Barbarians from of old, through discipline and science, and even through religion, grown more barbaric still, profoundly incapable of every divine feeling, unreceptive down to their very marrow of the happiness of the holy Graces, insulting any cultivated soul with every degree of hyperbole and squalor, dull and devoid of harmony, like the shards of a vase someone has tossed away—these, my Bellarmin! were my consolations!
> My language is harsh, and yet I have to say this, because it is the truth: I can think of no other nation that is more fragmented than the German. You'll find artisans, but no human beings, thinkers, but no human beings, priests, but no human beings. . . .—Is it not like a battlefield, where hands and arms and all the other limbs lie scattered about, while the blood that has been shed seeps into the sand? (CHV 1:754)

This is the mild part of Hölderlin's πόλεμος, for Hyperion's attack soon picks up speed and strength. At the end of his letter, Hyperion sighs, "Enough! . . . I speak for all who live and suffer in this country, as I have suffered" (CHV 1:757). True, Heidegger might have embraced Hölderlin's polemic, trusting that he, Heidegger, would be the one to mend the shards and transform barbarians into Greeks—in other words, trusting that a *thinker* might succeed where a *poet* had failed.[4] In a handwritten, unpublished note from the year 1939, Heidegger scolds Nietzsche for being "insufficiently German," as if that were an insult. The Hölderlin whom Heidegger prefers to Nietzsche was anything but inferior to Nietzsche in this "insufficiency," however. And when Nietzsche's mother scolds him precisely in the way Heidegger does, Nietzsche replies, "Even if I should be a very bad German—I am at all events a *very good European*" (KSAB 7:233). If only Heidegger had been able to make such a claim!

The fourth chapter of *Geschlecht IV* promises to take up the theme of *sacrifice* in this discourse of friendship and strife, yet very little is said here on sacrifice as such—it seems to be an issue for the future. Rather, what Derrida focuses on is Heraclitean πόλεμος as an *ontological* concept rather than an anthropological or political one. Again, the word *Walten*, "ruling sway" or "dominion," the root of *Gewalt*, "force" or "violence," comes to stage center in Derrida's thinking, a place it will occupy up to the end of his life. In this respect, the most important passage in Heidegger's *Introduction to Metaphysics* (1935), which Derrida reads in great detail over many pages of his own text, is the following, from Heidegger's chapter on "The Grammar and Etymology of the Word '*sein*'" (EM 47):

> φύσις means the rising upsurge, or the self-unfolding that tarries in itself. In this dominion [*Walten*], rest and motion are locked away and opened up on the basis of an original unity. Such dominion [*Walten*] is the overwhelming coming-to-presence that is still unmastered in our thinking, the coming-to-presence in which *that which* comes to presence essentially unfolds as a being. Yet such dominion first emerges from concealment—which means to say, in Greek, that ἀλήθεια (unconcealment) happens—when dominion struggles to become a world [*sich als eine Welt erkämpft*]. By means of world, beings first become what they are.

Heidegger now presents Heraclitus's fragment (Diels-Kranz B 53) in the Greek, which we may translate roughly as follows: "War [πόλεμος] is

---

4. Heidegger *did* read Hölderlin's polemic, and he *does* manage to exclude himself from the "barbarism" of the Germans of his own time. In his *Black Notebooks* Heidegger refers twice to the passage from the second volume of *Hyperion*, both alluding to it and citing it directly, without drawing its consequences for his own philo-Germanism. See 95:12 and 96:114.

both the father [πατήρ] and the king [βασιλεύς] of all things, proclaiming who shall be gods and who humans; some he determines as slaves, others he makes free." Heidegger's own translation might be rendered as follows: "Confrontation [*Auseinandersetzung*] is indeed the progenitor [*Erzeuger*] of all (that comes to presence), (letting it arise), but (also) the dominant preserver [*waltender Bewahrer*]. For confrontation lets some appear as gods, others as human beings, producing (and exhibiting) some as slaves, but others as free." Heidegger now comments:

> The πόλεμος named here is a dominant strife [*waltender Streit*] that precedes everything divine and everything human; it is not a war after the human fashion. The struggle about which Heraclitus is thinking lets those beings that essentially unfold separate from one another in an opposition, lets position and status and rank first be drawn into presencing. In such separation, clefts, distances, breadths, and jointures open up. In such a setting-apart-from-one-another [*Aus-einandersetzung*] world comes to be. (Confrontation neither divides the unity nor does it destroy the unity. It shapes the unity; it is gathering [*Sammlung*] (λόγος). Πόλεμος and λόγος are selfsame.) (Ibid.)

The principal effort in Derrida's discussion is to reflect on the anomaly that whereas in the postwar discussions Heidegger's emphasis falls on Heraclitean φιλεῖν, as in fragment B 123, φύσις κρύπτεσθαι φιλεῖ, "Upsurgence loves to hide," in 1933 and in 1935 the emphasis falls on πόλεμος as either *Kampf* or *Auseinandersetzung*, either "struggle" or "confrontation." And yet in both cases the overarching result for Heidegger is gathering and unification, *(Ver-)Sammlung*. It is only fair to repeat that the French translation of *Kampf* as *combat* is somewhat prejudicial, certainly all the more so as one examines the 1935 *Einführung*. Derrida is usually hypersensitive to such translation issues, but here he often accepts *combat* as an adequate rendering. Of course, in some cases, it is. Yet when Heidegger uses the word *Auseinandersetzung* in 1935, he assures us that he is not talking about some sort of "competition" or "race" among beings. And the word *Streit* is already associated with that striving between world and earth in which beings reveal themselves—especially in works of art. Although I do not recall a specific reference to Nietzsche in this regard, I imagine that Heidegger is here strongly influenced by Nietzsche's "Homer's Contest" and related early writings. Nietzsche's emphasis on the ἀγών, "competition" or "contest," in every aspect of Greek life surely must have impressed Heidegger. And although it may seem very odd to us, the very first meaning of ἀγών is "gathering" or "assembly," meaning principally the gathering of spectators at athletic games and contests. In that sense, Heidegger's identification of striving with gathering is not at all far-fetched. As for "discord," Ἔρις, Nietzsche reports that Pausanias claims to have seen some tablets containing Hesiod's *Works and Days* that record the existence of *two* goddesses by that name. The one Eris, who incites to war and violence, is universally hated, but the other, says Pausanias, sees to it that even the incompetent person goes to work and even the dullard struggles to comprehend. The good Eris is somewhere between Envy and Ambition, and, in spite of her dubious reputation, she merits praise (KSA 1:786).

To be sure, it is a grim turn that we are forced to make, from Homer's contest to the eve of World War II, and nothing I am writing here is meant to assuage Derrida's disquiet. No one who heard the "Rectorate Address" in 1933 had the least trouble translating everything he or she heard into the less sophisticated language of the *Völkische Beobachter,* and this discredit lies at Heidegger's feet and will lie there forever. As Derrida himself admits, however, the 1935 *Introduction to Metaphysics* gives us far more trouble, far more to think about.

As we have already noted, Heraclitean πόλεμος does not refer to a war of human making. It speaks of an initial separating out, after the fashion of Hesiod's *Theogony,* of beings and their encompassing world. This *Aus-einander-setzung* will be a word in Heidegger's vocabulary all the way into the 1960s; the confrontation with Nietzsche's thinking, for example, will bear that title. Derrida is struck by Heidegger's avoidance of the word *father* in Heraclitus B 53, and in his perplexity he cannot add much to what Heidegger says about the *Erzeuger.* Yet this "progenitor" is a hint in the direction of *Geschlecht,* inasmuch as "progenitor" or "engenderer" is a striking—and enigmatic—rendering of at least one facet of the father. Derrida notes that Heidegger may be trying to de-anthropologize his translation of Heraclitus, avoiding the eminently human figures of father and king. Perhaps (though Derrida does not say so) Heidegger is trying to avoid any Judeo-Christian allusions to a "heavenly" father. And his translation of *king* as *waltender Bewahrer,* which does not exactly roll off the tongue, is equally enigmatic: perhaps what Heidegger wants to stress, however, is that whatever violence (*Gewalt*) may be implicated in the word *Walten,* the dominion in question is a preserving and a safeguarding (*Gewähr*), and only to that extent a gathering.

However, *Walten* remains the sticking point for Derrida: it smacks of that "spiritual revolution" of which Heidegger felt himself the leader and by means of which he felt he could influence the National Socialist "movement." By 1935, of course, Heidegger is no longer rector, and the inner migration has begun. Yet Derrida continues to insist that when the word *Walten* appears in Heidegger's lectures and essays it is "not without a certain violence" (PA 407/207). Perhaps that is merely because Heidegger heaps up so many forms of the word: *überwältigend*, "overwhelming," *bewältigen*, "to get under control, to master," and, over and over again, *Walten* itself, as dominion and ruling sway, not to mention *sich erkämpfen*, the cosmic struggle for world. Everything *but* violence, *Gewalt*, in the familiar political sense of the word, appears here; and yet, to Derrida's ear at least, everything nevertheless rings with the jarring sounds of force and compulsion. Derrida: "The power, the force, or the violence of this *Walten* is the originary φύσις that can come about only in striving, *s'efforçant*," that is to say, forcing itself on us (PA 408/207). True, it is "spiritual" force—yet after *De l'esprit* one is less certain than ever about the characteristics and the limits of this spiriting force. Perhaps the forcing that most disquiets Derrida simply results from the fact that Heidegger insists on gathering *everything* into his assembly: love or hate, amity or discord, peace or war—it does not really matter, it all gets gathered. *One is all*. For a thinker of *différance*, this is a nightmare.

Although Derrida fails to mention it here, love and hate, gentleness and dissension are not always matters of indifference to Heidegger. At least where *Geschlecht* is concerned, as we have already seen and as we shall see again, there are two strokes, and it matters very much which one strikes. For one stroke results in a onefold twofold that is at least initially gentle, whereas the other is the curse of discord. Although Derrida does not mention this aspect of his *Geschlecht* project here, I do not believe for one minute that he has forgotten it.

There is, of course, a second reason for disquiet. In many of the texts of the 1930s, Heidegger includes the founding and the directing of a *state*, along with thinking and poetizing, as the essential activities of struggle and striving. To repeat, when *Kampf* and even *Walten* are being spoken in the Germany of the 1930s, an "essential equivocation" is possible, perhaps even inevitable, an equivocation that cannot be formalized or even formulated and that can be so readily misheard by ears other than Heidegger's. In his lectures on Hölderlin's "Germanien," a name that seems to lend itself to mishearing, Heidegger cites Heraclitus B 53 once again. Here the "king" is no longer *der waltende Bewahrer* but *der Beherrscher*, the ruler (39:125). Yet what rules in the Western world is *die Not*, the calamity of complacency, of needlessness and heedlessness with regard to the ontological difference. Needed is an entirely new orientation, a new beginning in which there "rules," *waltet*, a "supreme intensity in our own nation's belonging to beyng" (39:135). Needed are new ears, a new way for new ears to hearken, and new songs for German ears to heed. Yet the "sacrifice" to which Derrida now draws our attention has nothing redemptive about it. If a people is to find the truth of its historical existence, says Heidegger, it needs to listen to the voices of its poets. However, these voices will *not* be heard. Indeed, the great poets are our "firstborn," and the firstborn must be sacrificed, *[es] müssen die Erstlinge geopfert werden* (39:146). Here Heidegger does not seem to be bothered by the Judeo-Christian allusion to Jacob and Isaac, or to the older story of Cain and Abel.

The somber mood of sacrifice permeates Heidegger's 1936–38 *Contributions* as well, if we may allude to that work again, and it is a mood set by a number of lines from Hölderlin's "The Titans." The poem begins by saying that now is *not* the time, *Nicht ist es aber / Die Zeit*. No covenant binds us now to the gods, and yet the gods will not go to meet "nonparticipants." Thus the poet, in order to seek repose, meditates on the dead:

> Viele sind gestorben.
> Feldherrn in alter Zeit
> Und schöne Frauen und Dichter
> Und in neuer
> Der Männer viel
> Ich aber bin allein. (CHV 1:390; 39:137)

> Many have died.
> Warrior kings in ancient times
> And beautiful women and poets
> And in the new
> Many men.
> But I am alone.

Although Heidegger, in contrast to Carl Schmitt, rarely mentions "the enemy," he does make an important reference to *enmity* in his lecture course on "Germanien" and "Der Rhein." While interpreting Hölderlin's emphasis (in "Der Rhein") on the importance of one's origins and birth for a personal and perhaps collective destiny, a destiny that will always involve struggle, Heidegger speaks of the *Feindseligkeit* that can come to rule (*walten*, as always) in an "original hostility," *urprünglicher Feindschaft* (39:245). Yet there is something "blessed" (*selig*) in such opposition and enmity, for *Feindschaft* helps to shape whatever "purely originates." Therefore, says Heidegger, even enmity is an essentially unifying force. Although neither Heidegger nor Derrida mentions it, this sense of the importance of opposition arises very early in Hölderlin's work: the entire project of *Hyperion* rests on the "elliptical" interpretation of a human life, which has two conflicting foci, namely, one's natural endowment and one's schooling in the world at large; these two foci are forever in disharmony, and life is never a perfect circle or sphere but is always elliptical. No matter how *feindlich* the second of the two foci may be, however, there may also be something "blessed" about it, at least in view of the end result, namely, the formation of a human life. And yet toward the end of his own life Hölderlin finds that the two focal points have faded to undistinguishability. And the voice of his friend? She is long gone.

So it goes with the great poet, the firstborn who must and will be sacrificed. But what of the thinker? Heidegger himself is the poet's mediator, observes Derrida, and so it is Heidegger himself whose loneliness is being evoked. Derrida writes: "The mediator always says in truth: *Ich aber bin allein.* You do not hear me, when will you hear me hearing Heraclitus, Hölderlin, and some others? When will you stop sacrificing me? When will you hear the voice of that strange friend that your *Dasein* carries with itself (*bei sich trägt*), of that enemy-friend that speaks to you in the heart of a *Feindseligkeit*, of this originary enmity that forever gathers us for the best and the worst?" (PA 418–19/215–16). It is not too much to say that Derrida himself, who came to Europe from "another heading," that of North Africa, himself knew the taste of such loneliness.

Perhaps a concluding remark will not be out of place. By this point in the *Geschlecht* project, it is clear that the framework of Derrida's seminar, "Philosophical Nationality and Nationalism," has significantly altered the direction taken by the original *Geschlecht* article. "Philopolemology" has a new set of texts, several new objectives, and a new sense of disquiet, a disquiet that every reader of the 1987 *Of Spirit* will take to be justified. As always, *Versammlung* or "gathering" is at the core of Derrida's disquiet. Yet in the texts studied in *Geschlecht IV*, especially those from the 1930s, it is the gathering of *Kampf* and *Auseinandersetzung*, struggle and confrontation, that Derrida wants and needs to understand. Heidegger's insistence that there is such a thing as "a people's historical Dasein," and that Dasein stands in urgent need of *decision,* and furthermore that both the *Volk* and its historical Dasein are *one,* so that *the* decision will be grandiose, all-encompassing and all-compelling, is nothing short of militant. Heidegger's confidence in the Greek-German "spiritual" axis and his scarcely hidden contempt for all that runs counter to that axis in the history of the Western world, and especially for everything that comes out of the Mediterranean, whether from its northern or its southern shores, are equally disturbing. Most disquieting perhaps is Heidegger's frighteningly limited perspective on the destruction and the deaths of World War II. In the transition from the fourth to the fifth lecture hour of *What Is Called Thinking?* which, to repeat, was the first lecture course Heidegger was allowed to teach after having been banned from university teaching by the postwar denazification committee, Heidegger urges his students to visit an exhibit on German prisoners of war. He asks them to heed the exhibit's "soundless voice" and never to let that voice fade from their "inner ear" (WhD? 159). Who could object to Heidegger's desire to encourage *Andenken,* "commemoration"? In the same lecture course he invokes the sufferings of his divided land, and who could deny the pain of divided families in the East and West of Germany? I do not know a single German national of my own generation or the preceding one who bears no scars from the terrible experiences of those terrible times.

And yet. Where do we find in Heidegger's works a single passage in which he urges his students to visit the death camps, to develop an "inner ear" for the suffering of others? (Luckily, as far as I can see and hear, almost every German alive today has developed such an ear without Heidegger's assistance.) Where do we find, in his evocation of the historical existence of a "people," as though they were one, the slightest reference to German Jews or to the shtetl Jews of eastern Europe, to the Roma clans, to members of different classes, to members of the Social Democratic and Social Revolutionary parties, who themselves have a very highly developed sense of "decision," to city dwellers and country dwellers, for all of whom the nature and the extent of the suffering differ dramatically from those of the mainstream? Perhaps Derrida's deepest worry is that Heidegger's compulsion to gather and to resist at all costs dissemination and dispersion, even when such gathering paints itself in Heraclitean colors, is precisely what obscures Heidegger's perspective and inhibits his imagination and his empathy with regard to the others? When Heidegger makes his plea for a hearing that "holds firm," *das standhaltende Hören,* and when he praises the hearing that occurs in the "inner ear" for heeding only what has "genuine subsistence," *eigentlichen Bestand* (39:202), one has to remember that *Bestand* is also the metaphysical remnant of "permanence of presence," *Beständigkeit des Anwesens,* in the form of the technological stockpile. The more decisively Heidegger tries to "gather," the more likely he is to collapse back into the metaphysics he dreams of overcoming or of leaving to its own devices. It is as though his decisionism obstructs the capacity for decisions. It is as though Heidegger's one ear, the inner ear that is instructed to hear only one thing, and Heidegger's one hand, along with the one friend who seems to have no face and no gender, deprive him of the richness of experience that two ears, two hands, and the friends for whom one yearns and suffers can provide. Perhaps what troubles Derrida most deeply is that the procedure of *Destruktion,* which enables Heidegger to dismantle and think critically about the history of ontology, is never applied by Heidegger himself to what he calls *das Erbe,* "inheritance," in the sense of a cultural legacy and a national heritage. For the procedure of *Destruktion,* which serves as the very model for Derrida's own deconstruction, if applied to matters of cultural and national inheritance, would at least have slowed the pace of Heidegger's rush to choose a hero and assemble his generation and his people into a *Kampfgemeinschaft.*

Without hoping to do justice to the many paths that Derrida opens up here in *Geschlecht IV,* paths as sinuous as those of anyone's ear, we can certainly say that the fourth generation takes him and us far away from the themes of the *Geschlecht* series as a whole—at least, as far as we know it. It takes us principally in two different directions: first, in the direction of the critical questions we have raised concerning Heidegger's militancy, decisionism, and Germanism; secondly, in the direction of the very book in which *Geschlecht IV* is published, namely, *Politques de l'amitié* (1994). Discussion of that book's themes—friendship, fraternalism, and the dilemma of a democracy that wants *both* to possess some sort of identity *and* to display the qualities of hospitality and openness toward strangers—will have to wait for another occasion. Throughout that book, however, one continues to hear the question toward which the missing *Geschlecht,* the third, is urging Derrida and all of us. In a thinking such as Heidegger's, which insists always and everywhere on gathering and unification, what can distinguish between those two strokes that have struck our *Geschlecht,* the first, which coins a more gentle twofold, and the second, which condemns the once amicable twofold to discord, dispersion, and all the evils of war?

After Derrida presented *Geschlecht IV* as the keynote address at the second Loyola University conference in September 1989, I drove him out to O'Hare Airport. When he got into the car, he seemed very tired. Perhaps he was feeling the weight of the entire conference on his shoulders, since he had attended every paper and engaged generously in the discussions after each paper before presenting his own long and rich contribution. *Geschlecht IV* would mark the end of the *Geschlecht* series, its fourth and final generation. Yet it would not be the end of Derrida's preoccupation with Heidegger. As he settled into the passenger seat, Derrida said, murmuring the words more to himself than to me, "Heidegger—we will never get rid of his corpse." The voice of the friend? In any case, the voice of an endless haunting.

5

# *Geschlecht III*

## A Truncated Typescript

In the present chapter I want to report on two things—or at least on one and a half things. Principally, I want to offer an account of the typescript that Derrida distributed to the participants in the March 1985 colloquium organized by John Sallis at Loyola University of Chicago. There Derrida presented the paper that became *Geschlecht II*, that is, "Heidegger's Hand." The thirty-three-page typescript that he gave to the participants and that he himself called *Geschlecht III*, was the beginning of his transcription—as far as I have been able to discover it was never completed—of the detailed notes for his 1984–85 seminar in Paris. The second matter is the series of exchanges I had with Derrida concerning that typescript, exchanges that were very important for my own work on Heidegger and Trakl. It is not false humility but a reality check when I say that our exchanges were certainly much more important for me than they were for Derrida, even though he was, as always, very generous in his remarks to me in later years about them. As I look over my marginal notes to the thirty-three-page typescript, notes that I sent to him and later discussed with him, many of them mere references to other texts of Heidegger's, it is obvious to me now that the bulk of them were no news to him. That is to say, most of my remarks merely corroborated and encouraged the direction of his thinking. Every now and then, but really quite rarely, I urged caution or ventured a doubt or an objection.

I should explain that I photocopied Derrida's DINA-4 typescript onto the right half of a sheaf of sheets measuring eleven by seventeen inches, leaving a large space on the left for my marginalia. I mailed the oversized document to him sometime in the late fall of 1985 or early winter of 1986, that is to say, not many months after the Loyola Conference in which *Geschlecht II* was presented. Whether or not the original still exists I do not know; I did not find it among Derrida's papers at IMEC in Caen. I had made a photocopy of it for myself before sending it off, and it is from this photocopy that I am now working.[1]

The typescript has special importance for me, inasmuch as my own work, such as it is, involved Trakl early on. A *foyer* I was privileged to share with Derrida involved the eleventh chapter of the *Intimations* book (IM), a chapter dedicated to him just before the book went into print. (Derrida cites the chapter number incorrectly in *Geschlecht II*, listing it as the fourteenth rather than the eleventh—and last—of the book; yet I have always been grateful for the citation.) When he first saw a copy of *Intimations* at Perugia in 1986, he read aloud in one breath the chapter number, title, and dedication as they appeared on the opening page of the chapter: "Eleven . . . Strokes of Love and Death . . . for Jacques Derrida." He turned to me and said with a smile, "Frankly, I prefer the eleven strokes of love." That was at the Collegium Phaenomenologicum, which I was directing that summer of 1986, to which Derrida contributed a lecture during the concluding week. During the months that preceded the Collegium, we had corresponded about *Geschlecht III*. Some of my queries and observations concerning his typescript, I believe, became important to him—for example, those having to do with Heidegger's 1929–30 lecture course, which had only recently appeared and which had much to say about the problem of *animality*, a problem he had already broached in *Geschlecht I*. Yet, to repeat, as I look over my marginalia to Derrida's typescript now, I am struck by how insignificant many of them are; and yet Derrida himself always expressed gratitude for them. Such graciousness, I repeat, since it cannot be repeated often enough, was typical of him.

Let me try to follow the movement of the typescript pages—even if the first thing that must be noted is that they contain the mere beginnings of a transcription. Derrida appends a note to the end of the script, saying that due to lack of time he was unable to edit his notes to some five later sessions of the seminar—perhaps a hundred pages' worth of text, *environ une centaine de pages*. These are the pages we will take up in the

---

1. In a letter dated November 8, 1985, I tell Derrida that I have been rereading the typescript (which I there call "the second half of *Geschlecht II*") and that I have made many marginal notes on the text, promising to bring it with me on my upcoming visit to Paris or to mail it to him. He does not acknowledge receipt of the notes until March 13, 1986. His reception of my notes to the typescript, which he calls *"un 'draft' de Geschlecht III,"* notes that were clearly excessive, was as usual overly generous. The same letter refers to the planned conference on Heidegger at the University of Essex in mid-May 1986. I will cite the typescript and its marginalia in the body of my text by page number in parentheses. Finally, I intend to deposit a copy of the typescript (with my notes) at IMEC in April of 2014, so that it is available to the public.

next chapter. He asks those to whom he has distributed the typescript not to circulate it or cite it (as I am constantly tempted to do here): the typescript is entirely provisional and incomplete. I will for the most part continue to follow to the letter Derrida's instruction not to cite, though I will refer my own marginal notes to the typescript.

The typescript begins by stressing that it intends to follow the *rhythm* of Heidegger's Trakl essay, which is anything but regular or rectilinear. Rather, Heidegger often goes in circles, very much like the Robinson Crusoe that Derrida will later contrast with Heidegger's self-proclaimed *Weg*, the path of thinking that presumably moves forward. Yet each of Heidegger's paths advances by leaps and bounds, some of them calculated, most of them responding to another thinker or poet—in this case to the phantom of the other who is called Georg Trakl. In the present seminar, Derrida is everywhere concerned with Heidegger's *manner*, his *manière*, his way of *handling* Trakl's poetry *now*. After a lecture on Heidegger's hand, *la main de Heidegger*, this stress on *manière*, *manœuvre*, and *maintenant* should hardly surprise us. Questions of method thus dominate this third generation in its opening phase, namely, the method that must surrender the usual forms of discursivity in order to follow the rhythms of Trakl's poetry.

Here I urged Derrida—superfluously, one must say, inasmuch as he needed no such urging—to look again at Heidegger's remarkable insistence on rhythm in *Unterwegs zur Sprache* (US 38, 65, 75). For here Heidegger claims that *rhythm* is the name in metaphysical aesthetics for the wave that flows from the concealed site (*die Woge der verborgenen Ortschaft*) of Trakl's poetry. I noted that such a wave has to do with the "source," *die Quelle*, that Heidegger writes about in his *Erläuterungen zu Hölderlins Dichtung* (EHD 123, 130, 138, 146); it is the hidden source of the wave of poetry as such. As hidden, it has to do with what Trakl will call *das Fremde*, the foreign and strange.[2]

---

2. I had written about the theme of rhythm in Heidegger during the late 1970s, so that the starting point of Derrida's seminar had great importance for me—hence my supererogatory urging. The work on rhythm was later published in two places, first as "The Wave's Source: Rhythms of Poetic Speech," in *Heidegger and Language*, ed. David Wood (Warwick, England: Parousia Press, 1981), 25–50; revised and expanded, it then appeared as the third chapter of LV, "The Source of the Wave: Rhythm in the Languages of Poetry and Thinking." Although Trakl remained the focus, the issue of rhythm as "coinage," "articulation," and even "fettering," arose in quite different places—for example, in Heidegger's work on Aristotle and Derrida's on Paul Valéry, in Hölderlin's account of the caesura in tragedy and Heidegger's account of the rhythm of presencing and absencing in the granting of time and being.

Derrida thus "follows" Heidegger according to the manner and rhythm in which Heidegger "follows" Trakl, the poet himself "following" the stranger, the brother, and the sister—all of them embodied in what Trakl evokes as "blue game," *ein blaues Wild*. The word *suivre*, which has *je suis* as its first-person form, confounding "following" with "being," hence with Heidegger's *Sein*, was surely one of Derrida's favorite words. It forms the heart of one of his finest titles, *L'Animal que donc je suis*, "the animal that I am—and that therefore I (am to) follow." Yet "following" in the present instance, as in all the others, will not mean compliance: Derrida announces his intention to go slow precisely when and where Heidegger speeds up, and perhaps to leap forward when and where Heidegger seems to procrastinate or to avoid. Once again, Derrida emphasizes the two poles of Heidegger's philosophical confrontation with *Geschlecht,* the 1928 lecture course on the transcendence of neutral Dasein and the 1953 Trakl piece—on which the Paris seminar will focus. While it would be foolhardy to assert that these two dates span Heidegger's career of thinking, as though one could reduce it all to these references to *Geschlecht,* there seems to be some rapport or relation between them, even if that rapport itself (*Bezug, Zug, ziehen, entziehen,* etc.) withdraws from sight. At the outset, Derrida notes that the primary problem will be the two strokes that constitute *Geschlecht,* especially the second stroke, the one that introduces dissension or discord into the twofold (2). *Geschlecht* is in the first place a "mark," not even a sign, for twofolds, that is, for the word itself and for the "thing" referred to. Yet what could this "thing" be? We have already heard how many senses the word can have, and in how many combinations it can appear. Derrida cites *Geschlechtsverkehr,* sexual activity or "traffic"; I jotted alongside his reference the word *Geschlechtsverhältnis,* sexual "relation." Here the "thing" seems to be relation or rapport as such, the relation of two remarkably different forms of a twofold, the first apparently neutral, the second discordant, deleterious, destructive, "dissensional." What does it mean, then, to "relate" 1928 to 1953?

For about six or seven pages of text (2–8), Derrida focuses on the problem of the *type* of reading that both Heidegger and he himself are attempting, *type* understood in the sense developed by Philippe Lacoue-Labarthe's *Typographies*.[3] The type of reading, for Heidegger,

---

3. Derrida enters a long note on Lacoue-Labarthe's *Le sujet de la philosophie: Typographies I* (Paris: Flammarion, 1979), early on in the typescript. I added a note on Lacoue's *Typographies II,* which has the title *L'imitation des modernes* (Paris: Galilée, 1986), and which develops the theme of the uncanny, *das Unheimliche* (see esp. 229–55). This could contribute much, I added, to the questions of the foreign, *das Fremde,* and of "philosophical nationality and nationalism" in general.

involves the reciprocal relationship of *Erläuterung* and *Erörterung*, that is, of traditional commentary on, or elucidation of, particular poems (but chosen how? in what order? and upon what basis?), and the more demanding placement—that is, the *situating*—of Trakl's unique unsung poem in its rightful and essential place. Are these two types, strokes, or blows of reading—for every τύπος is also a *Schlag*, a "stroke" or "beat" that is the very root of *Geschlecht*—truly reciprocal? Or is there here an order of method, if not of implication? At all events, Derrida stresses that his own reading of Heidegger's Trakl can never be tranquil or self-assured. Above all, it cannot tranquilly accept—or even comprehend the meaning of—Heidegger's insistence that in Trakl there are two strokes of *Geschlecht*, the first neutral, the second malignant. No known procedure of reading—whether hermeneutical, philological, critico-theoretical, or poetic—will adequately characterize Heidegger's *manner;* none will tell us how Heidegger *handles* Trakl's poetry. Inasmuch as Heidegger himself incessantly raises the question of *Dichten und Denken*, always wanting to allow or enable his own thinking to be shaped as a response to poesy, the hand of Heidegger—presuming it, the hand, is only one—must be scrupulously observed, its every gesture examined and queried.

With regard to the *Ort* implied in *Erörterung*, "placement," Derrida notes Heidegger's acceptance of the supposition that *there is a place*, that a locale already exists for Trakl's singular unsung poem or *Gedicht*, and that such a locale can be located. A "discussion" of poetry, that is, *eine Erörterung* in its everyday sense, seems to guarantee the *Ort* and *Ortschaft*, the "place" and its "locale," which serve as the very root of *Er-ört-erung*. It clearly cannot be a point in geometric space that Heidegger is seeking; poetry is not a "thing" that lies at hand before us, an item in and of *Vorhandenheit*. To Derrida's references to Heidegger's 1957 *Der Satz vom Grund* and 1955 *Über die "Linie,"* I added a reference to Heidegger's "Conversation with a Japanese" (US 121). There Heidegger, as a "questioner," seeks a process by which mere commentary (*Erläuterung*) can become a placement (*Erörterung*). In that "Conversation," Heidegger refers to the Trakl article in question. The reference is important because it shows that placement is more fundamental, more "founding," in Heidegger's view than any sort of commentary can ever be. The relation between commentary and placement is therefore not reciprocal: *Erörterung* is the τέλος of every *Erläuterung*.

Yet what enables a commentary to locate the proper place of a poem? What signs *point to* this locale or place? Derrida cites Heidegger on the "original" meaning of the word *Ort* as the point of a spear or lance, *die Spitze des Speers*. There, at the peak, tip, or point, all is gathered.

Gathering, *Versammlung,* is the privileged signifier for Heidegger, as the phallus is for Lacan. One thinks in this regard of Derrida's invocation of the *élytre, stiletto,* and *stylus,* but also of the closed or opened umbrella, in his 1979 *Éperons,* or *Spurs: Nietzsche's Styles.* In the typescript, as in the 1984–85 seminar itself, Derrida does not shy from expressing a certain irony: Heidegger permits himself to write freely about the point of the spear either because, when it comes to psychoanalysis and all the other sciences of man, he is "above that sort of thing" or because, like Nietzsche, he is a little bit lost there—because, in the end, he is somewhat "inexperienced" in matters of sexuality and sexual difference (9–10). Perhaps it is that very inexperience that enables Heidegger to be confident that even if thinking often pursues an *Irrweg,* a confused and confusing path, it will eventually arrive at the place sought.

At this point I entered a series of remarks on the issue of "gathering," *Versammlung,* citing first of all Heidegger's "Logos: Heraclitus B 50" (VA 222): "The laying that gathers [*die lesende Lege,* that is, λόγος as λέγειν, and λέγειν as ὁμολογεῖν] gathers all sending to itself inasmuch as, bringing it forward, it lets it lie before us—holding every sort of presencing and absencing to its place [*auf seinen Ort*] and in its orbit, safeguarding everything by gathering it into the totality [*alles ins All versammelnd birgt*]." How does the λόγος do this? By means of the Ἕν (πάντα), "the unique-one as the unifying [*das Einzig-Eine als das Einende*]" (VA 220). Perhaps too eager to agree with Derrida, I asserted that everything in Heidegger's *Versammlung* comes to the same. In the fifth chapter of *Derrida and Our Animal Others* (2013), I paid more attention to the πάντα, and to what Heidegger acknowledges as the differentiating διαφερόμενον in all gathering. Yet in my much earlier notes to the typescript I referred to Heidegger's emphasis on the gathering power of the *-sam* even in the word *einsam,* "solitary" or "lonely." Even here, according to Heidegger, there is a gathering rather than an isolating. In "The Way to Language" Heidegger writes: "*Sam* is the Gothic *sama,* the Greek ἅμα" (US 265), the very ἅμα about which Derrida writes in "Ousia and Grammè" and in *Shibboleth.* Finally, I mentioned the lecture course from which the "Logos" article derives, published as volume 55 of the Heidegger *Gesamtausgabe.* There Heidegger writes, "Gathering [*Ver-sammlung*] is the original containment in a gatheredness [*Einbehalten in einer Gesammeltheit*], which, however, also . . . first admits all dissemination and dispersion [*Verstreuung und Zerstreuung*]. Gleaning and gathering, thought in this way, are more original than dissemination and dispersion" (55:269). Whereas for Derrida dissemination leaves only traces of sense, recognizing as it does the archaic non-origin of all meaning, for Heidegger dissemination is that paradox of a mightiness of essence that peters out into a scattering of forces, a kind of ontic-existentiel entropy. In the Heraclitus lecture course Heidegger contrasts the force of philosophy with the sheer distraction manifested by a student who goes to the movies instead of studying (55:397).

True, Heidegger's "Placement" begins with apparent caution and even modesty. Derrida cites the opening lines of Heidegger's Trakl essay and comments in detail on the problem of translating the lines into French:

> Placing [*Erörtern*] here means initially indicating the place [*in den Ort weisen*]. That then means paying attention to the place [*den Ort beachten*]. Both the indication of the place and the attention paid to it are the preparatory steps of a placement [*die vorbereitenden Schritte einer Erörterung*]. Yet we already dare [*wagen*] quite enough if in what follows we limit ourselves to these preparatory steps. The placement ends, as accords a path of thought, in a question. It asks after the locale of the place. (US 37)

Derrida remarks on this final phrase, *nach der Ortschaft des Ortes*, urging his students to resist understanding the substantive *Ortschaft* as a readily calculable, confidently located, and handily identified place. "Gathering" is not a rush to judgment. And yet already here, several years before *Of Spirit*, Derrida raises the question of the question, of that *Nachfragen* which Heidegger privileges here and almost everywhere. Heidegger's *Denkweg* is always a questioning *toward* and *after*, inasmuch as the preposition *nach* means both. Yet Derrida corrects himself here—as he also will do in *Of Spirit*, where, prompted by Françoise Dastur, he invokes the importance for Heidegger of address, assent, and response (*Zuspruch, Zusage*)—by saying that it is not so much the question that is privileged; rather, in the *toward* and *after* of questioning we notice that it is the *path* itself that yields the question. Derrida remarks once again, as he already has in *Geschlecht II*, that given this emphasis on the path it is odd that Heidegger offers no analysis of the foot in addition to the hand. I noted that Heidegger even employs the old word *wëgen*, "way-ing," "opening a path" (US 261), so that the foot would seem to be more essential than the hand on the path of thinking. For Heidegger, however, as we have heard, the foot neither speaks nor thinks, as the hand seems to do. It may be that Derrida is thinking of Bataille's "The Big Toe," a text that does not shy from the foot.[4] The closest Heidegger comes to acknowledging the foot is that pair of "peasant" shoes that causes such a stir in art history circles and on which Derrida famously comments in *The Truth in Painting.*

Heidegger, in a gesture typical of him, sets aside all the disciplines that might otherwise aid his "placement" (*Erörterung*) of the poem. Neither history nor sociology nor psychoanalysis—a rare reference for Heidegger to make, even by way of rejection, as though implicitly recognizing that there is a great deal in and about Trakl that would draw the analysts—nor any of the social sciences, with all their formulae, can aid the task of placement. And if the psychoanalyst, smiling wryly, should observe that Heidegger is ignorant of the phallus as the privileged signifier, Heidegger would reply, without a smile, that signification requires a topology if it is ever to take place, so that the search for the *Ort* comes first (10). Not even philology or *Literaturwissenschaft* of the usual sorts will aid the placement, even if Heidegger himself invokes the "original meaning" of German words such as *Ort* as signposts along his way. Always and everywhere the genius of the German language will be Heidegger's guide. Fichte is not far, Derrida remarks. We may therefore expect that the "original" sense of *Ort* as "the point of a spear" will be such a signpost. Heidegger will not refer to the weapon again, nor even to the hand that holds it. What is important for him, the point of the point, is the gathering, *Versammlung,* where everything comes together.

At this point, so to speak, I referred Derrida to a passage in *The Fundamental Problems of Metaphysics: World—Finitude—Solitude,* a then recently published lecture course that years later would become a key text for him, a passage that lent another sense to the point of the spear. There Heidegger defines the fundamental mood of boredom, profound boredom, as "a distension of the horizon of time [*das Weitwerden des Zeithorizontes*] and the dwindling of the point of a moment [*das Entschwinden der Spitze eines Augenblicks*]," in this way suggesting that the lance is a vector of original time, a vector that has as its tip or point the glance of an eye, the moment of insight (29/30:228–30). No matter how patient and painstaking a placement must be, however, we may say that the original time of placement is pointed and sudden: in his search for the origin, *den Ur-Sprung,* Heidegger counts on what at the very end of his introductory remarks he calls *einen Blicksprung an den Ort des Gedichtes* (US 39), a

---

4. Georges Bataille, "The Big Toe," in *Visions of Excess: Selected Writings, 1927–1939* (Manchester, UK: Manchester University Press, 1985), esp. 20–21.

leaping glance, regard, or view, itself a kind of *Augenblick,* that will guide our vision to the place of the poem (8). Literary critics will, of course, fault Heidegger for taking unaccountable leaps, from one poem or even one line or word of poetry to another, without any justification. Heidegger is prepared to accept such criticisms. His method will be one of strokes, leaps and bounds, jumps, even as he at times takes pains to go slow, step by step. Such is his method. If the method has anything axiomatic about it, it would be the affirmation that there will be—or there will have to have been—gathering, *Versammlung.* For only in and through gathering does the place take place. Even for a commentary or elucidation, to say nothing of a situating or placement, gathering *is* the point.

If the psychoanalyst insists on having the last word or the last laugh, she or he will remark that it is odd that a text that in the end involves brothers, sisters, lovers, and the strokes of sexuality begins with a blithe reference to the point of a lance. Derrida credits both Heidegger and the analyst, deciding for undecidability: perhaps the imperturbable Heidegger is simply not vulgar enough to concede to psychoanalysis the reduction that it craves; perhaps also an inexperienced Heidegger is unable to see beyond the tip of his nose in matters of, say, sexuality—or of politics (10).

Heidegger insists that Trakl's solitary poem, into which all his individual poems are gathered, as though running down the shaft of a lance to its point, remains *unspoken.* Such is the case with every great poet, says Heidegger, who does not doubt that he can take the measure of great poetry, and of great art in general, as that which is gathered in a singular and silent place. I noted in the margin the irony of a unified place, the singular space of a single unsung poem, that will have to do with endless twofolds: *Zwie-falt, Zwie-spalt, Zwie-tracht* brought together in a *Zwie-gespräch* or dialogue. What one must do—accepting Heidegger's alternation of the (non)metaphor of the lance—is follow the radically different figure of the wave, *la vague, die Woge,* that is, follow the *rhythm* in Trakl's poetry toward its source (11–12). Derrida defines the Greek sense of this word ῥυθμός as the regular, undulating flow of water, but I noted that for Heidegger the sense is generally not flow but *Gepräge,* articulation, coinage, imprint, or even chain and fetter—in short, the τύπος—as Lacoue-Labarthe emphasizes. Here Heidegger follows the lead of the classicist Thrasybulos Georgiades (LV 62–64). Insofar as there is a rhythmic wave, however, Heidegger asserts that it bubbles from a hidden source, so that the search for the place of the unspoken poem must in any case not follow the flow but trace it back toward its source. In a marginal note I recalled Hölderlin's *Andenken* and *Der Ister*: the Danube flows into the Black Sea, that is, into the foreign, and yet the poet follows it in the direction of *Hauß und Heimat,* house and homeland. If one is to understand *rhythm* without reference to a metaphysical aesthetics or to technical prosody, one must perhaps take it to be the relation of the unspoken poem and the written poems of the poet. The movement back and forth, from poems to unspoken poem, and from the silent poem to the individual poems, manifests the periodicity of the wave of rhythm.

The two senses of rhythm, namely, coinage versus flow, and the two figures, to wit, point of the lance versus wave, reminded me of the first text by Derrida that I had read carefully, that is, *Spurs.* I jotted a note into the margin of the typescript affirming once again the figure of the wave. Hölderlin, in *In lieblicher Bläue,* asks whether there is a measure on earth, and his answer is that there is none. So it is, I wrote, for the *Erörterung.* The point of the *épée* is also an *éperon,* the spar or spur of the ship in Derrida's first Nietzsche book, the ship that causes Nietzsche, in *The Gay Science,* to exclaim, "It's the women!" And, precisely as in that book, the point of the spur is both resisted and set in motion by an apotropaic veil or billowing sail, or even the open umbrella. The spar of the sailing ship does not penetrate the sail that enables it to move. As confused and confusing as all these figures seem to me now, at the moment they seemed to be decisive for Derrida's reading of Heidegger's "method."

Yet how do the rhythms of particular poems relate to the macrorhythm that Heidegger presumes he is following rather than himself setting? Where to start? Of course, one must start with the individual poems, inasmuch as the unspoken poem is unheard, a sign not read. Yet if one comes to the poems with wooden ears and a leaden heart, with a head full of ideas about what poetry is but without a prior intimation concerning the silent place from which the poems flow, is there any chance at all that an experience of poetry will arise? Derrida recalls for his students the dilemma of the "hermeneutic circle," from which one does not exit, but into which, as Heidegger says, one must enter "in the right way." Heidegger himself calls the relation between commentary (or elucidation or clarification: *Erläuterung*) and placement (or situation: *Erörterung*) a *Wechselbezug,* an "alternation" or a "reciprocal" relation. It is in fact, Derrida says, a *rhythmic* relation. Those who cannot dance to it, no matter how sophisticated their rhetoric and aesthetic, will gain nothing by either commentary or placement. Derrida takes some pains with the word *Erläuterung,* which is "clarification" in the sense of a wine that clarifies through long sedimentation. *Das Lautere* is the pristine, limpid, clear—a ray of light that shines through everything a poem says. That is what a "commentary" ought to see and say. In a marginal note I asked him whether *das Lautere,* the clear, might have any relation to *das Lauten,* the "sounding" of a poem, as in Heidegger's *Ge-läut der Stille.* "To clarify," in Greek, is κλύζω; to sound is κλύω. Could they have a common source, just as φωνή and φαίνω, sound and light, seem to be related? Even if classical philologists should cry out in dismay?

What precisely determines the thoughtful conversation between thinking and poetizing, the conversation or *denkendes Zwiegespräch* to which Heidegger constantly appeals? For Heidegger, to persist in such a conversation or exchange, with the verses of any given poem achieving their rhythm as they flow from the silent source of the unspoken poem, is the crucial matter. He distinguishes between two sorts of conversation or dialogue with poetry: the "proper" or "appropriate" conversation is that between poets, although such an appropriate dialogue does not exclude the possibility of a second dialogue, itself quite necessary, namely, that between thinking and poetizing. Not *philosophy* and poetry, in any case, but *Denken und Dichten.* What the two dialogues share, according to Heidegger, is an "exceptionally significant" (*ausgezeichnet*) relation to language. Derrida adds that such an exchange between thinking and poetizing involves both speech (*parole*) and signs—the very signs and signings marked in the word *significant*. Yet with what end in view—especially in the case of the dialogue between poetizing and thinking? For Heidegger, the "place" of "placement" is essential. Learning to *dwell within language* is the goal of such a dialogue. Mortals in our time must, according to Heidegger, learn the art of dwelling anew. The exchange with poetry, which would be the thinker's apprenticeship in dwelling within language, has scarcely begun in our time, he says (US 39). He also concedes that such dialogue may endanger the poem, obscuring it rather than either elucidating or situating it. The worst danger would be that the thinker interrupt the repose of the poem, the repose in which it *sings* rather than *speaks*. Song (*Singen, Gesang*) is the proper possibility of poetry, says Heidegger. Derrida notes that he is unsure whether he ought to refer to the *charm* of poetry, *charm* in its Latinate-Valérian sense, the sense of *carmen*. Heidegger resists such exportation to the Latin-Mediterranean region, and yet there is reason—especially in matters of music, dance, and song—to enter into the foreign. Even to go south.

At this point I jotted a note on the transition from saga to song, from *Sage* to *Gesang*. Heidegger insists on the importance of this transition, at the heart of which, he says, is the experience of pain, *Schmerz*. Pain, which

Heidegger says also includes the possibility of joy, is in fact the result of the interplay between joy and mourning. Such pain plays a significant role in the poetry of Trakl, but also, in Heidegger's view, everywhere in poetry (US 26–27, 61–64, 235). In my exchanges with Derrida, both by letter and in conversation, I urged him to take up this question of *Schmerz*, which I felt he had left largely out of account. In a marginal note to the typescript I ventured the possibility that Heidegger's *carmen* or *charme* would have to do with ecstatic temporality, which in *Being and Time* Heidegger describes as *Entrückung*, the raptures of temporality. This, I ventured further, was the sense of the passing of time in Trakl's *geistliches Jahr*, the "spiriting" year. Without knowing very clearly what I was saying, I suggested that for Heidegger *Singen*, μέλος, *Lied*, and *Gesang* all serve as the "gathering of saying" (US 229: *Versammlung des Sagens*). Yet there is nothing triumphant in such gathering. Rather, if *carmen* is incantation and chant, rune and rhythm, cult hymn and epigram, and if the interplay of joy and mourning can be described as a struggle, an ἀγών, then there may be agony in it, and that would surely be a word for *Schmerz*. However far-fetched these jottings of mine were, I felt that they may have had some impact when, years later, I heard and then read one of the last (and most difficult) sections of *De l'esprit* (DE 173–76), where *Schmerz* plays an important role.

Derrida doubtless remains suspicious of this appeal to song. Heidegger seems to pretend that he is not *reading* Trakl's poems, as the rest of us must do, but *hearing* Trakl's song, as though he has unmediated access to the voice of the poet. Phono-logo-centrism is not far. In a note, I objected, perhaps feebly, that the "song" is not in the idealizing throat of the thinker-philosopher himself, that it is not the mere auto-affection of hearing and understanding oneself while speaking; in the case of Trakl, at least, the song is sung by the defunct brother who appears at eventide on the forest rim—far away and utterly foreign. Yet Derrida's suspicions concerning Heidegger, not Trakl, are not confined to the question of the poet's song. For Derrida, the appeal to some sort of *Zwiegespräch*, a conversation between two, is itself a *maneuver*, a sleight (or slight) of hand (16). Heidegger's is a gesture of modesty and imperiousness at one and the same time, modest insofar as it submits thinking always and everywhere to the poetry of the poet, dedicating itself to the mere "placement" of the poem, imperious insofar as it rules out of court all the contributions that literary criticism and other disciplines might otherwise make to such a placement. Heidegger claims for his own thinking an access to the *essen-*

*tial* experience of poetry and language in general. At times it seems that not even the poet will have much to tell the thinker about the essential place of the poem. To be sure, Heidegger concedes that one must begin with the "spoken poems"; there is no immediate access to the unsung poem, no yellow brick road to Oz. Yet in some sense it does not matter *which* poems Heidegger comments on, if indeed all the poems are marked by a certain consonance, a certain unity, as though rising on the crest of a single wave of rhythm, chanting in *Einklang* or accord, and thus in some way announcing their appurtenance to the unsung, singular poem.

According to Heidegger, the *Grundton* or tonic of Trakl's unspoken and singular poem is determined by the emphatic *Ein* of *E i n Geschlecht*. That will have been (Derrida uses the future perfect tense here) the place of placement, the place for a conversation (*Zwiegespräch*) that emphasizes a twofold. The choice of the poems for commentary will have been guided by the determination of the *one* (17). The *one* of "*one* Geschlecht" will leap into Heidegger's view, his *Blicksprung*, and reveal itself as the source of all gathering. I commented on this portmanteau word, *Blicksprung*, not a common expression in today's German; a neologism, then, formed from two of Heidegger's favorite words: the *Blick* of *Augenblick*, the "moment of insight" or sudden "glance of an eye," joining the *Sprung* of *Ursprung*, the "origin" that can be reached only by a "primal leap." Yet, as Derrida will later argue (23–25), Heidegger's daring leap proceeds by the method of "metonymic transition," that is, by selecting a series of passwords (words such as *blue, soul, downgoing*) for his *Erläuterung* of Trakl's poems, a series that will allow him to glide or leap from one poem to the next—all in the name of the unspoken poem that the *Erörterung* is claiming to situate.

By this time in his analysis, Derrida has reached the end of Heidegger's untitled prelude or introduction to "Language in the Poem." Although the introduction consists of only three pages in the forty-five-page essay, in Derrida's view it decides everything that is to follow. In a note, I insisted that it decides *almost* everything, inasmuch as the strangeness of the brother-sister theme, which is at the heart of Heidegger's and Trakl's *Geschlecht*, still has some surprises in store. Even though my harping on this theme of brother and sister must have been irritating to Derrida—I myself find it irritating all these years later—I was and still am certain that Derrida granted the validity of the objection. If I had a "thesis" I wanted to defend, it would be that in Trakl's poetry the strangeness of the brother-sister relation, along with that of the lovers, caused Derrida to postpone his transcription of the 1984–85 seminar, postpone it indefinitely.

The remainder of Derrida's thirty-three-page typescript moves through the first part of Heidegger's tripartite essay and never really reaches the second and third parts—all in all, it treats a mere fifteen of Heidegger's forty-five pages! The call for Derrida's one hundred missing pages, that is, for the *Geschlecht III* that few as yet have seen, therefore arises from the desire to read Derrida's discussion of those thirty-five remaining pages of Heidegger's text, pages that have everything to do with the second stroke or *Schlag* of *Geschlecht*—the stroke that introduces dissension into the lives of brothers, sisters, and lovers.

Heidegger commences with the line *Es ist die Seele ein Fremdes auf Erden,* "It is something strange, the soul on earth," from "Springtime of the Soul." That line is repeated four times in the following dozen pages of the first part of Heidegger's essay. It is decisive for the first part his *Erläuterung* or "commentary" on Trakl's poetry, and it calls for the second part. Yet Derrida decides to "precipitate" matters, to move ahead more quickly, even though he realizes that this emulates Heidegger's own gesture and may result in a certain violence. It becomes clear in the course of the first major section of Heidegger's essay that the "place" of Trakl's unspoken poem, its singular *lieu* or *Ort,* the *one* of its "*one* Geschlecht," is gathered in the word *Abgeschiedenheit,* "apartness," or even "departedness." Heidegger follows the stranger—*dem Fremdling,* though not the sister, not *der Fremdlingin,* one must add—into the situation of apartness, so that the question of the foreign and strange, *das Fremde* and *ein Fremdes,* now arises (18–22). I noted for Derrida the pejorative use of the word *Abgeschiedenheit* in *Being and Time.* There Heidegger uses the word as though it meant sheer escapism. To it he counterposes *die vorlaufende Entschlossenheit,* the open resolve that runs ahead in a proper being-toward-the-end, enabling us to be *equal* to (mächtig *zu werden*) the power that death exerts in our lives, in spite of all the distractions of contemporary existence; thus Dasein sallies forth and disperses all the subterfuges and false escapes that would obscure the situation of its mortality. Wanting to have a conscience, *Gewissenhaben wollen,* is not some sort of apartness that flees the world, *keine weltflüchtige Abgeschiedenheit* (SZ 310). Open resolve grants Dasein the possibility of attaining power (the *mächtig* of *mächtig zu werden* is quite close to the *Mächtigkeit des Wesens* that we have seen at work in 1928); resoluteness is thus not some sort of flight from the world into monastic apartness. Here one can measure the distance between 1928 and 1953: Heidegger the phenomenologist takes arms against otherworldliness, whereas Heidegger the thinker of being follows the stranger into ever greater remoteness and apartness, even if he does reject the Platonic-Christian sense of otherworldliness. Like the Kafka who says that there is never enough night when he is writing, the thinker can never be far enough apart from the snares of everydayness.[5]

Derrida hears in the word *Abgeschiedenheit* its double tonality. A recluse or solitary knows the meaning and the importance of living apart. And the defunct, the deceased, the dead, if they know anything at all, know what it means to be departed. The French translation says *Dis-cès*, playing upon *décédé*, deceased, but retaining the *dis-* of separation and the critical capacity, as in dis-cernment, the perspicacity of the recluse. The coinage—itself the result of a *Schlag* of *Geschlecht*—attempts to retain the being under way of departure and to indicate a dying that is fateful but not fatal. In a second note, I suggested that this might be related to the theme of the unborn, *des Ungeborenen*, a theme that haunts Trakl throughout his poetry. The poet seems to be in the position of Karl Kraus, Franz Kafka, and no doubt many writers and artists who lived during the first great wave of psychoanalysis: not yet born, the seven-months' child awaits the carrying to full term that would be either birth or death. Such *Dis-cès* would thus have to do with *Untergang*, the "downgoing" that is also a persistent theme in the poems. If one follows the stranger in Trakl's poetry at all, one follows him *in den Untergang hinab*, in downgoing. Finally, or better, by way of commencement, Derrida notes that the "situation" of Trakl's poem leads us ineluctably to the question of animality (18).

---

5. I did not know at the time of my exchange with Derrida that Adorno, in "Parataxis," chooses this very word, *Abgeschiedenheit,* to name the essential place of *Hölderlin*'s poetry—or, more specifically, the effect of the *language* of that poetry. Adorno's essay was written in 1963, ten years after Heidegger's Trakl piece. It is an essay that is ardent to refute Heidegger on Hölderlin and on all things, but one that reverts to Heidegger *nolens volens* over and over again. Here too there are phantoms at work. See Theodor W. Adorno, "Parataxis," in *Noten zur Literatur,* ed. Rolf Tiedemann (Frankfurt am Main: Suhrkamp, 1981), 447–91; for an English translation, see *Notes to Literature: Volume Two,* trans. Shierry Weber Nicholson (New York: Columbia University Press, 1992), 109–49; notes on 338–41. These two points having been made, I should add that the relative neglect of *Untergang* in Derrida's typescript struck me as its most serious lacuna. My marginalia urge Derrida to pursue the placement of "apartness" in the direction of downgoing (*Untergang*), pain (*Schmerz*), and the possibility of song in agony—the darker side of Heidegger's placement of Trakl, the side that seems to me to be more faithful to the *Grundton* of Trakl's poetry—even if *Geschlecht III* forces me to doubt the grounds of every *Grundton,* no matter how somber. I must have continued to hound Derrida about song, pain, and downgoing over the years. In September 1989 he sent me a copy of the first edition of *Glas,* which was by that time out of print, inscribing it with the remark that this work of the early- to mid-1970s "was already founded on *Schmerz, Trauer und das Sterbenkönnen.*" When I reflect on the importance of Hegel's sister Christiane and Jesus's Mary Magdalene in *Glas,* I am compelled to concede the point.

Heidegger's situation or placement of Trakl, descending into apartness, is, Derrida says, *labyrinthique* (19). Where are the Ariadnic threads that will guide him and us? Once again, the principal thread for Heidegger is strangeness, foreignness, *ein Fremdes*. Yet in a typical gesture it is the Old High German meaning of the word *fremd*, the original-originary meaning of the word, that will save us. Derrida underlines the paradox: what is to be understood is the foreign, the strange, but it will be understood exclusively in the idiom of Heidegger's own language. This is what rankles Derrida. This is what compels him, in a course titled "Philosophical Nationality and Nationalism," to read Heidegger's Trakl essay. Admittedly, no possible translation could ever confidently cross the frontier of *fremd*. Yet does Heidegger ever approach that frontier? One can put the matter quite crudely: Heidegger plumbs the foreign precisely by never venturing into it; indeed, he insists that everything foreign can be thought only *in unserer Sprache*. Yet he seems to see this not as a fatal entanglement but as the very clearing of thinking. For Derrida, the idiomatic imbroglio of thinking is the uncanny as such—the German *Unheimlichkeit*, which is a kind of being not at home precisely when one is at home. For Heidegger, the idiomatic tangle seems to offer the thread of Ariadne. For Derrida, that thread is forever raveling. Derrida both adores and despises—is struck by both wonder and horror at—Heidegger's remark during the *Spiegel* interview that his French friends (meant is Jean Beaufret) confess to him that when they engage in thinking they have to think in German. Heidegger takes this as a straightforward confirmation of the Freiburg-Athens Axis, whereas Derrida takes it as a sign of how charming French friends can be and how easy it is to deceive oneself.[6]

In a long marginal note, I tried to defend Heidegger, or to interpret the paradox in a friendlier light. I did not do so well. The note says that if Heidegger ever truly confronts this problem of the foreign—the problem that Hölderlin confronted so thoughtfully in his letter of December

---

6. Benoît Peeters reports a meeting between Pierre Aubenque and Heidegger in 1967 during which the great Aristotle scholar—and admirer of the young Derrida—tries with Heidegger's help to translate the concept of *différance*, with an *a*, into German. The closest they can come in German to the double sense of the Latin *differe*, namely, to differ and to defer, is *verschieden sein* and *verschieben*. In spite of the apparent homophony, *scheiden* and *schieben* have distinct radicals. Aubenque quotes Heidegger as saying, "On this point, the French goes farther than the German" (BP 232). The French but also the Latin, one might add. Aubenque does not report whether Heidegger made this concession in French or in German, but one hopes it was the latter—as proof that Heidegger was truly thinking when he made it.

4, 1801, to Böhlendorff (CHV 2:912–14), a letter Heidegger cites quite often—then it is in his reading of Stefan George's "Das Wort." There (US 225) Heidegger concedes a certain failure, *Versagen,* a failure to "transport" something from afar, *von ferne,* across the frontier of "my country's rim," *meines landes saum.* To be sure, Heidegger is always sensitive to issues of translation: recall his labors over the saying of Anaximander (H 297, 302–303, 313, 318, etc.). And there is that *bon mot* from the Parmenides lectures, which Derrida loves to cite, "Tell me what you think of translation and I will tell you who you are," an expression that Derrida could only affirm. Yet Heidegger understands the *mein land* of George to be beyond all philosophical and poetic nationality and nationalism. For Heidegger these would be banal problematics, too ontic and precisely too regional for serious consideration. Thus Heidegger, apparently unaware of the idiom he shares with George, is able to take *mein land* to mean "the poetically preserved possession of the country" that is occupied by poet and thinker alike, *das dichterisch verwahrte Eigentum des Landes.* It is all in the *neighborhood* of poet and thinker. For Heidegger, *Nachbarschaft* is nearness, propinquity, and Heidegger's presumptive neighborhood is the Western world and Western philosophy since Plato. For Derrida, however, the *unheimlich* and the *fremd* can never be a matter of neighborhood, no matter how intimately they close in on us.

Heidegger, in his own language, is in search of a determination of and destination for the West, to wit, the reversal and overcoming of, or coming to terms with, Platonism. The sense of that reversal or coming to terms becomes clear when Heidegger insists that Trakl, when he sings that the soul is something strange on earth, does not mean that the human soul has another destination and that it is only temporarily inconvenienced by its "sidetracking" on earth. If our *Geschlecht* were *dahin nur verschlagen,* in the sense that we were merely "cast adrift" or "boarded up" on the earth, that would indicate that Trakl is a mere Platonist. Likewise, Heidegger insists that Trakl's *blaues Wild,* "blue game," *un bleu gibier,* has "nothing bestial" about it—as though the bestial were but the shadow side of a Platonism that has not yet been overcome in metaphysical philosophy. It is not as though, for Trakl, the soul has merely failed to find on earth its proper "cast" or "clan," *den rechten Schlag.* Later in the Trakl essay there will be talk of two strokes, the two *Schläge* that coin humankind, so that Derrida is attentive—as the French translation is not—to this very early appearance of *Geschlecht,* the word and the thing. His complaint is not that the translation is inadequate but that the matter for thinking, at least if philosophical nationality and nationalism are at issue, requires the most painstaking attention to every stroke of *Geschlecht*. Heidegger's desire to situate the poem of Trakl well outside of Platonism is what strikes Derrida as problematic. Heidegger speaks of "Platonic doctrine," namely, the view that the earth is the site of the soul's "corruption," *Verwesung*. Trakl will be gripped by the corrupt figure of humankind, but, insists Heidegger, such corruption has nothing to do with the Platonic complaint—at least as Platonism understands it. Derrida does not so much want to deny this as to note how the neighborhood of the thinker and the poet involves what one would have to call encroachment if not invasion: thinking will tell the poet what he never can have meant.

Heidegger cites an entire series of neuter expressions, parallel with *ein Fremdes,* that imprint their mark on the soul in Trakl's poetry. The soul is "something" mortal, obscure, solitary, sick, pale, silent, and so on. In a note, I stressed the neuter form as itself the foreign aspect of Trakl's words, "*Es* ist . . . ein Fremd*es*." Very often these neuter forms get translated into something far less strange in French. *Ein Fremdes* becomes *l'étranger,* "the stranger," instead of some*thing* strange, *l'étrangeté*. Many years ago, Véronique Fóti corrected a mistranslation of mine, when I took *ein Anderes* to be "another," in the sense of another person, instead of "something other" or "something else," and I have always been grateful to her. Hence, my desire to make Derrida aware of the strangeness of the form.

Derrida is right to note that when Heidegger asks, *Doch was heisst 'fremd'?* he is reverting to the form of his question *Was heisst Denken?* This question means not so much "What is it that we call thinking?" but "What is it that calls on us to think?" The question for Heidegger's situation or placement of Trakl is therefore: What does the word and thing called *fremd* call on us to think? At all events, Derrida says, Heidegger will cross no frontiers in order to reply to this question—unless a dictionary of Old High German is such a frontier, a frontier of time if not of place. Heidegger never avails himself of the treasures concealed in the Latin, Italian, Spanish, or French, to name only a few. *Extraneus, straniere, extrañar*—these words would lead him to consider frontiers, borders, insides, and outsides of sundry kinds. The Old High German *fram* means not the unfamiliar, not what the English cognate *from* implies, namely, a departing movement into the foreign; rather, says Heidegger, *fram,* taken "properly," "appropriately," "authentically," *eigentlich,* means moving forward, under way toward something that is held in reserve for us. For Derrida, this interpretation of the *fram* is an effect of the gathering, *das Versammeln,* that will prevent even "apartness" from becoming too strange, too foreign for us. But who, us?

At this point I entered a note from the biography of Georg Trakl—a note that Heidegger would have banished from the realm of thinking simply because it is biographical. Yet it struck me as remarkable that the Trakl children, raised in Salzburg, spoke almost exclusively French to one another. Their *bonne*, Marie Boring, a native of Alsace, spoke French with them, and this became the language of their childhood. Georg and Gretl addressed only their parents and the locals in German. How strange therefore to be reading—in Derrida's wonderful French—of Heidegger's insistence on *unserer Sprache*, especially when the Trakl *Kinder*, rapt to their ostensibly more tranquil childhood, would have replied *dans notre langue*, which is of course *la langue de l'autre*. Even Heidegger's favorite poetic formula—Trakl's use of the *Es ist* . . . in "Psalm" and "De Profundis"—was an expression Trakl learned from the *il y a* of Rimbaud's "Enfance," as Heidegger himself well knew.[7] Because childhood comes to play a vital role in Heidegger's placement of Trakl, I wanted to let Derrida know that however inadequate he might sometimes feel when trying to think (in) Heidegger's German, as we all do, Trakl and he would have understood one another perfectly well. If there were a *Gespräch* between Trakl and *Derrida*, then it would be Heidegger who would be on the outside listening in, or trying to, Heidegger trying to think in French. There are delicious ironies in the unaccountable encounters of poetry and thinking, especially when one believes one may safely exclude biography.

Heidegger does not doubt that he can follow what is strange in Trakl's poetry. The strange, which can also be a strange little boy or little girl, *Fremdling, Fremdlingin*, does not "err" or "wander," but is "determined" to have a destination. The stranger is following a call, *einem Ruf*,

---

7. See OB 118. Even though I do not cite it in my note to Derrida, we may examine here the use of the *il y a*, but also the reference to the "the forest rim," in the third section of Rimbaud's "Enfance," from *Illuminations*:

III

Au bois il y a un oiseau, son chant vous arrête et vous fait rougir.
Il y a une horloge qui ne sonne pas.
Il y a une fondrière avec un nid de bêtes blanches.
Il y a une cathédrale qui descend et un lac qui monte.
Il y a une petite voiture abandonnée dans le taillis, ou qui descend le sentier en courant, enrubannée.
Il y a une troupe de petits comédiens en costumes, aperçus sur la route à travers la lisière du bois.
Il y a enfin, quand l'on a faim et soif, quelqu'un qui vous chasse.

reminiscent of the call of conscience in fundamental ontology, so that Heidegger can follow the stranger who is following the call "into his own," *in sein Eigenes*. Always and everywhere, the "own," the *eigen* of *Eigenem* and *eigentlich*. No real danger of wandering off, straying, and getting lost in the foreign. One could almost say, remarks Derrida, that following what is strange or alien is merely a form of repatriation. The semantics of what would be *extraneus* are forcibly turned homeward. The current sense of the word *fremd* would be rendered foreign by its "proper" sense (21–22).

Derrida reverts now to the question of Trakl's ostensible escape from or successful avoidance of Platonism. Whether in fact "the Platonic doctrine" can be located or identified at all in the dialogues of Plato is a question that Derrida sets gently aside. At all events, Trakl will be placed in a situation outside of Platonism, a place congenial to Heidegger's overcoming of metaphysics. The soul is in fact searching for the earth as its promised destination. To demonstrate this, Heidegger now "leaps," says Derrida, to another poem, "Sebastian Dreaming," an exorbitant leap that can be justified only if one accepts the premise that Trakl has but one (unsung) poem. Derrida calls this leap, albeit with some hesitation, a "metonymic transition." The hesitation has to do with Heidegger's insistence that rhetorical analysis always has its technical tools in hand, ready to tinker with what the thinker is called upon to contemplate. Yet the word *metonymic* may be justified, for Heidegger seeks in other poems the word *ein Fremdes,* trusting that the new usage will clarify (by way of *Erläuterung*) the twenty-second line of "Springtime of the Soul." He cites three lines from the third part of "Sebastian Dreaming," lines that refer not only to "something strange" but also to *Untergang* and to the color blue, which will themselves prove to be metonyms:

> O wie stille ein Gang den blauen Fluß hinab
> Vergessenes sinnend, da im grünen Geäst
> Die Drossel ein Fremdes in den Untergang rief. (T 51)

> Oh, how serene a walk down the blue river
> Thinking forgotten things, when in green branches
> The thrush called on something strange to go down.

The metonymic leap—the leap of a *Blick-sprung*—occurs when Heidegger, remembering that the soul is something strange, feels justified now in saying that *the soul* itself is called into decline or downgoing.

Soul = strange = downgoing = toward and not away from the earth. By means of yet another metonymic leap, this time in a poem called "Autumn Transfigured," Heidegger takes the Platonic sting out of *Untergang*: "Das geht in Ruh und Schweigen unter," "In repose and silence all goes down." The leap seems justified, inasmuch as "Autumn Transfigured" invokes that same blue river, yet Derrida emphasizes the "seems." Nothing can explain these substitutions and linkages, Derrida asserts, and while on some level I had to agree, I entered a long note that showed my greater tolerance for Heidegger's metonymies. Nothing explains them, that is true, I wrote. Yet is not this *Untergang* a constant refrain in the poetry of Trakl? The soul is called into downgoing: Derrida wants to resist Heidegger's discourse on finitude, but do not Trakl's poems call us back to the earth and into downgoing? The problem for me was that the downgoing could not leave intact the language of "one's own." Yet even so one must follow this threnody or thanatography of Trakl's. When Heidegger asks, "In which silence?" and then immediately replies, *In die des Toten,* the silence of the dead one, Derrida is reluctant to follow him. It is not death in general that is being invoked here, but the death of a father or of a brother, of the father in *Traum und Umnachtung* or of Elis, the boy who died in early childhood. Lacking in wisdom, if not in nerve, I reminded Derrida of his own *Otobiographie* of Nietzsche and of what he there calls the logic of ob-sequence, that strange meditation on death, survival, and the mourning of the dead. As the very word suggests, ob-sequence is a process of *following*. And it follows the *downgoing*.

At this point, Heidegger reverts to the first poem cited, "Springtime of the Soul," though only to continue his commentary on the two other poems cited, namely, "Sebastian Dreaming" and "Autumn Transfigured." Derrida is perturbed by this return, but again I ventured in the margins to remark that this is in fact the sign of a new beginning—that is to say, of a break or caesura—in Heidegger's placement. The break indicates the rising of a second wave in the rhythm of the placement.

> Es ist die Seele ein Fremdes auf Erden. Geistlich dämmert
> Bläue über dem verhauenen Wald ... (T 78)

> Something strange is the soul on earth ...

But now—how are we to translate *Geistlich dämmert*? A blueness hovers over the clear-cut wood; these will be further metonymies on Heidegger's path. Yet what can the *Geist* of *geistlich* mean here?

It is the azure or blueness of either dawn or dusk, inasmuch as *Dämmerung* refers to both the rising and setting of the sun, the onset of day and night. But "spiritual"? "Ghostly"? "Spectral"? Several pages later Heidegger will invoke *das geistliche Jahr,* a phrase I felt might best be rendered as the *spiriting* year. Such "spiriting" evokes the coming and going of *Gang, Aufgang,* and *Untergang.* Here I reminded Derrida of Heidegger's strange question, in "The Anaximander Fragment," as to whether we dwellers of the Evening Land, *das Abendland,* find ourselves today at dawn or at dusk. Heidegger does not seem to be in search of some desperate coherence for either his placement or his commentary; he seems to be acknowledging the pain of the spiriting year. Pain? Without being able to be clear, either then or now, I associated the spiriting year, perhaps because of its transiency, with the theme of *Schmerz,* the theme I was constantly urging Derrida to take up, here once again referring him to sundry pages of *Unterwegs zur Sprache* (US 26–27, 45, 61–62, 235, etc.). And, again not lacking nerve, I referred him to the problematic of "datability" and "anniversary," developed in his own *Shibboleth: For Paul de Man.*

Heidegger leaps to yet another poem, spurred by the spiriting year and its azure, whether it be the cerulean of morn or the violet of night, the poem called "Summer Inclines to Its End," *Sommersneige.* This poem will grant Heidegger other colors, green and silver, for further metonymies, and it will bring him to the stranger he wishes to follow:

> Der grüne Sommer ist so leise
> Geworden und es läutet der Schritt
> Des Fremdlings durch die silberne Nacht.
> Gedächte ein blaues Wild seines Pfads,
>
> Des Wohllauts seiner geistlichen Jahre! (T 75)
>
> The green summer has grown so
> Quiet and the stranger's footfall
> Rings through the silvery night.
> Were a blue deer to remember its path,
>
> The consonance of its spiriting years!

He begins by commenting on the words that everyone feels to be perfectly comprehensible without commentary: *so leise.* "So discreetly," the French translation says; here I have written "so quiet," though one might venture "so hushed." Heidegger once again reverts to Old High German, *gelisian* giving the Germans their word *gleiten,* the English their word "to glide," the French their word *glisser.* Heidegger, of course, cites only the German *gleiten.* The hush of summer's end, summer having run its course, glides imperceptibly into autumn, as the day glides into night and night into a new day—the spiriting year.

Perhaps we are by now beginning to get a sense of Derrida's predicament, the imbroglio of *Geschlecht III.* It is not difficult to see how daring Heidegger's leaps and bounds are, his metonymies, his recursions to the Old High German. And yet. Trakl's verses are themselves so daring— even if they are hushed. I remember not one but several occasions when Derrida confessed to me how difficult Trakl's poetry was, how overchallenged he felt. I could only sympathize—and empathize. Even now, after all the years I have spent alongside Trakl's poetry, I am agape. *Gedächte?* Is that subjunctive a contrary-to-fact? And is the foundling stranger, *der Fremdling,* to be identified with *ein blaues Wild?* And can there be *a* "blue game," as though the collective noun could be singularized? We want such *Wild* very much to be a deer, *Rotwild,* even if we have to paint it blue, but could azure game *be?* And if it could be, would it be "thinking" or "remembering," *Gedächte?* Heidegger at least seems to be in a better position to deal with these idiomatic and idiosyncratic difficulties than either Derrida or I. If Derrida never published *Geschlecht III,* should I not have followed my own inclination to let this all go, since it is far too difficult?

Heidegger's are not really leaps at all, says Derrida, but hushed glidings, one metonymy slipping almost soundlessly into the next. Even if we suspect, as I noted in the margin, that some unexpressed intention is gathering it all, that some overarching intention is gathering the whole to some determined site, Heidegger guides us by slipping from one line of verse to the next, one word to the next. In fact, his path will always turn on the axis of a particular word, turning ever so *leise, leise* being its law. "In another poem," says Heidegger, "Another poem sings . . ." "Another poem says . . ." "Elsewhere. . . ." Yet all these metonymies take us in the direction of this gentle animal, this impossibly blue "game," which, because it remains outside of Platonism, has nothing bestial about it. If this be *Wild,* it is precisely not wild; if this be brute, it is neither brutal nor brutish. As Derrida rightly sees, Heidegger's situating of Trakl's poetry takes him to the crucial question of animality—and the problematic animality of that living being that has speech. Perhaps more important to Heidegger than being outside of Platonism is an exit from the Aristotelian definition of the human being as ζῷον λόγον ἔχον. No one is of greater assistance to

Heidegger in this respect than Nietzsche, who redefines the human being as *das noch nicht festgestellte Tier,* the animal that has not yet been successfully designated or even properly discovered. If the traditional earmark of the human is that it has *Vernunft,* that it is capable of seizing the truth and grasping ideas, Heidegger elsewhere counters, as we have heard, that the ape possesses a *Greiforgan,* an organ for grasping, but has no hand. Some other gifts will have to define both humans and other animals.

At this point in Derrida's text, with the introduction of the problem of animality, I inserted a long series of passages from volume 29/30 of the Heidegger *Gesamtausgabe.* Already in the letter to Derrida cited earlier, it was the theme of animality—and the related theme of the *birth* of Dasein—that elicited my most extensive set of comments on the typescript. If I may quote the letter: "Meanwhile, I wanted to recommend volume 29/30 of the Heidegger Gesamtausgabe to you because of its *long* discussion of animality, in sections 45–63—but also of *Vereinzelung,* individuation, in sections 2 and following—a discussion that is woefully inadequate, however! Here Heidegger allows a regressive analysis of the *als* to distinguish humanity from animality: the text cries for deconstruction." To the letter I attached two passages, one from *Being and Time* and the other from the "Letter on Humanism," having to do with birth and thus, if only by indirection, with "the unborn" and the theme of "animality." I did not doubt that Derrida was already aware of them, but they seemed to me to provide certain grounds for rethinking Heidegger's response to Trakl's "unborn" *Geschlecht.* The later passage, from the "Letter," here in translation (W 157; BW 206), reads:

> Of all the beings that are, presumably the most difficult to think are living creatures [*das Lebe-Wesen*], because on the one hand they are in a certain way most closely akin to us [*uns . . . am nächsten verwandt*], and on the other hand are at the same time separated from our ek-sistent essence [*Wesen*] by an abyss [*durch einen Abgrund*]. In opposition to them, it might also seem as though the essence of divinity were nearer to us than what is so alien in living creatures [*das Befremdende der Lebe-Wesen*]; nearer, namely, in an essential remoteness [*Wesensferne*] which, while remote, is nonetheless more familiar to our eksistent essence than our scarcely conceivable, abyssal bodily kinship with the beast.

I commented on this passage, which came to play an important role in my *Daimon Life,* in ways that now seem quite obvious: between the *Lebe-Wesen* and the *Ek-sistenz* of Dasein or the mortal human lies an abyss, a falling-away of all grounds, *the* abyss that we call "the body." It is the body that is alien to us. Addressing Derrida in the familiar form, I wrote, not shying from telling him what to do, "You must find a way to show how—no, *whether* and how—downgoing for Heidegger means embodiment. Embodiment is the path to the unborn. Or are the unborn, in their more gentle childhood, without body? *Leib und leblos?* Without body, without life? No, the path to the living creatures, *Lebe-Wesen*, leads us down into the abyssal loss of essence, corruption, *Ver-Wesung*. . . . Is the site of Trakl's poetry that of the sister in dark corruption, *Schwester schwarzer Verwesung*? Yes, also that."

The earlier passage (really two closely connected passages) to which my letter referred him was that remarkable concession on Heidegger's part that the fundamental ontology of *Being and Time* may have been led astray insofar as it ignores one of the two essential "ends" of Dasein, to wit, its birth:

> However, death is only the "end" of Dasein, formally speaking only the *one* end that encompasses the whole of Dasein. Yet the other "end" is the "beginning," namely, "birth." Only the being that is "between" birth and death represents the whole we are seeking. Accordingly, the prior orientation of our analysis remained "one-sided," in spite of its tendency toward the whole *that we exist* and in spite of its genuine explication of our appropriate and inappropriate being toward death. Dasein became our theme by way of its existing "ahead," so to speak, leaving all that has been "behind" it, as it were. We failed to observe not only our being toward the beginning [*das Sein zum Anfang*] but also and above all the *stretch* of Dasein *between* birth and death. What we overlooked in our analysis of being a whole was precisely the "nexus of life" [*"Zusammenhang des Lebens"*] in which Dasein constantly maintains itself one way or another. (SZ 373)

One page later Heidegger continues to reflect on the birth of Dasein, as though existence were in fact not only alive but also viviparous:

> Understood existentially, birth is not—no, not ever—something past in the sense of being no longer at hand, just as it is improper to say that death has the mode of being of something not yet at hand but coming toward us from out there somewhere.

> Factical Dasein exists as caught up in birth and, caught up in birth, it is already dying in the sense of its being toward death. Both "ends" and their "between" *are* as long as Dasein factically exists. . . . As care, Dasein *is* the "between." (SZ 374)

My comments on these remarks of Heidegger's went in the direction of Trakl's "unborn *Geschlecht*."[8] Are Trakl's "unborn" *gebürtig*? I asked. As the no longer decomposed *Geschlecht*, no longer the accursed figure of humankind, are they im-mortal? "Certainly not! Yet how are we to find the path to the mortals, the path that descends into *Untergang*? Perhaps not at either end of Dasein, but precisely there in-between?" All of this, of course, is by way of anticipation. The typescript has yet to take up in a focused way the problem of Trakl's (and Heidegger's) "unborn" generation. Let us then return to the typescript and the marginal notes.

For it is at this point that I referred Derrida to a number of passages in volume 29/30 of the Gesamtausgabe. As I look at these notes I am astonished to find that they are the selfsame passages that continued to haunt and hound me during the years 2010–13, the years of *Derrida and Our Animal Others*. If I am astonished to find Derrida returning in 2002–03 to a text of Heidegger's that he had already read in depth at the time of *De l'esprit*, 1986–87, the astonishment now boomerangs. As indiscreet as it may be, I want to quote these marginal notes at length. Like all the notes, they are written in a mix of French and German, but I will translate them here, keeping the editing otherwise to a minimum:

> I've already written you about Heidegger's 1929–1930 course at Freiburg, one year after the year 1928, which concerns you in *Geschlecht I*. The course has two principal divisions, the first investigating "profound boredom" as a fundamental attunement of Dasein, the second—and this is remarkable—discussing in the most detailed way the problem of the organism and of life as a "biological" determination. One could perhaps say that Heidegger is here looking for what there might have been *before* the bestrewal, *die Streuung*, that Dasein *is*. Heidegger takes up the analyses of Uexküll and Buytendijk, analyses of

---

8. At about this time I gave a paper to the Heidegger Circle that took Heidegger's *Gebürtigsein* seriously: I interpreted the later moment of birthing—and what is called the *afterbirth*—as an exceptional instance of the ecstatic temporality of Dasein. The paper was not well received, as I recall. There seems to be some resistance to taking the *life* of Dasein seriously.

the world and environment, *Welt/Umwelt,* of animals. All of it is fascinating, and I am unable to summarize it here. But the most astonishing aspect is that Heidegger approaches something quite new with respect to the problematic of death. Here are a few extracts, first, on the "sex drive" (29/30:363–64): "One of the most striking examples of this peculiar characteristic in all the behavior [of animals], that they eliminate one another [*dieses eigentümlich beseitigenden Charakters*], is the comportment of insects in that sphere of drives that we call the sex drive [*Geschlechtstrieb*]. It is well known that many females devour the male after copulation. After copulation the sexual characteristic [*der Geschlechtscharakter*] vanishes, so that the male now has the character of prey and so is eliminated. . . . Animal behavior as such is in each case in itself an elimination."

At this point I invited Derrida to compare Heidegger's account of *Beseitigen* to Hegel's philosophy of nature. Then I noted another set of passages from the lecture course (29/30:387–88), these ones on the problem of death. Already it was clear to me that even though Heidegger was trying to reserve the word *dying* (*Sterben*) for Dasein, resorting to the less honorific "perishing" or "coming to an end" (*Verenden*) for other life-forms, there was something in his own self-critique that worked against such a distinction. These were the selfsame passages that came to occupy me in the fourth chapter of *Derrida and Our Animal Others,* the chapter titled "Is There a Touchstone for All Philosophy?" The following note, from 1985, contains my first mention—my earliest awareness, I believe—of the problem and the promise of *Erschütterung,* the "agitation" or even "shattering" that tends to unify what Heidegger was seeking to hold apart, namely, the death of Dasein and of all other living beings. The note begins by quoting Heidegger, then comments on his "touchstone":

"The touchstone [*der Prüfstein*] for determining the suitability and originality of every inquiry into the essence of life and vice-versa [that is, presumably, the life of essence] is whether the inquiry has sufficiently grasped the problem of death, and whether it is able to bring that problem in the correct way into the question concerning the essence of life. . . . Because benumbment [*Benommenheit*] belongs to the essence of the animal, the animal cannot die, but only perish, inasmuch as we attribute dying to the human being."

And yet at the same time (at 29/30:396) Heidegger recognizes that there is "an *essential shattering*," *eine* wesenhafte Erschütterung, in the "essence of the animal," and it is Heidegger who emphasizes this. He says that we cannot understand it "as long as we fail to take into account the fundamental phenomenon [*Grundphänomen*] of the life-process and thereby of death." And so the course stammers and stumbles, precisely as did the *Grundprobleme* course of 1927 (Gesamtausgabe 24:387): "To enter here into a discussion of the finitude of time is impossible, because it is bound up with the difficult problem of death—and this is not the context or the place to discuss that." And this is precisely what happens with the logic course on Leibniz (Gesamtausgabe 26, §12), where the final words are *nihil originarium* and "impotence of Dasein," leading to the overturning of fundamental ontology into metontology.

That's 1928.

And 1953?

The "corrupted or dis-essencing *Geschlecht*" is always already the unity of brother and sister . . . in love and in death, *l'amour / la mort*. Animality, in Heidegger, remains, as Nietzsche says, "not yet determined," *noch nicht festgestellt*. Yet, understood as a question, it is a poem that strikes us.

By now it is clear to Derrida that Heidegger's entire "placement" or "situating" of Trakl rotates about the history of metaphysics from Plato to Nietzsche. It is Platonism's denigration of the animal—along with Aristotle's zoological definition of humankind—that is the issue. Trakl, envisaging in his "apartness" something like "blue game," must be all about the possibility of a new *Geschlecht*, a new generation, a new human race, a new "repatriation" of the soul and the body of humankind on the earth. It is at this point in the texts of both Heidegger and Derrida that the discussion of "essence" and "disessence" or corruption, *Wesen* and *Verwesung*, takes a new turn. In order to identify the as yet undetermined animal, humankind, one must commit the current stock of humanity to its corruption or disessencing. Derrida notes at this point in his text (27) all the *ver-* words that mark the failure of humanity in all of ontotheological metaphysics, its loss (*Verlust*), its abandonment by being (*Verlassenheit*), its fall and its falling prey (*Verfallen*), and its inability to develop in accord with its essence, hence, its *Ver-Wesung*. Yet the displacement of the word *corruption* to "disessencing" seems odd, and I noted this to Derrida.

Should not precisely the new *Geschlecht* accept what Platonism calls "corruption" rather than reject it? If one abandons the decaying corpse of prior humanity, disgusted by its corruption, is one not celebrating Platonism rather than twisting free of it, as Nietzsche demands of us? And would not this abnegation of corruption imply the continued condemnation of and contempt for the "animal"? Would this not be a *continuation* of Platonism?

At all events, the new gathering that Heidegger seeks in Trakl's poetry, or poem, is one that rescues the holy and the blue of heaven. Such a gathering will be gentle, appeasing, without war or quarrel. The twofold of brother and sister, man and woman, will be affirmed—in its *first* coinage—as a "more gentle twofold." Only after the second *Schlag* strikes will the twofold turn to dissension and violence. This is the story of the two strokes of *Geschlecht,* the story about why there have to be two strokes, and in what order they must come, the story that Derrida now wants to examine.

The new destination for our *Geschlecht* involves a "wandering ahead" that is actually the return to what Heidegger calls "a more tranquil childhood" and "the gentleness of a onefold twofold" (27). Here the constellation of brother and sister in Trakl's poetry rises and becomes fixed in the night sky, the "nocturnal weir" of Trakl's poem. Here one is struck for the first time—whether by the first or the second stroke or *Schlag* of *Geschlecht* is unclear, although there is no reason to believe it is the second, accursed stroke—by the lunar voice of the sister, the Selenic voice (28). Yet Derrida has scarcely mentioned this constellation and that lunar voice, which promises the more tender sexual difference of brother and sister, when his typescript begins to draw to a close—full of remorse, as he says. Not, to be sure, before it has posed the crucial question of the second *coup* or *frappe*. And not before it again hears Heidegger citing Trakl's "Autumnal Soul" on azure and game:

> Bald entgleitet Fisch und Wild.
> Blaue Seele, dunkles Wandern
> Schied uns bald von Lieben, Andern.
> Abend wechselt Sinn und Bild. (T 60)
>
> Soon fish and game glide away.
> Blue soul, darkling voyage
> Soon severed us from loved ones, others.
> Evening alters sense and image.

Who are the "others" from whom the new *Geschlecht* presumably takes its departure? To Heidegger, they represent the disessenced, the decomposing form of humankind, the *Schlag* or coinage of humankind as it has prevailed hitherto—let us not call them *degenerate,* cautions Derrida. Even so, it is alarming that Heidegger ignores the prior word *Lieben,* set in apposition to *Andern,* as though the new *Geschlecht* despises and scorns those it leaves behind. Now once again it is "our language," *unsere Sprache,* that guides the placement, this time explicitly in the direction of *Schlag* and *Geschlecht.* Derrida cites Heidegger as follows (US 49–50): "The wanderers, who follow the stranger [*dem Fremdling*] immediately see that they are separated 'from loved ones,' who now have become 'others' for them. The others—that is the coinage of the decomposed figure of humanity [*das ist der Schlag der verwesten Gestalt des Menschen*]." And then, after a paragraph break in Heidegger's text, the introduction of *Geschlecht* occurs. "Our language names the essence of human being, which is struck in a certain coinage [*aus einem Schlag geprägte*] and is stamped in this coinage [*und in diesen Schlag verschlagene Menschenwesen*], the '*Geschlecht.*'" This is the first appearance of the word *Geschlecht* in Heidegger's text—twelve pages into that text. Derrida's own reading has been magnetized by this word, however, from the very start of his own *Geschlecht* series, which here confronts its proper name for the first time. Something else, then, about the predicament of *Geschlecht III* becomes clear. The typescript is almost at an end, and yet its proper subject has only now been broached, and it has been broached only after Derrida himself has "leapt" many pages ahead in Heidegger's text—a text he wants to read in a *tempo adagio,* indeed *lentissimo.* His predicament is reflected comically in John Barth's "Lost in the Funhouse," in which the narrator reflects that the story is limping along, not really moving, so that the narrative will never, at that rate, get *out of* the funhouse—which is something like what we children used to call the funnyfarm—in order to complete the story. It has taken Derrida twenty-eight pages of typescript to get to *Geschlecht,* which has magnetized his project from the beginning; and in order to get to his topic he has had to skip an entire series of metonymic leaps or sidesteps in Heidegger's text. Among the topics he has skipped is *Schmerz,* the aching pain that somehow binds Trakl's blue to what others call the holy and that mysteriously transforms what is said into song. Here Heidegger has leapt not only from one poem to another but back to an earlier text of his, one that meditates on the line, *Schmerz versteinerte die Schwelle,* "Pain petrified the threshold," or "Ache turned the threshold to stone," from the poem "Winter Evening" (US 26–27; see Appendix A). In that earlier text,

"Language," Heidegger repeats Trakl's line over and over again, then says something about gathering, something that ought to become important for Derrida's irritation concerning the gathering:

> Yet what is pain? Pain tears. It is the rift. But it does not tear to bits, bits that scatter. Pain tears apart, that is true, it separates, but in such a way that it simultaneously draws everything to itself, gathering it in itself. Its tearing is, as the separating that gathers, at the same time the drawing that sketches out and articulates what is held apart in separation, as though it were a plan or an outline. Pain is what articulates tearing, the tearing that separates and gathers. Pain is the jointure of the tear. It is the threshold. (US 27)

Derrida might be vexed about the operations of "our language" here once again: the *Riss* can be both a rending and a sewing, a divorcing and a joining, an outline (*Aufriss*) and a preliminary sketch (*Vorriss*), and even the threshold of a coming and a departing. No doubt Derrida would immediately think of Freud, who also thought and wrote *in unserer Sprache*, for whom pain both rends and gathers: even in paraphrenics, says Freud, "organic pain and discomfort" call all libido back home, back to some suffering Narcissus. Freud will not be ashamed to cite Wilhelm Busch, who also wrote *in unserer Sprache* of the poet whose toothache compels the poet's soul to retreat into the narrow cavity of a molar. *"Einzig in der engen Höhle des Backenzahnes weilt die Seele,"* writes Freud in his "Introduction to Narcissism" (SA 3:49). Busch's humor—his *Scherz,* which is always on the cusp of *Schmerz*—and Freud's two-feet-on-the-ground would perhaps draw Heidegger's "pain" back to the stony threshold of earth and prevent the blue from becoming all too holy.

There is no hint of Derrida's taking such an aguey direction in *Geschlecht III*. The typescript downplays the theme of pain. Yet it does so in order to cite—if only by way of a promise—the Selenic voice of the sister, *die mondene Stimme* that haunts Trakl's entire oeuvre as though it were indeed but one poem. For the lunar voice of the sister announces that couple or twofold of a sexual difference that is still more tender. For the voice of the sister, evoked by the brother, is also a voice of the lovers, *der Liebenden,* who may or may not—that is the question—have suffered the second blow of *Geschlecht,* the stroke of discord and dissension. It is to this second *Schlag* that Derrida's text is under way. The second *Schlag,* which Heidegger calls a curse, πλήγη, and which in turn is the root of the English word *plague,* introduces discord (*Zwietracht*) into the relation of the sexes. When, asks Derrida, did the curse of this second stroke advene? With Eve and Adam? With Platonism? With Christianity? Derrida's answer I will have to quote, even if it means breaking my promise. When does the second stroke strike?

Before we hear Derrida's reply to this crucial question, let us return for an instant to the decomposing humankind that is "cast adrift" or "boarded up" and "imprisoned," *verschlagen,* in the decomposing *Geschlecht.* Derrida notes that the most common usage of the adjective *verschlagen* is to suggest someone who is crafty, sly, deceitful—a kind of Iago. Is Heidegger deaf to the adjective when he uses the verb to mean "driven off course"? Surely not. For the second stroke, the stroke of evil, has already struck the disessenced form of humanity, whose craftiness is merely a symptom of its errancy and malignancy. Heidegger's appeal to a childhood that would be "more gentle," a twofold of brother and sister not yet marred by dissension, is meant to counteract the corruption and the violence. Here I entered another long note that asks some rather obvious—yet horrendously difficult—questions, questions that I asked Derrida to consider.

> Does one not have to interrogate quite closely this "more silent" or "more tranquil childhood," *die stillere Kindheit,* to which Heidegger appeals, a childhood that promises something like simplicity, *Einfalt,* that is, the unifold, the disappearance of the twofold? *Einfältig* in everyday German means simple-minded, stupid, *bête.* Does Heidegger mean by this the brother and sister during their period of latency? Without the mark or the remarking of sexual difference? My suspicion—and I ask you to refine it—is that Heidegger wishes to replace the "horizontal" character of the *Geschlecht* of lovers with the "vertical" *Geschlecht* of succeeding generations, and these in terms of Western history and destiny. (The pages on "generation" in *Being and Time* (SZ 384–85) are so troubling!) Does not Heidegger want to gather man, *l'homme,* as *das Menschenwesen,* precisely by leaving the sister behind, not allowing her to become *la femme*? See also US 66–67, which I ask you to read with all your eyes. There Heidegger says:
> 
> "Thus apartness is neither simply the state of the one who died early nor the indeterminate space of his sojourn. Apartness, in the manner of its very conflagration [*ihres Flammens*],

is spirit, and spirit as the gathering. Such gathering brings the essence of the mortals back to their more silent childhood, safeguards them as the type that has not yet been brought to full term [*den noch nicht ausgetragenen Schlag*], the type that will coin the *Geschlecht* to come. The gathering of apartness rescues the unborn from what has suffered demise [*das Abgelebte*] in a future resurrection of a dawning humankind [*in ein kommendes Auferstehen des Menschenschlages aus der Frühe*]. The gathering, as the spirit of the gentle [*Geist des Sanften*], at the same time stills the spirit of evil. The turbulence of evil rises to extreme malevolence there where it irrupts from the discord of the sexes [*Zwietracht der Geschlechter*] and invades the fraternal-sororal [*das Geschwisterliche*].

"Yet at the same time the gathered fraternal-sororal twofold of the human *Geschlecht* lies concealed within the more silent unifold of childhood. In apartness the spirit of evil is neither denied and annihilated nor released and affirmed. Evil is transformed. In order to survive such a "transformation" the soul must turn itself toward what is great in its essence. The grandeur of such greatness is defined by the spirit of apartness. Apartness is the gathering by which the essence of humanity is taken under protection, back to its more silent childhood [*in seine stillere Kindheit . . . zurückgeborgen*], such childhood being brought back to the dawn of another inception. As gathering, apartness possesses the essence of the place [*des Ortes*]."

These two paragraphs, in my view, contain the most problematic aspects of the Trakl essay. One has to rejoin the discussion you have begun here on pages 9–10 concerning the discourse of psychoanalysis, which Heidegger would like to ignore.

What I was thinking of in this long note is no doubt Heidegger's appeal to some sort of latency period in which sexuality is ostensibly not yet marked. The use of *stillere* and *stillen* is also remarkable, inasmuch as *stillen* means to nurse. What does it mean to "nurse" evil, and why is evil at its extreme associated with the invasion of discord into the fraternal-sororal realm? Would this be yet another stroke, a *third* stroke, by which a regrettable yet predictable discord between the heterogamous sexes invades with unspeakable malignancy the brother-sister relation? Is Heidegger here pointing *without* pointing to the relationship between Georg and Gretl

Trakl? Does such a pointing *without* pointing reveal something like an underlying yet never questioned incest motif in Heidegger's thinking—precisely in the thinking that is famous for never having entertained questions of sexuality? Would not a Derridian double-reading be essential here, one that would be as generous as possible to a text that dares to think about a new coinage of humankind, a lineage that would overcome the corruption, violence, and malignancy of its earlier forms, yet also a reading that would wonder whether the most archaic of all thoughts and desires in this human-all-too-human species are here inflicting themselves upon the hapless and helpless Heidegger? Such a double-reading would be the predicament as such—and only Derrida would be capable of carrying out such a reading. It would carry him beyond the framework of "philosophical nationality and nationalism," back to that of the two grandfathers, Freud and Heidegger, but always and everywhere in order to gain insight into, or develop a better ear for, the magnetic poetry of Georg Trakl. What sort of text could satisfy all these demands?

The typescript now (29) returns to the passage in which Heidegger introduces the word and the thing called *Geschlecht*. Heidegger writes (US 50): "This word means the human race [*Menschengeschlecht*], in the sense of humankind [*Menschheit*], and also the *Geschlechter*, in the sense of tribes, clans, and families, all of this being coined in its turn [*wiederum*] by the twofold of the sexes [*Zwiefalt der Geschlechter*]." It is the *wiederum* that now draws Derrida's attention. All the other senses of *Geschlecht* are *in turn*, or *once again*, or *for their part*, stamped by the twofold of the *Geschlechter*. By rights, of course, one should allow this last word to stand in all its ambiguity, and not to translate it as "sexes"; yet it is Heidegger's introduction of the "twofold" that makes such a translation all but inevitable. Once again, then, willy-nilly, the text is brought back to the question of sexual difference, the question that Heidegger ostensibly never raises.

Here once again Derrida notes that Heidegger's twofold is itself doubled or redoubled. If the result of the first blow is the gentle childhood of the twofold of the sexes, so is it also the destination of the new *Geschlecht* that "wanders ahead." If its wandering ahead takes it *back to* the promised essence of humankind, what will prevent the second, accursed, blow from striking again? Is there not only a *third* blow, but an *nth* blow, in the cycle of the disessenced essence? Heidegger suggests that there are but two blows or strokes delivered to the twofold, the first marking them as brother and sister, or at least as male and female, the second introducing dissension into the twofold. The first stroke produces the first *Geschlecht*, which itself is double, yet still at peace with itself, still true to its essence. However, a second *Schlag* advenes—when? how? why? and above all whence?—which seems to be evil, indeed, to embody evil or malignancy as such. Heidegger does not yet speak of evil, to be sure, even if my marginal note to Derrida leaps ahead in order to invoke it. At this point Heidegger speaks merely of the "curse" that is somehow already implied in the word *Schlag*. Not simply *the* word, however, but *unser Wort "Schlag."* Yet if the curse is impacted in the very word *Schlag*, the root of *Geschlecht*, is not the very first stroke a "curse" and a "plague"? Even if Heidegger insists that it is not, is not the "curse," which falls from nowhere at no identifiable time for no accountable reason, a *supplement* to *Schlag* as such, both inside and outside the system of *Geschlecht*? Does the poet ever identify himself as dwelling outside of or beyond the curse? Does the poet ever dream Heidegger's dream?

Derrida observes that Heidegger does not quote the line from "Dream and Delusion," in the collection *Sebastian Dreaming*, which invokes the accursed race, tribe, family, or sex, "O des verfluchten Geschlechts." Derrida notes that even though the French translation avoids the words *curse, accursed,* perhaps in order to hold at a distance any "religious" connotation, Heidegger himself, however resistant he may be to any Christian reading of the poems, does not by any means avoid the Christian lexicon. To try to avoid it would simply distort both Trakl's poems and Heidegger's placement of them. *Fluch* is malediction, and πλήγη is the blow or stroke—by hand, lightning, calamity, or word of mouth—of such malediction. Derrida continues the quotation (US 50): "*Curse* in Greek is πλήγη, our word 'Schlag.' The curse of the decomposing species [*des verwesenden Geschlechts*] consists in the fact that this old species has been severed [*auseinandergeschlagen*] into the discord of the sexes [*Geschlechter*]." The dual now enters into a duel, the twofold disessences and engages in battle, the battle of the sexes, the quarrel between generations, the war of the worlds. The duplex enters into duplicity. This is the second blow or stroke, the bad one, that re-marks the species and its sexes. They become isolated in "unbridled individuation" and "blind savagery." The French translation of Heidegger's text renders such savagery, *Wildheit des Wildes,* in a way that recalls Trakl's *ein blaues Wild*, calling it a reversion to *la sauvagerie . . . du gibier*. This is of course a very odd decision, inasmuch as "blue game" is a figure of the poet himself and of those closest to him. It is not a figure of the "others," viewed as the accursed *Geschlecht*, from which the poet would proclaim his distance.

Heidegger's text folds back constantly on its doubles and redoublings. The force and the enigma of his entire text, says Derrida, derive from this strange doubling of sexes, of blows that drive them apart, of destinies that result in decomposition but also the hope of a new beginning—which is not new at all but earlier than the dawn. And if the second *Schlag* cannot be neatly distinguished from the first, will not the day unfold as it always does? At this point in his own text (30), Derrida refers back to the very beginning of his project, which focused on the 1928 lecture course at Marburg and which developed the premises of what Heidegger is here thinking in the phrase, *Nicht das Zwiefache als solches, sondern die Zwietracht ist der Fluch,* "Not the twofold as such, but discord is the curse." Sexual difference as such is not accursed, but only that which determines it to be oppositional, one sex in dispute with the other, and even, most wretchedly, brother and sister at war. Whence, then, the opposition and the discord? When does the curse strike? with Adam and Eve? with Platonism? with Christianity?

"*Réponse: plus tard.*" "Response: later."

The first sense of the "response" is that the curse falls well after Adam and Eve, after Platonism, and after Christianity—later than all these. The second sense of the "response" is that Derrida will postpone the question until later in the seminar—and that is doubtless the case, inasmuch as he pledges to work his way through Heidegger's Trakl text quite painstakingly, and there is much work remaining to be done.

At this point I entered a note in the typescript begging him not to be such a tease. *When,* later? Can one be more precise about the order of the two blows, about *das Zwiefache* and *die Zwietracht*? And why the fatal resemblance that the prefix *Zwie-* lends to both? As far as the second blow is concerned, how can one sidestep the uncanny yet compelling logic of the supplement? Will not any response to the *when?* question always have to come *later,* inasmuch as a fatal anachrony is at work in the two strokes? Just as there is good and bad writing, with the condemnation of writing suggesting both that bad or merely derivative writing always comes first and that good writing, *primal* writing, comes but lately, after the fact, in the philosopher's old age perhaps, so too the supplement of the second stroke, the accursed supplement, is impossible to locate in time, in sequence, in epoch, and in history—including the history of being.

Surely this is one of the secrets of Derrida's fascination with the Trakl text: the second blow will always have come first, even as it withdraws into concealment. It is explicable only as undecidably within and without the destiny of our double *Geschlecht*. Surely it will prove impossible—in spite of Heidegger's insistence—to keep these blows apart, to separate them out, and equally impossible to deny that sexual difference and ontological difference are structurally identical, or at least perfectly parallel. If the difference between being and beings, which is initially granted in Western history, is soon cursed by oblivion of being, so too is sexual difference initially granted, only to be cursed at some point by discord and dissension. Nor will it be possible to assert in either case that the histories of Platonism and Christianity play only a negative role in sexual and ontological difference. The blows or strokes of *Geschlecht,* like the granting of clearing and concealing in *Ereignis,* will prove to be both curse and resource, dejection and hope. Each blow will strike what comes before and will coin what follows.

Nevertheless, persisting with Heidegger's attempt to distinguish between the two, I asked in the margins of Derrida's typescript whether one might be justified in saying that the second stroke, the blow of dissension and evil, sows in Heidegger the seeds of the dream or phantasm of a quieter, more tranquil childhood, a childhood that surely never took place. The dream of a more sane and serene childhood in which siblings are not yet quarreling and in conflict—is this not the phantasm of an intrauterine interiority, of a self-presence that gathers itself together in order to avoid dispersion? Hearkening in the womb to the soufflé that is the voice of the friend?

In the end, and at the end of the typescript, Derrida's own questions mount. If good and bad writing repeat one another indissociably over and over again, what sense are we to make of Heidegger's insistence that there is a more tranquil childhood to which a new *Geschlecht,* a *Geschlecht* that is *one,* may revert, a childhood to which, indeed, it may be "resurrected"? We will immediately want to know—although Derrida himself does not state the matter so baldly—whether we can understand that reversion as anything other than a regression to the period of latency. If the second *Schlag* drives the concordant twofold into unchained individuation and isolation, as Heidegger's text suggests, Derrida asks how we are to understand that individuation as a curse. For individuation is otherwise always praised and sought after in Heidegger's texts, especially in *Being and Time,* where it is a mark of the resolute Dasein that has attained insight into its own mortality. Derrida cannot avoid referring to the sense of *Vereinzelung,* the French *démariage,* as an isolating, in eugenics and in agriculture, of unwanted plants and populations (31), and I could not refrain from chiding him a bit for this distraction from the central questions of the Trakl article. Here I referred once again to the 1929–30 course, which calls *Vereinzelung,* "individuation," and even *Einsamkeit,* "solitude" or "loneliness," a fundamental concept of metaphysics. Such individuation would be an effect of the "profound boredom" that may be interpreted as a fundamental attunement of Dasein, precisely in the way that *anxiety* served as the fundamental mood of *Being and Time*. *Vereinzelung* might then be the measure of a certain expanse in Heidegger's career of thought, indeed, from 1928 to 1953, in which it first of all designates the very authenticity of a Dasein that accepts its being-toward-the-end, but then is decried as an individuation that has run amok and become destructive. Does individuation begin as a sign of appropriateness and authenticity but end as a mark of disessencing?

At all events, Derrida's text seemed to me to get back on track—or on the path of Heidegger's thinking—when it refers to the transition from the first to the second stroke, from the initial gentle fold of genders and sexes to a twofold that is driven off course and shipwrecked, *verschlagen* and *zerschlagen*. For the discord of the sexes becomes utterly destructive of the species, and the quarrel appears to spread from abrasive couples to brother and sister, and from thence to entire families, tribes, and nations. It then becomes impossible for our *Geschlecht* to find its way back *in den rechten Schlag*, which would be its way back home, back to the more tranquil childhood. Yet it is this hope of a return with which Heidegger ends his paragraph. The way back can occur only with that *Geschlecht* "whose twofold [*Zwiefaches*] wanders ahead, on its way out of discord into the gentleness of a onefold twofold [*in die Sanftmut einer einfältigen Zwiefalt*]; that means it is something 'strange,' and it thereby follows the stranger [*dem Fremdling*]" (US 50).

And strange it is, this migration out ahead, as "our word" *fram* suggests, moving toward rather than away from; it moves toward a difference without dissension, a twofold without a fold, or at least without duplicity. Derrida recalls here Heidegger's reversion to his own starting point, *ein Fremdes*, in "Springtime of the Soul," and indicates, at the end of the first part of Heidegger's text, the identification of "the stranger" as himself *der Abgeschiedene*, the one who is apart—or departed—the one who is dead without being dead, the one who has taken his departure from the others and so is an other to the others. That one, *jener*, names the place of Trakl's poem. The place is called apartness, *Abgeschiedenheit*. Heidegger now pledges to take a second step (*einen zweiten Schritt*) toward that place that so resembles death, yet is not death. And with a reference to that second step, taken in the second part of "Language in the Poem," Derrida's typescript ends.

The final page of *Geschlecht III*, page 32 spilling over onto page 33 with the single word *remarquer*, consists of fragments, very brief paragraphs, all of them pointing toward the utter strangeness of that simplicity of the sexes that ostensibly prevails prior to the curse. It is as though Derrida wants us to remember the promise, made in *Geschlecht I*, of a pre-dual, pre-differential sexuality, positive in its intention and mighty in its essence. Yet one must wonder whether the promise can possibly hold. Heidegger appears to leave us with the more gentle childhood of a unifold twofold—strange, foreign, unheard-of, yet also idyllic, bucolic, oneiric, thalassic, perhaps amniotic. Perhaps also, as we shall see, utterly phantasmatic—haunted by a phantom of the other.

6

## *Geschlecht III*

### The Phantom of the Other

The *Geschlecht III* typescript, by moving quickly ahead and skipping over many pages of Heidegger's "Language in the Poem," pages that Derrida would no doubt have wanted to read very carefully, reaches the end of the first part of Heidegger's tripartite essay. The figures, images, and strategies of Heidegger's reading that I very much wanted Derrida to comment on and to read doubly, as it were, arise only in the second part of Heidegger's essay. After learning that the 1984–85 course, "Le fantôme de l'autre," was most likely the course that Derrida had been transcribing in the typescript, I betook myself in April 2012 to Caen to examine Derrida's notes.[1]

A handwritten title appears on the first page of the typewritten lecture notes: "Le nationalisme et les revenants," nationalism and its ghosts. Much later in the typescript appears another handwritten title: "LE FANTÔME DE L'AUTRE," the phantom of the other. "Other," as always in Derrida, is not *autrui*, not the Sartrean "other people," but the more neutral "otherness," which for Derrida certainly includes "the others" but also refers to the Freudian unconscious, the death that occupies Heidegger and Blanchot, the animals that we subjugate but do not comprehend, and virtually all that strikes us as uncanny—*le tout autre*, the altogether other. The very titles (or subtitles) of the seminar, with their *revenants* and their *fantôme*, tell us much about the inspiration for Derrida's 1987 *De l'esprit*.

We also find among the lecture notes a new typescript of the same material, but neither the notes nor the new typescript contains the material

---

1. In the Derrida Archive at IMEC, in Caen, I was able to locate the notes from "Nationalité et nationalisme philosophiques: le fantôme de l'autre," Derrida's 1984–85 seminar, in Boite 52, code "DRR 175 (1984/85; 1987/88)."

of the typescript Derrida distributed to the participants of the first Loyola conference in October 1985. The only date that appears—and it appears at random—in the initial typescript of the lecture notes is "21 novembre 1984." At any rate, it seems clear that Derrida presented the material on Heidegger's second Trakl essay, "Die Sprache im Gedicht: eine Erörterung von Georg Trakls Gedicht," in the fall and winter of 1984 and spring of 1985. The early part of the seminar contains the material that goes into *Geschlecht II*, for example, the material on Fichte's "Reden an die Deutsche Nation." There is also material here on the postwar German-Jewish-American nexus in philosophy, including material that would interest anyone working on the thinking of Hannah Arendt; we find here also discussions of Adorno and de Tocqueville, although with a greater amount of material on Arendt, including the Günter Gaus interview, "Es bleibt die Muttersprache" ("What Remains Is the Mother Tongue").[2]

The material that most interested me, however, is found in the final folder, containing Séances six to thirteen of "Le fantôme de l'autre." Here is where the bulk of the material (some of it published in *Geschlecht II*) designed for the proposed *Geschlecht III* appears. Séance eight is devoted to the themes of *Ort* and *Erörterung*, "place" and "placement," which is the first topic taken up in the Loyola typescript; farther into the lecture notes, on page 21, there is a description of curse as *Schlag*, the "blow" or "stroke" that Derrida renders as *coup* or *frappe*. Séance nine is largely handwritten, "improvised," while the remainder is already in typescript, although, from all appearances, not revised. Séances nine to thirteen would, in my judgment, be the five sessions that, as Derrida notes at the end of the *Geschlecht III* typescript, "restent à transcrire."

The first page of the ninth session is typewritten, pages 2 through 5 are handwritten, and the rest typewritten. The handwritten pages take up Derrida's response to Heidegger's insistence that Trakl has nothing to do with Christianity, a theme that will also be treated later on in the course.

---

2. This material intrigued me, and I took time to examine it, making a note to inform Arendt scholar Peg Birmingham about it. I recall from my own conversations with Arendt, most of them surrounding the translation and publication of Heidegger's works, her profound love of German literature and language. It was clear to me that for her, as for Benjamin, Adorno, and many others, the Third Reich, in addition to all its other crimes, had corrupted in an unforgivable way an entire culture, tradition, and language. Anyone who is insensitive to language will find this odd: Should the focus on the murder of millions be obscured or sidetracked by thoughts of culture? Yet for Arendt and many others—Derrida among them—the murder of the language and the literature was part of the crime, perhaps at the core of it.

The first matter taken up in the ninth session is the word *geistlich*, "spiritual" or "spiriting," as in "the spiriting year," *das geistliche Jahr*. Derrida is here already deep into the second part of Heidegger's essay, which by way of a "second step" tries to say more about the "place" or "situation" called "apartness," *Abgeschiedenheit*. So far in this second section Heidegger has taken up or reverted back to the following themes: the path of the stranger toward death, or a kind of death; the "madness" of the departed one; the boy Elis, who as one who dies young embodies the gentle twofold of the sexes; the paths of the stranger through "the spiriting year," and time as the arrival of a new dawn in what "has been." Heidegger now cites two lines from the poem "In Hellbrunn," which evokes the beautiful park on the outskirts of Salzburg frequented by Trakl, and Derrida reprints and comments on these lines:

> So geistlich ergrünen
> Die Eichen über die vergessenen Pfaden der Toten.
>
> So hauntingly verdant are
> The oaks above the forgotten paths of the dead.

Here the word *hauntingly* tries to translate *geistlich*, earlier rendered as "spiriting." It is precisely the impossible translation of this word that intrigues Derrida, that along with Heidegger's insistence that Trakl "avoids" the more expected word *geistig*. Heidegger asserts that the latter word remains trapped in the Platonic gap between the realms of thought and sensation, the gap or χωρισμός between the νοητόν and the αἰσθητόν, so that Trakl's avoiding the word indicates his "place" beyond Platonic metaphysics. For this Platonizing distinction belongs to the decomposing *Geschlecht*; hence, Trakl speaks or sings always of the *geistliche*, and not the *geistige*. Derrida refers to "Grodek," a poem that Heidegger cites only many pages later in his "placement"; there, Trakl invokes *Die heisse Flamme des Geistes*, a line and a theme, we recall, crucial to the book *Of Spirit* (see especially DE 158–59). Derrida marks the difference between this fiery spirit and the pneumatic tradition of metaphysics: *Geist*, the Old High German *gheis*, means that which is caught up, transported, beside itself, enflamed. This is for Derrida an exceptional example of the idiom, which is what the entire seminar is about, namely, the untranslatability of idiom and the specificity of philosophical nationality and nationalism. Derrida refers also to his treatment of Hegel in *Glas*, no doubt thinking especially of Hegel's treatment of the religion of the sun and his *brûle-tout* of nature (Gl 100, 265–70, and elsewhere). For Heidegger, the flame of spirit contains within itself both good and evil, that is, the possibility of both *Sanftmut* and *das Zerstörerische*, both "gentleness" and "the destructive."

Yet Derrida expresses his astonishment that Heidegger avoids altogether the relation between *Geist* and ghost, spirit and *le revenant, le fantôme*. Such avoidance is clearly what lends the entire seminar its title, *le fantôme de l'autre*. The avoidance has everything to do with the problematic of *fremd/fram*, that is, with the reduction of the "foreign," "alien," and "strange" to a place that lies just ahead of us on "our" path, the "toward which" of our heading home. These handwritten pages of Derrida's notes—almost impossible to decipher—stress Heidegger's insistence that Trakl's "place" is entirely outside of both the Platonic and the Christian spheres. Trakl would be so outside of these spheres that he could not even be said to be anti-Christian or anti-Platonic. Yet this doubling of the reference to the tradition, that is, presumably, Heidegger's reference to a Platonizing Christianity and a Christian Platonism *along with* the denial that either of these has anything to do with Trakl's use of the word *geistlich*, represents for Derrida an exceptional instance of the phantasmatic: when the alien is said to be that which lies ahead of us on our path, when the *fremd* is said to be that *fram* which we are heading *toward*, as it were, then something is haunting Heidegger's text, something that Heidegger himself seems desperate to avoid. And although it may seem perfectly obvious to my readers by this time, it may be worth noting that Derrida's choice of the title for his address to the Collège internationale de philosophie in March 1987, later published as *De l'esprit*, seems to derive precisely from this moment of the 1984–85 seminar: Heidegger is haunted by certain phantoms, phantoms of the "other," ghosts that he himself has raised and can no longer lay to rest, but which he seeks to avoid. Avoidance and the phantom, the idiomatic and the phantasmatic, now occupy the center of Derrida's reflections on Heidegger.

From this point on, with pages 6 and following of the seminar notes, the text is typed and the decipherment of Derrida's meaning considerably easier. Pages 11–12 of the ninth séance, on the *stillere Kindheit*, the "more reposeful childhood," and on *das Knabenhafte* and *Mädchenhafte*, that is, Heidegger's account (at US 55) of the essence of boyhood and girlhood, constitute important additions to what we find in the *Geschlecht III* typescript. To repeat, that typescript of thirty-three pages seems to get only as far as the eighth séance of the seminar, although this is hard to judge: the organization of the notes presented in seminar is much more repetitive

# Geschlecht III: The Phantom of the Other

than the typescript, as we might well expect. Yet the remarks in sessions nine and ten on the brother and sister are altogether missing from the transcription, so that these are the sessions that the present chapter will follow quite closely. Here we may be permitted to cite the notes, first in French and then in translation.[3]

On page 11 of the notes for séance nine, Derrida takes up the figure of Elis, the boy who, having died young, is one of the phantoms that appears and reappears (also under the names Sebastian and Helian) most persistently in Trakl's poetry:

> Elis nommerait donc un lieu plus ancien et plus paisible que le vieux Geschlecht (vieille espèce ou vieux sexe) qui a reçu le mauvais coup, le deuxième coup de la malédiction qui y installe le deux de la dissension, la différence sexuelle comme dissension. Et il s'agit bien de différence sexuelle, du Geschlecht aussi comme sexe et non seulement comme espèce, comme le traduit la traduction française, qui manque ici une détermination essentielle du passage. Elis va vers une sexualité, si vous voulez, plus ancienne que celle du vieux sexe déchiré par la différence sexuelle de type agonistique et oppositionnel.

> "Elis" would thus name a site more ancient and more peaceful than that of the old *Geschlecht* (the old species or the old sex), the latter having undergone the bad stroke, the second, accursed stroke, which instaurates the twofold of dissension, sexual difference as dissension. What is involved here is indeed sexual difference, *Geschlecht* also as sex and not merely species as the French translation says, missing here an essential determination of the passage. Elis is heading toward a sexuality that is older, if you will, than that of the old sex that is torn apart by a sexual difference that is agonistic and caught up in opposition.

Derrida continues, turning now to the theme of "youth," that is, of boyhood and girlhood:

---

3. I have edited the French text only slightly, only where obvious typos occurred. These seminar notes will, one hopes, some day be more carefully edited and published. For the moment, I am selecting only those passages that seem to me crucial to the theme of the brother, sister, and lovers in Trakl's poetry. For these too are phantoms that Heidegger raises and yet somehow avoids.

Et de fait, que dit H. aussitôt après? eh bien que dans la figure du jeune Elis, das Knabenhafte, l'être de garçon, ne réside pas dans une opposition (in einem Gegensatz) avec l'être de la fille (zum Mädchenhaften). Das Knabenhafte ist die Erscheinung der stilleren Kindheit, ce qui est étrangement traduit en français par le garçon Elis est l'apparition de l'enfance profonde, alors que le texte dit: l'être-garçon (das Knabenhafte, naturellement sous entendu, celui d'Elis) est le phénomène ou l'apparaître (Erscheinung) de l'enfance plus paisible (silencieuse, apaisée, etc.). Cette enfance en laquelle le garçon et la fille ne s'opposent pas, elle abrite et réserve en elle "die sanfte Zwiefalt der Geschlechter," le tendre dédoublement, "la tendre ou douce dualité des sexes," donc une différence sexuelle, un deux qui ne s'est pas encore déterminé et déchaîné dans l'opposition, aussi bien l'adolescent que l'adolescente, aussi bien le *Jüngling* que, citation, "la figure d'or de l'adolescente," die goldene Gestalt der Jünglingin.

And what does Heidegger say soon after this? Well, that in the figure of the young Elis *das Knabenhafte,* the being of the boy, does not reside in an opposition (*in einem Gegensatz*) to the being of the girl (*zum Mädchenhaften*). *Das Knabenhafte ist die Erscheinung der stilleren Kindheit,* which is oddly translated into the French as: the being of the boy Elis is the apparition of profound childhood, whereas what the text says is that the being of the boy (*das Knabenhafte,* naturally implying the boyhood of Elis) is the phenomenon or the appearance (*Erscheinung*) of the more peaceful childhood (more silent, more appeased, etc.). Such childhood, in which boy and girl do not oppose one another, conceals and holds in reserve within itself *die sanfte Zwiefalt der Geschlechter,* the tender doubling, "the tender or gentle twofold of the sexes," thus a sexual difference, a two that is not yet determined by or unleashed into opposition. This includes the male adolescent as well as the female adolescent, the *Jüngling* as well as, and I quote, "the golden figure of the adolescent girl," *die goldene Gestalt der Jünglingin.*

Derrida does not pause to comment on the extremely rare idiom, *die Jünglingin,* the "female youth" who exists, as far as I know, only in Achim von Arnim's 1809 "Eurial und Lukrezia," in Rilke's 1910 *Malte Laurids Brigge,* and in Trakl's poetry. She is clearly related to the *Fremdling* and the *Jüngling* in Trakl, and to the otherwise unknown *Mönchin,* "female monk." The suffix -*ling* is identical with the one that appears in the English "foundling" or "yearling," a diminutive form itself suggesting either smallness of size or gentleness and tenderness of aspect. Whereas the German language does not normally refer to a young girl as *Jünglingin*, the masculine *Jüngling* commonly refers to a male at puberty or in adolescence. It is odd that Heidegger himself does not comment on the strangeness, in "our language," of Trakl's word. The coinage itself suggests a blurring of the lines between boy and girl, perhaps in that "more reposeful" childhood that enchants Heidegger and that he seems to affirm without much reflection. Nor does Derrida comment directly on the way in which—in Heidegger's text, although not in Trakl's poems—*das Knabenhafte* seems to absorb within itself, at least during that more serene childhood, *das Mädchenhafte*. Every girl a tender tomboy, every boy the promise of a new, nonoppositional *Geschlecht*. At the very end of his seminar Derrida will take up the theme of the "fraternalization" of all things female, and of the sister above all.

Derrida continues (session nine, page 12), summarizing Heidegger's text (US 55), noting that Elis will not decompose after his death; he will instead, himself a phantom of the other, lead the friend and the brother back toward the early, the matutinal. For Heidegger, Elis is the promise of a more archaic and more serene childhood. This more serene childhood now appears indeed to be intrauterine: Heidegger again cites "our" language, the Old High German *giberan*, from which the modern word *geboren*, "born," derives. The stranger pertains to the *Geschlecht* that is *noch nicht zum Tragen gekommen*, that has not yet been "borne out" or brought to full term. Derrida comments on *tragen*, the French *porter*, especially in the phrase *porter un enfant jusqu'à son terme*. As we have already seen in chapter 4, *Austrag* is a crucial term for Heidegger in other texts, for example, his essay "Logos: Heraclitus B 50," in which the word carries the burden, precisely, of *difference*.[4] *Ein ausgetragenes Kind* is one that has been carried for the full nine months of a pregnancy. For Hei-

---

4. See chapter 5 of *Derrida and Our Animal Others*, in which *Austrag* is seen as carrying the entire burden of the διαφερόμενον, of difference and differencing, in Heidegger's response to Heraclitus. It is important to note that from the mid-1980s until the end Derrida thinks the *Austrag* and its *tragen* principally in two registers, neither of which has to do preeminently with the epoch of metaphysics: first, in terms of the voice of the friend that every Dasein *carries* with itself, and second, in terms of the friend who dies and whose death, *pace* Freud, means the end of the world. Each time, uniquely, the end of the world. Each time, uniquely, responding as Celan responds to catastrophe: *Die Welt ist fort, ich muss dich tragen*. See Jean Birnbaum, who cites Derrida's 2003 *Béliers* in this respect, in Jacques Derrida, *Apprendre à vivre enfin* (Paris: Galilée, 2005), 16–17. See the English translation by Pascale-Anne Brault and Michael Naas, *Learning to Live Finally: The Last Interview* (Hoboken: Melville House Publishing, 2007).

degger's Trakl, however, the negative is stressed. For the *unausgetragene Kind* is precisely the stranger, the youth, whether girl or boy, who in some sense remains unborn, *Ungeborenes*. Yet Heidegger is more likely (at least in other texts) to use the word *Austrag* with reference to the promise of a more incipient beginning, a commencement that remains concealed in the history of metaphysics, a promise not yet fulfilled or borne out in the history of the West but intimated in his own "other thinking." *Austrag* is therefore intimately bound up with the destinal in Heidegger's thinking, with *Schickung* and *Geschick,* and therefore with *Ereignis* and the granting of the clearing and of presence, as well as the thinking of *difference* as the Greek carrying-through or carrying out—the difference between beings and being and all the vicissitudes of that difference in Heidegger's long career of thought. All this is brought to bear in an important passage in the *first* Trakl essay (US 25), the opening essay of *Unterwegs zur Sprache,* called simply "Language." Derrida refers to the passage during his seminar—one of his very few leaps outside of "Die Sprache im Gedicht"— doubtless because *différence* and *différance* have been on his mind since the beginning:

> La dif-férence (Unter-schied) dans son unicité et son intimité est ce qui unit la diaphora et ce qui porte à terme en ayant porté d'un bout à l'autre (der durchtragende Austrag). La figure ou le procès du porté à terme (comme on le dit de l'enfant), la figure de la portée comme dif-férence, c'est Austrag, qui devient comme un synonyme de différence dans le texte de Heidegger. . . . Ici Elis, le mort étranger, déploie l'essence humaine vers ce qui n'est pas encore arrivé à terme, ce qui n'a pas encore été porté (noch nicht zum Tragen . . . gekommen). Et H. ajoute entre parenthèses: vieil allemand giberan: donc ce qui n'est pas encore né (unborn, ungeboren). Et c'est un mot, Ungeborenes, de Trakl. Ainsi ce qui est encore unausgetragen (non porté à terme . . .) et par là plus en repos et plus serein dans l'être du mort, le poète, dit H., le nomme das Ungeborene: l'ingénéré, dit la traduction française.

> The dif-ference (*Unter-schied*) in its unicity and intimacy is that which unites the διαφορά and also that which carries to term, having carried from one end to the other (*der durchtragende Austrag*). The figure or the process of carrying to term (as one says of an infant), the figure of being-carried as dif-ference,

this is the *Austrag*, which comes to be a synonym for difference in the Heideggerian text. . . . Here Elis, the dead stranger, deploys the human essence in the direction of that which has not yet arrived at its term, that which has not yet been borne (*noch nicht zum Tragen . . . gekommen*). And Heidegger adds in parentheses: the old German word *giberan*, thus, that which has not yet been born (the English *unborn*, German *ungeboren*). The latter (*Ungeborenes*) is a word of Trakl's. Hence, that which is still *unausgetragen* (not carried to term . . .) and by that very fact that which is more reposeful and more serene in the being of the dead, is, says Heidegger, what the poet names *das Ungeborene*. The French translation says *l'ingénéré*, the ungenerated.

As Derrida continues his analysis (13; US 55), the tale of the serene unborn, those who are in some sense merely on the other side of the living, those who have not yet come to bear or to be borne out, as it were, becomes even more uncanny. His notes continue:

Et Heidegger cite un autre vers, un autre poème (Heiterer Frühling), "Clair printemps":

> Und Ungebornes pflegt der eignen Ruh.
> Et l'ingénéré veille son propre repos.

Cet ingénéré veille et garde (wahrt) l'enfance plus sereine pour l'éveil à venir du Menschengeschlechtes (de l'espèce humaine— ou du sexe à venir). Le jeune mort vit ainsi. Il prévoit, il voit d'avance l'azur de la nuit spirituelle. Les blanches paupières qui protègent son regard brillent dans la parure nuptiale (plutôt d'une épouse) qui promet (verspricht)—tout cela est une méditation sur la promesse . . . qui promet die sanftere Zwiefalt des Geschlechtes, le plus tendre dédoublement du genre, dit la traduction, du sexe aussi, qui promet une différence sexuelle sans dissension.

And Heidegger cites another verse, from another poem ("Heiterer Frühling"), "Cloudless Spring": *Und Ungeborenes pflegt der eignen Ruh*. "And the ungenerated keeps to its proper repose." The ungenerated keep watch over and protect (*wahrt*) the more serene childhood for the coming awakening of the *Menschengeschlecht* (of the human species—or of the sex to come). Thus the young dead one lives. He is clairvoyant, he sees in advance the azure of the spiriting night. His white eyelids, protecting his gaze, shine in the nuptial adornment (which belongs rather to the bride) that promises (*verspricht*).—All of this is a meditation on the promise . . . which pledges *die sanftere Zwiefalt des Geschlechts*, "the more tender doubling of the genre," as the French translation says, but of sex also, promising a sexual difference without dissension.

Derrida says no more about the nuptial adornment—of the bride—in the eyes of the unborn youth. He pursues instead a reflection (unfortunately truncated) on the meaning of "gold" in Trakl's poetry, especially with regard to the *regard*, the gaze, and vision. We also recall that the unlikely *Jünglingin* is envisaged as a "golden" figure. He then notes that the corruption of the disessenced *Geschlecht* does not, historically and temporally considered, come *after* the beginning—that is to say, not after the promised commencement of this new, more matutinal, more incipient *Geschlecht*. Rather, such disessencing *precedes* the commencement of the unborn sex or the unborn generation. Thus the question of the *when?* of the second blow, of the stroke that introduces discord and savagery into the twofold of the sexes, is raised—and immediately frustrated—once again. To think this strange temporality that Heidegger is insisting on (see especially US 57), says Derrida, we would have to rethink both the linearity and the circularity of Aristotelian-Hegelian time. Here Derrida refers to his own "Ousia and Grammè," discussed all too briefly in the Introduction to the present volume.

Derrida now (14–15), leaping far ahead in Heidegger's text, engages the problem of the tension in Heidegger's proscription of all dissemination of meaning—while affirming nonetheless the essential polysemy or *Mehrdeutigkeit* of poetic language. It is here that Heidegger discusses *die ungebornen Enkel*, "the unborn grandchildren," of Trakl's last poem, "Grodek," named after a catastrophic battle early during World War I. The poem concludes in this way: "Oh, prouder mourning! you brazen altars / Spirit's hot flame feeds today on an overwhelming agony, / The unborn grandchildren." *Die ungebornen Enkel*, reads the final line. *Enkel*, says Derrida, is like the Old French *nepos*, which derives from the Greek νήπιος, child, or the young of a litter, which in turn becomes the Modern French *neveu*, "nephew" or "descendant." (Oddly, in English we hear in the German word its relation to *uncle*. In English as well, especially during the seventeenth century, the word *nephew* means more "grandchild" than "nephew." The OED mentions that the word was often a euphemism for the child of a priest: "Shall I call you uncle, father?" asks the little nephew, anxious to please.) The French word too means "progeny" initially, the little ones who come after, long before it comes to mean "nephew." Descartes, for example, uses the word in order to invoke the generations to come. The German word derives from the very odd form *eninchili*, a diminutive form (combining both *-chen* and *-le* or *-ling*) of the late Old High German *ano*, "our" word *Ahn*, or "ancestor," suggesting that the generations to come are in fact tiny reincarnations of the ancestry. *Der Enkel* is the ancestor who has come again, returning as the little one. Hermann Paul notes that the proper meaning of *Enkel* is "Little Grandfather" (HP 163B). Derrida adds a typewritten note: "Neveux: génération sautée," referring perhaps to Heidegger's comments on the skipped generation—inasmuch as those who have fallen in the war will engender no young (US 65: "The *Enkel* mentioned here are by no means the unengendered sons of the sons who have fallen, those who derive from the decomposing *Geschlecht*").

Heidegger's insistence on this "by no means" is something that in *Lunar Voices* I described as shocking, and even today, decades later, the coldness of Heidegger's reasoning disarms me completely. Heidegger writes, "Yet if it were only a matter of the cessation of the continued reproduction of prior *Geschlechter* [*Fortzeugung bisheriger Geschlechter*], then the poet would have to jubilate over such an end." The image of Trakl celebrating the agonies that he, as a medic, was unable to prevent or alleviate, the horrible deaths that surely led to his own suicide, is nothing less than horrific; it reminds one of the harshest aspects of Heidegger's political utterances and deeds of the 1930s, or his silences of the 1950s.[5]

Derrida's response to Heidegger's remark is much more sedate, although the dismay shines through, as we shall now see. Yet there may be something in Derrida's consideration of the words *Enkel* and *neveu* that for him ameliorates Heidegger's remark. Progeny are as such, at least in a sense, always the skipped generation: the child enters on the scene not as the son or daughter of mother and father but as the spittin' image of

---

5. Heidegger's *Black Notebooks* contain passages of this sort. In 1941 he writes that the war will bring about nothing other than the full accomplishment of technology, "the final act of which will be that the earth detonates itself and humanity as we now know it will disappear" (96:238). As though by way of consolation, Heidegger adds, "Yet this is no misfortune, but the first purification *of being* of its most profound disfigurement due to the dominance of beings" (ibid.). Earth exploded and mortals destroyed—for the sake of being's purification. Heidegger's "last god" may jubilate over such pyrification, but Trakl assuredly does not.

its grandparentage. The male child is quite literally the father of the man who is his father, and the female child is the mother of the daughter who is her mother. And so on. Derrida writes:

> Ici H. s'intéresse à ce mot Enkel, pour remarquer que les neveux, les descendants ne sont pas les fils inengendrés des fils tombés à la guerre (lecture courante du poème), ils ne nomment pas dans le poème l'interruption dans la propagation des générations (Geschlechter) car alors, l'espèce étant en voie de corruption, le poète devrait plutôt s'en réjouir (du moins dans la logique que lui prête H.). Il s'agit pour H. d'un "stolzeren Trauer" (d'un deuil plus haut, plus élevé, plus fier, plus altier) qui dans sa flamme regarde la paix de l'ingénéré (die Ruhe des Ungeborenen). Les ingénérés, les inengendrés sont neveux parce qu'ils ne peuvent pas être des fils, c'est à dire des rejetons, des descendants directs, immédiats du "verfallenen Geschlechts," de l'espèce ou du sexe déchu. "Entre eux et cette espèce ou ce sexe (Geschlecht) il y a une autre génération (Generation, cette fois). Elle est autre parce que d'un autre ordre, puisque d'une autre provenance, celle du matin, de l'origine de l'inengendré." (14–15)

> Here Heidegger takes an interest in this word *Enkel,* remarking that the *neveux,* the descendants, are not the unengendered sons of the sons who have fallen in the war (that is the current way of reading the poem); the *Enkel* of the poem do not designate the interruption in the propagation of generations (*Geschlechter*), inasmuch as, because the species is on the path of corruption, the poet would instead have to rejoice over this (at least according to the logic that Heidegger attributes to him). For Heidegger it is a matter of a *stolzeren Trauer* (a higher, more elevated mourning, a prouder, loftier mourning) which in its flame gazes on the peace of the unborn (*die Ruhe des Ungeborenen*). The ungenerated, the unengendered, are descendents because they cannot be born of sons, cannot be offshoots or direct descendents, immediate descendents of the "fallen *Geschlecht,*" of the deposed species or sex. "Between them and this species or sex (*Geschlecht*) there lives another generation (this time: *Generation*). It is other because it is of another order, in accord with its essentially other provenance from the dawn of the unengendered" (US 65–66).

Several paragraphs later (US 67), Heidegger refers to a "coming resurrection of the human *Geschlecht* from out of the dawn." What enables such a resurrection is the skipped generation. Yet the French translation, Derrida notes, refuses to translate *Auferstehung* as "resurrection," which is the only possible sense of the German word. Derrida is surely right in this, but as far as I can see, he neglects to cite Trakl's "sweet song of the resurrected," even though Heidegger's ignoring these lines from Trakl's *Abendländisches Lied,* or "Western Song," invites such a reference. The line occurs in the final strophe of the "Western Song," the very poem in which we find the decisive reference to *E i n Geschlecht*. The final lines of "Abendländisches Lied":

O, die bittere Stunde des Untergangs,
Da wir ein steinernes Antlitz in schwarzen Wassern beschaun.
Aber strahlend heben die silbernen Lider die Liebenden:
E i n *Geschlecht*. Weihrauch strömt von rosigen Kissen
Und der süße Gesang der Auferstandenen. (T 66)

Oh, the bitter hour of downfall,
When we gaze on a stony face in black waters.
Yet radiantly rise the silver eyelids of lovers:
O n e *Geschlecht*. Incense streams from pillows all roses
And the sweet song of the resurrected.

Later on in the course, Derrida will analyze more closely Heidegger's use of this poem, "Abendländisches Lied," and he will not shy from criticism. Yet here it is important for us to note that Heidegger ignores the fact that the "resurrected" are lovers, lovers reclining on pillows, and not some vertically destined boy-girl pair, nor brother and sister, *Geschwisterliches,* not some matutinal transformation of siblings who are regressing to their more serene childhood. Concerning the lovers and the beloved, we recall Heidegger's desire to have the poet leave them behind: this becomes apparent in his interpretation of the line *Schied uns bald von Lieben, Andern,* which we examined in the foregoing chapter. For Heidegger, the "loved ones" are those the poet now scorns, "the others" whom he cannot wait to abandon, inasmuch as they—and not he himself—pertain to the decomposing *Geschlecht*. Yet Derrida does not at this point, or at any point, reject Heidegger's reading outright. He restrains himself and remains close to Heidegger's text. And thus he comes to his startling conclusion—startling, at least, if one has banished psychoanalysis from both commentary and placement—that the sibling relation, even during that more serene childhood, is anything but asexual:

> Ce rassemblement du jeune mort ou de l'ingénéré prépare la résurrection à venir du Geschlecht. Comme esprit de douceur il apaise l'esprit du mal, c'est à dire de cette malfaisance qui atteint son comble dans la dissension (le Zwietracht) des sexes qui vient éclater, faire irruption jusque dans le Geschwisterliche, dans le rapport entre frère et soeur. La dissension sexuelle, la différence sexuelle comme Zwietracht, comme dualité agonistique c'est donc ce qui perturbe une différence sexuelle sereine, celle qui aurait lieu entre frère et soeur avant la malédiction et le mal, la mauvaise flamme de l'esprit. Ce Geschwisterliche, ce rapport entre frère et soeur, ne serait donc pas a-sexué, mais rapport sexuel dans une différence sans dissension.

> This gathering of the young dead man or of the ungenerated prepares the resurrection to come of the *Geschlecht*. As the spirit of gentleness he appeases the spirit of evil, that is, of the malfeasance that reaches its zenith in the dissension (*Zwietracht*) of the sexes which now explodes, intervening even in the relation of siblings (*Geschwisterliche*), the relation between brother and sister. Sexual dissension, sexual difference as discord, as agonistic duality, is that which disturbs a serene sexual difference, that which would take place between brother and sister prior to the curse and prior to evil, the wicked flame of spirit. This *Geschwisterliche*, this relation between brother and sister, is thus not asexual, but is a sexual relation within a difference that is without dissension.

At this point (15), Derrida announces that he will leave the rest of the discussion of brother and sister in Heidegger's essay to the reading of his students. How regrettable! He thus ventures no comment on the strange negotiation in Heidegger's text (US 69–70) whereby the stranger becomes a brother to the brother, and thereby, altogether mysteriously, a brother to the sister, in some way appropriating her or at least claiming to appropriate the lunar voice of the sister, *die mondene Stimme*. (I have developed this problem in *Lunar Voices,* and I will return to it in the final chapter of this volume. Let me here merely add that Heidegger's absorption of girlhood into boyhood displays this same tendency.) Nor does Derrida comment on Heidegger's disturbing neglect of the theme of the lovers in Trakl's poetry; it is as though, under the guise of rescuing the human race, Heidegger forces Trakl's brother and sister back to their ostensibly uncomplicated childhood—which, we may object, may not have been so serene. In other words, the entire question of sexual difference in Trakl's poetry hangs on the story of the *lovers* who establish o n e *Geschlecht*. Whether they do so as brother and sister should therefore be not so much a biographical question as *the* question of Heidegger's "placement," the unasked question of a possible *third* stroke, the question that in Heidegger is reduced to silence. Derrida himself does not broach the possibility of such a third blow, by which discord between the sexes invades the space of brother and sister—perhaps because the third is already implied in the relation of the two strokes to one another. Be that as it may, I would have wanted to ask Derrida whether we might well call the "one" *Geschlecht* of lovers *the* phantom of the other in Heidegger's text.

Yet for the moment we must continue to follow Derrida's seminar notes, which, to repeat, move on to the question of polysemy, that is, the *Mehrdeutigkeit* of poetic language, which Heidegger feels confident he can prevent from becoming dispersion and dissemination of meaning. As we might expect, Derrida is much less confident than Heidegger in this respect. In Derrida's view, developed in pages 16–19 of the notes for this ninth session, Heidegger remains classically Aristotelian in that he will embrace polysemy only if the various meanings of a word are subject to an ordering, a hierarchy, and an ultimate unity. For Heidegger, poetry is *mehrdeutig* but never out of control, never dispersed or scattered: the poetic preserves its "place" at and as the spearpoint, which is never the double-edged sword of meaning but always the singular gathering point, *der Ort,* of the poem. Nothing like dissemination of meaning is available to or accessible in Heidegger's thinking, except as *Heimatlosigkeit* and *Ver-wesung,* homelessness, rootlessness, decomposition, disessencing. There is in every verse of poetry *eine zweideutige Zweideutigkeit,* a redoubled ambiguity, Heidegger concedes, but he will vigorously deny that one of these redoubled couples is a result of the malign stroke, the second blow, the stroke of evil inflicting on all meaning a fatal hemorrhaging.

Allow me to intervene at this early point in the discussion. Whereas Derrida's complaint seems justified with regard to the Heidegger of 1953, matters may be quite different in 1928, or in 1927. When we study once again section 38 of *Being and Time* on *Zweideutigkeit,* "ambiguity," we find that we are left in a far less determinate and identifiable *Ortschaft.* For the ambiguity in which everyday Dasein moves is pervasive, and one does not see how any kind of open resolve, running ahead toward the end of Dasein, could dispel it. Indeed, everything Heidegger says here frustrates our desire to see distraction, dispersion, the craving for novelty, and "falling prey" routed. One of the most radical claims in *Being and Time* is about this irreducible twofoldness of meaning or significance; it is as though Heidegger early on has become a careful reader of Herman Melville's *Pierre; or, The Ambiguities,* in which, incidentally, the brother-sister relation is central to the catastrophe of the plot. Heidegger writes, in lines we examined earlier, "Everything looks as though it were all genuinely understood, grasped, and expressed, and yet at bottom it is not; or it all looks as though this were not so, and at bottom it truly is so" (SZ 173). And this happens not merely to everyday folk who are caught up in dailiness, but also to philosophers who avidly attend conferences and speak their everyday piece there (20:376).

Yet let us return to 1953, and to Derrida's complaint. Is Heidegger truly so confident that the poems of Trakl can be rescued from ambiguity, or from a polysemy that would inhere in the images of Trakl's poetry, causing them to explode across the page: the blood-bespattered linens, dust dancing in the stench of gutters, siblings shivering in the park, the weeping unborn, the sister's mouth whispering among dark twigs? "Autumn Transfigured" says, as we have already heard,

> Wie schön sich Bild an Bildchen reiht—
> Das geht in Ruh und Schweigen unter.
>
> How splendidly image and cameo line up—
> In repose and silence all goes down.

For Heidegger, says Derrida, "this plurality of meaning (*das Mehrdeutige*) of poetic saying does not disperse, does not disseminate, is not scattered to the winds this way and that in an indeterminate polyvalence (*flattert nicht ins unbestimmte Vieldeutige auseinander*). It gathers itself. The plurality gathers, the polysemy converges, and, given this condition, there is a poetic space, a *Gedicht*."[6] For Heidegger, polyphony and polysemy alike rest on a tonic, a *Grundton,* and there is nothing insecure or indeterminate

---

6. "[C]ette pluralité de sens (Mehrdeutige), du dire poétique, ne s'éparpille pas, ne se dissémine pas, ne devient pas éparse dans le vent deci-delà d'une polyvalence indéterminée (flattert nicht ins unbestimmte Vieldeutige auseinander). Elle se rassemble. La pluralité se rassemble, la polysémie converge, et c'est à cette condition qu'il y a un lieu poétique, un Gedicht" (16).

about this *Grundton*. What Heidegger despises most is what he calls (US 75) the insecurity and indeterminacy *des poetischen Umhertastens*, "the gropings of a poetizer" (18). The result of Heidegger's allergy to dissemination, in Derrida's view, is this: "There is a place, a homeland, a poem, and in the end an absolute univocity of language," *il y a un Ort, une patrie, un Gedicht, et finalement une univocité absolue de la langue* (19).

To be sure, Heidegger is forced to distinguish this univocity from the techno-scientific, modern-Cartesian univocity that would reflect a false security in certitude; and so a division into two is necessary. There turns out to be a good univocity and a bad univocity, just as there is a good sexual difference and a bad one, a good *Geschlecht* and a corrupt one. The irony is that in Heidegger's scheme of things sloppy poetizing and exact science wind up on the same side of the line, and this too cannot be good.

Session ten of the seminar continues to follow the good and the bad, the doubling gesture in Heidegger's clarification and placement of Trakl's poetry. Three questions are posed here: (1) whether Heidegger's insistence that Trakl's poetry is beyond Platonism and is unmarked by Christianity can be maintained at all; (2) what happens when Heidegger's German idiom confronts—and is even translated into—the Latinate French; and (3) why the *Ort* must be, for Heidegger, a site of gathering. All these questions have to do with the unsaid of the poem, its tonic or *Grundton*, which for Heidegger is captured in the emphatic *E i n* of *Geschlecht*. The unsaid has to do with a silence that encompasses even the Old and Middle High German, a silence that releases the untranslatable idiom of *Geschlecht*. It also has to do with the double *Schlag* (the strokes of good and evil), and with Trakl's putative non-Christian, non-Platonic status, that is, with the particular "place" or *lieu* of the poet (1–2).

Yet the session now (3–4) takes a surprising turn. Derrida refers to Heidegger *Gesamtausgabe* volume 54:119, where—as we have already heard in chapter 2, on Heidegger's hand—Heidegger talks about the deterioration of writing that has resulted from the use of the typewriter and the dictaphone—the reduction of language to a *Verkehrsmittel* or mode of transportation. The writer dictates to the machine, *"und er diktiert in die Maschine,"* laments Heidegger. Derrida shows that this dictation is the selfsame *dict* of *Gedicht*, and that such a *dict* traces the line of a rapport between German and Latin, which for Heidegger is always a line of corruption and mistranslation. And the putatively singular *Gedicht* of Heidegger's Trakl is encapsulated in the emphatic *Ein* of the *E i n Geschlecht*, the singular place where all *Geschlecht* is gathered, namely, at the "indivisible point of the spear," the *Ort* of Trakl's unspoken and univocal poem. It all comes back to the tension between polysemy and dissemination, the tension between *Mehrdeutigkeit* in the language of poetry and utter *Zerstreuung* with the subsequent loss of meaning. Heidegger would protest that the unifold or *Einfalt* of poetic language, in its gathering, does not reduce meaning to uniformity, but is rich and multifaceted. There has to be a pathbreaking movement, *Be-wegung,* in the poem and in its letter, even if the letter is indivisible and the sound unspoken. Yet to insist on *différance* as *dissémination* would in Heidegger's view be the very death of gathering. Derrida now insists that this is more than a "tension" in *Heidegger's* situation. Rather, both gathering and dissemination pertain to deconstruction itself, especially when deconstruction invokes the phantasmatic:

> S'il n'y avait que du rassemblement, du même, de l'unique, du lieu sans chemin, ce serait la mort sans phrases. Et ce n'est pas ce que veut dire H. puisqu'il insiste aussi sur le mouvement, le chemin de l'étranger, le chemin vers les autres, etc. Il faut donc qu'entre le lieu et le non-lieu, le rassemblement et la divisibilité, les rapports soient autres, une sorte de négociation et de compromis (différance) soit sans cesse en cours qui oblige à refondre la logique implicite qui semble guider H. Dire qu'il y a de la divisibilité ne revient pas non plus à dire qu'il n'y a que de la divisibilité ou de la division (ce serait aussi la mort). La mort guette des deux côtés, du côté du phantasme de l'intégrité du lieu propre et de l'innocence d'une différence sexuelle sans guerre, et du côté opposé, celui d'une impropriété ou d'une expropriation radicale, voire d'une guerre du Geschlecht comme dissension sexuelle. Je ne me sers pas du mot fantasme à la légère, en faisant comme si nous savions déjà grâce à la psychanalyse ce qu'il en est du phantasme. En vérité c'est un des concepts les plus obscurs de ladite psychanalyse. Non, il s'agit au contraire d'élaborer le concept de phantasme à partir de cette "grande logique," de ce que je nomme ici par ironie puisque ce que je veux dire c'est que la grande logique de la philosophie la plus continue, celle qui suppose une extériorité de l'essence et de l'accident, du pur et de l'impur, du propre et de l'impropre, du bien et du mal, cette grande logique . . . reste malgré tout à l'oeuvre, malgré les puissants mouvements déconstructeurs chez Heidegger contre la grande logique hegelienne (voir ce qu'il dit du Logos comme rassemblant). (6–7)

If there were only gathering, the same, the unique, the place without path, then, not to mince words, this would be death. And this is not what Heidegger wants to say, inasmuch as he insists on movement, on the path of the stranger, the path toward the others, and so on. It must be that between place and nonplace, between gathering and divisibility, the relationship is otherwise. There must be a sort of negotiation and compromise (*différance*) that is ceaselessly in play, something that would oblige us to reconstitute the implicit logic that appears to guide Heidegger. To say that there is divisibility does not come down to saying that there is only divisibility or division. (This too would be death.) Death lies in wait on both sides, with the phantasm of the integrity of the proper place and the innocence of a sexual difference without war, and also on the opposite side, that of impropriety or radical expropriation, or of a war of *Geschlecht* as sexual dissension. I do not use the word *phantasm* lightly here, as though thanks to psychoanalysis we already knew what is phantasmatic about all this. In truth, the phantasm is one of the most obscure concepts in psychoanalysis. No, on the contrary, what this involves is our elaborating the concept of phantasm by taking as our point of departure the "grand logic," a term I am using ironically here, because what I want to say is that the most continuous grand logic of philosophy is in spite of everything still at work here, the grand logic that presupposes an exteriority between essence and accident, pure and impure, proper and improper, good and evil, remaining still at work in spite of Heidegger's powerfully deconstructive movements against the grand logic of Hegel. (Observe what he says of the Logos as gathering.)

I take that final parenthetical remark to be referring to Heidegger's "Logos" essay, which is all about *Versammlung*, although there would surely be occasions, in Hegel's lesser or greater *Logics,* where the concept gathers all difference into its *besitzergreifenden* grasp. Heidegger concedes the plurivocity of Trakl's *Grundton*, the plurivocity of its consonance or *Einklang,* and he even admits that Trakl has to borrow words and images from the representational world (*Vorstellungswelt*) of Christianity, "*Worte, die zur biblischen und kirchlichen Vorstellungswelt gehören,*" says Heidegger (US 75). Yet Heidegger insists that this polysemy can be reduced and the Platonic-Christian residues expunged when it comes to identifying the *place* of Trakl's poem. Heidegger appears to be very prudent and very cautious, yet ultimately he claims that his own thinking back or thinking toward (*Nachdenken*) the place of Trakl's poem cannot take up in any positive way "Christian" notions, whatever these may be (8).

Perhaps a caveat is in order here. If I am right, it is not that Derrida wants to restore Trakl to a place within the various Christian or Platonic traditions; it is rather that he wants to challenge Heidegger's confidence that any *Nachdenken* can control the effects of polysemy and plurivocity. It is this lack of prudence on Heidegger's part that disturbs Derrida, with its dogmatism and its potential or actual violence. When Trakl ends a poem he calls "Psalm" with the line, *Schweigsam über die Schädelstätte öffnen sich Gottes goldene Augen,* "Silently over the Place of the Skull open God's golden eyes," we do not know what the silence over Golgotha and those feline eyes might mean. If this is a psalm, and it is, its first line says, *Es ist ein Licht, das der Wind ausgelöscht hat,* "It is a light that the wind has extinguished." It is hard to read in the dark. That is perhaps all that Derrida wants to affirm at the moment. Yet he will soon go much farther, if only in the dark.

Heidegger's is a plurivocity he feels he can dominate by force of a gathering, *une plurivocité dominable, rassemblable.* Whence the power of such dominion? It arises from Heidegger's confidence in the purity and mutual exclusion of opposites, the confidence that Nietzsche's analysis of the first great error or prejudice of metaphysics (*Beyond Good and Evil,* sections 2, 24, and elsewhere) ought to have subverted forever. Heidegger's strategy of distinguishing the two strokes, the good from the evil, thus seems to be entirely dependent on at least one strand of the Christian-Platonic tradition. The place of malediction or curse, and the place of the corruption of our *Geschlecht,* the place that Heidegger claims to be able to identify, will in fact be the place that has produced the tradition of metaphysics and morals. What Heidegger is claiming is that he has insight into a more originary ground or founding moment, one that is not radically dependent on the corrupted form. It is the claim to this more originary repetition that causes Derrida to doubt, the claim that seems to him, if one may understate the matter, "problematic" (9). Derrida goes to considerable lengths to show why Heidegger's insistence that Trakl is not *ein so entschiedener Christ,* not "so decidedly Christian" (US 76), is "coarse," if not *grossière* and basically "crude." In any case, no matter how one may judge Trakl's relation to past traditions, Heidegger here loses every sense of plurivocity (10–12). It is demonstrably true that in his penultimate poem, "Lament," Trakl invokes not the Christ but the sister who greets the dead heroes on the battlefield. According to Heidegger, this shows that he is not a "decided Christian." Trakl seems, although neither Heidegger nor Derrida traces the allusion, to be closer to some sort of Wagnerian or Nordic invocation of the Valkyrie. Derrida nevertheless assures his students that if they would grant him a bit of time he could show them that the figure of the sister and that of Christ could in fact be substituted, or set in alternation, the one for the other. He means this not flippantly, but "gravely," "in fear and trembling." Derrida, in fact, takes that time, and we ought to take the time to follow his demonstration. For, if earlier I lamented Derrida's decision to leave the remainder of this theme (brother and sister, or brother-sister-lovers) to his students, as though he had no more to say about it, the following remarks on what might otherwise be called a matter of theology respond in an astonishing way to my lament. For the sister and a certain Christ seem to meld, says Derrida,

> Et précisément dans le corpus, si je puis dire, de Trakl. Comment déterminer le sexe du Christ et comment caractériser, dans la différence sexuelle, l'expérience proprement chrétienne, décidément chrétienne, qu'un homme (à supposer que T. soit un homme, décidément un homme, onesidedly a man, comme un de ses commentateurs a osé dire de Joyce) ou une femme a du rapport au Christ? Fils de Dieu, le Christ est frère de tous les hommes et de toutes les femmes, en même temps qu'il est l'image ou l'intercesseur du père. Mais un frère dont la virilité n'est jamais simplement manifeste ou unilatérale, un frère qui se présente dans une aura d'homosexualité universelle, ou dans un différence sexuelle apaisée, pacifiée (tendre, dirait justement Trakl), hors des moments de tentatation où le mal est tout proche, un frère donc qui n'est peut-être pas autre qu'une soeur. Et d'un fils né d'une vierge elle-même née d'une immaculée conception, la détermination sexuelle ne peut être assez assurée pour qu'on puisse dire tranquillement: là où le poète nomme la soeur à la place du Christ, il ne nomme pas le Christ, il n'est pas chrétien plus, son poème n'est pas chrétien. C'est d'autant plus impossible ou précipité que H. lui-même ne manque pas de prêter attention à ce couple étrange du frère et de la soeur dans les poèmes de Trakl. Je dis couple parce qu'il témoigne d'une différence sexuelle qui, pour n'être pas encore ou déjà plus celle de la guerre ou de la dissension, de la différence

sexuelle comme antagonisme (Zwietracht), n'est pourtant pas sans désir, au sens où Hegel disait (à propos d'Antigone) que le rapport entre frère et soeur était begierdelos: peut-être sans désir manifeste dans l'espace où le désir fait la guerre, après le deuxième coup, mais non sans désir tendre, rapport à l'autre comme double homosexualité, réflexion sans appropriation du désir de l'autre où le frère devient la soeur et la soeur le frère, etc. Et qui peut tranquillement affirmer que ce n'est pas là l'essence du rapport au Christ, l'essence ou du moins la destination, la destinée qui se cherche, ce vers quoi est chemin, toute expérience chétienne de la sainte famille, voire de la famille tout court? (cf. Glas: je ne me permets de citer ce titre que parce que c'est au moment de la mort de Tr. que H. rappelle à ceux qui font de Tr. un chrétien que celui-ci aurait dû parler du Christ et de Dieu et non de la soeur, soeur qui est toujours la soeur à la voix de lune (mondene Stimme, la voix sélénique comme dit la traduction), voix de lune qui résonne dans la nuit spirituelle, comme le disent les derniers vers (eschaton [?] aussi) de *Geistliche Dämmerung* (figure eschatologique de la soeur). Cette figure sélénique de la soeur (l'eschaton, la lumière nocturne qui salue, etc.) est-elle si étrangère à la figure du Christ? Et le Christ, comme la soeur, est-ce une figure dont le sens soit si décidable? (14–15)

And this, if I may say so, precisely in the corpus of Trakl. How are we to determine the sex of Christ and how are we to characterize, within sexual difference, the experience that is properly Christian, decidedly Christian, the experience that a man (supposing Trakl is a man, decidedly a man, "one-sidedly a man," as a commentator once dared to say of Joyce) or a woman has by way of a relation to Christ? Son of God, Christ is the brother of all men and all women; he is simultaneously the image or the intercessor of the father. Yet he is a brother whose virility is never simply manifest or unilateral, a brother who presents himself within an aura of universal homosexuality, or in a sexual difference that has been appeased, pacified (or tender, as none other than Trakl would say), beyond all the moments of those temptations where evil is quite close, thus a brother who can be nothing other than a sister. And if it is a matter of a son born of a virgin herself born by way of an immaculate conception, the sexual determination cannot be adequately assured to the point where one could say quite tranquilly that wherever the poet names the sister instead of Christ both he and his poem are no longer Christian. That is all the more impossible, all the more precipitous, given the fact that Heidegger himself does not fail to draw attention to the strange couple of the brother and the sister in Trakl's poems. I say "couple" because the word testifies to a sexual difference that, even though it is no longer or not yet a difference of war or dissension, that is, sexual difference as antagonism (*Zwietracht*), is nevertheless not without desire. Hegel says (with regard to Antigone) that the rapport of brother and sister is without desire, *begierdelos*: perhaps it is without manifest desire, in that space where desire instigates war, desire after the second blow, yet it is not without tender desire as a rapport with the other, a double homosexuality, a reflection of desire without an appropriation of the other, a desire in which the brother becomes the sister or the sister becomes the brother, and so on. And who may tranquilly assert that this is not the essence of a relation to Christ, the essence or at least the destination, the destined end that is sought, the destiny toward which one is under way, the entire Christian experience of the Holy Family, which is to say, of any and every family?—See *Glas*, which I allow myself to cite only because Heidegger reminds all those who make of Trakl a Christian that it is precisely at the moment of Trakl's death that that he ought to have invoked Christ and God, not the sister, the sister who is always the sister of the lunar voice (*die mondene Stimme*, the Selenic voice, as the French translation says), the voice of the moon that resounds in the spiriting night, as the final lines (themselves also the ἔσχατον [?]) of *Geistliche Dämmerung* say, the eschatological figure of the sister. Is this Selenic figure of the sister (the ἔσχατον, the nocturnal light that greets, etc.) so entirely foreign to the figure of Christ? And is the Christ, like the sister, a figure whose meaning is so decidable?

The reference to *Glas*, the death knell, is striking here, and one could and should spend a great deal more time tracing the theme of the

Magdalene, "the sister," who anoints the feet of the one who is about to die.[7] For the moment we simply observe how readily Trakl's poetry invites interpretation, by way of Heidegger, to both a psychoanalytic sense of phantasm *and* a theological sense of the Christian life as a redoubled homosexuality. True, this is not a Christianity that would do well in the Bible Belt; yet it is one that might help us to understand the virulence and the violence of that Belt. Clearly, the strange "couple," brother and sister, *sol et luna,* is a theme that invites endless interpretation, a theme that is "strange" in its origins and unpredictable in its consequences.

Derrida concludes this session by saying that Heidegger's confidence is perhaps most surprising when at the end of this part of his discussion he contrasts the usual appeals to "Christian redemption" to Trakl's own reference to "the unborn grandchildren." Why the sister? asks Heidegger. Derrida replies to Heidegger's question, but why *not* the sister? especially if she is not so decisively opposable to Christ? "Especially if, in the end, a poem does something other than translate in a decidable manner the univocal thought or experience of a poet. . . . And, above all else, [if] both he and his poem may be Christian without being Christian, or without knowing it, or without wanting it."[8] Derrida repeats here Heidegger's phrase, as though struck by its naïveté or its dogmatism, *ein so entschiedener Christ,* and he enters a marginal note: "Foi = [and the rest of the note not even the archivists can decipher!]."[9] Trakl, in his "Lament," refers to die eisige Woge / Der Ewigkeit, the icy wave of eternity that may devour the golden image of humankind. Heidegger asks, "Is that thought in a Christian way?" Derrida replies, in a manner that seems at first to be merely flippant, *"eh bien oui, pourquoi pas."* It would certainly not be the Christianity of blind faith, and certainly not the faith professed in the Belt or taught *ex cathedra* anywhere. Yet Derrida, the last Jew, is surely right when he stubbornly avers, "In any case, one does not see in the name of what one can decide that it is not, at least not without some other sort of process." When Heidegger, equally stubborn, concludes by saying, "It

---

7. Allow me to refer to chapter 7, "Knell," of Krell, PB, esp. 157–68.

8. "Enfin surtout si un poème fait autre chose que traduire de manière décidable la pensée ou l'expérience univoque d'un poète. . . . Surtout il peut, lui ou le poème, être chrétien sans l'être ou sans le savoir ou sans le vouloir" (16).

9. Michael Naas would no doubt tell us that this is a reference to what will become "Faith and Reason." See Naas, *Miracle and Machine: Jacques Derrida and the Two Sources of Religion, Science, and the Media* (New York: Fordham University Press, 2012).

is not even Christian despair [*christliche Verzweiflung*]," Derrida objects: Why suppose that Christian despair (whatever that is) should remain identifiably Christian if it *is* despair? Why suppose that it preserves its identity as Christian? Perhaps when the Christian despairs—and Derrida ventures to say that we could probably find lots of evidence for this in the literature—what he or she despairs of is the ability to recognize the putative form of Christian despair in his or her own despair. "The Christian despairs of Christianity, or he does not truly despair."[10] A Shiite has never despaired of Christianity, remarks Derrida, but neither has a Christian, to the extent that he or she despairs in forms that are identifiably Christian—again, whatever that could possibly mean.

At this point Derrida enters a parenthesis: "le *Zwei* de *Verzweiflung*, cf. Hegel: doute: deux . . ." This is clearly a reference to *Verzweiflung* as the path of despair that natural consciousness takes, unable, as weak skepticism, to distinguish between what is foreign and what is its own in all its notions, thoughts, and opinions (PG 67–68). To weak skepticism, Hegel opposes a skepticism that goes all the way, taking the turn to self-consciousness, reason, and spirit as absolute knowing. Perhaps what Derrida wants to identify in the twofold of *Ver-zwei-flung* is the phantasm of a double blow or stroke in which one of the two can be clearly identified as the good, the other as evil. Such a phantasm would surely embrace a *Mehrdeutigkeit* that nonetheless resists the dissemination of meaning and the predicament of undecidability. Christian despair—or whatever can be clearly said to be *not even* Christian despair—would surely for Derrida be one of those undecidables. Yet not only the twofolds and the doublings are confounding; so, likewise, are the unities, univocities, and the ones. At the end of this session Derrida promises to take up the *Ein* of *E i n Geschlecht* in the third—and quite brief—part of Heidegger's "Die Sprache im Gedicht."

In the course of the eleventh séance, Derrida takes a detour from the Trakl text and its "placement" of the poem (3-4). He turns instead to the problem of Heidegger's references to Hölderlin's *vaterländische Umkehr*, to that poet's ostensible return late in his active life to his "fatherland" and to the very notion of homeland or *Heimat*, especially as Heidegger develops the theme in the "Letter on Humanism." There Heidegger speaks of *Heimat*, as he himself says, in a way that is "*nicht patriotisch, nicht nationalistisch*." Derrida points out the irony: on the one hand, this is a clear

---

10. "Le chrétien désespère du christianisme ou alors il ne désespère pas vraiment" (16–17).

condemnation of all chauvinistic identifications with a fatherland, and yet, on the other hand, because Heidegger uses these Latin-based words (*patriotisch* and *nationalistisch*) pejoratively, he demonstrates his unshakable faith in "our language" and his fear and suspicion of, or contempt for, all Latinate and Mediterranean forms. All pejoration in Heidegger, claims Derrida, occurs in Roman, Latinate forms; all affirmation and celebration occur in Germanic forms, especially archaic German forms. Even if he claims to be speaking in terms of the history of being, a history and a being that encompass all, or at least everything and everyone that is of the Land of Evening, Heidegger will always and everywhere identify inadequate modes of discourse and thought as Latinate. One must say, although Derrida does not do so here, that this is more true in 1953 than in 1928: at the very time (after World War II) when one expects and wishes that Heidegger will become more open to the "foreign," his reversion to Germanic forms intensifies.[11]

But to continue with Derrida's account. Heidegger rejects, as does Hölderlin, *den Egoismus des Volkes*—the "egoism" once again in Latin. Also in the case of Trakl, says Heidegger, it is always a matter of the Land of Evening, *das Abendland,* and not of the Occident, not of the *regio* or the *régionale,* never anything Latin but always and everywhere the Old and Middle High German (4). Likewise, the Levant is never relevant for Heidegger's thinking. Unlike Hölderlin, for whom an "Orientalizing" of the Greek is absolutely essential, Heidegger never refers to *l'Orient,* but, with the possible exception of "The Anaximander Fragment," always to *dem Abendland,* what others might call *le Couchant.* (The very thought of Heidegger referring to the *le Couchant* is enough to make us smile—it is as though one were confusing Heidegger with Lacan.) Thus it is that Heidegger reverts to the discourse of Fichte, which Derrida considered in some detail in *Geschlecht II,* for which "German" means "human," but only if "human" be uttered as *Menschheit* or *das Menschengeschlecht.*

This inflation of the German language in the direction of humankind as a whole, as we have seen, is not altogether foreign to Husserl's

---

11. I recall one of the principal interpreters of Heidegger's thought in Germany telling me—many years ago now—with enthusiastic approbation how Heidegger's later thinking expunges all the Latinate expressions that we find in *Being and Time,* evidence that Heidegger's thinking was becoming more and more his own, rejecting the foreign influences of metaphysics and even phenomenology. This was the same conversation in which that interpreter, referring to the edition of Nietzsche's works being prepared at that time by Giorgio Colli and Mazzino Montinari in Weimar, wondered aloud what those "damned Italians" were doing to Nietzsche's text. I shuddered as I left his office.

gesture in the *Crisis of the European Sciences*. Germany and the Western world as such take themselves to mean and to be *humanity* (5). Similarly, for Heidegger, thinking pursues the history of being, history understood as *Geschichte*, quite beyond the representational *Historie* that superficially recounts tales of various world regions through time. Thus Heidegger rejects the "cosmopolitanism" of eighteenth-century figures such as Goethe. That is why Hölderlin's relation to the Greeks surpasses that of Goethe and Winckelmann, and is putatively in direct touch with the matutinal event of Greek thinking. Heidegger adds a remark to his "Letter on Humanism" to the effect that the "young Germans" during the war who "knew of Hölderlin" faced death differently than the way prescribed by the public sphere of "German opinion," meaning clearly that of the Third Reich. Derrida adds the simple self-instruction: *Commenter*. His commentary would certainly have developed the double edge of Heidegger's claim: one resists the official "German opinion" only by achieving a still more German understanding of life and death, an understanding for which Hölderlin, he who reverts to the presumptive fatherland, is the principal architect, not to say *Bauleiter*.

Derrida now returns to the question of *Abgeschiedenheit*, "apartness" or "departedness," as the place of Trakl's poem. The word is translated by the French edition of Heidegger's text as le *Dis-cès*. Not decease or death is the desired sense, but departure (7). The *Ort* is therefore not a stable place, but a departing, a going down, a being under way. The double sense of the word *partage* fits here, inasmuch as it designates both a sharing in and a departing from. The third and final part of Heidegger's essay has to do with the *Ortschaft* of this *Ort*, and it reflects this sense of *partage*. The *Ort* is the *pays* of promise. Promise, *Versprechen*, accompanies this *Ortschaft*, at least in the performative if not constative evidence of Heidegger's text. "Our language," *unsere Sprache*, calls this "place" in which we "dwell" (*Wohnen*) *das Land* (8). But it is the land at eventide, *das Abend-Land*. Heidegger makes no reference to eventide in other languages and idioms, to *le soir, la sera, la tarde*—the last stemming from *tard*, "late," from the Sanskrit *sr*, meaning *aller, suivre, se suivre*, which would conform perfectly to what Heidegger himself says of Trakl's "spiriting year." Nevertheless, Heidegger makes no reference to these Gallo-Latinate roots, even though his education equipped him for such references, at least in the Latin. Heidegger is said to have admired the French word *garde, garder*, but that, says Derrida, is probably because it comes from the German *warten*, related to *wahr*.

If I may insert a remark. It is not as though Derrida is "hurt" that Heidegger ignores the French language or any other Latinate tongue, nor "irate" that Heidegger seems to despise the magnificent Mediterranean, apparently unaware that the Aegean is a corner of it. It is more a kind of astonishment that Heidegger can be so insensitive to words and phrases that would work so well for what he is trying to think. That is, if the entire family of Sanskrit languages were drawn into his ken—to say nothing of languages farther east and south, or farther west and south—this could only enrich, not vulgarize, the matter of his thinking. And it might prevent, or at least minimize, the danger of a certain naive assurance concerning what is one's own and what is foreign. For it often seems that even though Heidegger reads and interprets Hölderlin's letter to Böhlendorff he is utterly unable to make Hölderlin's devotion to the foreign a part of his life. For Derrida himself, having arrived in Europe from another cape, another continent, devoted as he nonetheless is to the French language almost to the point of monolinguism, the world of languages is larger and more full of surprises, good surprises, than it can ever be for Heidegger. Ultimately, Heidegger's limitation is not offensive, but baffling. And sad.

The Evening Land is to be thought in terms of a new beginning, a promise, even though Heidegger here offers very little detail about this *Versprechen* (11–12). Rather, promise works as a performative in his discourse, and is related to many words that do populate his discourse: *Ruf, Entscheidung, Verheissen,* and so on, "the call," "decision," a "pledging" and a "calling" that are very much a promising. There is surely a sense of *le don* in the *Es gibt* (which Derrida does not mention here, but on which he has commented extensively elsewhere) and in the *Schickung des Seins, das Gewähren von Zeit und Sein, das Ereignis,* and so on, "the sending of being," "the granting of time and being," and "the propriative event." Such donation, Derrida observes, often has to do with the discourse of the hand in Heidegger. As we saw in chapter 2, promise lies in the hand of Heidegger, as it were, especially in the book *Was heisst Denken?* There the discourse of *heissen* and *Verheissung* is omnipresent. In the second Trakl essay, "Die Sprache im Gedicht," the *Abendland* is said to be "earlier," more matutinal, richer in future, and as such "more promising," *versprechender,* than our corrupt present—in other words, "closer to the morning to come, because older than the old morning," *"plus près du matin à venir parce que plus vieux du matin ancien,"* meaning by the latter the old "Platonic-Christian" morning (13). Is this a cycle, asks Derrida, or is the cyclical absent from Heidegger? "I do not think it is absent," replies Derrida, and then, as a note to self: *"Dessiner cercle au tableau?"* One must wonder what the eternal return of the same, reinterpreted through the eyes of Heidegger's Trakl, would have looked like as a diagram on the board! At all events, the *Abendland* is also *Anbeginn*, "commencement," so that if there is circularity in Heidegger's thinking of history it is not the eternal return of the same in any of its usual interpretations. It is rather the hoped-for return of what was—somewhere, somehow, perhaps among the oldest sages of Greece—reserved for the West, *vorbehalten*, promised but never achieved, never received, never carried to full term, never *ausgetragen*. Thus the apparent paradox of the placement (*Erörterung*) as both a gathered sameness and a departure, both a convocation and a separation.

Derrida does not hesitate to say (and, as we have seen, he will elaborate on this at the end of *De l'esprit*) that both Christians and Jews might well be happy to latch onto this moment of Heidegger's thinking as the affirmation of some sort of "messianism" or even eschatology—the West in transition to its matutinal essence. However, Derrida concludes this session instead with a reference to the *Übergang* that is represented by Nietzsche's *Übermensch*, which Heidegger himself cites in *What Is Called Thinking?* It is the transition that promises a humankind that is no longer captivated by the "grasp" of reason—the *Ver-nehmen* of *Vernunft*—which still, as Heidegger says, thinks humanity on the basis of bestiality. One notes throughout Derrida's 1984–85 course anticipations of the "thread" that in the 1987 *Of Spirit* he will call "the essence of animality." It will never be absent from his thought after that, all the way up to his very last seminar in 2002–03. And, as he would insist, it will never have been absent even before that.

Perhaps this is the right moment to take up once again the *promise* of the "more gentle twofold," not as Heidegger envisages it, but as Derrida himself *dreams* of it. For it is clear that the entire *Geschlecht* series is magnetized by such a promise—the promise of a radically different sexuality for the future of humankind. It is not too much to say that if Heidegger were not promising such a thing, or at least not dreaming of such a promise, Derrida would not be reading Heidegger's 1953 Trakl essay with such fervor. Although Derrida is reluctant to speak here of the promise as he himself sees it, focused as he is on Heidegger, he is eloquent about it in his correspondence with Christie V. MacDonald, which we cited much earlier, back in chapter 1. Derrida concludes that correspondence by referring to the possibility of a loving relation that is not marked by the codes of traditional gender and sexual discriminations. He asks:

> Would it be a relation, then, that is not asexual—very far from it—but is otherwise sexualized, beyond the binary difference that governs the decorum of all codes, a relation beyond the

opposition feminine/masculine and therefore also beyond bisexuality, beyond homosexuality or heterosexuality, which come to the same? Because I dream of rescuing at least the chance to pose such a question, I want to believe in the multiplicity of sexually marked voices, in an indeterminable number of interwoven voices, in the mobility of unidentified sexual marks whose choreography can lead the body of each "individual," traversing it, dividing it, multiplying it, whether that body is classed as "man" or "woman" according to the criteria of usage. Surely it is not impossible that this desire for an innumerable sexuality may come to protect us, like a dream, against an implacable destiny that immures us all in perpetuity within the number 2. And should such pitiless closure, fight against it as we may, arrest our desire and pin us against the wall of opposition, insisting that there will always be only two sexes, neither one more nor one less, the tragedy would be our developing a taste for this opposition, which at bottom is altogether contingent; the tragedy would be that we might be forced to affirm and love the contingency, instead of dreaming of the innumerable. Yes, perhaps; why not? Whence the "dream" of the innumerable, if it is a dream? Does not the dream, all by itself, demonstrate that of which it is dreaming, that which is there precisely in order to make us dream? And so, I ask you, what would be the dance? Would there be any dance at all if one didn't exchange the sexes for an indeterminate number, and if one didn't exchange the law of the sexes for many variable rhythms? In a quite rigorous sense, the word *exchange* clearly will not suffice, however, because the desire remains one of escaping from the single combinatory and inventing incalculable choreographies.[12]

During the questioning period that followed his presentation at the University of Essex in May 1986 Derrida was asked whether, concerning a particular point under discussion, he wasn't "dreaming." He replied, his voice rising in a fit of humorous passion, "Of course I'm dreaming—one

---

12. See *Points of Suspension,* 114–15. The passage is terribly difficult to translate. I am grateful for Christie V. MacDonald's translation, which here and there I have altered, however. My thanks too to Michael Naas for his assistance.

has to dream, you can't stop dreaming!" He took a breath or two and his voice lowered to a more subdued tone, not jaded but wise to the world: "But I try not to dream all the time." We return now from dreams to the phantom of the other.

In session twelve of "The Phantom of the Other," Derrida once again focuses on the emphatic or spaced-type (*gesperrt gedruckt*) phrase *E i n Geschlecht* and to the ostensibly double *Schlag* of *Geschlecht*. He finds Heidegger's exceedingly sparse quotation from Trakl's "Abendländisches Lied" highly problematic, and he objects to Heidegger's "audacious" interpretation of the punctuation in the poem. These would be instances in which Heidegger's "commentary" on a particular poem is distorted by his confidence in a "placement." Heidegger emphasizes the importance of two appearances of a colon in Trakl's poem. The first line, in which both "soul" and "blow" or "stroke" appear, reads, *O der Seele nächtlicher Flügelschlag:* ("Oh, the soul's nocturnal wing beat:"). Heidegger says that what follows this colon (*Doppelpunkt, deux points*), which is to say all the rest of the twenty-two-line poem, is an explication of the colon itself—its "wingstroke," as it were. Twenty-one lines of poetry follow, full of punctuation, commas, semicolons, and periods, but Heidegger ignores them all. Then, in the antepenultimate line of the poem, the second colon appears, and after it, in the penultimate line: *E i n Geschlecht*. This is the *one* that has gathered Heidegger's interpretation from the outset, and the *Geschlecht* that has gripped Derrida for a decade. Derrida gives himself instructions to use the blackboard:

Tableau[:]
O der Seele nächtlicher Flügelschlag:
20 vers
............................................ :
E i n Geschlecht............

The generous spacing between the lines indicates how parsimonious Heidegger has been with his quotation. More disconcerting still is the fact that Heidegger also neglects to cite the line that precedes the second colon, whereas Derrida takes pains to present it: *"Aber strahlend heben die silbernen Lider die Liebenden: . . ."* (In an alternative translation to the one I ventured earlier, "But radiantly the lovers raise their silvery eyelids: . . ."). This reference to the *lovers* would of course be crucial for the ways in which the first words of the next line, "*E i n Geschlecht*," would be heard, crucial for whether one hears *Geschlecht* as generation, tribe, lineage, sex, the "house" of brother and sister, the embrace of lovers, and so on. To emphasize the colon and yet to ignore the embrace of lovers, whose wing beat (*Doppelpunkt, deux points*) leads directly to the unifying One, "lovers: / One . . . ," seems a bizarre way to "comment" on the poem. The *E i n* is *betont*, Heidegger says, and that means not merely emphasized but "intoned," "sung," as Heidegger says all poetry must be. This *one* is the *Grundton* of Trakl's poetry. Yet Heidegger does not say exactly that. He says: "*Es ist, soweit ich sehe, das einzige gesperrt geschriebene Wort in den Dichtungen Trakls.*" "It is, as far as I can see, the only word in the poems of Trakl that is written in spaced type." Spacing is therefore of the essence. For his part, Derrida makes no reference here to the space of writing or to spacing as such. Yet he notes the way Heidegger leaps from colon to colon, skipping not only twenty lines of verse but also the very word to which the second colon is attached, and he comments, rather dryly: "That may appear to be exorbitant, like a leap of the eye (*Blicksprung*), a leap of interpretation with one stroke of the wing. These are impressive strokes of wing and eye." ("*Cela peut paraître exorbitant, comme coup d'oeil (Blicksprung), comme saut d'interprétation d'un coup d'aile. Il y a là un coup d'aile et un coup d'oeil impressionants*" (4). Thus, the word *Schlag* continues to operate in Heidegger's discourse with regard to both *Geschlecht* as such and its "situation" in Trakl's poetry—or, better, in Heidegger's own "placement" of it. A placement from which the lovers are absent.

Why are they absent? Are they absent because they represent the innocents of the first stroke, or are they the quarrelsome pair of the second stroke? Or are they indeed the victims of the malignant "third" stroke, none of which Heidegger ever defines or determines as such? Derrida does not pose these questions in the manner I have asked them here. Yet his bitingly critical reading of Heidegger's interpretation of Trakl's "Western Song" invites them.

Heidegger also uses the word *bergen,* to safeguard and conceal, in order to say that the tonic of Trakl's poem is hidden and inaudible in this spacing of the *E i n. Das Gedicht schweigt,* and so remains secretive. Derrida's text (5), for its part, interweaves German and French constantly in order to show the untranslatable, idiomatic character of both languages, and the "spacing" that is involved in the writing of each. "*Die Einheit des einen Geschlechtes entquillt dem Schlag . . .*" Derrida comments: "*donc ce coup qui rassemble (versammelt) le Zwietracht der Geschlechter, la dissension des sexes ou des genres, simplement, de façon simple (einfältig) dans le tendre, le plus tendre (sanftere) Zwiefalt.*'" If one is permitted to put Derrida's French into some kind of English (although that would be merely to re-mark the spaces between the German and French), one might say: "Thus the stroke that gathers (*versammelt*) the *Zwietracht der Geschlechter* [the discord of the sexes], the dissension of the sexes or genders, does so simply, in a simple fashion (*einfältig*), into the tender, more tender (*sanftere*) *Zwiefalt*." Perhaps it is time to note that it is this "simple fashion," this ostensible onefold of simplicity, that Derrida resists from the very beginning of his research and writing. In the publication notice to his edition of Husserl's *Origin of Geometry,* Derrida indicates the problem that he has with the "origin" and "the simple." He speaks of "an originary complication of the origin, an initial contamination of the simple" (BP 93). When Heidegger envisages a more gentle *simplicity* for the twofold of the sexes, the gesture can only disquiet Derrida, now as then. He continues for the next several pages of his lecture notes to read Heidegger's text quite closely, interweaving the German and the French, now focusing on the *Schlag* as *coup* or *frappe,* as stroke or blow, but also as coinage and lineage, *souche* (in the sense of a genealogical line), which is the word that the French translation always prefers—in order thus to obfuscate the reference to sexuality. Even in France, or especially in France, one will have wanted all along to say that, no, Heidegger says really nothing about sexuality.

> Le coup, ou la souche, der Schlag est donc ce qui rassemble (et donc constitue le lieu), qui rassemble simplement, dans la simplicité (einfältig), la dissension (la dualité agonistique) dans la dualité douce et tendre. Le coup rassemble le Zwietracht en Zwiefalt. Il est donc le coup, il frappe entre deux fois deux, deux dualités ou différences du Geschlecht (deux différences sexuelles, mais non seulement sexuelles et la signification de sexualité est ici enveloppée dans la polysémie du Geschlecht. C'est peut-être quand elle s'en sépare et se détermine comme seulement sexuelle que le Zwietracht apparaît, et la guerre des sexes. C'est cette simplicité et cette douceur de la différence qui s'annonce comme le futur ou le très ancien dans le départ ou le dis-cès, par delà l'occident platonico-chrétien. Cette douce différence, en tant qu'elle tient à un coup, ou aussi bien à une souche en tant qu'elle est un empreinte. Cette empreinte frappe le un—l'unité du un dans les deux—et l'on va voir que le un ne s'oppose pas au deux, à vrai dire ne s'en distingue même pas. On doit dire aussi, bien que ce ne soit pas le propos explicite de H., que cette frappe de l'un dans le Geschlecht est aussi la

frappe du mot qui rassemble dans l'un et dans l'unité rassemblante du mot Geschlecht cette multiplicité de significations, dont tous les coups viennent en une seule marque, un seul mot, mot qui dit aussi le rassemblement (Ge-) sceller leur consonnance. (6)

The stroke or lineage, *der Schlag*, is thus that which gathers (and therefore constitutes the place). It gathers simply, into simplicity (*einfältig*), the dissension (the agonistic duality) into the gentle and tender duality. The stroke gathers the *Zwietracht* into a *Zwiefalt*. It is thus the stroke that beats two times two, two dualities or differences of *Geschlecht,* two sexual differences, albeit not only sexual, and the signification of sexuality is enveloped here in the polysemy of *Geschlecht*. It is perhaps when the sexual sense separates itself and determines itself as only sexual that discord appears, discord and the war of the sexes. It is the simplicity and the tenderness of the difference that is announced as the future of what is very old in the departure or the *dis-cès,* moving beyond the Platonic-Christian Occident. This gentle difference, insofar as it is tied up with a stroke, and also because it is bound up with a lineage, is an imprint. This imprint coins the one—the unity of the one into the two—and we come to see that the one is not opposed to two, and, truth to tell, cannot even be distinguished from it. One may also say, although this is not what Heidegger has explicitly in mind, that this stroke of one within the *Geschlecht* also coins the word that gathers into one, into the very gathering unity of the word *Geschlecht,* its multiple significations, from which, in one single mark, all the strokes come, one single word, a word which itself says gathering (*Ge-*), signing and sealing their consonance.

The "one" of the "onefold" or the "simplicity" of the more tender twofold is of course not meant arithmetically, and it has nothing to do with *Vorhandenheit* or objective, representational thinking. It is not a question of unisex or of vulgar, crass indifference, nor of androgyny or hermaphroditism. Heidegger is pointing toward an altogether other experience of sexual difference; as the very first of his *"Geschlecht"* articles shows, Derrida takes Heidegger's effort in this respect quite seriously. Even if the phantasmatic should abound here, Heidegger's effort is nonetheless impressive. Indeed, it is idiomatic, a *singulare tantum*, one of a kind, as the gathering prefix *Ge-*, unique to the German, indicates. Here, as everywhere, Derrida therefore takes some pains to correct the French translation:

> Dans le ton marqué (betonten) de *u n* Geschlecht se cache (verbirgt sich) cet unissant (jenes Einende: et non pas cette unité, comme dit la traduction) qui unit ou réunit (einigt) à partir de l'azur rassemblant (et non "appareillant") de la nuit spirituelle." "Le mot (ici toute l'expression Ein Geschlecht) parle à partir du chant (donc de l'intonation marquée, de l'accentuation: accent c'est le chant dans la parole) dans lequel le pays du soir est chanté (worin das Land des Abends gesungen wird)." (7)

> In the emphatic tone (*betonten*) of *o n e Geschlecht* there lies concealed (*verbirgt sich*) this unifying (*jenes Einende,* not "this unity," as the translation says), which unites or reunites (*einigt*) on the basis of the gathering (and not "preparatory") azure of the spiriting night. "The word (here meaning the entire phrase *O n e Geschlecht*) speaks on the basis of the song [hence in the emphatic intonation of accentuation: accent is the song in speech] in which the evening land is sung [*worin das Land des Abends gesungen wird*]." (US 78)

What strikes Derrida throughout is the singularity of Heidegger's gesture, the singularity of gathering, even if there is more than one stroke in question, that is, even if it is always and everywhere a question of the twofold:

> Il faut bien insister sur la singularité du geste et de ce Ein. C'est que l'unissant qui tient à la singularité de ce coup, Schlag, ou de cette frappe, cet unissant donne lieu à une simplicité qui n'est pas autre chose que la duplicité ou à une duplicité simple. Il n'y a plus, ou plutôt il n'y avait pas et il n'y aura pas, il n'aura pas eu d'opposition entre le Zwiefalt et le Einfalt quand le mouvement sera allé au bout de sa course, au bout de la nuit spirituelle. Dans le paragraphe précédent, einfältig (simplement, selon un seul pli) était un adverbe. Dans le paragraphe suivant c'est un nom. Dans le paragraphe précédent, le coup rassemble, disait H., la dissension (Zwietracht) des sexes simplement (ein-fältig)

dans la dualité (Zwiefalt; le double pli) plus doux, plus serein. Dans le paragraphe suivant, "le coup," dit H., der Schlag qui s'imprime (der sie prägt) dans la simplicité de "<u>Ein</u> Geschlecht" (in die Einfalt des "<u>Einen</u> Geschlechts," etc.

Que fait donc ce coup, cette frappe? Der Schlag schlägt, cette frappe frappe, dit H., et ce qui ressemble, selon un geste justement typique de H., à une tautologie signifie aussi, plus profondément, que nous avons là affaire à la signification de ce qui ne peut pas laisser place à un métalangage, qui ne peut pas se laisser définir par autre chose que soi sauf à avoir introduit la signification à définir dans la définition définissante. Toute prédication au sujet de Schlag suppose quelque Schlagen, doit être frappée, imprimée, suppose le coup, comme toute définition de la Sprache suppose assez le langage pour qu'on ne puisse dire la langue est ou fait ceci ou cela, puisque ces valeurs d'être et de faire sont inadéquates en ce qu'elles présupposent la Sprache: il faut donc dire die Sprache spricht, das Ereignis ereignet, der Schlag schlägt. Ces significations ne peuvent pas être dérivées. Mais comment la frappe frappe-t-elle? (8)

One must insist on the singularity of the gesture and of this *One*. The unifying that holds to the singularity of this stroke or *Schlag*, this blow, gives place to a simplicity which is nothing other than duplicity, or a simple duplicity. There is no longer—or, rather, there never was and never will be, there will not have been—any opposition between the *Zwiefalt* and the *Einfalt*, once the movement will have run its course, at the end of the spiriting night. In the preceding paragraph *einfältig* (simply, in accord with one fold) was an adverb. In the following paragraph it is a noun. In the preceding paragraph the stroke gathers, says Heidegger, the dissension (*Zwietracht*) of the sexes simply (*einfältig*) into the duality (*Zwiefalt*, the double fold), which is gentle, more serene. In the following paragraph, "the stroke," says Heidegger, the *Schlag* that coins it (*der sie prägt*) in the simplicity of *o n e Geschlecht* (in the onefold of the "*E i n e n Geschlechts*"), etc.

So, what does this stroke, this blow, do? *Der Schlag schlägt*, the stroke strikes, says Heidegger, and what resembles a tautology, in accord with a gesture absolutely typical of Heidegger, also signifies at a more profound level, since here it is a matter of a signification of what cannot give way to a metalanguage, cannot be defined by anything other than itself, that is, except by introducing the signification to be defined into the definition that defines it. Every predication on the subject of *Schlag* presupposes some sort of striking, has to be coined or imprinted, and thus presupposes the stroke, just as every definition of language presupposes the language by which one can say that language is or does this or that, because these values of being or doing are inadequate insofar as they presuppose language: thus one has to say that language speaks, *die Sprache spricht,* the event eventuates, *das Ereignis ereignet,* the stroke strikes, *der Schlag schlägt.* Such significations cannot be derived. Yet how does the stroke strike?

One hears the strange echo of Céline in the phrase *au bout de la nuit spirituelle,* and yet *everything* about the spiriting night is strange, so strange that its language becomes a reiteration of the same, pure tautology. How does the stroke strike? Derrida poses three responses to this question (9–10).

First, the *frappe* does not close or seal anything off; rather it opens, by way of *frayage,* "effraction" reminding us here of Derrida's early yet decisive essay, "Freud and the Scene of Writing." The stroke *lässt einen Weg einschlagen.* The idiom is untranslatable into French. In English we would say, hoping to avoid the baseball idiom, the stroke lets us strike out on a new path.

Second, even though the path opens up a future, it remains essentially the return to an "early" time, a dawn or a kind of pre-dawn, prior at least to the antiquity of Platonic Christianity. Derrida chooses the word *la veille,* nightwatch, to capture the sense of this guarding or watching over the arrival of the more matutinal commencement. And the idea of gathering, of the stroke that gathers all discord into tender duality and gentle simplicity, is also a return to childhood, a more tender childhood that is both more ancient and younger (10). The stroke "brings us back to the more serene childhood," *zurückbringt in die stillere Kindheit.*

Third, the return enables us to see the relation of the present seminar, "Le fantôme de l'autre," to the generic topic of the entire series, "Nationalité et nationalisme philosophiques." For the decomposing race is caught in the bootless alternative of nationalism and cosmopolitanism. Heidegger insists, in spite of every precaution he takes concerning chauvinism, on some sort of return to a *Heimat,* a homeland that was promised but never delivered, never securely sent. Every nationalism, Derrida ventures to say, places a high value on the theme of return. The appeals to rebirth, to a new voyage, a novel adventure, also pertain to the nationalist's rhetoric. Even something like "colonial expansion" is present in this problematic relation to a *patrie* or *Vaterland* that has always disappointed us, to say the least, but that holds so much (false) promise. My homeland will rise again! cries the nationalist. Derrida realizes that Heidegger would cry "foul!" at this analysis, but he persists.

Yet if he has ventured too far on the critical side, Derrida now works on the more generous side of deconstruction's double reading (11–12). He asks whether there is not indeed something altogether idiomatic about Heidegger's "conversation" with Trakl, idiomatic in a sense that requires respect. Where else could one find this manner of proceeding in thinking's involvement with poetry, with the thinker engaging in such an intense *Zwiegespräch* with poetry? Not in Greece, nor in Rome, not in England or America. And if such a dialogue happens today in the French language, one can be sure, says Derrida, that it is borrowing from Heidegger. Perhaps such a dialogue is no longer possible in today's Germany—as Hans-Jürgen Syberberg would certainly agree (recall his remarks toward the end of the otherwise uninteresting film *Der Ister*, to the effect that no one today, including the filmmakers, can really understand what Heidegger's lectures on poetry, especially Hölderlin's poetry, were all about). Yet it remains true that a conversation in the Heideggerian manner is possible nowhere else, in no other idiom. There seems to be something like *une certaine poéticité allemande*, says Derrida, in Heidegger's "situatings" of Hölderlin and Trakl, something that is to be found nowhere else. Even as Derrida pushes the question of philosophical nationality and nationalism he also asks:

> Est-il abusif de prétendre que cette juste frappe, en tant qu'elle parle et appelle la douceur, a un rapport essentiel avec la possibilité de la langue, l'allemande, dans laquelle cela se dit; et donc que le pays du soir (qui n'est pas l'Occident) et que chante la poésie de T. a un rapport essentiel avec cette Sprache; et donc que une certaine Allemagne—non pas l'Allemagne nationale de fait, etc. (vous connaissez maintenant toutes ces distinctions) est le lieu de cet appel de l'Occident par delà l'Occident européen métaphysico-chrétien: l'Allemagne appelée autant que lieu de l'appel? (14)

> Is it wrongheaded to claim that this just stroke, insofar as it speaks of and calls for gentleness, has an essential rapport

with the possibility of the language, the German language, in which it is said? And thus that this land of evening (which is not the Occident) which the poesy of Trakl sings has an essential rapport with this *Sprache*? And thus that a certain Germany—not the nation Germany as it exists in fact, you are by now familiar with all these distinctions—is the place of this call of the Occident that lies beyond the European metaphyico-Christian Occident: a Germany called for rather than the site of the call?

In short, Heidegger is calling *for*, rather than *to*, a possibility that remains German—even if that word can only misspeak itself. Derrida loves Paul de Man's play on words, *die Sprache verspricht (sich)*, language promises—and yet inevitably misspeaks, makes mistakes, and mistakes itself. So it is when Heidegger or perhaps anyone says the name *German*. Or the name *germain*—recall Derrida's "Envoi," his address in 1980 in Strasbourg to the Societies for Philosophy in the French Language. There the matters of idiom and of dissension are of equal importance, and it is time to take a closer look at them.

Derrida justifies his focus on Heidegger—which from an envoy to the combined philosophical societies for philosophy in the *French* language needs some justification—in terms of both the matter of representation (but as Heidegger's *vorstellendes Denken*) and the all-important issue of *Anwesenheit*, "presence." It is not enough, Derrida warns, to take Heidegger's emphasis on "presence" to be nostalgia for a Greek experience that has gotten lost in modern "representation." "*Anwesenheit* is not simple; it is already divided and differentiated, marking the place of a scission, division, and dissension (*Zwiespalt*)" (Ps 129). That last word seems odd. In *Geschlecht III*, which we are now examining, it is most often *Zwietracht* that is translated as *dissension*, and yet all the *Zwie*-words, with the sole exceptions of *Zwiefalt* and *Zwiegespräch*, appear as marks of discord in Heidegger's text. Furthermore, *Geschlecht III* envisages—perhaps through Heidegger's eyes—the possibility of a predual sexuality, which Heidegger himself designates as "unifold," *einfältig*. The "fold," however, is also present in the 1980 "Envoi": "the fold of dissension would open, announce, or envisage everything that in what is to come is determined as *mimesis*, imitation, representation, with the entire cortege of oppositional couples that will shape philosophical theory: production/reproduction, presentation/representation, originary/derived, and so on" (ibid.). Perhaps it is time to recall that the purpose of the *Geschlecht* series is to contemplate sexual difference in terms of, or at least alongside, ontological difference. Derrida is surely contemplating and deconstructing the male-female and even the brother-sister relation as two among those foundational oppositions in philosophy. A very Nietzschean position, one will say, and rightly so. Yet Derrida is more precise—and no doubt less ironic—about truth's becoming a woman, albeit a woman who is excluded, repressed, or oppressed throughout the epoch of metaphysics and morals. Epochality, to be sure, is a word that sticks in Derrida's throat; it is not a word that for him *s'entend-parler*. What must be thought through is the idiom of the "sending," *das Geschick des Seins,* which presumably sends both the possibility of thinking originary presence and the fatal imbroglio of representational thinking. Such *vorstellendes Denken* extends from Descartes through Lacan, says Derrida, even if it holds the promise of a certain remembrance of what the earliest Greek thinkers *almost* thought:

> Even if there is dissension (*Zwiespalt*) in what Heidegger calls the great Greek epoch and in the experience of *Anwesenheit,* this dissension is gathered in [*se rassemble dans*] the λέγειν. It is safeguarded and protected, thus assuring a sort of indivisibility of the destinal. It is in making foundational this gathered indivisibility of the sending [*de l'envoi*] that the Heideggerian reading can detach the epochs, including the most powerful, the longest, and the most dangerous of all epochs, that of representation in modern times. (Ps 136)

As in all his earlier meditations on Heidegger, however, Derrida contests the gathering, the destinal, and the detachable, identifiable, and thus "reduced" epochs. He formulates his question to Heidegger in the following way:

> [E]verywhere where the sending of being divides itself, defies the λέγειν, eludes its destination, is it not the case that the Heideggerian schematic is contestable in principle, historically deconstructed? deconstructed in the historicality that it still implies? If there was representation, it is perhaps the case (and Heidegger would recognize this) that precisely the sending of being was originally menaced in the totality of its being [*originairement menacé en son être-ensemble*], in its *Geschick,* by divisibility or dissension (what I would call *dissemination*). (ibid.)

Such a threat or menace to the sending of being, a menace that at least parallels the menace of the second *Schlag,* can be thought in various ways. Many years ago I proffered the thesis, unanimously rejected by everyone who knows anything about Heidegger, that being is fundamentally a gigolo, not so much menaced as menacing.[13] My reasoning based itself on Heidegger's insistence that it is not "we" who have forgotten being but being that has forgotten "us"; being "withdraws" in concealment and releases mortals to the tinsel of beings for the entire epoch of philosophy. Which, as we remember from *Geschlecht IV,* is an epoch of mourning. Being *abandons* beings, and especially the being who ought to have been intimate with it, ought to have lived in an *understanding* of it. Being, a gigolo? Heidegger is not composing the *Don Giovanni* of metaphysics, my colleagues reprimanded me, and they were surely right. Even so, in Spain alone, 1,003 mortals have been abandoned by being.— But let that pass. Let us agree that the epochal sending of being itself is menaced. In either case, whether menaced or menacing, the gleaning and gathering of being in λέγειν is anything but guaranteed; indeed, we can scarcely represent to ourselves what Heraclitus might have meant by the word. We recall, as Heidegger certainly also does, that Heraclitus was also fond of the word διαφερόμενον, perhaps "differance." Near the end of "Envoi," Derrida projects a "difference" that would not be "of being as presencing"; it would not be a "self-sending of being." Rather, he says, it would disseminate *multiple* sendings, sendings of the other and of others, *des envois de l'autre, des autres* (137). No doubt, such sendings would be phantasmatic—hence, phantoms of the other. To which we must return, in order to close.

Yet perhaps further reflection on *dissémination,* as opposed to Heideggerian polysemy, or *Mehrdeutigkeit,* is called for here, precisely with regard to the eminent case of a thinking of poetry in terms of the "fold."

---

13. This may have been—I can no longer remember; embarrassment inhibits memory—in the paper called "Spiriting Heidegger," in the volume *Of Derrida, Heidegger, and Spirit,* edited by David Wood (Evanston: Northwestern University Press, 1993), 11–40. My notes tell me that it is a revised version of a paper that appeared originally in *Research in Phenomenology* XVIII (1988): 205–30. Or it may have been in a paper called "Of Spirit and the Daimon: Jacques Derrida's *De l'esprit,*" delivered at the Society for Phenomenology and Existential Philosophy, then published in *Ethics and Danger: Currents in Continental Thought,* ed. Charles E. Scott and Arleen B. Dallery (Albany: State University of New York Press, 1992), 59–70. Unfortunately, the word and the thing called *gigolo* appears also in chapter 6 of *Daimon Life,* but in an essay on "paranoetic thinking," which confuses Heidegger's "abandonment *by* being" with President Schreber's predicament.

For Heidegger, the fold, as the onefold twofold, the two folding back into one, is essentially about gathering, *Sammlung, Versammlung.* In chapter 2 we noted the importance of the "fold," *le pli,* for Derrida as well as for Heidegger, suggesting that for Derrida the fold is *never* a gathering. Indeed, *le pli* is one of the principal terms of and for dissemination.

If we look briefly at "The Double Séance," Derrida's very difficult text on Mallarmé, the figure of the fold joins that of other key words for dissemination—*blanc, voile, feuille, milieu, hymen,* and so on. Derrida first invokes the word in order to discuss the undecidability of "appearance," which is both *Erscheinung* and *Schein,* the to-appear of beings and their *mere* appearance, that is, their dissemblance. The fold between these two is indeterminate or indefinite, *son pli indéfini* (D 239–40). Such indefiniteness and undecidability subvert presence and the truth of presence. One may say that this *pli* or *Falt* implies the fault or default of presence. In Mallarmé's terms, the mimicry of Pierrot can never be expunged, and every *Einfalt,* every folding into one, is *einfältig,* simply simplistic. The entire corpus of Mallarmé, says Derrida, is enfolded within *les plis d'un tissu* that cannot be decoded (D 242). Derrida expands the lesson and argues that *every* text folds back on itself, *s'y plie,* and thus engages a "double scene" (D 250). The analysis culminates in the remark that the fold multiplies itself into a manifold—better, a *manifolding* that Heidegger would attribute to a transcendental mightiness of essence, Derrida to a merely quasi-transcendental trace of forces—and is therefore never at one with itself: *"Le pli (se) multiplie mais (n'est) pas (un)"* (D 258–59). Such a multiplying of folds bears witness to "the excess of the signifier," a "surplus," "supplement," and even a "vicariance" at work in the text (D 265). Such multiplication, *"sans fin des plies, replis, reploiment, pliage, éploiement, déploiement,"* is unstoppable, so that "each determinate fold applies itself to configure the other [*se plie à figurer l'autre*] . . . and to re-mark writing's folding upon itself" (D 301). The fold has nothing to do with philosophical reflexivity in the sense of a thinking's reflecting back upon itself. Indeed, says Derrida, philosophical reflection "is merely an effect of the fold as text" (D 302). Inasmuch as Heidegger eschews reflexivity of the usual sorts, from Descartes to Hegel, one may hope that this folding of the text has nothing to do with Heidegger's "other thinking," his "other commencement." Can the possibility of gathering be rescued, particularly in the case of poetry, and above all in the case of Trakl's poetry?

In the present case, that of Heidegger's Trakl, the "fold" has to do with a particularly uncanny effect of textuality. It has eminently to do with sexual difference. During the thirteenth and final session of "The

Phantom of the Other," Derrida returns to the theme of the possibility of *la différence sexuelle sans pli* (1). The speaker of English is perhaps for the first time struck by this *sans pli*, which is simply the English "sim-ply," and by the double effect of simplicity, the without-fold: keep it simple, yet do not be simplistic, do not become a simpleton. The same double stroke, as it were, occurs with the German word *einfältig*, which nowadays, to repeat, has the preeminent sense of simplemindedness and even silliness. In either case, the word *Einfalt*, "onefold," "unifold," is odd, inasmuch as the onefold still has a fold, a single fold, that makes of the one thing folded a twofold by granting it two "leaves" or "wings," as it were. It is around these idiomatic *bisarreries*, reminiscent of Mallarmé but also of every poetic text, indeed of every literary text and perhaps every "commentary" and every "placement" of such texts, that Derrida's seminar rotates.

Perhaps there has been too much unfamiliar language at play in Derrida's seminar thus far. And perhaps this is always the case when one is dealing with Heidegger's discussions of poetry. Derrida imagines—or perceives—that his students are fed up with all this Heidegger. It may be that some grumbles have reached his ears. Even though I have cited the words of his defense elsewhere, in *Derrida and Our Animal Others* (AO 102–103), they are worth hearing again because they display the nature of Derrida's dedication to Heidegger's work. As I have also noted in *Our Animal Others*, I am not clear about the sense of the word *méfiance* in what follows:

> J'imagine l'impatience de certains, non seulement devant la lenteur appuyée de cette lecture, mais devant le temps de ce séjour auprès de H. Encore H.! Et ce retour de H. et ce retour à H.! Est-ce que cela ne suffit pas? Est-ce encore actuel?
>
> Ce qui m'intéresse aujourd'hui, c'est précisément le retour de H. et le retour à H. et c'est lui que je veux aussi étudier. Le H. qui revient ou auquel on revient n'est pas le même que celui qui en France fit son apparitions juste avant et juste après la guerre, ni celui qui réapparut encore dix ans après, quand les premières traductions abondantes et une nouvelle lecture de Husserl, et l'éloignement de la guerre ont changé un peu l'espace de sa réception, comme on dit. Et celui d'aujourd'hui est encore autre, la question politique qu'on lui adresse n'est plus la même, le corpus dont on dispose, maintenant que ses oeuvres complètes commencent à paraître (méfiance . . .) et que

de nouvelles traductions sont à notre disposition, ce corpus a une autre configuration, on entrevoit de nouveaux paysages.

Ce que j'appellerai, sans être sûr de ces mots, la force, la nécessité, mais aussi l'art d'une pensée ne se mesure pas à la durée et à la permanence de sa présence rayonnante, elle ne se mesure pas à la fixité d'un éclat mais au nombre de ses éclipses—et vous voyez que nous continuons, disant cela, à parler dans le texte sur Trakl, qui est aussi un texte sur l'année le jour et la course du soleil. Après chaque éclipse que cette pensée est capable d'endurer, elle réapparaît encore autre au sortir du nuage, et le "même" texte, le même legs n'est plus le même, il tourne sur lui-même et surprend encore. Un penseur qui n'accepte pas la loi de cette éclipse et qui ne calcule pas avec elle n'est pas un penseur, du moins est-ce un calculateur qui ne sait pas calculer avec le non-calcul qu'est le plus grand risque, celui de l'éclipse sans retour, celui de l'Étranger absolu qui ne revient pas. (2–3)

I imagine some of you are impatient not only with the insistent slowness of my reading but also with the amount of time we are taking on Heidegger in general. What? Heidegger again? Why this return of Heidegger, and this return *to* Heidegger! Haven't we had enough? And is any of this relevant?

What interests me today is precisely the return of Heidegger and the return to Heidegger, and it is precisely this that I want to study. The Heidegger who returns or to whom one recurs is not the same Heidegger who made his appearances in France immediately before and immediately after the Second World War, nor the one who reappeared ten years later, when many new translations of his works appeared, accompanied by a new reading of Husserl; these things, along with the growing distance from the War, changed in some small way the space of his reception, as we say. And the Heidegger of today is yet again another. The political question one addresses to him is no longer the same, and the corpus to which we can refer, now that his complete works are starting to appear (something suspicious there . . .) and now that we have access to new translations, takes on a different configuration. One glimpses a different landscape.

What I should call—without being sure of these words— the force, necessity, but also the art of a thinking is not measured by the duration and the permanence of its radiant presence; it is measured, not by the fixity of its impact, but by the number of its eclipses. And you will note that in saying this we are continuing to speak of the text on Trakl, which is also a text on the year, the day, and the course of the sun. After each eclipse that such thought is able to endure, it reappears once again, and differently, as it emerges from behind the clouds, and the "same" text, the same legacy, is no longer the same. It rotates on its axis, and once again it surprises us. A thinker who does not accept the law of this eclipse and who does not count on it is no thinker; at best he is a calculator who no longer knows how to calculate with the incalculable, which is the greatest risk, that of eclipse without return, that of the absolute Stranger who does not return.

At this late point in his seminar (5–6), Derrida returns to some lines from Trakl's "Sommersneige," lines that appeared much earlier both in Heidegger's text (US 68) and in his own transcript of the seminar, which we examined in the preceding chapter: *"Gedächte ein blaues Wild seines Pfads, / Des Wohllauts seiner geistlichen Jahre!"* ("Were a blue deer to remember its path, / The consonance of its spiriting years!"). Derrida refers to Heidegger's enduring resistance to the Aristotelian and Scholastic theme of man as the "rational animal" and his ongoing confrontation with Nietzsche's insistence that the human being is the "as yet undiscovered" or "as yet indeterminate" animal. The "blue" of "blue deer," or of "blue game," *ein blaues Wild,* signifies for Heidegger not the bestiality of humankind but *ein schauendes Denken,* a circumspective as well as intuitive thinking, but also a thinking back by way of a memory, which Heidegger reserves for mortal humans. Yet animals too have memory, as Derrida reminds his students, and as he will restate fifteen years later in *The Animal That Therefore I Am.* He notes that there is even a "biological" or "genetic" memory, and in the age of computers there is a "technological" memory as well. In a sense, the obviously "political" thematic of "Philosophical Nationality and Nationalism" is subtended by the theme of animal life, the theme to which Derrida will devote himself during his very last seminar. For the moment he elaborates all four of the "threads" that will go into the tapestry of his 1987 *Of Spirit.*

Naturellement, c'est cette limite entre deux mémoires, comme entre l'animal et l'homme, qui vient constamment en question dans ce séminaire, et c'est pourquoi j'ai beaucoup insisté sur la question de l'animalité avant d'aborder ce texte-ci. Cette question est aussi celle de la technique. Mais vous l'avez compris, il ne s'agit pas pour moi d'effacer toute limite ou toute distinction entre ce qu'on appelle la bête et ce qu'on appelle l'homme, mais de contester l'unité de cette limite comme opposition de part et d'autre d'une frontière qui serait celle qui sépare la mémoire et la non-mémoire, le donner et le prendre (et la mémoire est aussi une manière de prendre, de garder, de saisir . . .), la mémoire pensante et la mémoire biologique, la mémoire pensante et la mémoire technologique. Les différences entre les espèces dites animales, y compris l'homme, sont en très grand nombre (beaucoup plus d'une) et je parle là de différences structurelles dans la capacité disons engrammatique et dans l'économie de l'inscription, disons dans le pouvoir et la structure mnémoniques.

> Et donc dans l'expérience du territoire.
> Et du territoire sexuel.
> Et du retour, et de la "patrie." (5–6)

Naturally, it is this limit between two memories, as between animal and human, that is constantly coming into question in our seminar, and that is why I have strongly insisted on the question of animality before taking up this particular text. This question is also that of technology. But you will have understood that for me it is not a matter of effacing every limit or every distinction between what one calls "the beast" and what one calls "man," but of contesting the unity of this limit as oppositional on both sides of the one frontier, a frontier that would be what separates memory from nonmemory, giving from taking (and memory is also a manner of taking, safeguarding, seizing . . .), thinking memory and biological memory, thinking memory and technological memory. The differences among the species we call "animal," including man, are vast in number (many more than one), and in this context I speak of structural differences in the capacity we may call engrammatical and in the economy of inscription, in what we may call the power of mnemonic structures.

And thus in the experience of territory.
And of sexual territory.
And of return, and of "the fatherland."

For Heidegger, Trakl is a profoundly historical poet, "historical" in the sense of *geschichtlich* and *geschickt,* destinal; that is to say, he is a poet who, like Hölderlin, has a potentially fateful impact on German-speaking peoples. Trakl is not a bucolic poet, not one who spurns the great cities of our civilization and hies off to the countryside, even if forests, animals, farming folk, and hunters populate his poems. His *Gedicht* or singular unsung poem marks the homecoming, not to a familiar nation or country, to be sure, but to a new way of inhabiting or dwelling on the earth. It is as though by referring to this new *patrie* as precisely that, a "fatherland," and doing so in the face of Heidegger's protestations, Derrida wants to push his effort concerning philosophical nationality and nationalism as far as it can go. For the new site, the new locale, the new place called *earth* is still invoked within a very particular idiom, namely, that of Heidegger's arcane German (7–8). Yet the strangest aspect of this new historical-destinal beginning is what Heidegger describes as follows, with Derrida citing the German here: "*Seine Dichtung singt das Geschick des Schlages, der das Menschengeschlecht in sein noch vorbehaltenes Wesen verschlägt, d. h. rettet*" (US 80). "His poetry sings the sending of the stroke that drives—and that means rescues—the human *Geschlecht* into that essence which still remains reserved for it." Derrida stresses the promise of rescue and notes (perhaps not with adequate emphasis) the bizarre coupling of "driving" or "casting adrift," *verschlagen,* with "rescue," *retten,* as though these two very different words, these antonyms, were synonyms. Derrida does not recall here the use of *verschlagen* in "What Is Metaphysics?" which says, "*Die Angst verschlägt uns das Wort,*" anxiety deprives us of speech, bottles or boards up the mouth, casts us adrift, leaves us shipwrecked. Nor does he cite *Being and Time*: "What threatens . . . is so close that it corners us and deprives us of breath [*den Atem verschlägt*]" (SZ 186). Shipwreck and rescue, in one blow? Suffocation as salvation? Derrida does note that the French translation says merely "*frappe en séparant, en spécifiant,*" which, although double, is a very weak translation of *verschlägt,* at least in the light of Heidegger's earlier uses of the word both here and in prior essays and lectures. Yet Derrida is certainly aware that this *coup* or *frappe,* which in Heidegger's view is to coin a new humankind and to rescue the earth, is oddly bound up with the double *Schlag*—which now seems to be but *one* stroke—of good and evil, as well as with the redoubled, polysemic *Schlag* of generation and sexuality, of tribe, race, genus, and all the rest. And even though one does not want to leap from 1985 to 2003 in Derrida's own life, at least not without caution, it is surely not too much to say that in the *Schlag* of *Geschlecht* there is something both *gewaltig* and *gewaltsam*, both powerful and violent. The violence, ironically, would consist in the impossibly appeasing apposition of *verschlagen* and *retten*, as though the stroke of evil were all a part of the plan and represented what the military loves to call mere collateral damage. This is what fascinates and affrights Derrida, and keeps him on task (9–10).[14]

It is clear to Derrida that the *Schlag* that transforms the new *Menschengeschlecht* into "the essence that is still reserved for it," *sein noch vorbehaltenes Wesen*, is both archaic and originary and yet in some way still to come, *archi-originaire et à venir*, so that Derrida would "almost dare to call it messianism." In a handwritten marginal note he adds the underscored words *le salut*, "salvation," followed by several undecipherable words, perhaps including the word *venir* (12).[15] At all events, the rescuing *Schlag* takes the form of a return (13–14). Derrida identifies this with a return—a Hölderlinian *Heimkunft*—to *Heimat*, to the Land of Evening, *dem Abendland*. In this way he brings his "Fantôme de l'autre" back to the more generic theme of "Nationalité et nationalisme philosophiques." Yet, to repeat, this "homeland" is no fatherland in any normal sense. It is perhaps instead a kind of "brotherland," for even though Derrida does not say so explicitly here, there are many references in this seminar to the prevailing fraternalism of the fatherland—and in fact Derrida will end the seminar by invoking the theme of fraternity. Such fraternity or fraternalism is particularly important to me because of the unaccountable way in which Heidegger's stranger "gains a sister" in his reading of Trakl. In any case, the *patrie* is granted only in the remote return that is futural, to come, and no doubt still at an immense distance. At this point, in a

---

14. Page 9 is skipped in the typescript, which goes from 8 to 10; Derrida corrects the oversight by hand. From page 11 to the end of the typewritten notes an electric typewriter is being used, one with Courier type, as opposed to the older typewriter with Pica font. Remington has displaced Olivetti, while Macintosh looms in the wings.

15. The fact even the archivists have a difficult time deciphering Derrida's handwriting is a reminder of how important it is that the editing of Derrida's texts is done by those who are expert in reading his writing. Clearly, I am not among them. Every time Derrida wrote me a handwritten letter I dashed off to Pascale-Anne Brault, crying for help, which I received, but after painstaking efforts on her part—for which again, once again and forever, she has my deepest thanks.

*Geschlecht III*: The Phantom of the Other         219

rhetoric that is all too familiar, Heidegger tries to defend himself against the possible charge of "dreamy Romanticism" (US 80) by saying that there is nothing in Trakl's song for the throng of journalists and technocrats, nothing there for the realm of political economy, nothing there for the masses, *Massendasein*.

Derrida now initiates some concluding remarks on the "promise" (although this is seldom Heidegger's explicit word) of a new morning or a new start of the year, a matutinal commencement for a new *Menschenschlag* on the earth, promised of old yet still outstanding. Derrida does so, one must say, with a certain flair and with tongue fairly deep in cheek, thinking of Heidegger's scorn for calculative thinking and for the traditional Christian interpretations of Trakl's poetry, but thinking also of the promise of spring and of his own impending departure for the New World:

> C'est sur le poème Frühling [der Seele] dont le vers Es ist die Seele . . . est extrait que se ferme ou plutôt s'ouvre la conclusion du texte [de Heidegger]. Le printemps (premier temps, primus, commencement de l'année, Jahr, Gehen, première des saisons) qui commence entre le 19 et le 21 mars, donc aujourd'hui même[16]—et calculateur comme je suis, j'ai tout programmé pour que la dernière séance de ce séminaire qui fût consacrée à ce texte qui se termine par une ouverture et un envoi sur le printemps, et sur le voyage, pour que la dernière séance de cette lecture de Frühling der Seele de Trakl et de Heidegger lisant Trakl et situant ce printemps, cette ouverture à la fin, pour que cette dernière séance tombât, comme on dit, le jour du printemps à la veille de Pâques et d'un voyage dans le nouveau monde. (15)

> It is with the poem "Frühling [der Seele]" from which the line "Something strange is the soul," *Es ist die Seele* . . . is taken that Heidegger's text closes, or rather, opens its conclusion. Spring, *le printemps* (*premier temps*, *primus*, the commencement of the year or *Jahr* [derived from *Gehen*, "to go"], the first of the seasons), begins between the 19th and the 21st of March, hence precisely today—and, calculator that I am, I've

---

16. According to my historical calendar, this final session took place on Wednesday, March 20, 1985.

programmed everything so that this final session of our seminar, which was devoted to this text that comes to a close with an overture to the spring and a dispatch sent toward it, to and toward a voyage, so that the final session of this reading of Trakl's "Springtime of the Soul" and of the Heideggerian reading of Trakl that situates this spring, this overture to the end, so that the final session would fall, as one says, on the first day of spring and on the eve of Easter, as well as on the eve of a voyage to the New World.

Somewhat less tongue in cheek, Derrida notes that the poem "Frühling der Seele," with which Heidegger begins and ends his Trakl article, contains the word *gewaltig* (16). Derrida circles the word in his own typescript, circles it heavily and makes a marginal notation which, typically, no one at the archive can decipher. In any case, it is clear that this word, derived from *Walten,* is already important to him in the spring of 1985, which is the time of *Geschlecht II* and the seedbed, if one may say so, of the third and fourth *Geschlechter.* The phrase in Derrida's typescript reads: *"Et la mort même, disons cet être pour la mort du jeune homme, est une mort à laquelle s'ordonne, se plie la mort, le mourir prodigieux, puissant, extraordinaire, violent (gewaltig)."* "And death itself, or let us say, the young man's being toward death is a death that orders and folds itself into a death and a dying that are prodigious, powerful, extraordinary, and violent *(gewaltig).*" The words *violent, extraordinary, puissant* or *powerful,* and *prodigious* all seek to translate Trakl's word *gewaltig.* This German word will continue to fascinate Derrida up to the end of his teaching career. Meanwhile, in these closing moments of the present seminar, Derrida comments on a theme that will occupy him throughout his book *Politics of Friendship,* namely, the theme of fraternity and fraternalism:

> Mais qui chante ce chant et qui appelle cette mort? C'est le frère, c'est le frère qui meurt de cette façon puissante (gewaltig), puissante parce que discrètement elle accomplit, elle fait quelque chose, d'abord elle chante et le chant ne décrit pas, ne dit pas ce qui est, ne constate pas, il appelle et par là fait advenir, fait venir. C'est donc le frère qui chante, c'est lui le poète aussi qui meurt de cette mort, qui accomplit cette mort selon le printemps, qui "sait" chanter et mourir—comme il faut . . .—Le frère qui est le chantant (der Singende), qui meurt en suivant ce déclin qui n'est pas la chute (ihm stirbt der Bruder als der

singende nach). Ce n'est pas la soeur sélénique. Mourant en veillant, . . . l'ami suit l'étranger et traverse la nuit spirituelle de l'année du Départ—Abgeschiedenheit. (17)

Yet who sings this song, and who calls upon this death? It is the brother. It is the brother who dies in this powerful way (*gewaltig*), puissant because it accomplishes and achieves something quite discreetly. First of all, it sings, and its song does not describe, does not say what it is, does not constate; rather, it calls and thus causes to advene, to arrive. It is thus the brother who sings. It is he, the poet also, who dies this death, who accomplishes this death in accord with springtime, who "knows" how to sing and to die—as one must . . .—The brother, who is the one singing (*der Singende*), dies by following this declivity that is not a fall (*ihm stirbt der Bruder als der singende nach* ["the brother dies after him as the one singing"]). This is not the Selenic sister. Dying in safeguarding, . . . the friend follows the stranger and traverses the spiriting night of the year of departure—"apartness," *Abgeschiedenheit*.

In retrospect, it seems to me that these concluding remarks suffice to put in perspective the odd "gaining" of a sister that was the object of my constant complaint to Derrida, along with the plea that he take up the oddity, even the perversity, of the exclusion or appropriation of the sister in Heidegger's placement. For it has always struck me that of all the poets and writers I have read, Georg Trakl would be the very last to be so oblivious with respect to the sister, the very last to be deaf to her inimitable lunar voice. One of his most striking poems bears the title "To the Sister," and if, as Heidegger dreams, there is but one *Gedicht* in Trakl, that could have been its title. Trakl would be the very last to allow her lunar nature to be scorched by the solar splendor of brothers. The *chute* of Derrida's own typescript, and of the course, *chute* being one of his favorite words, is as follows:

Il y aurait beaucoup à dire, naturellement, compte tenue de E i n Geschlecht, de cet un de un sexe, une espèce dans le simple de sa différence, il y aurait beaucoup à dire de ce point de vue quant au fait que la figure du frère soit la seule à rassembler ce chant: ni la soeur, ni personne d'autre (ni le père, la mère, le fils ou la fille). Cela voudrait-il dire que toutes ces figures "familiales" sont des figures spécifiant le frère, que non seulement le père et le fils sont des frères, ce que peut confirmer une certain évidence mais que la mère, la fille et la soeur sont aussi des frères et surtout que ceux qui n'appartiennent pas à la famille "générique" ou généalogique sont des frères, le frère marquant ainsi la rupture avec la structure familiale, la rupture ou le dépassement ou l'émancipation, l'ami suivant le frère (figure de la patrie ou au-delà de la patrie dans la fratrie? Natalité, naturalité, nationalité ou le contraire, ou son au-delà? Question que je laisse suspendue. (17–18)

Naturally, there would be lot to say, taking the *E i n Geschlecht* into account, about this "one" and this "one sex," a species within the simple of its difference. There would be a lot to say from this point of view concerning the fact that the figure of the brother is the only one who gathers up this song: neither the sister nor anyone else (not the father, the mother, the son or the daughter). Would that be to say that all these "familial" figures are specific figures of the brother, that not only father and son are brothers, which a certain kind of evidence could confirm, but that mother and sister too are brothers, and above all that those who do not belong the "generic" or genealogical family are brothers, the brother thus marking the rupture with the family structure, the rupture or the surpassing or the emancipation, the friend following the brother (a figure of the fatherland or, beyond the fatherland, of the brotherland)? Natality, naturality, nationality, or else the contrary, the beyond of all that? A question I leave in suspense.

Derrida concludes by reciting one last time the poem "Frühling der Seele," which Heidegger too cites at both the beginning and the end of his second Trakl essay. And with this gesture so entirely Heideggerian, one must say, yet in a style unmistakably his own, Derrida draws the course to a close.

7

# The Magnetism of Georg and Gretl Trakl

> There is therefore **one** cause that brought the most primordial opposition into nature. This cause we can designate by means of the (unknown) cause of primordial magnetism.
>
> —F. W. J. Schelling

> Back of everything magnetism. Earth for instance pulling this and being pulled. That causes movement. And time? Well, that's the time the movement takes. . . . Come. Come. Tip. Woman and man that is. . . . Molly, he.
>
> —L. Boom

Very near the end of his life, Trakl jotted down two aphorisms, one in the spirit of Nietzsche and Heidegger, the other very much in Derrida's spirit. The first is almost a paraphrase of *The Gay Science*, number 324, which serves as the epigram to the 1961 publication of Heidegger's *Nietzsche* lectures of the late 1930s. Nietzsche himself seems to be remembering a letter he wrote during his teenage years to his younger sister—telling her that she must *either* be a believer, hence happy, *or* become a knower, and thus surrender all hopes of happiness. Trakl writes: "Knowledge will come only to the one who despises happiness" (T 256). The second aphorism, reminiscent of—or looking ahead to—the philosopher who remarked that virtually all his seminars circled about the theme of *amour*, reads, "My feeling in those moments of being that seem similar to death: All human beings are worthy of love. Coming to wakefulness you feel the world's bitterness; all your unabsolved guilt is there; your poem an imperfect retribution" (ibid.). And because Trakl refers here to *dein Gedicht*, in the singular, this may be an aphorism for Heidegger as well.

223

One of the most remarkable differences between Heidegger and Derrida generally is the latter's insistence that *life* and *work* are intertwined in such a way that one cannot simply abjure biography. It is not enough to say that Aristotle was born, worked, and died—even if Derrida agrees that birth and death are significant. No doubt, Heidegger is right to fear the subjectivism and biographical reductionism of our time, when gossip rules—although when and where did it not? Derrida himself is stringently critical of biographical and especially autobiographical discourses, and he is more likely to affirm the self-*tracing* of the life that runs through *every* autobiographical animal. Neither Heidegger nor Derrida has much faith in a tracing that is performed by the *cogito*, however, which derives from *cogo* and therefore means as much as a gathering performed by mere consciousness. In this lack of faith Heidegger and Derrida are one.

In this final chapter, it will be a matter of trying to trace at least something of the lives and works of Georg and Gretl Trakl. No doubt this attempt at an interweaving will be ungainly, the work of a beginner, especially when the biographical details are so scanty. Yet the attempt must be made. For "thinking" alone, whatever it may be, will not be able to place or situate the poem; nor will it be able to register the magnetic force exerted by the *Geschlecht* that bears the name *Trakl*.

How to explain the magnetism—felt by both Heidegger and Derrida—radiated by a man who despises happiness and who at least from adolescence on succeeds in banishing it from the remainder of the meager twenty-seven years of his life? How account for the magnetism exerted by a poet who after puberty tastes bitterness and guilt every day of that brief life, yet whose "poem," always close to the moments most reminiscent of death, desires to declare nothing other than love, and to every human being? To declare love—even if Trakl faults himself for the lack of it. In a letter to Ludwig von Ficker, dated June 26, 1913, Trakl writes from Salzburg:

> Here each day is gloomier and colder than the last, and it is raining without interruption. From time to time a ray of light from my final sunny days in Innsbruck penetrates the gloom and fills me with the most profound gratitude toward you and all the noble human beings whose goodness, in truth, I do not very much deserve. Too little love, too little justice and mercy, and again, always too little love; too much severity, arrogance, and all sorts of criminality—that is who I am. I am certain that I abstain from evil only out of weakness and cowardice, so that

I desecrate my very malevolence. I long for the day when the soul in this soulless body of mine, plagued by melancholy, will no longer wish to dwell, will no longer be able to dwell; the day when my soul abandons this figure of mockery composed of filth and rot, which is an all-too-faithful mirror image of a godless and accursed century.

God, only a tiny spark of pure joy—and one would be rescued; love—and one would be redeemed. (T 301)

It is time to bring my own effort in the present book to some kind of conclusion. Even though one of the lowest circles of hell is dedicated to authors who quote themselves, I decided early on in the writing of it to review my earlier published pieces on Trakl, Heidegger's Trakl, and Derrida's Heidegger, simply because the first piece, "Schlag der Liebe, Schlag des Todes," was important for my own initial encounters with Derrida, while the second and third, chapter 8 of *Daimon Life* and chapter 4 of *Lunar Voices,* were left largely without response from him. Not that Derrida was displeased with or uninterested in them—our conversations about them enable me to feel sure about that. When I urged him in 1992 to return to Heidegger's Trakl interpretation and to publish *Geschlecht III*, he laughed and said, "Why should I? You've already done it." I have no illusions or delusions about this, of course, and my insistence that he continue is what lies behind the book the reader has now in hand: even if Derrida leaves the question of the brother and sister in Trakl's poetry largely in suspense, advising his students to pursue it, and even if he leaves the theme of the lovers in Trakl's poetry more or less undiscussed, in spite of his own dedication to the mysteries of *amour,* it seems to me that the 1984–85 seminar, "The Phantom of the Other," eminently merits publication and discussion. What follows is no more than a concluding reflection on a number of the many phantoms—all of them altogether other—with which Derrida has blessed us in that seminar. Including the phantoms of Georg and Gretl Trakl.

Perhaps seven themes call for further thinking: first, but also last, as the alpha and omega of the present undertaking, the riddle of Georg Trakl's magnetism for both Heidegger and Derrida—especially the admiration that Heidegger has for this *poète maudit,* which is anything but clear; second, the problem of *Erläuterung* and *Erörterung,* "commentary" and "placement" or "situation," which are not simply alternating modes of interpretation, not simply in *Wechselbezug,* as Heidegger claims, but which indicate an aporia of thinking in the face of all poetry; third, related to the issue of "placement" as opposed to "commentary," the problem of Heideggerian *Mehrdeutigkeit*, or "multiplicity of meaning," as opposed to the less familiar and far more difficult notion of Derridian *dissémination;* fourth, the likewise related question of the idiomatic qualities of any and every language, and that means the issue of possible and impossible translation; fifth, Heidegger's strange reduction of the sister in Trakl's poetry to a mere appurtenance of fraternity, even though he is perfectly aware of the importance of σελάννα, the lunar voice of the sister; sixth, Heidegger's apparent confidence that the two "blows" of *Geschlecht* can be distinguished, the first coining the neutral difference of sexual duality, man and woman, the second introducing the curse of discord into the relations between them, especially when such discord invades the brother-sister relationship; equally problematic is the further confidence—or desperate hope—that a return to a "more serene childhood" is possible for the *Geschlechter;* and seventh, the problem of "Christian faith" and "Christian despair" in relation to Trakl's poetry.

Initially, however, I would like to enter a preliminary remark concerning the termination of the *Geschlecht* series. Derrida's presentation of *Aporias: Dying—Awaiting (One Another at) the Limits of Truth* on July 15, 1992, at Cerisy la Salle, was an extraordinary event. If the theme for this second *décade* (of the eventual four) at Cerisy in honor of Derrida's work was "Crossing Frontiers," Derrida chose to talk about the frontier we call *death*. Again it was Heidegger who occupied center stage, albeit not the Heidegger of spirit, whether in 1933 or 1953, nor the Heidegger of *Geschlecht,* whether in 1928 or 1953. Here it was once again a matter of Heidegger's *Being and Time* and its famous existential interpretation of death as the "possible impossibility of Dasein," along with Maurice Blanchot's alternative, which one might call the "impossible possibility of death." During his introductory remarks on limits and frontiers, Derrida observed: "In another conference it would have been necessary to explore these experiences of the edge or the borderline designated by what one calls the body proper and sexual difference" (AP 48/21). Yet that conference never materialized, even though Derrida's final seminar on animality constantly touched on the themes of sexuality and sexual difference.

At this same *décade* of 1992, I presented a paper with the title, "Passage à la soeur: autour de Trakl, Heidegger et *Geschlecht*," which became the basis for the fourth chapter of *Lunar Voices,* "The Lunar Voice of the Sister," mentioned a moment ago. Both the discussion with Derrida that followed my paper and his own remark in the "Aporias" lecture should have demonstrated to me—although I am not certain that I recognized it at the time—that the *Geschlecht* project had come to a close. Foolishly, I did not jot down any notes from the discussion that followed my own paper, but I recall Derrida asking me principally about the quandary that goes under the by now familiar terms *Erläuterung* and *Erörterung*. As I remember, he did not venture farther into the matter that occupied me then as now—the peculiar power of the figures of the sister and the lovers in Trakl's poetry, along with Heidegger's resistance to any discussion of that power. As I read again *Aporias* all these years later—more than two decades have passed—I am torn between the desire to discuss it here, because it is truly an extraordinary meditation—indeed, one of Derrida's most remarkable confrontations with Heidegger—and the necessity of recognizing that in it Trakl plays no obvious role.

The first (and last) of the seven themes mentioned above is that of Trakl's mysterious magnetism. I had been reading Heidegger's Trakl interpretation, especially in "Die Sprache im Gedicht," along with the poems of Georg Trakl to which Heidegger's reading initially sent me, since the early 1970s. I had also begun to learn more about Trakl's brief and troubled life, as well as about the life of his beloved sister Margarethe, "Gretl." Her life was as brief and as catastrophic as her brother's. Georg died of an overdose of cocaine during the first weeks of World War I; Gretl died of a self-inflicted gunshot wound three years later. The very first remark of my first published venture into Trakl, "Strokes of Love and Death," notes how bizarre the pair Heidegger-Trakl seems to be. We can easily understand Heidegger's devotion to Hölderlin. Everything about Hölderlin seems to justify Heidegger's devotion, even if not everything about Heidegger's devotion does justice to Hölderlin. Yet no matter how "Expressionist" Heidegger's own thinking and writing often prove to be, it is difficult to comprehend the fundamental ontologist's or the later thinker's dedication to Trakl's poetry, a dedication that began during Heidegger's student days and continued up to the end of his life. One of Trakl's companions called the poet "a Platonic criminal," and while that could mean many things, none of them seems likely to have drawn Heidegger to Trakl. The magnetism that Trakl exerts on Heidegger may of course arise from the echoes of Hölderlin that we hear throughout Trakl's verses. Klaus Mann remarks that Trakl "took up the lyre that slipped from Hölderlin's hands"; Kurt Pinthus adds that Trakl himself "glided *hölderlinisch* into an infinitely blue stream of fatal attenuation."[1] In our own days the lyre seems to have

---

1. For the source of these quotations from Kurt Pinthus, *Menschheitsdämmerung,* see IM, 189.

passed to Paul Celan, Ingeborg Bachmann, and others; certainly in the Anglophone world, albeit not in the German-speaking world, Trakl has well-nigh vanished. Among "Heideggerians," the Trakl essays of Heidegger are largely ignored: they seem not to "fit in" with Heidegger's usual preoccupations. They certainly do not aid any ethereal thinking of being or *Ereignis;* they surely do not edify in any way. And yet, as Derrida says of these essays, especially the second, "Die Sprache im Gedicht," they are remarkably dense and rich, as intense and as thought-provoking as any of Heidegger's lectures and essays on Hölderlin. Perhaps Heidegger, in spite of his problems with Rilke, would have had to affirm Rilke's response to Trakl's poetry. Rilke described his reaction to it in four words: *ergriffen, staunend, ahnend, und ratlos,* "gripped, astonished, intimating, and utterly at a loss."[2] He asked Ludwig von Ficker, "Who might he have been?"

*Derrida's* attraction to Trakl is surely as indebted to Heidegger's reading of the poet as my own was and is. That is to say, we have no evidence that Derrida had any "contact" with Trakl's poetry prior his study of Heidegger's two essays in *Unterwegs zur Sprache.* That is natural enough—and it testifies to the importance of *literary* as well as *philosophical* nationality and nationalism. It is safe to say that what both fascinates and perturbs Derrida about Heidegger's reading of Trakl is its confidence, the assurance with which it declares what Trakl's ostensible single poem, unwritten and unsung, says; to be sure, Heidegger often enough proclaims the tentativeness of his "placement" of Trakl's poetry, avowing that he scarcely dares to continue with it, and yet Derrida suspects that these proclamations are disingenuous. No doubt, he finds Trakl's poems far less amenable to such a confident "placement," in part because they are written and sung in *germain.* For Derrida, the magnetism of Trakl's poetry has to do with those declarations of love mentioned earlier: *aimance* and *aimer* are of a piece, and the title *Geschlecht,* although in the German idiom, itself identifies the nature of the magnetism in Derrida's case. For Derrida, the lover of Baudelaire, Mallarmé, Kafka, Maurice Blanchot, Georges Bataille, Jean Genet, Francis Ponge, Hélène Cixous, and Paul Celan, the magnetism of Trakl's poetry is not so difficult to explain, even if its "situation" remains undecidable. Ludwig Wittgenstein, who through the agency of Ludwig von Ficker provided a generous grant to Trakl during the final weeks

---

2. Rainer Maria Rilke, *Briefe aus den Jahren 1914 bis 1921* (Leipzig: Insel Verlag, 1938), 36–37. See also Rilke's letter to Ludwig von Ficker immediately preceding and a later one, dated February 22, 1917, to Trakl's childhood friend Erhard Buschbeck, *Briefe,* 126–27.

of the poet's life, says this about the poems: "I don't understand them; but their *tone* pleases me. It is the tone of the truly ingenious human being" (OB 145). Neither Derrida nor Heidegger mentions Wittgenstein's response, but it is in any case much closer to their own responses than one might have imagined. About Rilke's response too they remain silent. After one studies Trakl's poetic development, observing his meticulous revision of poem after poem, one is left with a remark by Trakl to Karl Röck, which the latter records as follows: "One cannot communicate oneself at all." *Man kann sich überhaupt nicht mitteilen* (OB 101).

To be sure, Derrida's Trakl and Heidegger's Trakl are two very different sorts of lodestones—in spite of the fascination that draws them both to him. For both Heidegger and Derrida, however, the question as to who Trakl may have been leads directly to the question of *Geschlecht*—the genus and generation of humankind, coined in and by the twofold of the *Geschlechter*. And that question leads directly to that of the *Schlag*, the blow, stamping, or coining of humankind that itself appears to be twofold: first, the blow or coinage produces the primal twofold of the sexes, and second, the blow, inexplicably become a curse and a plague, drives those sexes into dissension and internecine warfare. Ultimately, that second blow, which may become yet a third, when the dissension between man and woman penetrates the brother-sister pair in a way that Heidegger describes as superlative malignancy, leads Heidegger—but also Derrida, who has not given up on a certain utopia of sexual differences—to ask whether one may hope for a more gentle twofold. Heidegger seems to find it in a regression back to childhood, as though childhood and its latency were the primal scene of a gentleness or *Sanftmut* that later, in sexual maturity, is quashed. Derrida, who may be, *pace* Lacan, the most creative interpreter of psychoanalysis in our time, cannot follow such a move, which appears to be a return to something that never was, an impossible return to a past that never was present. Even so, as Derrida concedes, one can dream. The magnetism of Georg and Gretl Trakl—for once again the name Gretl, mentioned by neither philosopher, is drawn magnetically into the constellation—along with the magnetism of Trakl's poetry, seem to draw philosophers of any and every stripe into the realm of dream.

What in the end seems to frustrate Heidegger's phantasm of a radical transformation of the accursed coinage of humankind, namely, its transfiguration into a matutinal birth and burgeoning, a transfiguration promised at the dawn but not realized by nightfall, is that Trakl's poetry everywhere affirms the interlacing of dawn and dusk, innocence and guilt, greening and decaying. To be on Earth and to belong to the earth is to affirm that interlacing. It is a mistake to say, as I said in my first effort to read Heidegger's Trakl essay, that Trakl *contrasts* blue game and the decomposing *Geschlecht*. Trakl is not a poet of contrastings. He is a poet of accumulated intertwinings and imbrications, in which the poet's own mirror image is that of a female stranger—utterly uncanny in all its confirmations and contradictions. Oppositional thinking does not pertain to Trakl and is inadequate to his poetry. His law does not exclude the middle but embraces it. What is oddest about Heidegger's reading of Trakl is that while it rejects any "Christian" or "Platonizing" placement of the poems, the "apartness" of that poetry is thought in terms of a history of being that seeks rescue and even salvation for the *Menschengeschlecht,* provided there can be a radical purge of the "disessenced" creature. Such a purge, transfiguration, and salvation necessitate Heidegger's effort to distinguish between the two blows, the first innocent or at least neutral, the second evil. His effort thus culminates in the phantasm of the *transmutation* of evil. Such a transmutation, in Heidegger's view, would repel the invasion of quarrel and conflict into the relations between brother and sister; it would resist or "still" that invasion by realizing a more gentle, more tranquil childhood for the two of them. And even so, Heidegger is convinced that his own dream has nothing to do with Platonism or with Christianity.

The word *incest* of course does not appear in Heidegger's essays on Trakl. Derrida too circumvents the word, even if it is the word of Rousseau. For Heidegger, at least, the work of thinking and the word of poetry must be protected from brutal penetrations of biography and psychology, to say nothing of cultural anthropology and the law. And yet the shadow of discord and even of supreme evil haunts the siblings. If Hegel appears to be confident that in the brother-sister relationship the blood is never agitated (PG 325–26), Heidegger is no longer so certain. And Derrida is far from certain, as he dreams of a redoubled, universal homosexuality, or at least of a desire between siblings that does not lead to war. Even if one can and must exclude psychoanalysis and every other social science from a placement of poetry, the effects of those discourses is felt on every page of Heidegger's text. Avoidance, as Derrida demonstrates so effectively in *Of Spirit,* even if a sometime thing with regard to its efficacy, is everywhere present in Heidegger's essay. Avoidance operates a bit like the mood of anxiety as described in *Being and Time*: even when one turns one's back on the fundamental attunement of anxiety, it creeps up from behind, and nothing turns out to be harder to maintain than a complacent inauthenticity.

Heidegger's need to rescue Trakl and the rest of humankind from the decomposition and "disessencing" that Trakl so compellingly poetizes results in various forms of violence in his placement. One of them is so alarming that I need to reproduce my complaint about it here, even though already in *Lunar Voices* I made much of it. Because Heidegger wants to separate off the transmogrified race of a new humankind from what has gone before, he insists that Trakl can only rejoice when the accursed race falls in battle—one thinks of Ernst Macke, Franz Marc, and Trakl himself among the fallen. Heidegger comments on the final lines of "Grodek," "The hot flame of spirit is fed today by an overwhelming agony, / The unborn grandchildren," as follows:

> The "grandchildren" indicated here are in no sense the sons who remain ungenerated by the sons who have fallen [*die ungezeugt gebliebenen Söhne der gefallenen Söhne*], those fallen sons who stemmed from the decomposing *Geschlecht*. If that were all that is involved, namely, a cessation of further generation of prior *Geschlechter*, then our poet would have to jubilate over such an end [*müßte . . . jubeln*]. Yet he is in mourning. To be sure, it is a "prouder mourning," one that gazes ardently on the repose of the unborn. (US 65)

Heidegger recognizes that Trakl is in mourning, but he wants to deny that it is a mourning of the unborn offspring of the war dead. For such unborn would belong to the accursed race, and Heidegger is certain that Trakl joins him in wishing that race good riddance. Heidegger cannot conceive of Trakl's intimate belonging to the accursed race, cannot conceive of Trakl's affirmation of and fidelity to the disessenced *Geschlecht*. Yet Trakl's poetry everywhere proclaims the poet's belonging to and affirmation of that unhappy house, which is the only house there ever was. Trakl, the poet who served as a medic during the first weeks of the war, a medic without medicines, unable to alleviate the suffering of the wounded whose desperation cost him his own life, is not likely to have exulted over the agony and wretched demise of his fellows, however "disessenced." It is one thing not to allow biography to intrude upon a placement of poetry; it is another to project a brutal indifference onto the poet. Trakl does not dream of the demise of any *Geschlecht*. The cruelty of Silenos and the scorn of Mephistopheles are ultimately foreign to him, no matter how much he castigates himself for his hardness of heart, his arrogance, and his lack of love. When in "Autumn Soul" Trakl invokes the "dark wandering" that "soon separated us from loved ones, others," a separation (the -*schied* of *Abgeschiedenheit*) that causes him pain and grief, Heidegger is once again happy to celebrate the end of the accursed race. In Heidegger's view, the "others" are nothing other than "the coinage of the decomposed configuration of humanity" (US 49), ostensibly spurned by the poet for the sake of the new *Geschlecht*. Heidegger concedes that some love and veneration may still "remain attached" to these contemptible "others," but what he desires is that the figure of Elis, he or she of the lunar voice, become "the other with regard to these others [*der Andere zu den Anderen*]" (US 50). Heidegger hopes and trusts that the "others" cited in Trakl's line will be abandoned. In other words, the *Liebe* that is still attached to the "others" in Trakl's line, *von Lieben, Andern*, is an embarrassment to Heidegger, something that ought to be overcome. Loved ones? Heidegger never mentions them again. Lovers? Heidegger never mentions them at all. Trakl often does. His favorite novel is Goethe's *Wahlverwandtschaften*, "such a still and gentle book" (OB 111).

The lovers, invoked time and again in Trakl's poetry, some of it reproduced in Appendix B at the end of the present book, share the mild time of gentle embrace. They raise their roselike eyelids under the shadow of a tree, breathing sighs among its branches. Blond and beaming lovers cast darkling looks at one another and in dark conversation come to know one another as man and woman. Lovers glow afresh in wingèd things, cling to one another with longing arms, and they suffer more gently. (Indeed, *Sanftmut* seems to be preeminently theirs, even as they cling to one another, even as they make love.) Their breath flows more sweetly through the night as they blossom toward their stars. To be sure, there is a shadow side to their embrace. Their limbs are *schmächtig*, delicate but also fragile, sometimes utterly without strength, languishing, exhausted. The lovers die on their way across. Finally, the lovers are also mentioned in the very poem that gives Heidegger his principal question, the question of *Geschlecht*, the question that in turn magnetizes Derrida. We have seen and heard these lines from the "Western Song" already:

> Aber strahlend heben die silbernen Lider die Liebenden:
> E i n Geschlecht. Weihrauch strömt von rosigen Kissen
> Und der süße Gesang der Auferstandenen.
>
> Yet radiantly rise the silver eyelids of lovers:
> O n e *Geschlecht*. Incense streams from pillows all roses
> And the sweet song of the resurrected.

When Derrida in the final stages of his 1984–85 seminar comments on Heidegger's foreshortened and even foreclosed reading of this poem, we can sense the entire range of questions Derrida himself wants to raise, questions such as the following: Where, in Heidegger's treatment of Trakl, do we find an interpretation of the radiance of the lovers, the rays or beams of the lovers? Where do we find an inquiry into the eyelids of lovers, for example, or for that matter into the eyebrows of the sister, shaped and bent by God? (See "To the Sister," cited below and reprinted in Appendix B.) Do we find even the word *die Liebenden* in either of Heidegger's two Trakl essays? Do the lovers then count for nothing? Even when they immediately precede the colon that may well *gather* an entire poem to its meaning? Have the lovers no relation to Heidegger's dream of stillness, repose, and *Sanftmut*? What is the relation of lovers to childhood, to the childlike and even the childish? Can anything about that relation be decided in *epochal* terms, that is to say, for an entire *Geschlecht*? Or would not differences abound especially here? Would there not be, amidst all the failures gaffes gambles and losses, the occasional achievement of tenderness? the fortuitous combination of madness and gentleness? laughter without mockery? tears without crocodiles? Would thinking be able to entertain something like the polysemic pleasure of lovers? And what about these loving bodies, and the exhalations of these bodies? What is the incense that yellows the lovers' pillows, pillows otherwise all roses? Why is the lovers' song sweet? And why is it a song or even a hymn of "the resurrected"?

To be sure, in response to this last question Heidegger would be quick to deny that such "resurrection" is anything like the one depicted on the Isenheim altar, which shows an astonishingly radiant Christ bursting from the tomb. Derrida, for his part, would wonder whether such a Christ, or any follower of Christ, in addition to being a sister, might also be a lover. At all events, the lines quoted above are the very last lines of the *Abendländisches Lied*. And if the Occident named in the title of Trakl's song is (at least in part) also the site of Heidegger's history of being, how can his or anyone's account of the history of being ignore these lines? Dare anyone extract *one* word from *one* phrase, the *one* of O n e *Geschlecht*, and ignore the rest?

In *Lunar Voices* I could find no better way of describing Heidegger's placement of Trakl's poem than by declaring, rather naively and helplessly, that Heidegger turns the horizontality of the lovers into a vertical, transforming their horizon into the phantasm of an upward-bound humankind in the history of being. The irony of such ascensionalism, preferring the *y*-axis to the *x*-axis, would be that it collapses back into the Platonism from which it had hoped to rescue Trakl's poetry. The destitution of such ascensionalism is that it deprives itself of the "sweet song of the resurrected." And who apart from the moralist and the metaphysician would refuse to exchange the entire history of being for one stanza of that song? Sung by even the most tone deaf dissessenced lover?

I recall keeping these reminders alive at Cerisy la Salle in 1992. Whatever the excesses and failures of my remarks there, the resulting chapter in *Lunar Voices* does several things that I believe still have some future to them: (1) it challenges Heidegger's notions of the gentleness of childhood and the apparent clarity of the distinction boy-girl as envisaged by Trakl; (2) it challenges Heidegger's attribution to Trakl of the notion that a futural and matutinal generation of the unborn will be the culmination of Western history—that is to say, it challenges what here too I will continue to call Heidegger's "verticalization" of the horizon(t)al relation of brothers, sisters, and lovers in Trakl's poetry; (3) it invites us to think about Heidegger's tacit allusion to and acceptance of the incest prohibition in his interpretation of radical evil, an allusion that refuses to meditate on that prohibition; (4) it challenges Heidegger's bland suggestion that one can fraternize with the sister by becoming a brother to the stranger;[3] finally, (5) it bears witness to Heidegger's failure to recognize that the *one* of *E i n Geschlecht* is predicated not of brother and sister prior to the second stroke, nor even after the second stroke, but of the lovers, *Liebenden*.

What might one ask of Derrida, or now of his readers, with regard to the themes of the sister and the lovers in Trakl's poetry? One possibility would be to expand Derrida's *Politics of Friendship* by considering the way in which Heidegger too elevates *fraternity* to a central position even when it is a question of the sister. Recall the odd way in which, according to Heidegger, one "gains" a sister—discussed at some length in *Lunar Voices*. It is a ritual of the uncanniest sort. According to Heidegger, "A friend listens in on the stranger. Listening in this way, he pursues the one who is apart, and thereby himself becomes a wanderer, a stranger" (US 68). The friend with whom Heidegger seems to identify himself is all ears, and by listening to the stranger's song the friend becomes everything the stranger is. The friend is, or desires to be, the friend that every Dasein

---

3. Please note the printer's error in chapter 4 of *Lunar Voices:* on p. 103, line 6 from the bottom, the phrase should read: "becomes a *brother* to his sister."

carries with itself, the friend who haunts *Geschlecht IV.* These strange friends share everything, even their fraternal relation to a sister. It is not that the sister of the one becomes the sister of the other. The problem then becomes: How does one gain a sister?

The friend who listens invites the stranger to converse with him. He gazes on the stranger until the stranger returns his gaze. Through this exchange of regards, the friend becomes *a brother* to the stranger. The friend, become brother, presumably gains for himself all the mysterious serenity of the stranger. The stranger, who is perhaps the boy who died young, Elis, is himself the secret source of serenity and repose. Nevertheless, as though by way of some unexplained supplementation, Heidegger now adds a final detail concerning the initiation into brotherhood, the rite of passage from friend to brother: "However, when the friend who listens in sings 'The Song of the Departed,' and in so doing becomes a brother to the stranger, the stranger's brother, through the stranger alone [*durch diesen erst*], becomes a brother to his sister, the sister whose 'lunar voice resounds through the spiriting night'" (US 69–70). The lines of the "Gesang des Abgeschiedenen" (reprinted in Appendix A) that seem particularly relevant to Heidegger's winning of a sister are these:

> Und es leuchtet ein Lämpchen, das Gute, in seinem Herzen
> Und der Frieden des Mahls; denn geheiligt ist Brot und Wein
> Von Gottes Händen, und es schaut aus nächtigen Augen
> Stille dich der Bruder an, daß er ruhe von dorniger Wanderschaft.
> O das Wohnen in der beseelten Bläue der Nacht. (T 79)

> And a fragile lamp is lit, the good, in his heart
> And the peace of the repast; for bread and wine are sanctified
> By God's hands, and, gazing at you from nocturnal eyes,
> Quietly, the brother, may he find rest from thorny wandering;
> Oh, to dwell in the ensouled blueness of the night.

Singing these lines, the friend becomes a brother to the stranger, and, although nothing in this poem directly names or invokes the sister, the friend, according to Heidegger, "through the stranger alone, becomes a brother to his sister." One has to ask: *his* sister? Whose? Two remarks, one on the "his" of "his sister," the second on the sister as inevitably the sister to a "brother."

In the phrase *wird der Bruder des Fremdlings durch diesen erst zum Bruder seiner Schwester,* what is the antecedent of the possessive pronoun *seiner*? Is the sister in question consanguineous with the stranger, or rather with the stranger's friend and newly won brother? The French translation of Heidegger's "Language in the Poem" does not hesitate to answer the question concerning the sister, translating the phrase as follows: *"ce frère devient, pour sa propre soeur, à son tour un frère,"* roughly, "this brother becomes in turn a brother to his own sister."[4] At the instant the friend becomes a brother to the stranger, his fraternal relation to *his own* sister becomes somehow realized, becomes only now what it always should have been. The French words *pour sa propre* and *à son tour* correspond to nothing in the German text; they are expletives used to justify the translators' decision about whose sister this is. Had Heidegger written *"seiner* eigenen *Schwester,"* one would know that the sister is initially related to the stranger's *friend,* and the French translation would be apt. However, the word *eigenen* is not there; neither is anything that might mean "in [his or her] turn." Had Heidegger written *"des Fremdlings . . .* dessen *Schwester,"* one would know that the sister is first of all a sister of the *stranger,* and *only through him* a sister to her brother's new brother. In short, Heidegger's wording is ambiguous—or, as he would prefer to say, *mehrdeutig,* multiple in meaning. Yet one cannot get over the feeling that the sister is being manhandled. For in both cases the sister remains the sister to a brother, precisely as she does in Hegel's model of the ethical deed in the nascent community (PG 318–42; Gl 160–71/141–51, 184–211/163–88). She is a sister only by grace of the fraternal axis. No matter whose sister she may be *ab ovo,* the brother remains the axis, the pivotal point, the magnetic pole, the active and controlling center of the sibling relation. The friend and brother enters into relation with her—no matter whose sister she is, as though in their confusion they were bartering for a sister rather than a bride—exclusively by the action and efficacy of the male stranger. *Durch diesen erst,* that is, only through the male stranger, does the friend become a brother to the sister: no multiplicity of meaning here. Heidegger's stranger is never *die Fremdlingin.* She would be too strange, too *fremd.*

Or does the oddest multiplicity of meaning occur *nolens volens* precisely here? When the friend and brother-to-be listens in on the stranger, whose voice does he hear? Is not the stranger's a lunar voice? And is not the lunar voice always and everywhere in Trakl's poetry the Selenic voice

---

4. Martin Heidegger, *Acheminement vers la parole,* trans. Jean Beaufret, Werner Brokmeier, and François Fédier (Paris: Gallimard, 1976), 72.

of the sister? If the stranger "himself," the boy Elis, is lunar, *monden* (T 15), does not the closest of ties bind sister and stranger, and perhaps something more than ties? Does not the sister incorporate everything that is strange, including the extravagant, spiriting night, the night of decline and death—precisely as that *Jünglingin,* that impossible female youth? As each of these figures elides with and emerges from the other, it becomes more and more difficult to learn how one gains a sister. If the sister is *familial* in relation to all that is strange, there is precisely nothing *familiar* about her. She is the uncanny in all that is canny, the secret passage to the *(un)heimlich* as such. She is most uncannily lodged in the stranger's throat, as "his" larynx, "his" voice. She, *la voix,* gives herself out as her brother, her brother the philosopher. And everyone, including Heidegger, thinks it is the master who is speaking.

A second possibility for expanding such questions, far more difficult of execution, would be to read once again those pages in *De la grammatologie* (DG 361–78) that deconstruct the themes of autoeroticism and incest in Rousseau's *Essay on the Origin of Languages.* Here Derrida discusses a chain of supplements that bind erotic matters to the scene of writing. In a sense, these erotic themes dominate the entire second part of the *Grammatology,* so that summarizing them here is quite impossible. Suffice it to say that something of the logic of the supplement runs through Heidegger's "Language in the Poem" from beginning to end, from the very relation of "placement" and "commentary" to the two *Schläge* that coin but then distort and disrupt *die Geschlechter.* The need to locate the supplement *outside the system* and the entire problem of the *hinge,* that is, the impossible trapdoor (as in Kafka's *Der Bau*) between nature and culture, or between the pristine commencement and the "disessenced" or decomposed *Geschlecht,* propels Heidegger's text as much as it does Rousseau's. The innocence of the first stroke is mirrored in Rousseau's "feast," in the joyous dance of the (boy) cowherds and the (girl) water bearers at the well; the discord of the second blow would be that *funeste hasard* that never should have occurred, but did occur, introducing prohibition, temptation, violation, discord, and war into the play of the world. The attempt to explain—or explain away—catastrophe would be common to both texts. What catastrophe? Ultimately, the loss of *presence* and of *the origin,* the disappearance of "the true cradle of the nations," and the commencement of a ruinous age, that of incest prohibition, which for the first time distinguishes brother and sister from the lovers. Yet in Rousseau as well the two blows cannot really be distinguished—they parallel one another, and indeed the one seems to arise from the other. The "post-originary degradation" of civilization, as Derrida says, "is analogous to the pre-originary repetition" (DG 377). Might one not translate this as the inextricability, in spite of Heidegger's every effort, of the two blows or strokes in Heidegger's placement of Trakl's poem? Is it not with Heidegger as it is with Rousseau—that "the feast just as soon [straightway, immediately, directly: *aussitôt*] becomes war" (ibid.)? Yet such an *aussitôt* would devastate every hope for a new dawn to come in the history of being as *Ereignis*. It would reduce Heidegger's "other thinking" to sheer delusion—to a mere phantasm of the other.

A third possibility for advancing these questions, the most difficult of the three, is of course *Glas,* which announces *amour* as its theme— whether in the column of *dialectic* or that of *galactic*—and which focuses as much on the sister as it does on the lovers and on the question of incest. In both cases, one is dealing (also) with Hegel, so that the mind-bending complexity of the dialectic is everywhere guaranteed. Yet the logic of the cauldron too is everywhere present, as is that of the supplement: "Dialectic of nature: nature produces the prohibition of incest by splitting away from itself, but this rupture with itself is in its nature, in the nature of nature" (Gl 224A). It would be fruitful to consider the circularity of the unborn *Geschlecht* and the demise of the "disessenced" *Geschlecht* in terms of the nature of nature: the unborn *Geschlecht* is "older" than the accursed race of metaphysical man, but is also destined to be—or at least is promised as—its future, as though the sending of being will finally get around to delivering the mail that some renegade letter carrier has stowed in his cellar for millennia.

In *Daimon Life,* I translated a passage from Luce Irigaray's commentary on Heidegger's placement of Trakl's poetry in her *L'oubli de l'air: chez Martin Heidegger.* It seemed to me to promise a way to move from questions of brother and sister to questions involving the lovers. I reproduce the passage here:

> That man is heading into his decline, into the decomposition of whatever up to now has gathered man—this he [Heidegger] has said. At least, by way of the poet Trakl. . . . That the dusk would offer the chance of a new dawn, that this November would offer the hope of a new spring to come, a hope granted by a gaze that is lost in the night—this he has said. And again, that the destiny of this other sunrise has been confided to something foreign [*à l'étrange*], where all will be gathered, sheltered, and safeguarded otherwise. Where will the sojourn find another

site? Where will habitation take place, no longer on the site of hate, but in the lodgings of the only tenderness there is?

Yet it is in a young boy, a boy who is dead in order to safeguard a profound childhood, that this setting and rising would find their possible future. A young boy, demented: sensitized otherwise than man, the old man, of the West. A dream that is dead at morningtide, a dream dreamt for the insurrection of spirit [*de l'esprit*]. Abandoned to the passageways of an underground memory.

The apparition and evanescence of a profound childhood, ungenerated by the difference between boy and girl, would find their place in the figure of an adolescent. It would be on the side of man's having yet to be engendered that a chance would be reserved for what is to come. Would it still be of man [*Encore de l'homme*]?[5]

It is clear that both Irigaray and Derrida are skeptical about the chances of that dead boy, skeptical about the chance of a new dawn that is entirely caught up in figures of the previous day and its long night. And it is also clear that many readers—readers who no longer read Irigaray now that she has become essentialist rather than essential—will be skeptical about her claim concerning tenderness, *la tendresse,* namely, that it is one and that it bears some essential relation to woman or to the feminine, as if she or it were one. In any case, where will the sojourn of humankind find another site? Where will human habitation take place, if it yearns to flee the site of discord, dissension, and hate, seeking respite "in the lodgings of the only tenderness there is"? It is, of course, important not to attribute such lodgings to the womb alone or to a more tranquil childhood, which would be an oneiric continuation of that amniotic existence and a phantasmatic return to latency. Perhaps the only recourse, in a time that dreams the dream cited in the exergue of the present book, is to seek tenderness among lovers of every stripe, lovers of every shape and dimension, lovers of every persuasion, lovers who are persuaded of nothing other than one another.

---

5. Luce Irigaray, *L'oubli de l'air chez Martin Heidegger* (Paris: Minuit, 1983), 108–109. Since the time of *Daimon Life,* Irigaray's astonishing book, which, as she told me, she began to write in late May 1976, the moment she heard of Heidegger's death, so that *L'oubli* may be considered a work of mourning, has been translated by Mary Beth Mader and published by the University of Texas Press.

The sought tenderness would not sing paeans to incest. Robert Musil's *Der Mann ohne Eigenschaften,* his never-completed saga of the siblings Ulrich and Agathe, demonstrates quite convincingly that brother and sister will never become the Siamese twins they both dream of becoming. Yet the tenderness between the two characters augments in the course of the long novel and its endless sketches toward a completion. Theirs is a tenderness that does not regress to a more serene childhood, not even when every mode of expressed tenderness seems to be baffled by the world. Wherever that tenderness arises from, whatever its traces in the lives of men and women, it seems to be the elixir that might alter the accursed *Geschlecht*. Not by eliminating that *Geschlecht*, certainly not by letting it fall in war, but by bending it a bit, gently. We today do not appear to be finding the formula for such an elixir. Yet we can dream and we can concoct, and we can hope that our dreams and our potions become more inventive as our hopes become more modest.

It is clear to me that from the very beginning I accepted and affirmed Heidegger's view that Trakl is not a Christian poet, and that even his despair is not "Christian despair." I did not stop to ask myself what the latter—either a mystery or an oxymoron—could possibly be. By accepting Heidegger's reading I earned the wrath of other commentators in the field of German Studies who stressed the Christian metaphors and figures in Trakl's poetry. Yet I remained adamant in my apostasy, affirming Heidegger's denial of the Christian context of Trakl's poetry. As a possible defense, one could say that Heidegger may be reacting to the eminently "Christian" adoption of Trakl's poetry by the *Brenner-Kreis,* led after Ludwig von Ficker's death by Carl Dallago, an adoption so fervent and so total that critics are sometimes driven to speak of "the Trakl church." Yet Heidegger himself says nothing about the *Brenner* circle and seems to declare Trakl's non-Christian status *ex cathedra,* as it were. Derrida's criticisms of Heidegger in this respect (and I think for once one can call them *criticisms*) are therefore devastating. One only has to read a few stanzas in the volume of Trakl's collected poems, to read almost anywhere in it, and one will find at least something like the rags and remnants of Christian faith, Christian shame and guilt, perhaps even Christian despair—whatever that may be. In an earlier chapter I cited Trakl's astonishing "Psalm," reprinted in Appendix A. In this respect one may also cite a poem Trakl titles "Humanity," *Menschheit*:

> Humanity exposed to maws of fire,
> A drumroll, brows of dark warriors,
> Footsteps through a fog of blood; black iron reports,
> Despair, night in brains that mourn:

> Here the shade of Eve, the hunt, and red lucre.
> Clouds pierced by light, the Last Supper.
> A gentle taciturnity dwells in bread and wine
> And they are gathered, twelve in number.
> At night, asleep beneath the olive boughs, they cry out;
> Saint Thomas dips his hand into the wound.

It is a "doubting Thomas," to be sure, and doubtless a doubting Georg. Yet who or what could be more Christian than the doubter? It is safe to say that Trakl's is a Christianity that is something apart, *abgeschieden,* precisely as Heidegger says. It is also safe to say, as Derrida does say, that Trakl does not dream of simply banishing that tradition, does not dream of being able to set it aside or leave it behind him. If the cloister walls are "crowded by fairytales and legends," one may argue into the evening and all through the night about whether Christendom or Christianity can be reduced to bygone sagas. And when Saint Thomas dips his hand, not a finger but the entire hand, it is important to know that the wound is here called a *Wundenmal,* whereby *Mal* is a mole or a birthmark, perhaps Melville's "sad birthmark," also a scar, a stigma (see John 20:24–29). The one thing we may safely say is that Trakl's Christianity has nothing to do with certitude of sanctity, nothing to do with faith in salvation; it is safer to say, as Otto Basil does say, that Christianity is itself a baptism of fire for Trakl, perhaps even exposure to a kind of leprosy. The question of Trakl's "Christianity" appears and reappears throughout Basil's excellent monograph (OB 8–12, 135–36, and elsewhere). If Elke Lasker-Schüler, one of the greatest of the Expressionist poets, is right when she says that Trakl "was surely Martin Luther," then he is the Luther of rebellion and wrath, but also the Luther of the dark night of the soul. It seems safe to say that Trakl's Christianity is that of thorns without mercy, guilt without grace, sin without forgiveness; all the Sorrowful Mysteries and none of the Joyful or Glorious. It is therefore understandable that Heidegger, agreeing with Friedrich Georg Jünger, would want to resist the efforts of the *Brenner-Kreis* to transform Trakl's poetry into piety. Yet it is also quite clear that, as Basil says, "the question is far from being decided" (OB 10).

If paradise is lost, and poor berated Eve is now a shade, the seekers of paradise may head out for Otahiti, as Hölderlin once dreamt of doing, or Borneo, as Trakl proposed (T 275), or they may hope for sanctuary closer to home, where indisputably all is falling to human ruin. Perhaps what is most remarkable in all this is that Derrida, the Algerian Jew whose relation to his own religious tradition is entirely fraught, is the one who is most vigilant and cautious concerning Heidegger's thesis with regard to Trakl's ostensible scorn for Christianity. He, Derrida, will have been taught in this respect by Nietzsche, the pastor's prodigal son who nonetheless did not refuse to meditate on the extent to which, as he says, "we are still pious." Indeed, in Heidegger's reading of Trakl what is perhaps most striking for Derrida is not Heidegger's resistance to Christianity but his susceptibility to stories and themes one associates with Christ. What is the "more tranquil childhood" of which Heidegger dreams? "Suffer the little children to come unto me." And can Heidegger's dream of a vertical rescue of the accursed horizontal generation be anything other than the dream dreamt by what Lacan once scathingly called "the salvationist choirs"?

The magnetism of Georg Trakl himself—the poet rather than the poems—is not easy to explain. It is not entirely easy to be drawn to a man who writes to his sister, not Gretl but another sister, Maria, "I'm always sad whenever I'm happy—isn't that odd?" (T 262). Trakl is no doubt very good at unhappiness. His own father tells the boy that he is drawn to suffering, has a gift for it. There is also no doubt that the magnetism between Georg and Gretl is particularly strong in this respect. They form an alliance against their parents, especially against their mother, and against the harsh world. Yet Georg is also close to his older sisters, Maria ("Mizzi") and Hermine ("Minna"). To the latter, in a letter dated October 5, 1908, he confides the following paradox—the paradox of what he calls "animal drives" and "the ensouled ear for melodies" in his life:

> I believe it must be terrifying always to have to live this way, feeling the full force of all the animal drives that cause our life to wallow through all its phases [*die das Leben durch die Zeiten wälzen*]. I have felt the most terrifying possibilities in me; I have smelled, touched, and heard all the demons howling in my blood, the thousand devils with their thorns that drive the flesh to madness. What a horrifying nightmare!
> 
> Gone! Today this vision of reality has sunk back into nothingness again, things are remote from me now, their voice even more remote, and once again I eavesdrop, all ensouled ear, to the melodies that are in me, and my enraptured eye once again dreams its images, images that are more beautiful than any reality! I am at home with myself; I am my world! My whole beautiful world, full of infinite euphony. (T 261)

During the last two weeks of July 1910 Trakl complains to his friend Erhard Buschbeck that a mediocre poet has been mimicking his style. He refers to "my imagistic style," *meine bildhafte Manier*, "which in a stanza of four lines forges together four individual imagistic parts in order to form one single impression" (T 267). Such forging is "ardent" in his own case, he says, whereas his imitator "lacks the vital fever" (ibid.). At the same time, he writes to Buschbeck that he can configure only the smallest portion of the impressions that strike him ("what an infernal chaos of rhythms and images"), and that he feels like "a risible failure" when he cannot master these impressions—the "slightest external stimulus" transporting him to "cramps and deliria" (T 268). "Mastery" is surely a misnomer, however, since it is always a matter of subordinating himself to the image: "You have to believe that it is not easy for me, and never will be easy for me, to subordinate myself unconditionally to what is to be depicted [*dem Darzustellenden unterzuordnen*], and I have to correct myself over and over again in order to present the truth of what is indeed true" (T 274).

However devoted to Salzburg he may have been for his images, neither Salzburg nor Innsbruck nor Vienna appeal to him as dwelling places. A number of contemporaries report that Trakl is much more at home among workers and farmers than among the *literati* and the city sophisticates. Whereas his relations with the latter are marked by a scarcely concealed disdain and disgust, the disgust doubtless hiding doubts about himself, he is unfailingly kind to and patient with the "common" folk (OB 107, 112). If his more learned associates are magnetized by him, he himself feels drawn to farmers, hunters, and village folk. Above all, he is drawn to the village inn. In the fall of 1912 he writes to Buschbeck,

> I sense that it is winter, that it's getting cold, because of the calefaction I derive from my evening wine [*an der abendlichen Weinheizung*]. The day before yesterday I drank 10 (I tell you: ten!) quarter-liters of red. At four in the morning I took a moon and frost bath on my balcony, and in the morning I finally wrote a splendid poem that shivers with cold. (T 278)

Even after consuming two and a half liters of wine, however, Trakl seems never to lose control, never to slip into a maudlin or aggressive mood; and yet his friends find him on more than one occasion collapsed and unconscious in the snow (OB 104). The tone of his letters, in spite of that reference to a "moon and frost bath," is seldom jocular. To Karl Borromaeus Heinrich in Innsbruck he writes from Salzburg:

> I'd be so happy if you could come to Salzburg in March. My days are not easy here at home, and I muddle along between

fever and faint in sunny rooms that are unspeakably cold. Odd storms of metamorphosis, felt bodily to the point where I cannot bear them, faces of all things dark, absolutely certain that I am dead, enraptured to the point of stony paralysis; and dreaming on and on my mournful dreams. How dark this city of dry rot is, full of churches and images of death. (T 288–89)

Four days later he writes to Ludwig von Ficker, "It terrifies me to think how in recent days I've been developing an inexplicable hatred toward myself, and how in the most insignificant affairs of everyday life I seem to myself to be utterly grotesque" (T 289). During the second week of November 1913, a year before his suicide, the struggle seems to be already over: "I have slept through 2 days and 2 nights, and still today I'm suffering from an overdose of veronal. In my confusion and in all the despair of recent times I no longer know how I should live. . . . It seems to me that everything will end in the dark" (T 307). Two weeks later he adds, "O my God, what a Judgment has come crashing down on me [*ist über mich hereingebrochen*]" (T 311). In January of his final year, Trakl writes to Karl Borromaeus Heinrich:

Things are not entirely well with me. Between despair and drunken stupor I am lost, haven't the strength to alter my position, which becomes more menacing with each passing day, the only wish remaining would be that a storm descend on me and either purify me or destroy me. O God, through what guilt and gloom we are made to pass. May we not be defeated by it in the end. (T 313)

As a reserve medic, he reports for duty when war is declared. During the second week of September his medical unit serves at the battle of Grodek, where the Austrian troops are routed. Many wounded, no medicine. The wounded beg him to finish them off. Trakl tells his messmates, "I cannot live this way." When he hurriedly quits the mess tent he confronts a vast number of corpses hanging from the limbs of the surrounding trees. The Austrians have taken the local Ruthenians to be Russian sympathizers. Trakl's messmates, fearing that he will harm himself, take his weapons from him. On October 7 he is sent to a military hospital in Krakow for psychiatric observation. On October 27 he mails to Ludwig von Ficker in Innsbruck his two last poems, "Klage," and "Grodek." "I almost feel already beyond the world," he writes (T 324). He adds, in a rhetoric that seems to stem from a notary or a lawyer, "In conclusion I wish to add that in the case of my demise it is my wish and will that my dear sister Gretl be given all that I possess by way of money and all other objects." On November 3, 1914, at nine in the evening, he succumbs to an overdose.

Yet it is not only the war, although that would have been enough. A particularly acute distress descends on Trakl in March of that final year. Gretl, after an abortion that has induced excessive bleeding, is close to death. Georg travels to Berlin immediately and remains there from the fifteenth to the twenty-fifth of March, 1914. To Karl Borromaeus Heinrich, on March 19, 1914, Trakl writes, "A few days ago my sister suffered a miscarriage that resulted in extraordinarily vehement hemorrhaging. Her condition is alarming, all the more so since she has not eaten in five days" (T 313). Two days later he writes to Ludwig von Ficker:

> My poor sister is still suffering greatly. Her life is so filled with sadness that it tears my heart; yet she is so wonderfully courageous that I often appear to myself to be very slight compared to her. And she would merit a thousand times more than I to live within a circle of good and noble human beings, a favor that has been granted to me in such extraordinary measure whenever times were difficult.
>
> I plan to stay for a considerable number of days in Berlin, since my sister is alone all day and my presence may be of some use to her. (T 314)

No one knows what transpires there between them during those ten days in Berlin, but it seems to have been decisive. It would doubtless form the core scene, the turning point, of a drama concerning the two of them (OB 140).

What can or must be said about this sister, Margarethe, "Gretl"? She is the object of endless speculation, precisely because we know so little about her. We do not even know where in Berlin she is buried. It as though her self-destruction leads to a second death, her burial in a vault of shame and oblivion. We know that she ends her life at age twenty-five, three years after her brother's death. Her husband, the Berlin bookseller Albert Langen, has by that time left her, having realized that Gretl married him only in order to support her habit. We know that she was a brilliant and well-trained pianist, on her way to a concert career—until the cocaine and opium destroyed her "mechanics." We know that she is devoted to her brother, and that she takes the lead in his life in so many ways. Someone has to, as he himself says, inasmuch as he is only half-born, a kind of seven-month fetus, not yet ready to face the world. Biographers speculate that she and Georg have an incestuous relationship for several years, the Vienna years, but perhaps for many years prior to Vienna as well, and that here too Gretl, five years younger than Georg, appears to have taken the lead—although how can one possibly know such a thing? And, even "knowing" it, what can one possibly understand by it? The biographers and literary historians would know and understand a lot more if the entire correspondence between the two had not been destroyed, presumably by a family member, perhaps the mother. As it is, all we have are the phantoms of her that appear in her brother's poems. The sister combs her hair, plays a Schubert sonata in the next room, and speaks companionably with ghosts in the garden; she is found in an isolated forest clearing at noon amid silent animals, her mouth whispering in black branches. The eyes of her white face stare strangely in someone's evil dreams. Her own sleep is heavy, perhaps because it is steeped in stormy melancholy. She appears as a radiant youth—that is, as an adolescent boy—in autumn amid black corruption, then as a fiery demon with eyes of stone, then again as a pale figure with bleeding mouth. Revealing a silver wound, she murmurs, "Prick, black thorn." Her image emerges from the blue depths of a mirror, plunging her brother into darkness, as though he has met his Doppelgänger in her and therefore is already dead. She may be a child in the summer garden whom he violates. Above all else she is "strange," perhaps even "foreign," *die fremde Schwester,* as Trakl calls her in "Psalm," the alien sister who appears in someone's evil dreams.

In the end, at the end, on that very first battlefield of World War I, she greets the bleeding heads of fallen warriors—as though she were a Valkyrie. In his poem to her, "An die Schwester," the poet associates her with evening and autumn, the migration of birds, and blue game. He marks her slight smile and the melancholy above the arc of her eyebrows. She is Good Friday's Child, full of woe, marked by God and sought out by the stars. Everything about her "sounds," *tönt*:

> To the Sister
>
> Where you walk autumn and evening descend,
> Blue deer sounding beneath the trees,
> Lonely pond at evening.
>
> Softly the flight of birds sounds,
> Melancholy above the arc of your eyes.
> Your slight smile sounds.

God bent the arc of your eyelids.
At night, Good Friday's Child, stars seek
The arc of your brow.

Most persistent, beyond all the visual images, beyond even blue game, is the sound of her voice, her lunar voice, *die mondene Stimme*, reverberating through the "spiriting night." Heidegger does hear this voice, and he comments on it in "Die Sprache im Gedicht," whereas Derrida notes it but says little about it. The brother treads *die mondenen Pfade*, "the lunar paths," in search of a brother who dies young or who is yet to be born; all the while, he is entranced by the lunar voice of the sister. It is almost as though the ghostly "brother" of the poems were himself a sister; all we can be sure of is that boyishness (*das Knabenhafte*) in Trakl's life and work never dominates or absorbs *das Mädchenhafte*.

Heidegger recalls the way an ancient Greek poet invokes the moon and stars (US 48–49), although he neglects to tell us that the poet is Sappho. Nor does he remind us of the lunar *Geschlecht* that stands at the center of Aristophanes's tale in Plato's *Symposium*. In the 1928 Leibniz course Heidegger refuses to take Aristophanes seriously when it comes to questions of sexuality, even though Aristophanes begs the participants to take his speech in earnest. Nothing has changed about Heidegger's refusal by 1953. Yet should we not remember a detail or two of the comedian's story? For that story is meant to explain τὴν ἀνθρωπίνην φύσιν, "the nature of humankind," which in German—Schleiermacher's German, for example—might be translated as *den Schlag des Menschengeschlechts*. Originally there were three γένη, says Aristophanes, the purely male, fathered by the Helios the sun, the purely female, mothered by Gaia the earth, and an androgynous third genus, which has as its parent the moon, σελήνη, which in some mysterious way (Aristophanes does not explain how) "participates in both sexes" (190b 3). It is difficult to conceive (literally) how either the purely male or purely female can engender young and so constitute a genuine genus. The only genus that makes sense, generating itself generation after generation, is the moonstruck androgynous genus, the House of Loonies. As for the *coup* or *frappe* for which Derrida is searching, Aristophanes is not wanting: when the men, women, and androgynes try to storm heaven, Zeus strikes a blow that severs all these round people in twain; the second *coup*, of course, would be Zeus's moving their genitals around to the front, so that the halves can see what they are looking for. One could of course go on and on, but it is enough if we remark what a shame it is that neither Heidegger nor Derrida takes the time to reconsider Aristophanes's tale—feeling perhaps, as Agathe does in *Der Mann ohne Eigenschaften,* that the story is so familiar that one is embarrassed to mention it yet again. And, after all, there is very little about the magnetism of Georg and Gretl Trakl that lends itself to Aristophanic comedy, not when their untimely deaths mark them out for tragedy. For the androgynes in this case are brother and sister, and Freud's *Inzestscheu* does not seem to stop them (SA 9:309–10).

Yet is it permissible to invoke psychoanalysis in this way, as though it too were comedy, and can one simply pronounce the word *Inzestscheu* without giving it a thought? How *is* psychoanalysis to be invoked, granted that Heidegger's allergy to it is not sufficient reason to banish it? Otto Basil gives us insight into Heidegger's resistance to psychoanalysis, the insight (paradoxical, to be sure) that Trakl appears to be "an ideal case" of neurosis, inasmuch as he embodies the fatal combination of genius and sexual guilt (OB 13). It is all too easy, all too inevitable, that the poet be reduced to familiar psychoanalytic categories. Heidegger cries *no no no!* while Derrida replies *soit—ce sont des choses qui arrivent.* Yet I suspect that both Heidegger and Derrida would agree that that Georg Trakl, together with his sister Gretl, is not an ideal case of neurosis and infantile fixation but "a tragic human being in the sense of ancient tragedy" (OB 14). Like all tragedies, the one involving Georg and Gretl Trakl ends in an early death, and again we are summoned *in den Untergang hinab.*

As a trained and practicing pharmacist, Trakl had knowledge of—and access to—an entire series of drugs: nicotine, morphine, veronal, chloroform, opium, cocaine, and perhaps mescaline. These always in combination with alcohol. And all of them eventually shared with Gretl. In other words, an "ideal case" for medical toxicology as well, these two siblings. Georg's experiments with cocaine, chloroform, and opium-treated cigarettes begin during his high school years; he introduces Gretl into these mysteries during their years in Vienna, 1909–10, when she is seventeen, he twenty-two. Finally, or first of all, once again alpha and omega, the sexual relationship with Gretl seems to have developed fully in Vienna. It seems to be both a loving and a dependency relationship. In the end it is fatal to brother and sister alike (OB 15–17, 70–84). We know that during their Vienna years, Gretl also enters into a relationship with Erhard Buschbeck, the childhood friend of the two of them; and we know that at age twenty she marries Albert Langen, a much older man; we know too that Georg, as though he were the hero in one of his early plays, is devastated by a despair beyond jealousy.

Otto Basil chooses as the title of the chapter in which he discusses Gretl herself *Die Fremdlingin,* the foreign or alien woman, the unknown woman. And that she certainly is. Among all the children, Georg and Gretl look almost exactly alike—the childhood photographs of the two show an extraordinary likeness. One thinks again of Robert Musil's "Siamese twins," Ulrich and Agathe, in *Der Mann ohne Eigenschaften*. Trakl's poetry and prose poems reflect the experience of the mirror image that is his sister, of one self dissolving into another, neither one knowing the other or the self as such, however, so that even the gender identity of each fades, melts, or melds, the one into the other. She sometimes appears in her brother's poetry as the girl youth, *die Jünglingin,* and even as the woman monk, *die Mönchin*. Of all the children, these two are the musically gifted ones, although Gretl alone pursues the study of music. She is well on her way to becoming a concert pianist, specializing in Chopin, Liszt, and the Russian Romantics, studying with Paul de Conne in Vienna and Ernst von Dohnányi in Berlin—until, after Georg's death, the addiction and the loneliness overwhelm her. On November 2, 1917, after a pleasant evening with friends, Gretl ends her life in the most violent way.

November 2, 1917? That would be the eve of Georg's third anniversary.

As mysterious as Gretl's life and death remain, Otto Basil does not hesitate to say that even if Georg's guilt appears to make him the leading partner in the relationship, the reverse is probably the case. Basil calls Gretl "by nature an unrestrained woman, driven, demi-daimonic, half-genius, anti-bourgeois, and in the sexual relationship probably the more active one" (OB 16). Again, the caution would be that nothing about their relationship is recorded: the other siblings remain silent, the mother is as incommunicative as she always is, the father dead, the letters destroyed. At all events, Gretl is surely the more active one when it comes to Georg's involvements in the world; she is the one who helps him to find employment at "The White Angel" pharmacy and the one who bolsters his confidence in all things. To repeat, from early childhood on Georg and Gretl join forces against their mother, who is more interested in her collection of antiques than in the children, although she is interested enough to be the disciplinarian in the family. Their alliance against her is perhaps aided by their *bonne,* the young Alsatian woman who is devoted to her charges and who would love to convert them from Protestantism to her own fervent Catholicism. The Christianity of the children, although neither Heidegger nor Derrida allude to this, is formed in this double manner—both Protestant and Catholic, so that the children seem to have inherited all the disadvantages of the two traditions for their lives. By way of compensation, their Mademoiselle gives them the gift of French, which becomes the children's language and later enables Trakl to absorb the poetry of Baudelaire and Rimbaud. The death of their amiable and well-loved father in 1910 and the survival of their mother constitute one of those ironies that make up, or take down, a life. But to return to Gretl. If one dare say such a thing, this younger sister seems to be the one who assumes the responsibilities of a life, Georg's, that in his own view began far too soon, a life that could not gather the strength needed to face the world. It is as though Georg is premature throughout his life, whereas his sister is prematurely mature. Karl Kraus, thanking Trakl for the dedication of "Psalm" to him, publishes the following prose text in *Die Fackel*:

> Seven-months' children are the only ones whose gaze makes the parents feel responsible, so that the parents sit there like thieves caught in the act, right next to the one they've robbed. Seven-months' children have the gaze that demands the return of what was taken from them, and when their thinking suddenly shuts down, it is as though they were looking for the remainder, and they gaze back in the direction of what they are missing. There are others who apprehend in a thoughtful way that look, but theirs is a look that would like to give back to Chaos the excess they have garnered. These are the complete ones, the ones who were finished when it was too late. They came into the world with a cry of shame—a world that causes them to feel only one thing, one thing first and last: Back into your body, O Mother, where it was good! (Cited at OB 118)

Basil notes, on the basis of reports from Trakl's contemporaries, the poet's forward-leaning walk, as though bent with osteoporosis, and his perpetual fear of falling; notes also his unusually quiet monotone, despite the occasional outbursts; and does not fail to mention the timid disdain of his gaze (OB 45). Photographs show him to be short and stocky, his hair closely cropped in the military style. He wears a ridiculous knitted cap. If he smiles, the smile seems tenuous and forced. Usually he lets the smile go. His late self-portrait, painted in the studio of his friend Oskar Kokoschka, all greens and oranges with spectral eyes, causes us to worry. His surviving brothers, sisters, and friends insist nevertheless that Trakl was a jovial, fun-loving lad during his preadolescent years, that only later did he grow "moody, quarrelsome, arrogant, self-assertive, and weary of life" (OB 56). From puberty on, they say, a self-destructive tendency battles in him with an intense affirmation of life and Eros (OB

59). His early dramas feature a beloved woman's betrayal of the hero, the hero's jealousy, and his subsequent suicide (OB 65). His later puppet play, *Bluebeard*, pits the serial killer against the innocent thirteen-year-old bride Elisabeth, but a serial killer who in the end falls on his knees and prays to the crucifix: "He drags her off into the depths. We hear a deafening scream. After a while Bluebeard appears, dripping with blood, besotted, beside himself, and he falls—as though from a rifle shot—to his knees before a crucifix" (T 245). Yet what is the penultimate act of this "Bluebeard," whom Gretl no doubt teases as "Bluebird"? We recall the letter to von Ficker asking him to see to it that whatever wealth he possesses—it is mainly a matter of Wittgenstein's generous grant—in the case of his demise goes to his sister Gretl.

The ins and outs of these biographical remarks—all the "folds" we see in any account of people's lives, folds that dependably hide more than they reveal—how unreliable and prejudicial they seem! How foolish! And what are we to make of the poet's own images, the images of his poems? What are we meant to see in the arc of Gretl's eyebrows, bent or twisted by God? Roberto Calasso pictures myths as the folds of Apollo's cloak; with every flick of his cloak the god alters the myth. The folds of a life are surely as complex as those of a myth or a poem. In the preceding chapter we paused to consider the contrast between Heidegger's and Derrida's conception of the "fold," partly with regard to sexual difference but also with regard to textuality. It may have seemed at that moment that Derrida's Mallarmé has little to do with Heidegger's Trakl; it may have seemed that the doublings and duplicities, the multiplications of the fold in Mallarmé, are more extreme than in the case of Trakl. After all, is not Rimbaud the proper confrere of Trakl? In spite of the sharp contours of Trakl's images, however, one has to affirm the multiple ways in which Trakl's poetry folds back upon itself and displaces all decisions about meaning, even multiple meanings. The poems are so precise, and yet, as Heidegger concedes, formulas fail in the face of them. Their folding occurs, not in some reflexive way, but in such a way that the signifiers whelm the signified, or send the referent and the meaning-content packing, such that one *experiences* the dissemination of meaning and the failure of "gathering." As I look through the poems selected for Appendices A and B, and as I think back on the impossible project of translating them, I recall the folds that make any effort at translation—or, for that matter, any reading—nothing short of harrowing. For when a fold runs deep it becomes an abyss.

Allow me to conclude with some final reflections on those seven themes cited at the outset. As for alpha and omega, it is clear in this question of magnetism that I side with Derrida: it is impossible to exclude the life of the poet, inasmuch as the magnetism of the work draws us to that life as though to its concealed source. And yet the source remains concealed for every biographical inquiry. We experience there a kind of non-origin of origins. Whether reflection on the life enriches rather than impoverishes our devotion to the work seems undecidable. All we can be sure of is that the folds of a life are never ironed out into clear meanings in the poetry. Or, altering the image, one can watch the iron filings dance, but the magnetism itself one never sees.

Second, the aporia represented by "commentary" and "placement" seems to extend far beyond the present case, namely, Heidegger's and Derrida's responses to Trakl. We have all suffered from commentaries that seem to us utterly beside the point, and perhaps the only way to explain their irrelevance is to admit that commentaries often do not occupy the "place" of the work—even if, or precisely because, that place is a floating island. At the same time, every claim to situate or place the work is a prime instance of hubris. We are never close enough to the work in all its facets and folds to make such a claim tenable. One may admire Heidegger's temerity, but one must admire even more Derrida's demonstrations of the hubris. Heidegger loves Heraclitus's warning that hubris needs to be quenched sooner than a raging fire; he would therefore have to love the chief of the fire brigade, and that would be Derrida.

Third, on most days of the week we need to hope with Heidegger that polysemy can be contained, that *Mehrdeutigkeit* need not imply that meaning dribbles through our fingers. Yet there are days when we have to realize that all the poets of the past two centuries have been trying to show us what signifiers can do and do do, and that what they do makes the life of a thinker difficult. No matter how much we would like to reduce or restrain dissemination, we see it at work in every unpronounceable German word with maddeningly multiple meanings. And we see it at work in "our" language, at least when we are paying attention.

Fourth, in a remarkable moment of the 1984–85 seminar, Derrida confesses that in some sense one *must* think these unpronounceable German words *in German,* even if that is not "our" language. There *is* untranslatability. Yet precisely for that reason, one must shatter every foreclosure of thinking; one must try to think in more than *one* language; one must seek and learn to accept the incalculable gifts and insights of *other* languages. For other languages are phantoms of the other. The etymology of words in our own tongue holds surprises in store for us, no doubt about that; yet these shrink in comparison to the surprises that await us in other corners of the speaking world. To say nothing of other libraries, other archives, other poems. Furthermore, as Hölderlin knew and insisted, we come home to our own language only after many long residences abroad. In this regard Derrida's life and thought seem an extraordinarily instructive event. Inimitable but to be emulated.

Fifth, Heidegger hears the Selenic voice of the sister, the lunar voice, but he is much more attuned to the solar voice of boyhood, *des Knabenhaften*. He does not fraternize *with* the sister, but he does fraternalize her, reducing her role to that of a mere appendage. True, he sees the poet calling on his sister rather than on God at the moment of crisis, but he makes no inquiry into this very new or very old deity. In the end, he feels that if one is a good enough brother to the stranger one will get a sister too. Nowhere do we have the sense that he sees—in the stranger, in Elis, in Helian, in Sebastian—the sister stepping out of the blue mirror into which the poet is gazing.

Sixth, it remains entirely unclear how the theme of "the sister" and that of "the lovers" are bound up with one another. It need not be a question of incest, of the prohibition and the known or unknown breach—known perhaps only as trauma and shadow. Heidegger is clearly drawn to this theme; otherwise, there would be no talk of *Geschlecht* and nothing for Derrida to write. Yet just as the lives of the two Trakl children, Georg and Gretl, remain almost entirely unknown to us, and just as Gretl is unlocatable in both life and death, one has to confess a certain helplessness with regard to both commentary and placement. Heidegger circles the flame of sexual love like a moth, protecting his wings, not getting too close, yet unable to leave the place. For the place is *geistlich,* of spirit. Certainly, in 1928 he finds the flame of being mighty, positive in its bestrewal of light and heat and embodiment, although he fears the dispersion that bestrewal seems inevitably to become; by 1953 he seems to want to "transmute" the effects of the flame, at least the effect that we call *evil.* It may be that his insistence that Trakl and we leave Platonism and Christianity behind arises from the desire to transmute, and in some way to still, the rage of evil. Derrida, after the incredible experience of having composed *Glas,* in which stories of sisters, brothers, and lovers abound, is surely able to get much closer to the flame. His minute reading of Heidegger's several strokes—even if his students show some impatience with it all—is breathtaking. Never was the logic of the supplement so fatal to a "placement" as it is to Heidegger's of Trakl. And yet at the same time Derrida shares something of Heidegger's desire to rescue a certain promise, the promise of a reduction if not a cessation of hostilities, the promise of something either very old or very new or both. Why not dream of a cease-fire between and among all the sexes, genders, and generations, some of which we know and many of which we have not yet seen? The more generous side of Derrida's reading of "Language in the Poem" arises from this dream, the justification of which is that we can only dream it. It is this mix of generosity and fearsome critical powers that makes Derrida one of a kind, one *Geschlecht*, as it were.

Seventh, nowhere is Derrida's brilliance better demonstrated than in his treatment of Heidegger's allergy with regard to the "Platonic-Christian" interpretation of Trakl. Whereas Derrida has no interest in rescuing Trakl for any ecclesiastical or philosophical love-feast, he is surely interested to see how Trakl's poetry might stretch our expectations concerning such a feast. The sisterhood and universal homosexuality of his Jesus is equal to, and indeed far surpasses, anything Hegel has to say in "The Spirit of Christianity," the *Phenomenology of Spirit*, and the late lectures on the philosophy of religion. Derrida's invocation of Christ the Sister is equal to Schelling's most wayward speculations on the femininity of deity, at least when deity has the sense to seek rescue from the rough seas near Samothrace. Once ashore, she feels the madness of Samothracian magnetism, settles into its earths, and stays. As for Derrida's account of despair, whether it be Christian or utterly undecidable, one has to admit that it gives despair a new lease on life. One can only be grateful.

A final thought, at least for the moment. One might make the mistake of thinking that whereas Heidegger's "placement" of poetry makes a "strong statement," Derrida's must be correspondingly "weak," a *pensamento debile*, in Gianni Vattimo's apt and unforgettable words. There is some truth in this. Whereas Heidegger boldly proceeds to a placement of the unsung poem, such placement reflecting a long-term relationship with the poems themselves, Derrida offers no such independent reading of Trakl. Rather, he restricts himself for the most part to critical commentary and a call for caution. Yet if Derrida is a philosopher, and he is, his words concerning the very desire to write a philosophical text, to say nothing of a philosophical text that dares to confront a work of poetry, must apply to himself as much as to Heidegger. In an interview taken up into *Points de suspension* . . . , Derrida says:

> The philosopher is someone whose desire and ambition are absolutely insane; the desire for power among the great politicians is absolutely puerile and minuscule alongside the philosopher's desire. The philosopher, in a work of philosophy,

manifests simultaneously a pattern of mastery and a renunciation of mastery to an extent or scope that I find infinitely more powerful than what we see in others. . . . For me, philosophy, if I have the taste for it, is the cause of this excess; it is out of proportion with other types of discourses, and sometimes even with all the rules of art. (Po 149; BP 537–38)

It perhaps for this very reason that, as Derrida says elsewhere, every time he is confronted with a philosophical concept he feels like a fly who is about to be caught in the deadly goo of a strip of flypaper (BP 599). Hence the call for caution. The translator who approaches the task of rendering Trakl's lines, along with the man or woman who wishes to comment on the lives and deaths of Georg and Gretl Trakl, including the nature of their love for one another, must approach such tasks or desires on these frantic and fragile *pattes de mouche*. Perhaps the thinker who boldly desires to situate or place Trakl's poem needs to develop the same sense of disquiet. Such disquiet, no matter how frantic and fragile, could only strengthen the discourse of thinking.

Alpha and omega? These are letters, letters of language, (the) first and (the) last. In the present instance they are letters of poetic language. To which, following Heidegger and Derrida, we may now at long last turn, trusting that Appendices A and B are not vestigial organs.

APPENDIX A

# Poems Discussed in the Present Volume

Both Heidegger and Derrida refer to many more poems than are here reprinted. Yet the following seemed to me the most intensely discussed among them. I cite Georg Trakl, *Dichtungen und Briefe,* edited by Walther Killy and Hans Szklenar (Salzburg: Otto Müller Verlag, 1969–70), which is based on the historical-critical edition. Readers may also refer to the inexpensive paperback edition, Georg Trakl, *Das dichterische Werk,* by the same editors (Munich: Deutscher Taschenbuch Verlag, 1972). I have kept the endnotes to a minimum. As for the order of the poems, I have followed the historical-critical edition by reprinting the poems that appear in (1) the 1913 *Gedichte,* (2) the 1914 *Sebastian im Traum,* (3) the poems published in the *Brenner* and *Fackel* journals in 1914–15, and (4) the literary remains, often earlier forms of the published poems. Many of the oddities of spelling and punctuation in the poems, "corrected" in earlier editions, have been restored by the historical-critical edition.

Readers will be able to locate several published collections of Trakl's poetry in English translation. Without wanting or daring to suggest any criticism of them, I felt the need to try my own hand here. Perhaps a poet of genius would have been able to translate the sense of the lines while preserving the rhymes and meters of each poem. Yet whether the genii of two languages ever consent to let this happen I have to doubt. At all events, for the most part I have had to let the rhymes go, except for the occasional happy accident. And meters, or rhythms? What can one say of the hidden source of all poetry? I have tried to be sensitive to the meters of my translations, but without claiming that they resonate with the German originals. I hope that I may be forgiven whatever liberties are taken by my own translations, if only because the German originals appear *en face.* In the end one can perhaps agree with both Derrida and Heidegger: it is pointless to try to place Trakl's poetry, since its places are many and varied; and yet each of them is beyond all doubt a place apart.

## An den Knaben Elis

Elis, wenn die Amsel im schwarzen Wald ruft,
Dieses ist dein Untergang.
Deine Lippen trinken die Kühle des blauen Felsenquells.

Laß, wenn deine Stirne leise blutet
Uralte Legenden
Und dunkle Deutung des Vogelflugs.

Du aber gehst mit weichen Schritten in die Nacht,
Die voll purpurner Trauben hängt
Und du regst die Arme schöner im Blau.

Ein Dornenbusch tönt,
Wo deine mondenen Augen sind.
O, wie lange bist, Elis, du verstorben.

Dein Leib ist eine Hyazinthe,
In die ein Mönch die wächsernen Finger taucht.
Eine schwarze Höhle ist unser Schweigen,

Daraus bisweilen ein sanftes Tier tritt
Und langsam die schweren Lider senkt.
Auf deine Schläfen tropft schwarzer Tau,

Das letzte Gold verfallener Sterne.

## To the Boy Elis

Elis, when the blackbird in the black wood calls,
This is your downgoing.
Your lips drink the chill of the blue source in the rocks.

Let there be, when your brow slowly bleeds,
Primeval legends
And dark readings of birdflight.[1]

Yet you walk with soft steps into the night
With clusters of purple grapes hanging
And you raise your arms more beautifully in blue.

A briar sounds
Where your lunar eyes are.
Oh, how long, Elis, since you died.

Your body is a hyacinth
Into which a monk dips his waxen fingers.
A black cavern is the silence we keep,

From which at times a tender animal emerges
And slowly lowers its drowsy lids.
Onto your temples black dew drips,

Final traces of gold from fallen stars.

## Traum des Bösen
(1. Fassung)

Verhallend eines Gongs braungoldne Klänge—
Ein Liebender erwacht in schwarzen Zimmern
Die Wang' an Flammen, die im Fenster flimmern.
Am Strome blitzen Segel, Masten, Stränge.

Ein Mönch, ein schwangres Weib dort im Gedränge.
Guitarren klimpern, rote Kittel schimmern.
Kastanien schwül in goldnem Glanz verkümmern;
Schwarz ragt der Kirchen trauriges Gepränge.

Aus bleichen Masken schaut der Geist des Bösen.
Ein Platz verdämmert grauenvoll und düster;
Am Abend regt auf Inseln sich Geflüster.

Des Vogelfluges wirre Zeichen lesen
Aussätzige, die zur Nacht vielleicht verwesen.
Im Park erblicken zitternd sich Geschwister.

## Dream of Evil
(first version)

Golden brown reverberations of a gong—
A lover awakens in black rooms
His cheeks ablaze, flames flickering at the window.
On the river flash sails, masts, rigging.[2]

A monk, a pregnant woman there in the throng.
Guitar strings plucked, red dresses shimmer.
Chestnuts ferment in humid golden glow;
Black looms the mournful pomp of churches.

Out of pale masks the spirit of evil stares.
A townsquare darkens, menacing and somber;
In the evening on islands whispers stir.

Reading baffling signs of birdflight are
Lepers who may decay in the night.
In the park siblings gaze on one another tremblingly.

## Verklärter Herbst

Gewaltig endet so das Jahr
Mit goldnem Wein und Frucht der Gärten.
Rund schweigen Wälder wunderbar
Und sind des Einsamen Gefährten.

Da sagt der Landmann: Es ist gut.
Ihr Abendglocken lang und leise
Gebt noch zum Ende frohen Mut.
Ein Vogelzug grüßt auf der Reise.

Es ist der Liebe milde Zeit.
Im Kahn den blauen Fluß hinunter
Wie schön sich Bild an Bildchen reiht—
Das geht in Ruh und Schweigen unter.

## Autumn Transfigured

The year ends this way, overwhelmingly,
With golden wine and garden fruits.
Round about the woods hush wondrously
And are the lonely one's companions.

Then the farmer says: It is good.
You bells of evening long and languid
Give us at the end some gladness.
A flock of birds on their journey greets.

It is the mild time of love.
In a skiff gliding down the blue river
How splendidly image and cameo line up—
In repose and silence all goes down.

## De profundis

Es ist ein Stoppelfeld, in das ein schwarzer Regen fällt.
Es ist ein brauner Baum, der einsam dasteht.
Es ist ein Zischelwind, der leere Hütten umkreist.
Wie traurig dieser Abend.

Am Weiler vorbei
Sammelt die sanfte Waise noch spärliche Ähren ein.
Ihre Augen weiden rund und goldig in der Dämmerung
Und ihr Schoß harrt des himmlischen Bräutigams.

Bei der Heimkehr
Fanden die Hirten den süßen Leib
Verwest im Dornenbusch.

Ein Schatten bin ich ferne finsteren Dörfern.
Gottes Schweigen
Trank ich aus dem Brunnen des Hains.

Auf meine Stirne tritt kaltes Metall
Spinnen suchen mein Herz.
Es ist ein Licht, das in meinem Mund erlöscht.

Nachts fand ich mich auf einer Heide,
Starrend von Unrat und Staub der Sterne.
Im Haselgebüsch
Klangen wieder kristallne Engel.

## De Profundis

It is a stubble field where a black rain falls.
It is a brown tree standing there forlorn.
It is a hissing wind encircling empty huts.
How sad this evening.

Passing on by the hamlet
The gentle orphan girl gathers meager ears of grain.
Her eyes graze round and golden in the twilight
And her womb awaits the heavenly bridegroom.

Turning homeward
The shepherds found the sweet body
Decomposed in the briar.

A shadow am I remote from gloomy villages.
God's silence
I drank from the font in the grove.

Cold metal touches my forehead
Spiders seek my heart.
It is a light that dies in my mouth.

At night I found myself upon a heath,
Bathed in filth and dust of stars.
In the hazel bushes,
Once again resounding, crystalline angels.

## Heiterer Frühling
(2. Fassung)

### 1

Am Bach, der durch das gelbe Brachfeld fließt,
Zieht noch das dürre Rohr vom vorigen Jahr.
Durchs Graue gleiten Klänge wunderbar,
Vorüberweht ein Hauch von warmem Mist.

An Weiden baumeln Kätzchen sacht im Wind,
Sein traurig Lied singt träumend ein Soldat.
Ein Wiesenstreifen saust verweht und matt,
Ein Kind steht in Konturen weich und lind.

Die Birken dort, der schwarze Dornenstrauch,
Auch fliehn im Rauch Gestalten aufgelöst.
Hell Grünes blüht und anderes verwest
Und Kröten schliefen durch den jungen Lauch.

### 2

Dich lieb ich treu du derbe Wäscherin.
Noch trägt die Flut des Himmels goldene Last.
Ein Fischlein blitzt vorüber und verblaßt;
Ein wächsern Antlitz fließt durch Erlen hin.

In Gärten sinken Glocken lang und leis
Ein kleiner Vogel trällert wie verrückt.
Das sanfte Korn schwillt leise und verzückt
Und Bienen sammeln noch mit ernstem Fleiß.

Komm Liebe nun zum müden Arbeitsmann!
In seine Hütte fällt ein lauer Strahl.
Der Wald strömt durch den Abend herb und fahl
Und Knospen knistern heiter dann und wann.

### 3

Wie scheint doch alles Werdende so krank!
Ein Fieberhauch um einen Weiler kreist;
Doch aus Gezweigen winkt ein sanfter Geist
Und öffnet das Gemüte weit und bang.

## Cloudless Spring
(second version)

### 1

The brook that flows through yellow fallow field
Is bordered still by last year's desiccated reeds.
Through the gray sounds glide wondrously,
A breath of warm manure wafts by.

Pussywillows sway gently in the wind,
A soldier sings dreamily his melancholy tune.
A strip of bare pasture is tossed by the wind,
A child stands there, softly outlined, gentle.

Those birches there, the black bramble,
Also shapes dissolving, fleeing in the smoke.
Bright greens blossom while others decompose
And toads slip through the verdant wild leek.

### 2

I love you truly you feisty washerwoman.
The tide bears still the golden burden of the sky.
A tiny fish darts by and then goes pale;
A waxen face flees through the alders.

In gardens bells fade long and languid
A small bird warbles as though quite mad.
The tender grains swell silent and enraptured
And bees still gather with earnest application.

Come love now to the weary laborer!
A beam of soft light invades his hut.
The forest streams brisk and bare through the evening
And buds crackle cheerfully now and then.

### 3

How sickly all becoming seems!
A febrile haze encircles a hamlet;
Yet from the boughs a gentle spirit signals
And opens wide and deep the heart's core.

Ein blühender Erguß verrinnt sehr sacht
Und Ungebornes pflegt der eignen Ruh.
Die Liebenden blühn ihren Sternen zu
Und süßer fließt ihr Odem durch die Nacht.

So schmerzlich gut und wahrhaft ist, was lebt;
Und leise rührt dich an ein alter Stein:
Wahrlich! Ich werde immer bei euch sein.
O Mund! der durch die Silberweide bebt.

An ejaculation blooms, then quietly runs dry,
And the unborn cultivates its own repose.
The lovers blossom toward their stars
And their breath flows more sweetly through the night.

So painfully good and truthful is what lives;
And an old stone softly touches you:
Truly! I shall be with you always.
Oh, mouth! quivering through the silver willow.

## Psalm

(2. Fassung)

*Karl Kraus zugeeignet*

Es ist ein Licht, das der Wind ausgelöscht hat.
Es ist ein Heidekrug, den am Nachmittag ein Betrunkener verläßt.
Es ist ein Weinberg, verbrannt und schwarz mit Löchern voll
 Spinnen.
Es ist ein Raum, den sie mit Milch getüncht haben.
Der Wahnsinnige ist gestorben. Es ist eine Insel der Südsee,
Den Sonnengott zu empfangen. Man rührt die Trommeln.
Die Männer führen kriegerische Tänze auf.
Die Frauen wiegen die Hüften in Schlinggewächsen und
 Feuerblumen,
Wenn das Meer singt. O unser verlorenes Paradies.

Die Nymphen haben die goldenen Wälder verlassen.
Man begräbt den Fremden. Dann hebt ein Flimmerregen an.
Der Sohn des Pan erscheint in Gestalt eines Erdarbeiters,
Der den Mittag am glühenden Asphalt verschläft.
Es sind kleine Mädchen in einem Hof in Kleidchen voll
 herzzerreißender Armut!
Es sind Zimmer, erfüllt von Akkorden und Sonaten.
Es sind Schatten, die sich vor einem erblindeten Spiegel umarmen.
An den Fenstern des Spitals wärmen sich Genesende.
Ein weißer Dampfer am Kanal trägt blutige Seuchen herauf.

Die fremde Schwester erscheint wieder in jemands bösen Träumen.
Ruhend im Haselgebüsch spielt sie mit seinen Sternen.
Der Student, vielleicht ein Doppelgänger, schaut ihr lange vom
 Fenster nach.
Hinter ihm steht sein toter Bruder, oder er geht die alte
 Wendeltreppe herab.
Im Dunkel brauner Kastanien verblaßt die Gestalt des jungen Novizen.
Der Garten ist im Abend. Im Kreuzgang flattern die Fledermäuse
 umher.
Die Kinder des Hausmeisters hören zu spielen auf und suchen das
 Gold des Himmels.

## Psalm[3]
(second version)

*Dedicated to Karl Kraus*

It is a light extinguished by the wind.
It is a country inn abandoned by a drunkard of an afternoon.
It is a vineyard scorched and black with holes full of spiders.
It is a room they have whitewashed with milk.
The madman is dead. It is a South Sea island,
To receive the sungod. They beat the drums.
The men perform their war dances.
The women wrap their hips in grass skirts and passion flowers
When the sea sings. Oh, our lost paradise.

The nymphs have quit the golden woods.
The stranger is buried. Then a glittering rain sets in.
The Son of Pan appears in the form of a ditchdigger
Who lies asleep at noon on the glowing asphalt.
It is a group of little girls in the courtyard dressed in heartrending poverty!
It is rooms reverberating with chords and sonatas.
It is shadows embracing before a mirror gone blind.
At hospital windows convalescents warm themselves.
A white steamer in the canal transports blood red pestilence.

The strange sister appears again in someone's evil dreams.
Resting in the hazels she plays with his stars.
The student, perhaps a Doppelgänger, gazes at her from his window.
Behind him stands his dead brother, or he descends the old spiral staircase.
In the dark beneath brown chestnuts the figure of the young seminarian goes pale.
The garden has gone to evening. In the cloister bats flit.
The caretaker's children cease their play and seek the gold of the sky.

Endakkorde eines Quartetts. Die kleine Blinde läuft zitternd durch die Allee,
Und später tastet ihr Schatten an kalten Mauern hin, umgeben von Märchen und heiligen Legenden.

Es ist ein leeres Boot, das am Abend den schwarzen Kanal heruntertreibt.
In der Düsternis des alten Asyls verfallen menschliche Ruinen.
Die toten Waisen liegen an der Gartenmauer.
Aus grauen Zimmern treten Engel mit kotgefleckten Flügeln.
Würmer tropfen von ihren vergilbten Lidern.
Der Platz vor der Kirche ist finster und schweigsam, wie in den Tagen der Kindheit.
Auf silbernen Sohlen gleiten frühere Leben vorbei
Und die Schatten der Verdammten steigen zu den seufzenden Wassern nieder.
In seinem Grab spielt der weiße Magier mit seinen Schlangen.

Schweigsam über der Schädelstätte öffnen sich Gottes goldene Augen.

Concluding chords of a quartet. The blind girl, shivering,
    hurries through the lane,
And later her shadow gropes its way along chilly walls,
    surrounded by fairy tales and holy legends.

It is an empty boat making its way at evening down the
    black canal.
In the gloom of the old age home human ruins collapse.
The dead orphans lie buried along the garden wall.
Angels emerge from gray rooms, their wings flecked with filth.
Worms drop from their yellowed eyelids.
The church square is grimly dark and silent, as it was in
    childhood days.
On silver footsoles earlier lives glide by
And the shadows of the damned descend to sighing waters.
In his grave the white sorcerer plays with his serpents.

Silently over the Place of the Skull open God's golden eyes.

## Stundenlied

Mit dunklen Blicken sehen sich die Liebenden an,
Die Blonden, Strahlenden. In starrender Finsternis
Umschlingen schmächtig sich die sehnenden Arme.

Purpurn zerbrach der Gesegneten Mund. Die runden Augen
Spiegeln das dunkle Gold des Frühlingsnachmittags,
Saum und Schwärze des Walds, Abendängste im Grün;
Vielleicht unsäglichen Vogelflug, des Ungeborenen
Pfad an finsteren Dörfern, einsamen Sommern hin
Und aus verfallener Bläue tritt bisweilen ein Abgelebtes.

Leise rauscht im Acker das gelbe Korn.
Hart ist das Leben und stählern schwingt die Sense der
    Landmann,
Fügt gewaltige Balken der Zimmermann.

Purpurn färbt sich das Laub im Herbst; der mönchische Geist
Durchwandelt heitere Tage; reif ist die Traube
Und festlich die Luft in geräumigen Höfen.
Süßer duften vergilbte Früchte; leise ist das Lachen
Des Frohen, Musik und Tanz in schattigen Kellern;
Im dämmernden Garten Schritt und Stille des verstorbenen
    Knaben.

## Song of the Hours[4]

With darkling looks the lovers gaze on one another,
Blond, beaming. In all-pervading gloom
Their longing arms languorously entwine.

The mouth of the blessed ones shattered in purple. Their
    round eyes
Mirror the dark gold of the springtime afternoon,
Rim and blackness of the woods, evening anxieties in the green;
Perhaps an unspeakable flight of birds, path of the
Unborn at gloomy villages, the length of lonely summers
And now and then from decaying haze of blue emerges
    something no longer alive.

The yellow grain in the field rustles softly.
Life is hard and the steeled farmer swings his scythe,
The builder joins massive beams.

The leaves go purple in autumn; the monastic spirit
Traverses cloudless days; the grape is ripe
And the air festive in spacious courtyards.
Sweeter still smell yellowed fruits; soft is the laughter
Of the glad one, music and dance in shaded cellars;
In the twilit garden footfall and silence of the boy who died.

## Unterwegs

Am Abend trugen sie den Fremden in die Totenkammer;
Ein Duft von Teer; das leise Rauschen roter Platanen;
Der dunkle Flug der Dohlen; am Platz zog eine Wache auf.
Die Sonne ist in schwarze Linnen gesunken; immer wieder
 kehrt dieser vergangene Abend.
Im Nebenzimmer spielt die Schwester eine Sonate von Schubert.
Sehr leise sinkt ihr Lächeln in den verfallenen Brunnen,
Der bläulich in der Dämmerung rauscht. O, wie alt ist unser
 Geschlecht.
Jemand flüstert drunten im Garten; jemand hat diesen
 schwarzen Himmel verlassen.
Auf der Kommode duften Äpfel. Großmutter zündet goldene
 Kerzen an.

O, wie mild ist der Herbst. Leise klingen unsere Schritte im
 alten Park
Unter hohen Bäumen. O, wie ernst ist das hyazinthene
 Antlitz der Dämmerung.
Der blaue Quell zu deinen Füßen, geheimnisvoll die rote
 Stille deines Munds,
Umdüstert vom Schlummer des Laubs, dem dunklen Gold
 verfallener Sonnenblumen.
Deine Lider sind schwer von Mohn und träumen leise auf
 meiner Stirne.
Sanfte Glocken durchzittern die Brust. Eine blaue Wolke
Ist dein Antlitz auf mich gesunken in der Dämmerung.

Ein Lied zur Guitarre, das in einer fremden Schenke erklingt,
Die wilden Holunderbüsche dort, ein lang vergangener
 Novembertag,
Vertraute Schritte auf der dämmernden Stiege, der Anblick
 gebräunter Balken,
Ein offenes Fenster, an dem ein süßes Hoffen zurückblieb—
Unsäglich ist das alles, o Gott, daß man erschüttert ins Knie
 bricht.

O, wie dunkel ist diese Nacht. Eine purpurne Flamme
Erlosch an meinem Mund. In der Stille
Erstirbt der bangen Seele einsames Saitenspiel.
Laß, wenn trunken von Wein das Haupt in die Gosse sinkt.

## On the Way

In the evening they carried the stranger to his death chamber;
An odor of tar; the soft rustling of red plane trees;
The dark flight of jackdaws; in the square the nightwatch
 took up his post.
The sun has set in black linens; this past evening recurs
 again and again.
In the next room the sister is playing a Schubert sonata.
Very quietly her smile sinks into the dilapidated fountain
Which at dusk murmurs in shades of blue. Oh, how ancient
 is our House.
Someone whispers down in the garden; someone has
 abandoned this black sky.
On the dresser the smell of apples. Grandmother lights the
 golden candles.

Oh, how mild the autumn is. Our footsteps in the old park
 sound softly
Under lofty trees. Oh, how earnest is the hyacinthine face of
 twilight.
The blue source at your feet, mysterious the red stillness of
 your mouth,
Shadowed by the slumber of leaves, the dark gold of
 desiccated sunflowers.
Your eyelids are heavy with poppy and dream lightly on my
 brow.
Gentle bells quiver in the breast. A blue cloud
Is your countenance descending on me at twilight.

A song with guitar echoing at an unknown tavern,
The wild elderberry bushes there, a November day long gone by,
Familiar footsteps on the ascent at twilight, a view of
 brownstained beams,
An open window where a cherished hope still clung—
Unspeakable are all these things, O God; shattered, one falls
 to one's knees.

Oh, how dark this night is. A purple flame
Was snuffed at my mouth. In the silence
Dies the lonely thrum of strings in a troubled soul.
Let that be, when drunk with wine the head sinks into the gutter.

## Ein Winterabend
(2. Fassung)

Wenn der Schnee ans Fenster fällt,
Lang die Abendglocke läutet,
Vielen ist der Tisch bereitet
Und das Haus ist wohlbestellt.

Mancher auf der Wanderschaft
Kommt ans Tor auf dunklen Pfaden.
Golden blüht der Baum der Gnaden
Aus der Erde kühlem Saft.

Wanderer tritt still herein;
Schmerz versteinerte die Schwelle.
Da erglänzt in reiner Helle
Auf dem Tische Brot und Wein.

## A Winter's Eve
(second version)

When snow falls against the window,
Long tolls the vesper bell,
For many the table is laid
And the house is in good order.

Many a one who wanders
On dark paths arrives at the gate.
Golden blooms the tree of grace
Out of the earth's cool sap.

Wanderer, enter quietly;
Pain turned the threshold to stone.
Glistening there in pristine light
On the table bread and wine.[5]

## Die Verfluchten

### 1

Es dämmert. Zum Brunnen gehn die alten Fraun.
Im Dunkel der Kastanien lacht ein Rot.
Aus einem Laden rinnt ein Duft von Brot
Und Sonnenblumen sinken übern Zaun.

Am Fluß die Schenke tönt noch lau und leis.
Guitarre summt; ein Klimperklang von Geld.
Ein Heiligenschein auf jene Kleine fällt,
Die vor der Glastür wartet sanft und weiß.

O! blauer Glanz, den sie in Scheiben weckt,
Umrahmt von Dornen, schwarz und starrverzückt.
Ein krummer Schreiber lächelt wie verrückt
Ins Wasser, das ein wilder Aufruhr schreckt.

### 2

Am Abend säumt die Pest ihr blau Gewand
Und leise schließt die Tür ein finstrer Gast.
Durchs Fenster sinkt des Ahorns schwarze Last;
Ein Knabe legt die Stirn in ihre Hand.

Oft sinken ihre Lider bös und schwer.
Des Kindes Hände rinnen durch ihr Haar
Und seine Tränen stürzen heiß und klar
In ihre Augenhöhlen schwarz und leer.

Ein Nest von scharlachfarbnen Schlangen bäumt
Sich träg in ihrem aufgewühlten Schoß.
Die Arme lassen ein Erstorbenes los,
Das eines Teppichs Traurigkeit umsäumt.

### 3

Ins braune Gärtchen tönt ein Glockenspiel.
Im Dunkel der Kastanien schwebt ein Blau,
Der süße Mantel einer fremden Frau.
Resedenduft; und glühendes Gefühl

## The Accursed

### 1

Twilight falls. The old women walk to the well.
In the dark of chestnuts a laughing red.
From a shop streams a fragrance of bread
And sunflowers droop over the fence.

Noises at the riverside tavern now soft and faint.
A guitar strum; a jingling of coins.
A halo descends over that little girl there
Who waits, tender and white, before the glass door.

Oh! the blue luster she rouses in panes,
Framed by thorns, black and enraptured, motionless.
A wizened scrivener smiles like a madman
In waters terrified by wild tumult.

### 2

In the evening Plague hems her blue garment
And a gloomy guest quietly closes the door.
Through the window the maple's black burden sinks;
A boy lays his brow in her hand.

Often her eyelids close malevolent and leaden.
The child's hands run through her hair
And its tears plunge hot and clear
Into the sockets of her eyes black and bare.

A nest of scarlet snakes writhes
Languidly in her burrowed womb.
The arms release something lifeless
That hems a mournful tapestry.

### 3

The play of bells invades a small brown garden.
A blue hovers in the dark of chestnut trees,
The sweet cloak of a foreign woman.
Fragrance of Reseda[6]; and the ardent feeling

Des Bösen. Die feuchte Stirn beugt kalt und bleich
Sich über Unrat, drin die Ratte wühlt,
Vom Scharlachglanz der Sterne lau umspült;
Im Garten fallen Äpfel dumpf und weich.

Die Nacht ist schwarz. Gespenstisch bläht der Föhn
Des wandelnden Knaben weißes Schlafgewand
Und leise greift in seinen Mund die Hand
Der Toten. Sonja lächelt sanft und schön.

Of evil. The moist brow bends cold and pale
Over filth where a rat is burrowing,
Warmly rinsed by the scarlet glow of stars;
In the garden apples fall dully, softly.

The night is black. Warm air inflates ghostily
The white nightdress of the somnambulant boy
And softly reaching into his mouth is the hand
Of the dead. Tenderly, beautifully, Sonia smiles.[7]

## Herbstseele
(2. Fassung)

Jägerruf und Blutgebell;
Hinter Kreuz und braunem Hügel
Blindet sacht der Weiherspiegel,
Schreit der Habicht hart und hell.

Über Stoppelfeld und Pfad
Banget schon ein schwarzes Schweigen;
Reiner Himmel in den Zweigen;
Nur der Bach rinnt still und stad.

Bald entgleitet Fisch und Wild.
Blaue Seele, dunkles Wandern
Schied uns bald von Lieben, Andern.
Abend wechselt Sinn und Bild.

Rechten Lebens Brot und Wein,
Gott in deine milden Hände
Legt der Mensch das dunkle Ende,
Alle Schuld und rote Pein.

## Autumn Soul
(second version)

Hunter's call and bloodhound's bark;
Behind crucifix and brown hill
The pond's reflection gently blinding,
The hawk cries harsh and bright.

Above stubble field and path
A black silence already feels fear;
Clear sky seen through the boughs;
The brook alone streams soft and steady.

Soon fish and game glide away.
Blue soul, darkling voyage
Soon severed us from loved ones, others.
Evening alters sense and image.

Bread and wine of life lived well,
God into your mild hands
The human lays its dark ending,
All guilt and blood red pain.

## Ruh und Schweigen

Hirten begruben die Sonne im kahlen Wald.
Ein Fischer zog
In härenem Netz den Mond aus frierendem Weiher.

In blauem Kristall
Wohnt der bleiche Mensch, die Wang' an seine Sterne gelehnt;
Oder es neigt das Haupt in purpurnem Schlaf.

Doch immer rührt der schwarze Flug der Vögel
Den Schauenden, das Heilige blauer Blumen,
Denkt die nahe Stille Vergessenes, erloschene Engel.

Wieder nachtet die Stirne in mondenem Gestein;
Ein strahlender Jüngling
Erscheint die Schwester in Herbst und schwarzer Verwesung.

## Repose and Silence

Shepherds buried the sun in the barren wood.
A fisherman drew the moon
In a woven net from the freezing weir.

In blue crystal
The pallid man dwells, his cheek leaning on his stars;
Or his head droops slowly in purple slumber.

Yet always the black flight of birds touches
The one who sees, the holiness of blue blossoms,
The close stillness thinks things forgotten, extinguished angels.

Once again the brow is benighted in lunar stone;
A beaming youth
The sister appears in autumn and black decomposition.

## An einen Frühverstorbenen

O, der schwarze Engel, der leise aus dem Innern des Baums trat,
Da wir sanfte Gespielen am Abend waren,
Am Rand des bläulichen Brunnens.
Ruhig war unser Schritt, die runden Augen in der braunen
    Kühle des Herbstes,
O, die purpurne Süße der Sterne.

Jener aber ging die steinernen Stufen des Mönchsbergs hinab,
Ein blaues Lächeln im Antlitz und seltsam verpuppt
In seine stillere Kindheit und starb;
Und im Garten blieb das silberne Antlitz des Freundes zurück,
Lauschend im Laub oder im alten Gestein.

Seele sang den Tod, die grüne Verwesung des Fleisches
Und es war das Rauschen des Walds,
Die inbrünstige Klage des Wildes.
Immer klangen von dämmernden Türmen die blauen
    Glocken des Abends.

Stunde kam, da jener die Schatten in purpurner Sonne sah,
Die Schatten der Fäulnis in kahlem Geäst;
Abend, da an dämmernder Mauer die Amsel sang,
Der Geist des Frühverstorbenen stille im Zimmer erschien.

O, das Blut, das aus der Kehle des Tönenden rinnt,
Blaue Blume; o die feurige Träne
Geweint in die Nacht.

Goldene Wolke und Zeit. In einsamer Kammer
Lädst du öfter den Toten zu Gast,
Wandelst in trautem Gespräch unter Ulmen den grünen
    Fluß hinab.

## To One Who Died Young

Oh, the black angel that slowly emerged from the pith of the tree,
When we were gentle playmates in the evening,
At the edge of the fountain in blue haze.
Our step unrushed, our eyes round in the brown chill of autumn,
Oh, the purple sweetness of stars.

Yet that one descended the stony steps of the Mönchsberg,
A blue smile on his countenance, and strangely he metamorphosed
Into his more serene childhood and died;
And in the garden, left behind, the silver countenance of the friend,
Eavesdropping among the leaves or old stones.

Soul sang the death, the green decomposing of the flesh
And there was the rustling of the forest,
The intense lament of wild animal.
Always sounding from twilit towers the blue vesper bells.

Hour came when that one saw the shadows in the purple sun,
The shadows of foulness in barren boughs;
Evening, when the blackbird sang at the twilit wall,
The spirit of the one who died young appeared silently in the room.

Oh, the blood that flows from the throat of the sounding one,
Blue blossom; oh, the furious tear
Wept into the night.

Golden cloud and time. In a lonely chamber
You often invite the dead one to be your guest,
You walk in intimate converse under elms along the green river.

## Geistliche Dämmerung
### (2. Fassung)

Stille begegnet am Saum des Waldes
Ein dunkles Wild;
Am Hügel endet leise der Abendwind,

Verstummt die Klage der Amsel,
Und die sanften Flöten des Herbstes
Schweigen im Rohr.

Auf schwarzer Wolke
Befährst du trunken von Mohn
Den nächtigen Weiher,

Den Sternenhimmel.
Immer tönt der Schwester mondene Stimme
Durch die geistliche Nacht.

## Spiriting Twilight
(second version)

Stillness encounters at forest rim
A dusky deer;
On the hill the evening wind abates,

The blackbird's lament grows mute,
And the autumn's gentle flutings
Go silent in the reed.

On a black cloud
,You ride drunk with poppy
The nocturnal pond,

The star-filled sky.
Ceaselessly sounds the sister's lunar voice
Through the spiriting night.

## Abendländisches Lied

O der Seele nächtlicher Flügelschlag:
Hirten gingen wir einst an dämmernden Wäldern hin
Und es folgte das rote Wild, die grüne Blume und der lallende
 Quell
Demutsvoll. O, der uralte Ton des Heimchens,
Blut blühend am Opferstein
Und der Schrei des einsamen Vogels über der grünen Stille
 des Teichs.

O, ihr Kreuzzüge und glühenden Martern
Des Fleisches, Fallen purpurner Früchte
Im Abendgarten, wo vor Zeiten die frommen Jünger gegangen,
Kriegsleute nun, erwachend aus Wunden und Sternenträumen.
O, das sanfte Zyanenbündel der Nacht.

O, ihr Zeiten der Stille und goldener Herbste,
Da wir friedliche Mönche die purpurne Traube gekeltert;
Und rings erglänzten Hügel und Wald.
O, ihr Jagden und Schlösser; Ruh des Abends,
Da in seiner Kammer der Mensch Gerechtes sann,
In stummem Gebet um Gottes lebendiges Haupt rang.

O, die bittere Stunde des Untergangs,
Da wir ein steinernes Antlitz in schwarzen Wassern beschaun.
Aber strahlend heben die silbernen Lider die Liebenden:
E i n Geschlecht. Weihrauch strömt von rosigen Kissen
Und der süße Gesang der Auferstandenen.

## Western Song

Oh, the soul's nocturnal wing beat:
Once we shepherds walked near twilit forests
With the red deer, the green flower, and the purling font
    pursuing
Humbly. Oh, the primeval sound of the cricket,
Blood blossoming on the sacrificial stone
And the cry of the lonely bird above the pond's green stillness.

Oh, you Crusades and ardent martyrdoms
Of the flesh; purple fruits falling
In the evening garden, where long ago the pious apostles
    walked,
Warriors now, waking from wounds and dreams of stars.
Oh, the gentle cornflower cluster of the night.

Oh, you times of stillness and golden autumns,
When we peaceful monks pressed the purple grape;
And all around us glistened hill and wood.
Oh, you hunting parties, you castles; evening's repose,
When in their chambers human beings pondered righteousness,
Beseeching in silent prayer the living head of God.

Oh, the bitter hour of downfall,
When we gaze on a stony face in black waters.
Yet radiantly rise the silver eyelids of lovers:
*One* House. Incense streams from pillows all roses
And the sweet song of the resurrected.

## Siebengesang des Todes

Bläulich dämmert der Frühling; unter saugenden Bäumen
Wandert ein Dunkles in Abend und Untergang,
Lauschend der sanften Klage der Amsel.
Schweigend erscheint die Nacht, ein blutendes Wild,
Das langsam hinsinkt am Hügel.

In feuchter Luft schwankt blühendes Apfelgezweig,
Löst silbern sich Verschlungenes,
Hinsterbend aus nächtigen Augen; fallende Sterne;
Sanfter Gesang der Kindheit.

Erscheinender stieg der Schläfer den schwarzen Wald hinab,
Und es rauschte ein blauer Quell im Grund,
Daß jener leise die bleichen Lider aufhob
Über sein schneeiges Antlitz;

Und es jagte der Mond ein rotes Tier
Aus seiner Höhle;
Und es starb in Seufzern die dunkle Klage der Frauen.

Strahlender hob die Hände zu seinem Stern
Der weiße Fremdling;
Schweigend verläßt ein Totes das verfallene Haus.

O des Menschen verweste Gestalt: gefügt aus kalten Metallen,
Nacht und Schrecken versunkener Wälder
Und der sengenden Wildnis des Tiers;
Windesstille der Seele.

Auf schwärzlichem Kahn fuhr jener schimmernde Ströme hinab,
Purpurner Sterne voll, und es sank
Friedlich das ergrünte Gezweig auf ihn,
Mohn aus silberner Wolke.

## Septet of Death

Spring dawns in blue haze; beneath suckling trees
Something dark wanders in evening and decline,
Rapt to the blackbird's gentle lamentation.
Night silently appears, a bleeding deer
That slowly sinks on the hillside.

In humid air blossoming apple branches sway,
Something clasping ravels in silver,
Fainting in nocturnal eyes; falling stars;
Gentle song of childhood.

In greater splendor the sleeper descended the black wood,
And a blue source purled in the valley below,
So that he slowly raised the pallid eyelids
Of his snowy countenance;

And the moon flushed a red animal
From its den;
And the dark lament of women died down to sighs.

More radiantly, raising his hands to his star,
The white stranger;
Silently something dead abandons the ruined house.

Oh, the decomposed figure of humankind: joined of cold metals,
Night and terror of sunken forests,
And the singeing savagery of the animal;
Doldrums of the soul.

On a black skiff he glided down shimmering streams,
Full of purple stars, and bending down
To brush him tranquilly were the budding branches,
Poppy from a silver cloud.

## Sommersneige

Der grüne Sommer ist so leise
Geworden, dein kristallenes Antlitz.
Am Abendweiher starben die Blumen,
Ein erschrockener Amselruf.

Vergebliche Hoffnung des Lebens. Schon rüstet
Zur Reise sich die Schwalbe im Haus
Und die Sonne versinkt am Hügel;
Schon winkt zur Sternenreise die Nacht.

Stille der Dörfer; es tönen rings
Die verlassenen Wälder. Herz,
Neige dich nun liebender
Über die ruhige Schläferin.

Der grüne Sommer ist so leise
Geworden und es läutet der Schritt
Des Fremdlings durch die silberne Nacht.
Gedächte ein blaues Wild seines Pfads,

Des Wohllauts seiner geistlichen Jahre!

## Summer Inclines to Its End[8]

The green summer has grown so
Quiet, your crystalline face.
At the weir in the evening the flowers wilted.
A startled blackbird's cry.

Vain hope of life. Already preparing
For the journey is the swallow of the house
And the sun is sinking behind the hill;
Already the night invites a star journey.

Villages hushed; around them the sounds
Of abandoned forests. Heart,
Incline more lovingly now
Over the woman sleeping peacefully.

The green summer has grown so
Quiet and the stranger's footfall
Rings through the silvery night.
Were a blue deer to remember its path,

The consonance of its spiriting years!

## Jahr

Dunkle Stille der Kindheit. Unter grünenden Eschen
Weidet die Sanftmut bläulichen Blickes; goldene Ruh.
Ein Dunkles entzückt der Duft der Veilchen; schwankende Ähren
Im Abend, Samen und die goldenen Schatten der Schwermut.
Balken behaut der Zimmermann; im dämmernden Grund
Mahlt die Mühle; im Hasellaub wölbt sich ein purpurner Mund,
Männliches rot über schweigende Wasser geneigt.
Leise ist der Herbst, der Geist des Waldes; goldene Wolke
Folgt dem Einsamen, der schwarze Schatten des Enkels.
Neige in steinernem Zimmer; unter alten Zypressen
Sind der Tränen nächtige Bilder zum Quell versammelt;
Goldenes Auge des Anbeginns, dunkle Geduld des Endes.

## Year

Dark stillness of childhood. Beneath the greening ash trees
The gentleness of an azure gaze browses; golden repose.
The fragrance of violets entrances something dark; ears of
 grain sway
In the evening, seed and the golden shadows of melancholy.
The joiner hacks away at beams; deep in the twilit valley
The mill grinds grain; among hazel leaves a purple mouth
 opens,
A manly red bent over waters that say not a word.
Tranquil is the autumn, the spirit of the wood; golden cloud
Follows the lonely one, the black shadow of the grandchild.
Waning in the stony room; beneath old cypresses
Nocturnal images of tears have gathered to a source;
Golden eye of commencement, dark patience of the end.

## Frühling der Seele

Aufschrei im Schlaf; durch schwarze Gassen stürzt der Wind,
Das Blau des Frühlings winkt durch brechendes Geäst,
Purpurner Nachttau und es erlöschen rings die Sterne.
Grünlich dämmert der Fluß, silbern die alten Alleen
Und die Türme der Stadt. O sanfte Trunkenheit
Im gleitenden Kahn und die dunklen Rufe der Amsel
In kindlichen Gärten. Schon lichtet sich der rosige Flor.

Feierlich rauschen die Wasser. O die feuchten Schatten der Au,
Das schreitende Tier; Grünendes, Blütengezweig
Rührt die kristallene Stirne; schimmernder Schaukelkahn.
Leise tönt die Sonne im Rosengewölk am Hügel.
Groß ist die Stille des Tannenwalds, die ernsten Schatten am Fluß.

Reinheit! Reinheit! Wo sind die furchtbaren Pfade des Todes,
Des grauen steinernen Schweigens, die Felsen der Nacht
Und die friedlosen Schatten? Strahlender Sonnenabgrund.

Schwester, da ich dich fand an einsamer Lichtung
Des Waldes und Mittag war und groß das Schweigen des Tiers;
Weiße unter wilder Eiche, und es blühte silbern der Dorn.
Gewaltiges Sterben und die singende Flamme im Herzen.

Dunkler umfließen die Wasser die schönen Spiele der Fische.
Stunde der Trauer, schweigender Anblick der Sonne;
Es ist die Seele ein Fremdes auf Erden. Geistlich dämmert
Bläue über dem verhauenen Wald und es läutet
Lange eine dunkle Glocke im Dorf; friedlich Geleit.
Stille blüht die Myrthe über den weißen Lidern des Toten.

Leise tönen die Wasser im sinkenden Nachmittag
Und es grünet dunkler die Wildnis am Ufer, Freude im rosigen Wind;
Der sanfte Gesang des Bruders am Abendhügel.

## Springtime of the Soul

A scream while sleeping; the wind surges in black alleyways,
The blue of spring signals through breaking branches,
Purple dew of night and all about the stars go out.
The river glows a dusky green, silver the ancient avenues
And the towers of the city. Oh, soft inebriation
In the gliding skiff and the blackbird's dark calls
In the gardens of childhood. Already the blooms are lit in rose.

Waters purl solemnly. Oh, the meadow's moist shadows,
The pacing animal; all grows green, blossoming branch
Touches the crystalline brow; shimmering bobbing bark,
Softly sounds the sun in clouds of rose upon the hill.
Vast the silence in the pinewood, earnest shadows at the river.

Purity! Purity! Where are the terrifying paths of death,
Of the gray stony silence, where the cliffs of night
And the restive shadows? Beaming abyss of sun.

Sister, when I found you in a lonely clearing
Of the wood and it was noon and vast the animal's silence;
White light beneath the wild oak, and silver bloomed the
  thorn.
Violent dying and the flame singing in my heart.

The waters flow more darkly about the lovely play of fish.
Hour of mourning, silent glimpse of the sun;
Something strange is the soul on earth. Spiriting twilight
In a blue haze over the clearcut forest and the long
Tolling of a dark bell in the village; peaceful guardian.
Silently the myrtle blooms above the white eyelids of the
  dead one.

Softly sound the waters in the sinking afternoon,
And greens darken in the bank's wild growth, joy in a wind
  all roses;
The gentle song of the brother on the evening hill.

## Gesang des Abgeschiedenen

*An Karl Borromaeus Heinrich*

Voll Harmonien ist der Flug der Vögel. Es haben die grünen Wälder
Am Abend sich zu stilleren Hütten versammelt;
Die kristallenen Weiden des Rehs.
Dunkles besänftigt das Plätschern des Bachs, die feuchten Schatten

Und die Blumen des Sommers, die schön im Winde läuten.
Schon dämmert die Stirne dem sinnenden Menschen.

Und es leuchtet ein Lämpchen, das Gute, in seinem Herzen
Und der Frieden des Mahls; denn geheiligt ist Brot und Wein
Von Gottes Händen, und es schaut aus nächtigen Augen
Stille dich der Bruder an, daß er ruhe von dorniger Wanderschaft.
O das Wohnen in der beseelten Bläue der Nacht.

Liebend auch umfängt das Schweigen im Zimmer die Schatten der Alten,
Die purpurnen Martern, Klage eines großen Geschlechts,
Das fromm nun hingeht im einsamen Enkel.

Denn strahlender immer erwacht aus schwarzen Minuten des Wahnsinns
Der Duldende an versteinerter Schwelle
Und es umfängt ihn gewaltig die kühle Bläue und die leuchtende Neige des Herbsts,

Das stille Haus und die Sagen des Waldes,
Maß und Gesetz und die mondenen Pfade der Abgeschiedenen.

# Appendix A

## Song of the Departed One

*to Karl Borromaeus Heinrich*

Full of harmonies is the flight of birds. The green woods
Have gathered to cottages quieter now at evening;
The crystalline pastures of the deer.
The brook's splashing calms what is dark, the humid shadows

And the flowers of summer that toll beautifully in the wind.
Already the brow of the meditative human being is in twilight.

And a fragile lamp is lit, the good, in his heart
And the peace of the repast; for bread and wine are sanctified
By God's hands, and gazing at you from nocturnal eyes
Quietly, the brother, may he find rest from thorny wandering;
Oh, to dwell in the ensouled blueness of the night.

Lovingly also the silence in the room embraces the shades
   of the old ones,
The purple martyrdoms, lament of a great House
That piously comes to its end now in the solitary grandchild.

For the longsuffering one awakens more radiantly from
   black moments of madness
On a threshold turned to stone
And the cool blueness and the luminous waning of the
   autumn whelm him,

The silent house and the forest sagas,
Measure and law and the lunar paths of the departed ones.

## Klage

Schlaf und Tod, die düstern Adler
Umrauschen nachtlang dieses Haupt:
Des Menschen goldnes Bildnis
Verschlänge die eisige Woge
Der Ewigkeit. An schaurigen Riffen
Zerschellt der purpurne Leib
Und es klagt die dunkle Stimme
Über dem Meer.
Schwester stürmischer Schwermut
Sieh ein ängstlicher Kahn versinkt
Unter Sternen,
Dem schweigenden Antlitz der Nacht.

## Lament

Sleep and death, the gloomy eagles
Swoop about this head all night;
The golden image of humankind
May be swallowed in the icy swell
Of eternity. On terrifying reefs
The purple body shatters
And the dark voice raises a keen
Over the sea.
Sister of stormy melancholy
Behold an anxious skiff founders
Under stars, beneath
The taciturn visage of night.

## Grodek
(2. Fassung)

Am Abend tönen die herbstlichen Wälder
Von tödlichen Waffen, die goldnen Ebenen
Und blauen Seen, darüber die Sonne
Düstrer hinrollt; umfängt die Nacht
Sterbende Krieger, die wilde Klage
Ihrer zerbrochenen Münder.
Doch stille sammelt im Weidengrund
Rotes Gewölk, darin ein zürnender Gott wohnt
Das vergoßne Blut sich, mondene Kühle;
Alle Straßen münden in schwarze Verwesung.
Unter goldnem Gezweig der Nacht und Sternen
Es schwankt der Schwester Schatten durch den schweigenden
 Hain,
Zu grüßen die Geister der Helden, die blutenden Häupter;
Und leise tönen im Rohr die dunkeln Flöten des Herbstes.
O stolzere Trauer! ihr ehernen Altäre
Die heiße Flamme des Geistes nährt heute ein gewaltiger
 Schmerz,
Die ungebornen Enkel.

## Grodek
(second version)

At evening the autumn woods resound
With deadly weaponry, the golden plains
And blue lakes, above them the sun
Rolling on more gloomily; the night envelops
Dying warriors, the savage keen
Of their shattered mouths.
Yet silently in the pastureland
Red clouds, wherein dwells a wrathful God,
Gather up the bloodshed, lunar chill;
All roads converge in black decomposition.
Beneath the golden boughs of night and stars
The sister's shadow sweeps through the taciturn grove
To greet the spirits of heroes, the bleeding heads;
And softly sounding in the reeds the dark fluting of autumn.
Oh, prouder mourning! you brazen altars
The hot flame of spirit is fed today by an overwhelming
    agony,
The unborn grandchildren.

# Appendix A

## Notes

1. In a letter to his publisher Kurt Wolff, written at the end of May or beginning of June 1913, after the page proofs of *Gedichte* have been corrected and returned, Trakl replies to a query of Wolff's. The word *Laß*, he writes, should be understood in the sense of "to be patient," or "to forbear," *dulden*. The sense is therefore closer to letting-be or releasement than to abandonment or cessation.

2. In the last letter we have from Trakl (T 325–26), the poet alters the first stanza of "Traum des Bösen." The major change is to the first line, which now (in the *third* version, at T 197) reads: *Verhallend eines Sterbeglöckchens Klänge—*, "Reverberations of a little bell that tolls a death—."

3. In a letter to Kurt Wolff from mid-May 1913, Trakl returns the page proofs of his *Gedichte*. He asks the publisher to make the stanza breaks in "Psalm" clearer, even if that should force the poem to continue onto the next page. This would have the further advantage of allowing the *Rosenkranzlieder* (see Appendix B) to appear *en face*, so that they would achieve their "full effect." Wolff follows this instruction. In general, the correspondence shows how meticulous Trakl was with each of his poems—with the word choice of each poem, with its appearance on the page, and with the sequence of the poems in any given collection.

4. On July 8, 1913, Trakl sends a "new version" (the only version we possess, however) of his *Stundenlied* to Ludwig von Ficker, remarking that the new version has "slipped altogether into darkness and despair" (T 302). By this time in Appendix A we have advanced from the 1913 *Gedichte* to *Sebastian im Traum*, the manuscript of which Trakl mailed to the Kurt Wolff Verlag on March 6, 1914, some six months before his death. He never saw *Sebastian im Traum* in print.

5. Heidegger devotes to this poem a long commentary in his *first* Trakl article, "Die Sprache" (US 9–33). The last two lines of the second stanza and the entire third stanza are remarkably different in the first version of the poem, which has the title *Im Winter*, mailed to Karl Kraus ("as an expression of homage to a man who like no one else serves as an example to the world") on December 13, 1913. These are bitter days, as Trakl's letters attest, and something of that bitterness—or at least of the pain and distress—comes through in the following lines, which refer back to "Many a one who wanders" and who "On dark paths arrives at the gate":

(. . .)
Seine Wunde voller Gnaden
Pflegt der Liebe sanfte Kraft.

O! des Menschen bloße Pein.
Der mit Engeln stumm gerungen,

Langt von heiligem Schmerz bezwungen
Still nach Gottes Brot und Wein.

•

His wounds full of grace
Tended by the gentle force of love.

Oh! the naked pain of human being.
Who has mutely wrestled with angels
Reaches out, compelled by holy agony,
In stillness for God's bread and wine.

6. *Reseda* designates a series of Mediterranean and southern European flowering plants used since ancient times in homeopathy and in the dyeing of textiles. Mignonette, or *Reseda odorata,* and Dyer's Weed, or *Reseda luteola,* are the most common varieties. The generic German name for these plants is *Wau. Färberwau,* which yields a pale yellow-green dye, along with *Rapunzelwau,* are common in southern Germany and Austria. Sweet-smelling Reseda is the reference here: Pliny the Elder tells us that the name derives from the imperative form of the verb *resedo, resedere,* "to diminish, shrink." When the plant was applied to tumors in the hope that they would *recede,* the practitioner would chant *reseda, morbos, reseda.*

7. The very next poem in Trakl's *Sebastian im Traum* is titled "Sonja." See Appendix B.

8. For reasons he does not state, Trakl requests of Kurt Wolff in a letter dated June 10, 1914, that *Sommersneige* ("Summer Inclines to Its End") and four other poems of *Sebastian im Traum* be struck. Fortunately, this order was not carried out. Note in the penultimate line of the poem Trakl's reference to *ein blaues Wild,* "blue game," or "a blue deer," a repeated reference in his poetry and one that is impossible to translate. (*Das Wild* is a collective noun for "game," usually deer, so that in English one must say either "blue game," letting the plural stand, or "a blue deer," losing the reference to "game.") As for the word *blue,* one cannot help but think of Franz Marc's blue horses. It may well be that Trakl knew of Marc's paintings, perhaps through Elke Lasker-Schüler or Oskar Kokoschka. At all events, theories of color (Macke, Marc, Kandinsky, and Klee, among others) were all the rage during the first two decades of the twentieth century. And Marc's focus on animals—he spoke of his "animalization" of painting—may have been important for Trakl as well. Nonetheless, Trakl's odd use of the collective noun, *das Wild,* with the *indefinite* article, as though one could say "a game" as readily as one can say "a deer," is distinctly his own.

APPENDIX B

# Poems Undiscussed

Appendix B presents a number of Georg Trakl's poems that are not discussed in the present volume. Once again, the selection is in no way "representative" of Trakl's poetry. Rather, the focus here is on the two themes of "the sister" and "the lovers" in his poems. Neither Heidegger nor Derrida, it seems to me, does justice to these two themes, although Derrida is far more sensitive to them than Heidegger is. If thinking and poetizing are to continue to be in dialogue, as it seems to me they should be, especially for thinking's sake, the following poems may serve as a spur—or perhaps as a sail—to think about Trakl's poetry. Not all the poems that mention the sister or the lovers are included here, but, once again, only a selection. These are among the poems I would have wanted both Heidegger and Derrida to consider. Missing from both Appendices A and B, unfortunately, and only for reasons of space, are the prose poems of *Sebastian im Traum* and *Der Brenner*, "Verwandlung des Bösen," "Winternacht," "Traum und Umnachtung," and "Offenbarung und Untergang," along with that long masterpiece, "Helian."

I have not been entirely consistent in my translation of Trakl's colors, especially his Hölderlinian *Bläue*, although I have tried to respect his palette. How often I wished there were more words in English for quiet, silence, gentleness, softness, and slowness of pace! And how often I wished the (in)transitive or middle-voiced verb *schweigen* could be rescued somehow in the English, or the *es* of verbal phrases such as *es schweigt* or *es rauscht*. As readers will have seen by now, I have taken the liberty of translating *Geschlecht* in a way that has not yet been attempted so far in the book. I wanted to avoid the long list of "dictionary meanings," and at some point I remembered the use of the word *House* in classical Greek tragedy, Aeschylus's ἰώ, ἰώ, δῶμα δῶμα, "Alas, alas! the House, the House!" meaning of course not the palace of Agamemnon but the House of Atreus. When Trakl writes *Haus*, I write *house* with a lower case.

All such decisions are controversial, to say the least. English and German have such different requirements, in spite of their family relationship. Derrida knew better than anyone else about these idiomatic and idiosyncratic requirements of texts. And in this respect poetry makes demands to which no one is really equal. Least of all the author of the present volume.

## Allerseelen
*an Karl Hauer*

Die Männlein, Weiblein, traurige Gesellen,
Sie streuen heute Blumen blau und rot
Auf ihre Grüfte, die sich zag erhellen.
Sie tun wie arme Puppen vor dem Tod.

O! wie sie hier voll Angst und Demut scheinen,
Wie Schatten hinter schwarzen Büschen stehn.
Im Herbstwind klagt der Ungebornen Weinen,
Auch sieht man Lichter in der Irre gehn.

Das Seufzen Liebender haucht in Gezweigen
Und dort verwest die Mutter mit dem Kind.
Unwirklich scheinet der Lebendigen Reigen
Und wunderlich zerstreut im Abendwind.

Ihr Leben ist so wirr, voll trüber Plagen.
Erbarm' dich Gott der Frauen Höll' und Qual,
Und dieser hoffnungslosen Todesklagen.
Einsame wandeln still im Sternensaal.

## All Souls' Day
*to Karl Hauer*

The little men, little women, mournful mates
Today are strewing flowers blue and red
On their graves, which brighten quite reluctantly.
They act like wretched dolls in the face of death.

Oh! here they seem so full of dread and humility,
Like shadows lurking behind black bushes.
In the autumn wind the weeping unborn lament,
One also sees some lanterns wandering astray.

The sighs of lovers breathe in branches
And there the mother with her child decomposes.
The ringdance of those who live seems unreal
And marvelously routed in the evening wind.

Their life is so bewildering, full of turbid plaints.
Have mercy God on the hellish pangs of women,
And on these hopeless lamentations of death.
The lonely drift in stillness in the starry hall.

## Winkel am Wald
*an Karl Minnich*

Braune Kastanien. Leise gleiten die alten Leute
In stilleren Abend; weich verwelken schöne Blätter.
Am Friedhof scherzt die Amsel mit dem toten Vetter,
Angelen gibt der blonde Lehrer das Geleite.

Des Todes reine Bilder schaun von Kirchenfenstern;
Doch wirkt ein blutiger Grund sehr trauervoll und düster.
Das Tor blieb heut verschlossen. Den Schlüssel hat der Küster.
Im Garten spricht die Schwester freundlich mit Gespenstern.

In alten Kellern reift der Wein ins Goldne, Klare.
Süß duften Äpfel. Freude glänzt nicht allzu ferne.
Den langen Abend hören Kinder Märchen gerne;
Auch zeigt sich sanftem Wahnsinn oft das Goldne, Wahre.

Das Blau fließt voll Reseden; in Zimmern Kerzenhelle.
Bescheidenen ist ihre Stätte wohl bereitet.
Den Saum des Walds hinab ein einsam Schicksal gleitet;
Die Nacht erscheint, der Ruhe Engel, auf der Schwelle.

## Forest Nook
*to Karl Minnich*

Brown chestnuts. Slowly the old folks glide
Into quieter evening; softly beautiful leaves wilt.
At the cemetery the blackbird is joking with the dead cousin,
The blond teacher accompanies Angela.

Pure images of death gaze from church windows;
Yet a bloody background seems mournful and menacing.
Today the gate remained locked. The sacristan keeps the key.
In the garden the sister speaks amiably with specters.

In ancient cellars the wine is ripening to golden clarity.
Apples smell sweet. Joy is shining not so very far away.
On long evenings the children love to hear fairy tales;
Then too the gently mad are often shown the golden truth.

The blue flows full of Reseda; candlelight fills the rooms.
For those of modest means a decent place is prepared.
Down the forest rim glides a lonely destiny;
The night appears, the Angel of Repose, upon the threshold.

## Menschheit

Menschheit vor Feuerschlünden aufgestellt,
Ein Trommelwirbel, dunkler Krieger Stirnen,
Schritte durch Blutnebel; schwarzes Eisen schellt,
Verzweiflung, Nacht in traurigen Gehirnen:
Hier Evas Schatten, Jagd und rotes Geld.
Gewölk, das Licht durchbricht, das Abendmahl.
Es wohnt in Brot und Wein ein sanftes Schweigen
Und jene sind versammelt zwölf an Zahl.
Nachts schrein im Schlaf sie unter Ölbaumzweigen;
Sankt Thomas taucht die Hand ins Wundenmal.

## Humanity

Humanity exposed to maws of fire,
A drumroll, brows of dark warriors,
Footsteps through a fog of blood; black iron reports,
Despair, night in brains that mourn:
Here the shade of Eve, the hunt, and red lucre.
Clouds pierced by light, the Last Supper.
A gentle taciturnity dwells in bread and wine
And they are gathered, twelve in number.
At night, asleep beneath the olive boughs, they cry out;
Saint Thomas dips his hand into the wound.

## Rosenkranzlieder

### An die Schwester

Wo du gehst wird Herbst und Abend,
Blaues Wild, das unter Bäumen tönt,
Einsamer Weiher am Abend.

Leise der Flug der Vögel tönt,
Die Schwermut über deinen Augenbogen.
Dein schmales Lächeln tönt.

Gott hat deine Lider verbogen.
Sterne suchen nachts, Karfreitagskind,
Deinen Stirnenbogen.


### Nähe des Todes
(2. Fassung)

O der Abend, der in die finsteren Dörfer der Kindheit geht.
Der Weiher unter den Weiden
Füllt sich mit den verpesteten Seufzern der Schwermut.

O der Wald, der leise die braunen Augen senkt,
Da aus des Einsamen knöchernen Händen
Der Purpur seiner verzückten Tage hinsinkt.

O die Nähe des Todes. Laß uns beten.
In dieser Nacht lösen auf lauen Kissen
Vergilbt von Weihrauch sich der Liebenden schmächtige Glieder.


### Amen

Verwestes gleitend durch die morsche Stube;
Schatten an gelben Tapeten; in dunklen Spiegeln wölbt
Sich unserer Hände elfenbeinerne Traurigkeit.

## Rosary Hymns[1]

### To the Sister[2]

Where you walk autumn and evening descend,
Blue deer sounding beneath the trees,
Lonely pond at evening.

Softly the flight of birds sounds,
Melancholy above the arc of your eyes.
Your slight smile sounds.

God bent the arc of your eyelids.
At night, Good Friday's Child, stars seek
The arc of your brow.

### Nearness of Death
(second version)

Oh, the evening that comes to the gloomy villages of childhood.
The pond beneath the willows
Fills with the pestilential sighs of melancholy.

Oh, the wood that slowly lowers its brown eyes,
When from the skeletal hands of the lonely one
The purple of his enraptured days slowly slips.

Oh, the nearness of death. Let us pray.
In this night, on pillows still warm to the touch,
Yellowed by incense, spent limbs of lovers unravel.

### Amen

Decay drifts through the rotting parlor;
Shadows on yellow wallpaper; in dark mirrors
Our hands in ivory mourning form a vault.

Braune Perlen rinnen durch die erstorbenen Finger.
In der Stille
Tun sich eines Engels blaue Mohnaugen auf.

Blau ist auch der Abend;
Die Stunde unseres Absterbens, Azraels Schatten,
Der ein braunes Gärtchen verdunkelt.

Brown pearls trickle through fingers that have died.
In the stillness
Blue eyes of an angel open like poppies.

Blue also is the evening;
The hour of our demise, Azrael's shadow,[3]
Casting its gloom across a small brown garden.

## In der Heimat

Resedenduft durchs kranke Fenster irrt;
Ein alter Platz, Kastanien schwarz und wüst.
Das Dach durchbricht ein goldener Strahl und fließt
Auf die Geschwister traumhaft und verwirrt.

Im Spülicht treibt Verfallnes, leise girrt
Der Föhn im braunen Gärtchen; sehr still genießt
Ihr Gold die Sonnenblume und zerfließt.
Durch blaue Luft der Ruf der Wache klirrt.

Resedenduft. Die Mauern dämmern kahl.
Der Schwester Schlaf ist schwer. Der Nachtwind wühlt
In ihrem Haar, das mondner Glanz umspült.

Der Katze Schatten gleitet blau und schmal
Vom morschen Dach, das nahes Unheil säumt,
Die Kerzenflamme, die sich purpurn bäumt.

## In the Homeland

Odor of Reseda errs out the sickroom window;
An old townsquare, chestnuts black and desolate.
A golden beam penetrates the roof and bathes
The siblings dreamily and in confusion.

Decay swims in gutter water, softly coos the warm wind
In the small brown garden; very quietly enjoying
Its gold is the sunflower, which then dissolves.
The call of the nightwatch clatters through blue air.

Odor of Reseda. The walls grow bleak at dusk.
The sister's sleep is heavy. The nightwind musses
Her hair, bathed in lunar shimmer.

The cat's shadow slips blue and lean
From the sagging roof that hems approaching ill,
The candleflame that vaults in purple.

## Menschliches Elend
(Menschliche Trauer 2. Fassung)

Die Uhr, die vor der Sonne fünfe schlägt—
Einsame Menschen packt ein dunkles Grausen,
Im Abendgarten kahle Bäume sausen.
Des Toten Antlitz sich am Fenster regt.

Vielleicht, daß diese Stunde stille steht.
Vor trüben Augen blaue Bilder gaukeln
Im Takt der Schiffe, die am Flusse schaukeln.
Am Kai ein Schwesternzug vorüberweht.

Im Hasel spielen Mädchen blaß und blind,
Wie Liebende, die sich im Schlaf umschlingen.
Vielleicht, daß um ein Aas dort Fliegen singen,
Vielleicht auch weint im Mutterschoß ein Kind.

Aus Händen sinken Astern blau und rot,
Des Jünglings Mund entgleitet fremd und weise;
Und Lider flattern angstverwirrt und leise;
Durch Fieberschwärze weht ein Duft von Brot.

Es scheint, man hört auch gräßliches Geschrei;
Gebeine durch verfallne Mauern schimmern.
Ein böses Herz lacht laut in schönen Zimmern;
An einem Träumer läuft ein Hund vorbei.

Ein leerer Sarg im Dunkel sich verliert.
Dem Mörder will ein Raum sich bleich erhellen,
Indes Laternen nachts im Sturm zerschellen.
Des Edlen weiße Schläfe Lorbeer ziert.

## Human Misery
### (Human Mourning, second version)[4]

The clock, faster than the sun, strikes five—
A dark horror grips the lonely humans,
In the evening garden bare trees toss.
The face of the dead man in the window stirs.

Perhaps this hour will come to stand still.
Before turbid eyes blue images flutter
In rhythm with the ships that bob at the riverside.
On the quay a flock of sisters drifts by.

In the hazels blind and pallid girls at play,
Like lovers who cling to one another in their sleep.
Perhaps flies are singing over carrion there.
Perhaps too a child is weeping in its mother's womb.

Asters blue and red drop from someone's hands,
The mouth of a youth drifts off, strangely, wisely;
And eyelids flutter quietly in anxious confusion;
Through jet-black fevers wafts a smell of bread.

It seems one also hears horrid cries;
Skeletons shimmer through dilapidated walls.
An evil heart laughs aloud in splendid rooms;
A dog dashes past a dreamer.

An empty coffin drifts off in the dark.
A room seems bright and bleak to the killer,
While lanterns shatter in the stormy night.
Laurels crown the white temples of the nobleman.

## Elis
(3. Fassung)

### 1

Vollkommen ist die Stille dieses goldenen Tags.
Unter alten Eichen
Erscheinst du, Elis, ein Ruhender mit runden Augen.

Ihre Bläue spiegelt den Schlummer der Liebenden.
An deinem Mund
Verstummten ihre rosigen Seufzer.

Am Abend zog der Fischer die schweren Netze ein.
Ein guter Hirt
Führt seine Herde am Waldsaum hin.
O! wie gerecht sind, Elis, alle deine Tage.

Leise sinkt
An kahlen Mauern des Ölbaums blaue Stille,
Erstirbt eines Greisen dunkler Gesang.

Ein goldener Kahn
Schaukelt, Elis, dein Herz am einsamen Himmel.

### 2

Ein sanftes Glockenspiel tönt in Elis' Brust
Am Abend,
Da sein Haupt ins schwarze Kissen sinkt.

Ein blaues Wild
Blutet leise im Dorngestrüpp.

Ein brauner Baum steht abgeschieden da;
Seine blauen Früchte fielen von ihm.

Zeichen und Sterne
Versinken leise im Abendweiher.

Hinter dem Hügel ist es Winter geworden.
Blaue Tauben

## Elis
(third version)

### 1

Perfect is the hush of this golden day.
Under ancient oaks
You appear, Elis, in repose and round-eyed.

The blue of those eyes mirrors the slumber of lovers.
On your mouth
Their sighs, all roses, grew mute.

In the evening the fisherman gathered his heavy nets.
A good shepherd
Drives his herd along the forest rim.
Oh! how just, Elis, are all your days.

Quietly falls
The blue hush of an olive tree over bare walls,
The melancholy song of an old man dies away.

A golden skiff,
Elis, cradles your heart in the lonely sky.

### 2

A gentle carillon sounds in Elis' breast
At evening,
As his head sinks deep into the black pillow.

A blue deer
Bleeds slowly in the thorny undergrowth.

A brown tree stands there quite apart;
Its blue fruit fell from it.

Signs and stars
Slowly sink in the evening weir.

Behind the hill winter has come.
Blue doves

Trinken nachts den eisigen Schweiß,
Der von Elis' kristallener Stirne rinnt.

Immer tönt
An schwarzen Mauern Gottes einsamer Wind.

Drink at night from the streams of icy sweat
That trickle from Elis' crystalline brow.

Always sounding
Near black walls the lonely wind of God.

## Im Frühling

Leise sank von dunklen Schritten der Schnee,
Im Schatten des Baums
Heben die rosigen Lider Liebende.

Immer folgt den dunklen Rufen der Schiffer
Stern und Nacht;
Und die Ruder schlagen leise im Takt.

Balde an verfallener Mauer blühen
Die Veilchen,
Ergrünt so still die Schläfe des Einsamen.

## In Spring

Softly beneath dark footsteps sank the snow,
In the tree's shadow
Lovers raise their eyelids all roses.

Forever following the dark calls of mariners
Star and night;
And the oars quietly keep the beat.

Along ruined walls will soon be blooming
The violets,
Greening so silently the temples of the lonely one.

## Sonja

Abend kehrt in alten Garten;
Sonjas Leben, blaue Stille.
Wilder Vögel Wanderfahrten;
Kahler Baum in Herbst und Stille.

Sonnenblume, sanftgeneigte
Über Sonjas weißes Leben.
Wunde, rote, niegezeigte
Läßt in dunklen Zimmern leben,

Wo die blauen Glocken läuten;
Sonjas Schritt und sanfte Stille.
Sterbend Tier grüßt im Entgleiten,
Kahler Baum in Herbst und Stille.

Sonne alter Tage leuchtet
Über Sonjas weiße Brauen,
Schnee, der ihre Wangen feuchtet,
Und die Wildnis ihrer Brauen.

## Sonia

Evening comes to ancient garden;
Sonia's life, blue stillness.
Migrations of wild birds;
Bare tree in autumn and in stillness.

Sunflower, softly bending
Over Sonia's white life.
Wound, red, never shown
Lets live in darkened rooms

Where the blue bells toll;
Sonia's step and gentle stillness.
Dying animal greets in going,
Bare tree in autumn and in stillness.

Sun of bygone days shines
Above Sonia's white eyebrows,
Snowfall moistening her cheeks
And the wilds of her brows.

## Der Herbst des Einsamen

Der dunkle Herbst kehrt ein voll Frucht und Fülle,
Vergilbter Glanz von schönen Sommertagen.
Ein reines Blau tritt aus verfallener Hülle;
Der Flug der Vögel tönt von alten Sagen.
Gekeltert ist der Wein, die milde Stille
Erfüllt von leiser Antwort dunkler Fragen.

Und hier und dort ein Kreuz auf ödem Hügel;
Im roten Wald verliert sich eine Herde.
Die Wolke wandert übern Weiherspiegel;
Es ruht des Landmanns ruhige Geberde.
Sehr leise rührt des Abends blauer Flügel
Ein Dach von dürrem Stroh, die schwarze Erde.

Bald nisten Sterne in des Müden Brauen;
In kühle Stuben kehrt ein still Bescheiden
Und Engel treten leise aus den blauen
Augen der Liebenden, die sanfter leiden.
Es rauscht das Rohr; anfällt ein knöchern Grauen,
Wenn schwarz der Tau tropft von den kahlen Weiden.

## Autumn of the Lonely One

Dark autumn comes round full fruit and plenty,
Faded gleam of lovely summer days.
A pure blue rises from its decayed husk;
The flight of birds intones old sagas.
The wine is pressed, the mild silence
Filled with hushed answers to dark questions.

And here and there a crucifix on barren hill;
A herd strays through the red forest.
The cloud drifts across the mirror of the weir;
The farmer's calm gestures come to rest.
Very gently the blue wing of evening
Touches a roof of dried thatch, the black earth.

Soon stars nestle in the brows of the weary one;
In cool rooms a modest life unfolds
And angels slowly rise from the blue
Eyes of lovers, who more gently suffer.
The reed whistles in the wind; horror of old bones,
When the dew drips black from the bare willows.

## Im Dunkel
(2. Fassung)

Es schweigt die Seele den blauen Frühling.
Unter feuchtem Abendgezweig
Sank in Schauern die Stirne den Liebenden.

O das grünende Kreuz. In dunklem Gespräch
Erkannten sich Mann und Weib.
An kahler Mauer
Wandelt mit seinen Gestirnen der Einsame.

Über die mondbeglänzten Wege des Walds
Sank die Wildnis
Vergessener Jagden; Blick der Bläue
Aus verfallenen Felsen bricht.

## In the Dark
(second version)

The soul is silent about the blue springtime.
Beneath moist branches of evening
The brows of lovers sank in shudders.

Oh, the greening crucifix. In dark converse
Man and woman came to know each other.
At barren wall
The lonely one paces with his stars.

Above the forest paths bathed in moonlight
Sank the savagery
Of forgotten hunts; glimpse of blue haze
Breaks from ruined rocks.

## Das Dunkle Tal

In Föhren zerflattert ein Krähenzug
Und grüne Abendnebel steigen
Und wie im Traum ein Klang von Geigen
Und Mägde laufen zum Tanz in Krug.

Man hört Betrunkener Lachen und Schrei,
Ein Schauer geht durch alte Eiben.
An leichenfahlen Fensterscheiben
Huschen die Schatten der Tänzer vorbei.

Es riecht nach Wein und Thymian
Und durch den Wald hallt einsam Rufen.
Das Bettelvolk lauscht auf den Stufen
Und hebt sinnlos zu beten an.

Ein Wild verblutet im Haselgesträuch.
Dumpf schwanken riesige Baumarkaden,
Von eisigen Wolken überladen.
Liebende ruhn umschlungen am Teich.

## The Dark Valley

In the firs a flock of crows disperses
And green fogs of evening rise
And as in a dream a sound of fiddles
And maids dash to the dance at the inn.

One hears laughter and the cries of drunkards,
A shower sweeps through the ancient yews.
At windowpanes as pale as corpses
The shadows of the dancers drift by.

Fragrance of wine and mountain thyme
And calls echo forlorn through the wood.
Paupers gather on the stairs, listening in,
And senselessly commence a prayer.

A deer bleeds to death in a tangle of hazels.
Vast arcades of trees dully sway,
Overburdened by icy clouds.
Near the pond clasping lovers are now at rest.

## Sommerdämmerung

Im grünen Äther flimmert jäh ein Stern
Und im Spitale wittern sie den Morgen.
Die Drossel trällert irr im Busch verborgen
Und Klosterglocken gehn traumhaft und fern.

Ein Standbild ragt am Platz, einsam und schlank
Und in den Höfen dämmern rote Blumenpfühle[.]
Die Luft um Holzbalkone bebt von Schwüle
Und Fliegen taumeln leise um Gestank.

Der Silbervorhang dort vor'm Fenster hehlt
Verschlungene Glieder, Lippen, zarte Brüste.
Ein hart' Gehämmer hallt vom Turmgerüste
Und weiß verfällt der Mond am Himmelszelt.

Ein geisterhafter Traumakkord verschwebt
Und Mönche tauchen aus den Kirchentoren
Und schreiten im Unendlichen verloren.
Ein heller Gipfel sich am Himmel hebt.

## Summer Twilight

Suddenly through ethereal green a star glimmers
And in the clinic they sense the coming morn.
The thrush concealed in the bush twitters madly
And monastery bells ring dreamily afar.

A statue looms in the townsquare lonely and gaunt
And in the courtyards red flowerbeds are lit by dawn[.]
The air on wooden balconies quivers with humidity
And houseflies tumble lazily about some putrefaction.

The silver curtain in the window there conceals
Clasping limbs, lips, tender breasts.
Loud hammering rings from the tower's scaffolding
And the white moon decays in heaven's canopy.

A spectral dreamlike chord hangs in the air
And monks emerge from churchyard gates
And pace quite lost in the infinite.
A radiant mountain peak looms in the sky.

## Passion
(3. Fassung)

Wenn Orpheus silbern die Laute rührt,
Beklagend ein Totes im Abendgarten,
Wer bist du Ruhendes unter hohen Bäumen?
Es rauscht die Klage das herbstliche Rohr,
Der blaue Teich,
Hinsterbend unter grünenden Bäumen
Und folgend dem Schatten der Schwester;
Dunkle Liebe
Eines wilden Geschlechts,
Dem auf goldenen Rädern der Tag davonrauscht.
Stille Nacht.

Unter finsteren Tannen
Mischten zwei Wölfe ihr Blut
In steinerner Umarmung; ein Goldnes
Verlor sich die Wolke über dem Steg,
Geduld und Schweigen der Kindheit.
Wieder begegnet der zarte Leichnam
Am Tritonsteich
Schlummernd in seinem hyazinthenen Haar.
Daß endlich zerbräche das kühle Haupt!

Denn immer folgt, ein blaues Wild,
Ein Äugendes unter dämmernden Bäumen,
Dieser dunkleren Pfaden
Wachend und bewegt von nächtigem Wohllaut,
Sanftem Wahnsinn;
Oder es tönte dunkler Verzückung
Voll das Saitenspiel
Zu den kühlen Füßen der Büßerin
In der steinernen Stadt.

## Passion
(third version)

When Orpheus plucks his silvery lute,
Lamenting something dead in the evening garden,
Who are you Reposeful One under lofty trees?
The autumn reed sounds the lamentation,
The blue pond,
Dying beneath the greening trees
And following the shadow of the sister;
Dark love
Of a savage House,
From which on golden wheels the day departs.
Silent night.

Beneath gloomy pines
Two wolves mixed their blood
In stony embrace; something golden
Drifted off, a cloud above the footbridge,
Patience and silence of childhood.
Encountered again is the tender corpse
At Triton's pond
Dozing in his hyacinthine hair.
May the cool head at long last shatter!

For what a blue deer always follows,
Its gazing eye beneath the twilit trees,
Alert to this darker path
And moved by the euphony of the night,
Is gentle madness;
Or full of dark rapture
A thrum of strings sounded
At the cool feet of the penitent woman
In the city of stone.

346    Appendix B

## Notes

1. In a letter to Erhard Buschbeck during the second half of March 1913, that is, during the time when the two friends were planning the publication of Trakl's *Gedichte,* to be released by the Kurt Wolff Verlag in Leipzig, Trakl asks his friend to gather three poems together (*zusammenzuschließen*), namely, "An die Schwester," "Nähe des Todes," and "Amen" (T 291), as the *Rosenkranzlieder*. A month later, in a letter to Kurt Wolff, Trakl asks whether the collection as a whole should have a more informative title than "poems," *Gedichte,* and he proposes the title that the collection originally had for him, namely, *Dämmerung und Verfall,* "Dusk and Decay," a title, he says, that "expresses everything essential" (T 295). In the end, the neutral title *Gedichte* prevails.

2. The title of this poem in its first version is *An meine Schwester,* "To My Sister." Very often, it seems, Trakl, upon reflection, uses the definite article *the* instead of the more natural possessive pronoun *my*. I have tried to respect this decision of his, even though it sounds odder to the English ear than to the German. The use of the definite article seems to be a part of Trakl's strategy, discussed in a letter to Buschbeck in 1911 (T 173-74), to translate the "personal" into the "impersonal" and "more universal" form. Nevertheless, it seems to be a safe assumption—if any assumption is safe in Trakl's poetry—that "the" sister in question is Gretl.

3. "Azrael's shadow." The third edition (1874) of Wilhelm Vollmer's *Wörterbuch der Mythologie* contains (at 10:346) a reference to Azrael. The context is a reputedly *Persian* extrapolation on the story of Adam and Eve and the genesis of humankind. The story goes that God, desiring to make the human being out of a handful of soil from each of the seven layers of the earth, sent the angels Gabriel, Michael, and Azrafel down to earth to gather the requisite material. The earth, however, knowing of the curse that would befall it because of humankind's disobedience, begged the angels to desist, which they did. They returned emptyhanded to the Lord. God thereupon sent the angel Azrael, noted for his implacable will, down to earth. Azrael ignored the earth's pleas and tore handfuls of soil from each of her seven layers. The Lord honored Azrael's obedience and iron will by making him the Angel of Death for humankind.

4. The very last letter of Trakl's that we have (T 325-26), written less than a week before his death, contains what is now called the *third* version of "Human Mourning" (T 203-204). The poem is greatly abbreviated, and the third and fourth stanzas contain new material:

### Menschliche Trauer

Die Uhr, die vor der Sonne fünfe schlägt—
Einsame Menschen packt ein dunkles Grausen.
Im Abendgarten morsche Bäume sausen;
Des Toten Antlitz sich am Fenster regt.

Vielleicht daß diese Stunde stillesteht.
Vor trüben Augen nächtige Bilder gaukeln
Im Takt der Schiffe, die am Flusse schaukeln;
Am Kai ein Schwesternzug vorüberweht.

Es scheint, man hört der Fledermäuse Schrei,
Im Garten einen Sarg zusammenzimmern.
Gebeine durch verfallne Mauern schimmern
Und schwärzlich schwankt ein Irrer dort vorbei.

Ein blauer Strahl im Herbstgewölk erfriert.
Die Liebenden im Schlafe sich umschlingen.
Gelehnet an der Engel Sternenschwingen,
Des Edlen bleiche Schläfe Lorbeer ziert.


## Human Mourning

The clock, faster than the sun, strikes five—
A dark horror grips the lonely humans,
In the evening garden dead trees toss.
The face of the dead man in the window stirs.

Perhaps this hour will come to a standstill.
Before turbid eyes blue images flutter
In rhythm with the ships that bob at the riverside.
On the quay a flock of sisters drifts by.

It seems one hears the cry of bats,
A coffin being joined in the garden.
Skeletons shimmer through dilapidated walls
And there a madman lurches by in black.

A blue beam freezes in the autumn clouds.
The lovers clasp each other in their sleep,
Leaning on the starry pinions of the angels,
Laurels crown the white temples of the nobleman.

# Index

adolescence, 176–77, 224, 239, 246, 250; *see also* childhood, latency, youth
Adorno, T. W., 145, 172
Anaximander, 9–11, 55, 103, 115, 147, 152, 196
animality, 2, 28, 32, 49, 51, 56, 62, 64–65, 72–76, 82–87, 95–96, 132, 134, 136, 145, 153–59, 171, 177, 199, 213–17, 224, 226, 242, 246, 259, 289, 295, 301, 309, 335
anthropology, 20, 22, 27, 44, 74, 101, 122, 124, 230
anxiety (*die Angst*), 5, 14, 44, 84–85, 114, 168, 217, 230, 275, 305, 327
apartness (*die Abgeschiedenheit*), 144–48, 158, 162–63, 168, 173, 197, 221, 230, 302–3, 328–29
appropriateness/inappropriateness, 12, 32, 35, 41, 43, 46, 77–78, 83–84, 98, 107–9, 112, 141, 148, 155, 168
Arendt, Hannah, 172
Aristotle, 10–11, 21, 23, 40, 51, 78, 102, 109, 113, 133n2, 146n6, 153, 158, 180, 185, 215, 224
*Austrag, der* (settlement, carrying out), 108, 112, 177–79
avoidance, 38, 41, 48, 58, 62, 66, 69, 72–77, 83–84, 91, 94, 101, 103n5, 116, 124, 134, 150, 165–67, 173–75, 207, 230

Basil, Otto, 241, 248–50
Bataille, Georges, 228, 250
Baudelaire, Charles, 228, 250
*Befindlichkeit*, 14, 20–22
benumbment (*Benommenheit*), 28n5, 39, 42, 84, 86, 157
Berezdivin, Ruben, xi, xiv, 3
bestrewal (*die Streuung*), 16, 19, 27, 36–41, 45–46, 85–88, 156, 253; *see also* dispersion, distraction, positivity
*Bewegtheit* (animatedness, "movedness"), 8, 41, 78
biography, 149, 151, 185, 224, 230–31, 246, 251–52
biology, 20, 27, 44, 49, 52, 56, 63–65, 75, 81, 86, 91, 156, 215–16
Birmingham, Peg, 172
birth, 7, 19–20, 23, 30, 43–44, 49, 93, 98, 112, 119, 126, 145, 154–56, 208, 224, 229, 241
Blanchot, Maurice, 171, 226, 228
body, the human, 35–38, 43, 52, 56–58, 76, 85, 88, 91, 102, 134, 154–55, 158, 173, 200, 225, 226, 233, 244, 250, 253, 259, 265, 305
brothers, 17, 85, 87, 94, 97, 134, 139, 142–44, 151, 158–68, 175, 177, 183–86, 191–94, 202, 210, 218, 221–22, 225–30, 234–38, 240, 245–50, 253, 271, 301, 303

## Index

Buber, Martin, 31–33

Calasso, Roberto, 48–49, 251
Cassirer, Ernst, 28n5
Celan, Paul, 177n4, 228
childhood, iv, 17, 37, 57, 93, 105, 112, 145, 149, 151, 155, 159–64, 167–69, 174–77, 180–85, 207, 226, 228–30, 233–34, 239–42, 246–50, 253, 267, 271, 273, 281, 289, 295, 299, 301, 303, 309, 315, 317, 321, 327, 345
Christianity, 42, 44, 65–66, 70, 74, 79, 86, 89, 91–96, 99–105, 124, 126, 145, 162, 165–67, 172, 174, 187, 189–95, 198–99, 204, 207, 209, 219, 226, 230, 240–42, 249, 253–54
Cixous, Hélène, 110, 228
commentary (*Erläuterung*), 65, 120, 135, 139–41, 143–44, 151–52, 184, 197, 201, 213, 225–26, 237, 252–54
curse, 42, 46, 61–62, 89–90, 105, 120, 125, 156, 159–62, 164–69, 172, 175, 184, 190, 225–26, 229–32, 238, 240, 242, 281, 346

Dastur, Françoise, 71, 97, 103n5, 137
dawn, the, 10, 93, 96, 104, 152, 163, 166, 173, 182–83, 207, 229, 238–39, 295, 343; *see also* dusk, twilight
death, xii, 7–9, 16, 30, 43, 84, 93n4, 96, 98, 109–10, 128, 132, 144–45, 151, 155–58, 168, 171, 173, 177, 181, 188–89, 193, 197, 220–21, 223–27, 237, 239n5, 240, 244–45, 248–50, 253, 255, 277, 289, 295, 301, 305, 308, 315, 317, 321, 341, 346
decline (*der Untergang*), 49, 82, 150–51, 220–21, 237–38, 295; *see also* downgoing
decomposition (*die Verwesung*), 42, 46, 61–62, 66, 73, 89, 98–99, 102, 105, 156, 160, 162, 165–66, 173, 177, 181, 183, 185, 207, 230–32, 237–38, 265, 267, 287, 289, 295, 307, 315; *see also* disessencing
democracy, 114, 116, 128–29
demonic, the, 87–89, 242, 246; *see also* evil
Descartes, René, 7, 13–15, 23, 43, 56, 74–79, 87, 89, 181, 187, 210, 212, 224
despair, 82, 100, 195, 226, 240, 244, 248, 254, 308, 319
destination, 17, 66, 147–50, 159, 164, 192–93, 210
destiny (*Geschick*), 8, 14–15, 17, 80, 126, 147, 162, 166, 178, 183, 193, 200, 210, 217, 238; *see also* legacy
*Destruktion*, 5, 74–75, 79, 129
discord (*die Zwietracht*), 10, 17, 30, 42, 59, 62, 66, 88, 90, 96, 103n5, 115, 120, 124–25, 129, 134, 161–68, 180, 184–85, 203–4, 207, 209, 226, 230, 237, 239
disessencing (*die Ver-wesung*), 42–43, 46, 62, 66, 73, 158–65, 168, 180, 185, 230–31, 237–38; *see also* decomposition
dispersion (*die Zerstreuung*), 3, 19, 29–30, 35–46, 49, 58–59, 65–66, 78, 81, 88, 128–29, 136, 144, 167, 185–86, 253; *see also* bestrewal, distraction, negativity
dissemination, 19, 37n8, 38–40, 43, 45–46, 60, 63, 65, 81, 85, 128, 136–37, 180, 185–88, 195, 210–12, 226, 251–52; *see also* polysemy
dissension, *see* discord
distraction (*die Zerstreuung*), 36–37, 39–45, 78, 84–85, 88, 117, 137, 144, 167, 186; *see also* dispersion
domination (*Walten*), 83, 112, 122–26, 220; *see also* violence
downgoing (*der Untergang*), 145, 150–52, 156, 183, 248, 259, 263, 273, 293, 295, 317, 346; *see also* decline

# Index

dream, v, 17, 21, 29, 47, 81, 89, 105, 128, 150–51, 165, 167, 199–201, 219, 221, 229–33, 239–44, 246, 254, 261, 267, 271, 277, 293, 325, 327, 341, 343; *see also* phantasm
duality, 10, 16n2, 19, 24, 27–30, 35–36, 37n8, 45, 64, 96, 165, 169, 176, 184, 203–9, 226; *see also* twofold
dusk, 96, 152, 229, 238, 277, 291, 301, 325, 346; *see also* dawn, twilight

ear, the, 3–5, 111, 115
earth, 39, 79–81, 96, 123, 140, 144, 147–51, 158, 161, 181n5, 217, 219, 223, 230, 247, 254, 279, 301, 337, 346
ecstatic, the, 7–8, 11–12, 14, 30, 40–41, 43, 77–78, 95, 100, 108, 142, 156n8
Empedocles, 26, 100, 117, 119, 121
epochality, 7, 9, 13, 17, 73–76, 79, 85, 87, 90, 99–104, 112, 114, 166, 177n4, 210–11, 233
*Ereignis* ("event of [ap]propriation"), 10–12, 14, 43, 85, 98, 101, 112, 117, 167, 178, 198, 206–7, 228, 238
erotic, the, 2, 19–22, 29, 35, 113–15, 237, 250; *see also* love, lovers
Europe, 86–88, 90, 100, 102–3, 106, 122, 127–28, 197–98, 208–9
essence (*das Wesen*), 13, 27–30, 32–33, 35–37, 41–46, 52, 54, 61–62, 66, 71–73, 76, 79–80, 83, 85, 89, 92, 94, 96, 104, 107–8, 115, 137, 154–55, 157–60, 162–65, 168–69, 174, 178–80, 185, 188–89, 192–93, 199, 202, 212, 217–18, 230–31, 234, 237–38
ethics, 17, 22, 27, 38–39, 42, 45, 49, 81, 236
everydayness, 13, 22, 41–42, 46, 56, 78, 108–10, 135, 145, 185–86, 244
evil, 35, 45, 66, 72–73, 78, 87–90, 94, 103–4, 114, 129, 162–65, 167, 174, 184–85, 187, 189–92, 195, 218, 224, 230, 234, 246, 253, 261, 271, 283, 327
exemplarity, 20, 22, 27, 71, 75, 87
eyes, 51, 53, 58, 138, 143, 162, 180, 183, 190, 198, 201–2, 209, 232–33, 235, 242, 246–47, 250–51, 259, 265, 273, 275, 277, 281, 289, 293, 295, 299, 301, 303, 321, 323, 327, 329, 333, 335, 337, 345, 347

falling (*Verfallen*), 11, 39, 41–43, 45, 61–62, 77–78, 105, 158, 165–66, 181–82, 186, 221, 231, 240–44, 246, 250
fatherland, 10, 195–97, 217–18, 222; *see also* nation
fathers, 16, 63, 110, 123–24, 151, 181–82, 192, 222, 242, 247, 249–50
feet, 50–53, 57, 124, 161, 194
Fichte, Johann Gottlieb, 47–49, 54, 138, 172, 196
Ficker, Ludwig von, 224, 228, 240, 244–45, 251
flame, 66, 69, 70, 74, 78, 81, 85, 91–95, 99–103, 105, 173–74, 180, 182, 184, 231, 253, 261, 277, 301, 307, 325
foreign (*fremd*), 13, 14, 66, 113, 133–34, 140–42, 144, 146–50, 169, 174, 193, 195–98, 231, 238, 246, 248–49, 271, 277, 281, 295, 301, 327; *see also* strange
Freud, Sigmund, 8–9, 16–17, 26, 29, 34, 38, 47, 53, 108, 110, 118, 161, 164, 171, 177n4, 207, 248; *see also* psychoanalysis
friendship, x–xi, 4–5, 22, 32, 34, 48, 90, 107–15, 122, 127–30, 146, 167, 177, 220, 222, 228, 234–36, 242–43, 248–50, 289, 346; *see also* love
future, the, 7–8, 40, 96, 99, 101–4, 122, 143, 163, 198–99, 203–4, 207, 218, 234, 238–39; *see also* promise, temporality

Fynsk, Christopher, 107, 109

gathering (*versammeln, Versammlung*), 48, 50, 55, 58, 60, 63, 66, 74, 80, 85, 92, 103, 112–16, 119–20, 123–29, 135–39, 142–44, 148, 153, 159–63, 167, 184–90, 199, 201, 203–7, 210–12, 222, 224, 233, 238, 241, 250–51
*geistig* (spiritual), 47–48, 65–66, 69–79, 74, 77–83, 86, 89, 91, 95, 101, 173
*geistlich* (spiriting), 63–66, 69–70, 74, 79, 83, 86, 89, 91, 94–96, 101–2, 142, 151–52, 173–74, 79, 83, 86, 89, 91, 94–96, 101–2, 142, 151–52, 173–74, 192–93, 215, 253, 290, 296, 300; see also *gheis*
*Gelassenheit* (releasement), 80, 117–18
Genet, Jean, 16, 26, 228
gentleness (*die Sanftmut*), 26, 29, 59, 62–63, 92–93, 105, 118, 125, 129, 153–55, 159, 162–64, 168–69, 173–77, 184, 199, 203–8, 229–30, 232–34, 241, 265, 267, 277, 289, 291, 293, 295, 299, 301, 309, 311, 319, 329, 335, 345
*gheis*, 66, 94, 100–1, 173; see also flame
ghosts, 72, 81, 84, 88–91, 100, 106, 110, 152, 171, 174, 246–47, 283
Goethe, J. W. von, 34, 197, 232
grammatology, 7, 39, 51, 54, 237
grandchildren, 100, 180–81, 104, 231, 299, 303, 307
grandfathers, 17, 164, 181
Greek language, ancient, 7, 13, 25, 36, 54–55, 61, 70, 90–91, 103, 107, 111, 121–23, 127, 136, 139, 141, 165, 178, 180, 196–97, 209–10, 247
Grimm Brothers, the, 2, 100

hands, x, 3, 5, 9, 11, 25, 32, 44, 47–67, 69, 73, 76–77, 95–96, 107–8, 119, 121–22, 129, 131, 133, 135, 137–38, 142, 150, 154–55, 165, 171–72, 174, 187, 198, 204, 218, 225, 227, 235–36, 241, 281, 283, 285, 295, 303, 319, 321, 327; see also orientation
Hegel, G. W. F., 6–8, 11, 15–17, 22–23, 37, 41–43, 50, 77, 79–80, 83–85, 102, 108, 145, 157, 173, 180, 188–89, 192–93, 195, 212, 230, 236, 238, 254
Heraclitus, 9, 70, 100, 102, 108, 113–15, 119–28, 136–37, 177, 211, 252
heritage (*das Erbe*), 70, 72, 75, 91, 112, 129; see also legacy
hermeneutics, 6, 42, 95, 117, 135, 140
Hesiod, 102, 124
historicity (*Geschichtlichkeit*), 5–8, 109; see also epochality
history, 5–11, 41–43, 48–49, 55, 64, 66, 70, 72–74, 80–82, 87–88, 91–93, 103–5, 109, 114, 126–29, 138, 158, 162, 166–67, 178, 180, 196–99, 210, 217, 230, 233–34, 238, 246
Hölderlin, Friedrich, 29, 50, 70, 90–93, 102–3, 113, 115, 120–22, 125–27, 133, 139–40, 145–46, 195–98, 208, 217–18, 227–28, 241, 253
humanism, 86, 90–91, 154, 195, 197
humanity, 2, 37, 42, 48–49, 64–66, 73, 83–84, 86, 90–91, 101, 105, 154, 158–63, 181, 197, 199, 232, 240, 273, 285, 293, 303, 309, 319, 327, 346–47
humankind, 13, 37, 56, 61–65 85, 96, 105, 147–48, 156–64, 194, 196, 199, 215, 217, 229–33, 239, 247, 295, 305, 346
Husserl, Edmund, 5–6, 86–87, 196, 203, 213–14; see also phenomenology

idiom, 10, 15, 45, 47–49, 59–60, 65, 74, 146–47, 153, 173–76, 187, 197,

202, 205, 207–10, 213, 217, 226, 228
incest, 16, 66, 164, 230, 234, 237–38, 240, 246, 253
individuation, 31, 35–39, 43, 54, 62, 154, 165, 167–68, 200
Irigaray, Luce, 238–39

Jesus Christ, 145n5, 191–94, 254
Jews, Judaism, 103, 105, 128, 172, 194, 241
Joyce, James, 191–92, 223

Kafka, Franz, 145, 228, 237
Kant, Immanuel, 5, 12, 15, 21, 37, 52, 55n4, 56–57, 118
Klages, Ludwig, 82, 92, 119
Kleist, H. von, 121
Kraus, Karl, 60, 145, 250, 270–71, 308

Lacan, Jacques, 29, 37–38, 136, 196, 210, 229, 242
latency, 162–63, 167, 229, 239
Latin language, 1, 8, 13, 31, 36, 45, 49, 70, 90, 94, 103, 112, 141, 146n6, 148, 187, 196–97
Leavey Jr., J. P., 3–4, 59
legacy (*das Erbe*), 129, 215; *see also* heritage
Leibniz, Gottfried Wilhelm, 16n2, 22, 27, 31–32, 82, 158, 247
logocentrism, 55, 142, 210
love, lovers, 16–18, 21, 25, 29, 31, 34, 50, 53, 58–60, 85, 92–93, 105, 107–8, 111–20, 123–25, 132, 139, 143–44, 147, 158–62, 172n2, 175n3, 183–85, 191, 200–2, 209, 223–28, 231–34, 237–39, 249–55, 261, 263, 267, 269, 275, 285, 293, 309, 311, 315, 317, 321, 327, 329, 333, 337, 339, 341, 345, 347
lunar, xii, 38, 100, 159, 161, 181, 184, 193, 221, 225–26, 231–37, 247, 253, 259, 287, 291, 303, 307, 325; *see also* moon

MacDonald, Christie V., 16n2, 199–200
McNeill, William C., 33n7, 55
magnetism, ix–x, 2–3, 12–13, 18, 21, 24–26, 58–59, 66, 70, 85, 93, 113, 160, 164, 199, 223–25, 227–30, 232, 236, 242–43, 248, 252, 254
Mallarmé, Stéphane, 212–13, 228, 251
de Man, Paul, 152, 209
Mediterranean, 128, 141, 196, 198
Melville, Herman, 44, 177, 186, 241
memory, 57, 97–98, 211n13, 215–16, 239
metaphor, 3, 6–8, 13, 16, 139, 240
metaphysics, 5–6, 9–15, 17, 22–23, 29–30, 32–35, 42, 49, 51, 54, 72–73, 76–77, 80–93, 99, 101, 104–5, 112–15, 122, 124, 128, 133, 138, 140, 147, 150, 158, 167, 173, 177n4, 178, 190, 196n11, 208–11, 217, 234, 238
method, 19, 44, 65, 79, 84, 133, 135, 139–40, 143
metontology, 28n6, 29, 158
metonymy, 143, 150–53, 160
*Mitdasein, Mitsein* ("being-with-others"), 21, 23–24, 32, 35, 43, 108, 110
moment (*der Augenblick*), 1, 97–100, 113, 138, 143, 156n8, 190, 193, 223–24, 239n5, 252–53; *see also* eyes
monstration, monstrosity, v, 43, 50–55, 57–58, 75, 87, 200, 252
moon, the, 193, 243, 247, 287, 295, 339, 343; *see also* lunar
mothers, 16, 32, 49, 122, 172, 181–82, 222, 242, 246–47, 249–50, 277, 315, 327
mourning, 4, 63, 112–14, 120, 142, 151, 180–82, 211, 231–32, 239n5, 240, 244, 320–21
Musil, Robert, 60, 87, 240, 248–49

Naas, Michael, 177n4, 194n9, 200n12

nation, 49, 60, 64, 70, 82, 88, 90, 102, 113, 121, 128–29, 168, 172, 209, 217, 237; *see also* fatherland
nationalism, nationality, ix, 3–4, 11–12, 15, 17, 22, 47, 60, 87, 127, 134n3, 146–47, 164, 171n1, 173, 195–96, 207–9, 215, 217–18, 22, 228
Nazism, 49, 81, 106, 115–16, 125; *see also* Third Reich
negativity, 5, 19, 26–30, 35–45, 48, 74, 83, 91, 102, 112, 167, 178; *see also* nothing
neuter, ix, 1–2, 22–24, 27, 30, 35, 44, 148
neutral, ix, 22–24, 26–37, 39, 41, 43–46, 134–35, 171, 226, 230
Nietzsche, Friedrich, x, 4, 8–9, 15–16, 22, 54, 69–70, 81–82, 91–92, 101, 114, 122–24, 136, 140, 151, 154, 158–59, 190, 196n11, 199, 210, 215, 223, 242
nostalgia, 10, 93, 113–14, 120, 209
nothing, the (*das Nichts*), 5, 14, 23, 28, 40, 43, 78, 84–85, 88, 242; *see also* negativity

oblivion of being (*Seinsvergessenheit*), 9, 13, 42, 112, 114, 167, 245
Occident, the, 64, 90, 103, 196, 203–4, 208–9, 233; *see also* West, Western
ontic, 19, 21–24, 27–28, 31, 41, 50, 52, 72, 137, 147
ontological difference, 3, 8–10, 16, 19–48, 73, 84, 108, 112, 125, 167, 210
ontology, fundamental, 1, 5–6, 9–10, 12–13, 19–48, 50, 57, 72–77, 80, 82, 84, 98, 122, 129, 150, 155, 158, 227
orientation, 55–57, 125, 155; *see also* hands
Orient, the, 103, 196
original, origins, 5, 7–8, 11–12, 23, 27, 29–31, 35–36, 38–39, 43–44, 50, 62, 77–78, 80, 92–97, 100–5, 115–16, 120, 122, 125–27, 131, 135–38, 143, 146, 157–58, 182, 190, 194, 203, 209–10, 218, 237–38, 247, 252
others, xii, 21, 28n. 5, 32, 39, 43, 49, 60–61, 111, 123, 128, 136, 159–60, 165, 168, 171, 183, 189, 211, 232, 255, 267, 285, 339, 347; *see also* Mitdasein, Mitsein

pain (*der Schmerz*), 93, 128, 141–42, 145n5, 152, 160–61, 232, 269, 279, 285, 308–9
paranoetic thinking, 118–19, 211n13
Parmenides, 53–54, 157
past, the, 7–8, 105–6, 116, 155, 190, 229, 252; *see also* history, temporality
Paul, Hermann, 1, 48, 100, 181
Peeters, Benoit, 53n3, 146n6
phantasm, 102, 167, 169, 174, 188–89, 194–95, 204, 211, 229–30, 233, 238–39; *see also* dream
phenomenology, xi, 3, 6, 8, 12, 17, 23, 40, 69, 75, 78, 82, 116–18, 144, 196n11, 211n13, 254
phonocentrism, 55, 142, 210
placement (*Erörterung*), ix, 19, 25, 59, 62, 65, 70, 93, 95, 135–43, 145n5, 146–52, 158–60, 165, 172–73, 184–87, 195, 199, 201–2, 213, 221, 225–33, 237–38, 252–54
Plato, 6, 17, 21, 25–26, 55, 74, 90, 113, 147, 150, 158, 173, 247
Platonism, 42–44, 65–66, 70, 74, 79, 86, 91–96, 99–105, 119, 145, 147–53, 159, 162, 166–67, 173–74, 187–90, 198, 203–4, 207, 227, 230, 234, 253–54
plenipotence (*die Übermacht*), 28, 34, 36
*pli, le* ("the fold"), 63, 206, 212–13; *see also* simple, simplicity, twofold

poetizing (*Dichten*), 72, 86, 125, 141, 187, 231; *see also* rhythm, song
polemic, 34, 70, 82, 116–22; *see also* struggle
polysemy (*die Mehrdeutigkeit*), 60, 63, 65, 180, 185–90, 203–4, 211, 218, 233, 252
positivity, 19, 27–30, 35–39, 41–46, 112, 116, 169, 190, 253
presence, 6–16, 53, 72, 78, 97, 111, 115, 120–23, 128, 133n2, 136, 167, 178, 209–12, 215, 229, 237, 245; *see also* proximity
present, the, 7–8, 10, 12, 40, 42, 77, 97, 106, 108, 117, 119, 198, 229
promise, xii, 10, 38, 47–48, 50, 53, 59, 63, 65, 71, 92–99, 104–5, 122, 150, 157, 159–64, 169, 177–80, 195, 197–99, 207–10, 217–19, 229, 238, 253
propriation, see *Ereignis*
proximity, 12–14, 23, 54, 56, 79, 90, 115
psychoanalysis, 136–39, 145, 163, 183–84, 189, 194, 229–30, 248; *see also* Freud
psychology, 20, 32, 44, 57, 75, 230

questioning (*das Fragen*), 22–23, 36, 55, 71–72, 75–76, 81, 97–98, 137; *see also* thinking, *Zusage, Zuspruch*

race, racism, ix, 2, 22, 25, 31, 47–48, 52, 61–62, 81, 86, 91, 101, 105, 158, 164–65, 185, 207, 218, 231–32, 238
"Rectorate Address," the, 79–80, 86, 101, 113–16, 119–20, 124
religion, 20–21, 38–39, 45, 81, 88, 99–100, 105–6, 121, 165, 173–74, 194n9, 241, 254
repose (*die Ruhe*), 126, 141, 151, 174, 177–79, 186, 231, 233, 235, 262–63, 268–69, 270–71, 286–87, 288–89, 292–93, 316–17, 328–29, 336–37, 340–41, 344–45

resoluteness, resolve (*Entschlossenheit*), 8, 30, 80, 99, 113, 144, 167, 186
rhythm, xi, 133–34, 139–43, 151, 200, 243; *see also* poetizing
Rilke, R. M., 86, 176, 228–29
Rimbaud, Arthur, 149–51

sacrifice, 122, 126–27
Sallis, John, x–xi, 2–4, 53, 131
Schelling, F. W. J., 21–22, 26, 34–35, 70, 87, 89, 91–93, 103–4, 223, 254
Schleiermacher, Friedrich, 90, 247
Schmitt, Carl, 115, 120, 126
sciences, natural, 52, 81, 88, 121, 187, 194n9, 197; *see also* biology
sciences, social, 20, 136, 138, 230; *see also* anthropology, psychology
self, selfhood, 7, 9–10, 12–15, 23, 30–32, 34–35, 38, 45, 108
serenity, 150, 167, 177–80, 183–85, 206–7, 226, 235, 240, 289; *see also* repose, tranquillity
sex, sexuality, ix, 2–4, 8, 10, 16, 19–46, 47–48, 50, 59, 62–64, 66, 85, 93–94, 96, 103n5, 111–14, 132, 134–36, 139, 157, 159–69, 173–76, 179–85, 187–94, 199–206, 209, 212, 216–18, 221–22, 226, 229–30, 247–54
silence (*Schweigen*), 20, 22, 26–27, 55, 98, 103, 106, 139–41, 148, 151, 162–63, 176, 181, 185–87, 190, 229, 246, 249, 258–59, 262–67, 272–77, 284–95, 300–3, 306–7, 310–11, 332–33, 336–39, 344–45
simple, simplicity (*Einfalt, einfältig*), 50, 81, 162, 161, 191–92, 202–9, 212–13, 221–22
sisters, xii, 16–18, 85, 93, 100, 134, 139, 143–45, 155, 158–68, 175, 177, 183–86, 191–94, 202, 210, 218, 221–23, 225–30, 233–42, 245–54, 271, 277, 287, 291, 301, 305–7, 311, 317, 321, 325–27, 345–47

solitude, 32, 50, 73, 82, 103, 136, 138–39, 145, 148, 167
song, 43, 57–59, 63–64, 100, 126, 141–42, 145n5, 160, 183, 202, 205, 219–22, 232–35, 266–67, 270–71, 274–77, 292–95, 300–3, 326–29; *see also* pain, poetizing, rhythm
sons, 16, 181–82, 231, 271
spacing, 12, 43, 96, 201–2
strange (*fremd*), 30–32, 34, 39, 44, 62, 69, 96, 127, 133, 143–44, 146–53, 166–69, 174, 177, 180, 184, 193–94, 207, 217, 219, 226, 235, 237, 246, 271, 289, 301, 327; *see also* foreign, uncanny
stranger, the, 48, 62, 97, 129, 134, 144–45, 148–50, 152–53, 160, 168, 173, 177–79, 184, 189, 215, 218, 221, 230, 234–37, 253, 271, 277, 295–97
stroke (*der Schlag*), 25–26, 30, 45–46, 50, 61–62, 66, 90, 96, 104–5, 120, 125, 129, 132–35, 139, 144, 147–48, 159–68, 172, 175, 180, 185–87, 190, 195, 201–8, 213, 217–18, 27, 234, 237–38, 253
struggle (πόλεμος, *der Kampf*), 29, 62, 78, 107–8, 112–27, 142, 244
sun, the, 83–84, 95–96, 109–10, 152, 173–74, 215, 224, 238, 244, 247
supplement, logic of the, 16, 39, 42, 165–66, 212, 235, 237–38, 253

technology, 38, 52, 60, 71–72, 119, 128, 181n. 5, 215–16
temporality, 6–7, 11–12, 22, 30, 40, 43, 77–78, 95, 98, 142, 156n8, 180; *see also* future, past, present
"they" (*das Man*), 29–30, 44, 111
thinking (*Denken*), 57, 60, 90, 98, 128, 135, 141, 190, 209–10, 215
Third Reich, the, 172n. 2, 197; *see also* Nazism

thrownness (*die Geworfenheit*), 8, 28n5, 30, 39, 41, 43, 84
trace, 7–12, 34, 51, 74, 87, 89, 96, 100, 117, 136, 139, 187, 191, 212, 224, 240
tranquillity, 149, 159, 162, 167–68, 230, 239, 242, 295, 299; *see also* repose, serenity
transcendence, 14, 22, 27, 29–30, 32–35, 39–43, 52, 82, 85, 88, 134, 212
translation, xi, xii, 5, 10, 24, 28n6, 45, 47, 53, 60, 64, 70, 78, 90, 103, 109, 111–12, 123–24, 137, 145–48, 152, 154, 164–65, 172n2, 173, 175, 179–80, 183, 187, 193, 201, 203, 205, 214, 217, 226, 236, 251
truth, 9, 13–14, 22, 25, 29, 39–40, 74, 80, 117–18, 121, 126–27, 138, 154, 210, 212, 243, 254, 267, 269, 317
twilight, 89, 96, 265, 275, 277, 281, 289, 291, 293, 299, 301, 303, 343, 345; *see also* dawn, dusk
twofold (*die Zwiefalt*), 27, 46, 50, 59–66, 90, 92–93, 105, 125, 129, 134, 139, 143, 159–69, 173–76, 180, 186, 195, 199, 203–5, 212–13, 229

unborn, the, 100, 145, 154–56, 163, 178–82, 186, 194, 231, 234, 238, 268–69, 274–75, 306–7, 314–15
uncanny, the, 14, 32, 62, 84, 97, 115, 119, 134n3, 146, 166, 171, 179, 212, 230, 234, 237; *see also* foreign, strange
unconcealment (*die Unverborgenheit*), 29, 122; *see also* truth
undecidability, 104, 166, 195, 228, 252, 254
university, the, 78–81, 120, 128; *see also* "Rectorate Address"

Valéry, Paul, 87–88, 133n2

violence, 29, 36, 54, 80, 87, 95, 105–6, 117–18, 122–25, 144, 159, 162, 164, 190, 194, 218, 220, 231, 249; *see also* dominion
voice, xii, 9, 13, 32, 51–55, 100, 107–14, 126–30, 142, 159–61, 167, 177n4, 184, 193, 200–1, 221, 226, 232, 235–37, 242, 247, 253, 291, 305, 311

West, Western, 9, 55, 59, 63–66, 88, 114, 120, 125, 128, 147, 162, 167, 178, 183, 197, 199, 202, 232, 234, 239, 292–93; *see also* Occident

Wittgenstein, Ludwig, 228–29, 251
World War I, 116, 180, 227, 246, 304–7
World War II, 115–16, 124, 128, 196, 214
writing, 17, 25, 47, 51–56, 59–60, 95, 105, 120, 145, 166–67, 187, 202–3, 207, 212, 218n15, 225, 227, 237

youth, 99, 175–80, 237, 246, 249, 287, 327

*Zusage, Zuspruch* (assent, address), 71–72, 97–98, 137

Made in the USA
Middletown, DE
22 July 2015